Dialogic Inquiry

Towards a Sociocultural Practice
and Theory of Education

GORDON WELLS
University of Toronto

PUBLISHED BY THE PRESS SYNDICATE OF THE UNIVERSITY OF CAMBRIDGE
The Pitt Building, Trumpington Street, Cambridge, United Kingdom

CAMBRIDGE UNIVERSITY PRESS
The Edinburgh Building, Cambridge CB2 2RU, UK
40 West 20th Street, New York, NY 10011-4211, USA
477 Williamstown Road, Port Melbourne, VIC 3207, Australia
Ruiz de Alarcón 13, 28014 Madrid, Spain
Dock House, The Waterfront, Cape Town 8001, South Africa

First published 1999
Reprinted 2002, 2003

Printed in the United States of America

Typeface 10.25/13 Janson Text   *System* LaTeX 2_ε [TB]

A catalog record for this book is available from the British Library.

Library of Congress Cataloging-in-Publication Data
Wells, C. Gordon.
    Dialogic inquiry : towards a sociocultural practice and theory of
education / Gordon Wells.
        p.   cm. – (Learning in doing)
    Includes bibliographical references and index.
    ISBN 0-521-63133-5 (hb). – ISBN 0-521-63725-2 (pbk.)
    1. Learning, Psychology of.   2. Language and education.
3. Educational sociology.   4. Inquiry (Theory of knowledge)
5. Vygotskii, L. S. (Lev Semenovich), 1896–1934.   I. Title.
II. Series.
LB1060. W457   1999
370.1.5'23 – dc21   98-39349
                                                            CIP

ISBN 0 521 63133 5 hardback
ISBN 0 521 63725 2 paperback

Contents

Conventions of Transcription

Layout	Turns are numbered consecutively. Within turns, each new utterance starts on a new line. Speakers are indicated by name or initial letter of name.
-	Incomplete utterances or restarts are shown by a hyphen on the end of the segment that was not completed. Continuations after an intervening speaker are shown preceded by a hyphen.
.	One period marks a perceptible pause. Thereafter, each period corresponds to one second of pause, e.g., "Yes . . . I did"
?!	These punctuation marks are used to mark utterances that are judged to have an interrogative or exclamatory intention.
CAPS	Capitals are use for words spoken with emphasis, e.g. "I really LOVE painting"
< >	Angle brackets enclose segments about which the transcriber was uncertain.
*	Passages that were insufficiently clear to transcribe are shown with asterisks, one for each word judged to have been spoken.
———	When two participants speak at once, the overlapping segments are underlined and vertically aligned.
" "	Words that are quoted or passages that are read aloud are enclosed in inverted commas.
( )	Interpretations of what was said or descriptions of the manner in which it was said are enclosed in parentheses.
[ ]	Square brackets enclose descriptions of other relevant behavior.

Introduction

James, age 5, comes into the kitchen just as his mother has taken some cakes out of the oven. There is a loud, metallic "Crack."

James: Who did that?

Mother: I expect it was that tin contracting

James: Which tin?

Mother: The one with your pastry in

James: Why did it make that noise?

Mother: Well, when it was in the oven, it got very hot and stretched a bit . I've just taken it out of the oven, and it's cooling down very quickly, you see, and that noise happens when it gets smaller again and goes back to its ordinary shape

James: Oh! was it a different shape in the oven?

Mother: Not very different . just a little bigger

James: Naughty little tin . you might get smacked - if you do it again

(Wells, 1986, p. 59)

My central argument in this book is that education should be conducted as a dialogue about matters that are of interest and concern to the participants. This is how children learn about the world as they simultaneously learn to talk before they go to school; the above is just one of many spontaneously occurring examples of learning and teaching in the home that were captured on tape in my earlier study of first language development (Wells, 1985, 1986). Surely we should enable children to build on that firm foundation by encouraging their desire to understand and their willingness to observe and experiment, and to read, write, and talk with others about what interests them.

Lest this should immediately alienate those who believe that education should be about equipping students with the knowledge and skills that are culturally valued, I should make it clear immediately that I am also in agreement with that goal. But *how* students are educated is as important as what they are expected to learn, and it is on the "how" that I want to focus in this book.

In arriving at my present understanding about learning and teaching, I have been strongly influenced by Vygotsky's theory of learning and development. Indeed, my original intention was to title this book "Thinking with Vygotsky," in order to emphasize how I have used his ideas to shape my own. However, that title would have failed to recognize the equally important influence of others, whose contributions I shall refer to below. Nevertheless, I believe that Vygotsky has been the most influential.

For more than a quarter of a century, educational reform efforts have been locked in a sterile argument between those who advocate a "progressive," child-centred form of education and those who argue for a return to a more structured, teacher-directed curriculum that emphasizes basic knowledge and skills. However, with its recognition that cultural continuity and individual creativity are complementary and interdependent facets of all activity, and hence of the developmental learning trajectories of those who participate in them, Vygotsky's social constructivist theory offers a way out of this impasse. In the place of traditional transmissional teaching on the one hand and unstructured discovery learning on the other, his theory places the emphasis on the co-construction of knowledge by more mature and less mature participants engaging in activity together. It also focuses on semiotic mediation as the primary means whereby the less mature are assisted to appropriate the culture's existing resources and guided as they use and transform them for the solution of the problems that they consider important. In the place of competitive individualism, his theory proposes a collaborative community in which, with the teacher as leader, all participants learn with and from each other as they engage together in dialogic inquiry.

This form of dialogic inquiry is also what distinguishes contemporary efforts to realize a vision of education based on Vygotsky's ideas. In his brief working life, he did not himself put forward a fully articulated theory of education and, even if he had, his theory would not have been entirely relevant to the very different world in which we live today. The appeal to Vygotskyian theory, therefore, is not an attempt to revive a revolutionary, but outmoded, pedagogy; rather, his theory provides the point of departure for an ongoing inquiry by educators from many countries, as they bring his seminal ideas on learning and development to bear in constructing solutions to the contemporary problems of public education in their different societies. As Vygotsky might have put it, his theory is not a solution, but a powerful tool for mediating further understanding and action.

A second important influence has been that of Halliday, whose functional approach to language has provided support for my conviction that the explanation of language development is to be found in the study of conversational interaction. Like Vygotsky, he also believes that intellectual development is essentially a process of making meaning with others; so, although the setting of the classroom is different in many respects from that of the home, he too argues for the central role of discourse at all levels of education. However, where Vygotsky, as a psychologist, focused on the role of language in the construction of the "higher mental functions," Halliday has been concerned with language in its social uses and with the relationships between spoken and written texts and the situations in which they are created and interpreted.

Nevertheless, despite their different orientations, I have always found their ideas to be theoretically both compatible and complementary and, in recent years, I have attempted to exploit this complementarity in order to better investigate the discourse of learning and teaching in school. This book is the first fruit of that attempt.

These have been my intellectual mentors. But equally important have been the teachers and students with whom I have worked. I first learned about the power of inquiry for energizing learning from a Grade 3 class that I visited regularly more than a decade ago and, in that same classroom, I also learned how inquiry can be equally rewarding for a teacher who systematically investigates her or his own practice in an attempt to improve it. And, as I quickly came to realize, the two forms of inquiry are mutually supportive. That was my introduction to collaborative action research, which has been the mode in which I have worked ever since (Wells, 1994). At that time, however, there were few examples to serve as models and no tradition of funding for this kind of research.

Then – as is still the case now – much of what was taken to be known about learning and teaching in school classrooms was based on observational studies, usually large scale, carried out by visiting researchers, who spent little time in individual classrooms. Such was the nature of my own research in the Bristol study of Language at Home and at School (Wells, 1985, 1986). Whatever the advantages of this approach from a traditional methodological point of view, however, such studies have two serious limitations. First, what is observed is interpreted almost entirely from the researcher's perspective, which inevitably lacks an experiential understanding of the history and local context of the classroom communities involved. As a result, each classroom tends to be described in terms of generalized features rather than of what is specific to its individual mode of functioning. Second, whether the purpose of the research is to explain what is observed or to evaluate it against some notional ideal, the emphasis is on describing *the way things are*. Furthermore, as these studies are subsequently disseminated, their findings take on a normative status; what was found to be characteristic of the more successful classrooms becomes the ideal that should be reproduced in every case.

There is a second tradition of educational research, more oriented to bringing about change, that is based on intervention studies. Here, an attempt is made to introduce some new curriculum materials or an improved approach to pedagogy or classroom management that has been developed by "experts" outside the classroom. In this tradition, the emphasis is on making changes to what *is* in order to achieve what *ought* to be the case – according to the beliefs and values of the originator of the change. However, this is equally unsatisfactory. For although there is a strong commitment to bringing about improvement, two essential ingredients are missing: first, the grounding of change in the specific cultural and historical context of the classrooms involved and, second, the active participation of the individual teachers concerned in deciding what sort of changes to make and how best to try to make them.

From my developing sociocultural perspective, therefore, neither of these forms of research seemed to be appropriate. First, they fail to recognize that, to bring about change that leads to genuine development of understanding for all concerned, educational research needs to be a collaborative endeavor, involving classroom participants as well as university researchers in situated inquiries that start from current practice. And equally important, traditional approaches allow no place within the research design for new ways of learning and teaching to emerge as teachers, working with informed and supportive colleagues, explore what they and their students *might be able to achieve*.

I was extremely fortunate, therefore, that in 1991, the Spencer Foundation provided a generous grant to enable me to attempt a new approach to carrying out research in classrooms. Rather than do research *on* classroom interaction, the results and implications of which I would then attempt to impress on teachers, the proposal was, instead, to do research *with* teachers and students, with the aim that all of us should simultaneously better understand and improve the activities of learning and teaching and the part played by spoken and written discourse in these activities. This is not the place to describe in detail how our project has changed and developed, nor to present the results of our inquiries. However, it is symptomatic that, part way through, the group decided to change its name; since 1995, we have been the Developing Inquiring Communities in Education Project (DICEP).[1] All the examples on which I draw in the following chapters are taken from recordings made in the course of our co-investigations and my understanding of the practicalities as well as the potential of dialogic inquiry has come from the discussions I have had with the teachers and students concerned.

On this basis, I believe, it is reasonable to claim that these chapters are not simply academic theorizing. They are equally based on practical inquiries carried out in collaboration with teachers who are attempting to put the ideas of sociocultural theory to work in their classrooms in a multicultural urban metropolis. I would emphasize, therefore, that if the vision of education I present appears somewhat idealistic, it is nevertheless an ideal that can be, and is being, achieved in practice.

Plan of the Book

The book is arranged into three parts. The first establishes the theoretical framework, drawing particularly on the work of Vygotsky and Halliday and on other writers in the fields of cultural historical activity theory and linguistic interaction. The second part includes a number of classroom investigations in which the concern is to understand the forms that dialogic inquiry can take and the conditions that make this possible. In the spirit of action research, these are not reports of findings from work completed, but essays towards improved acting with understanding. The final part explores the significance of Vygotsky's construct of the "zone of proximal development" for learning and teaching through dialogic inquiry.

Part I: Establishing the Theoretical Framework

Vygotsky certainly recognized the key role of discourse in learning and teaching, as is clear, in particular, from his final work, *Thinking and Speech*. However, in his day, the discipline of descriptive linguistics was still relatively undeveloped and electronic means of recording had still to be invented. Consequently, his theory provides little detailed guidance for the study of classroom interaction. Fortunately, however, in recent years this gap has been substantially filled by the work of Halliday and his colleagues, whose approach to language as "social semiotic" is entirely compatible with Vygotsky's sociocultural theory. Part I starts, therefore, with an exposition of the relationship between the work of these two theorists. The occasion for the writing of this chapter was the publication by Halliday of a paper summarizing his work in developmental and educational linguistics under the title, "Towards a language-based theory of learning." I took up the invitation to write a response by showing how Halliday's work effectively complements that of Vygotsky to provide an even more comprehensive theoretical framework for understanding the role of language in young people's development, both at home and at school. This chapter introduces many of the themes to be developed in the remainder of the book. However, those readers who are not familiar with the work of either of these writers may find that this chapter is more approachable after they have read some of the others, in particular Chapters 4 and 5.

Chapter 2 narrows the introductory focus by addressing the nature of knowledge and its production and reproduction. In the age of the "'knowledge revolution'," it seems important to clarify what is meant by "knowledge," and what its place is in the curriculum; my conclusion is that, rather than with knowledge, our main concern should be with "knowing" and "coming to know." Adopting the genetic approach advocated by Vygotsky, I trace the emergence over human history of six modes of knowing, showing how this progression is dependent on the artifacts that mediate knowing in joint activity. In the second part of the chapter, I propose a model of the spiral of knowing as a way of thinking about the relationship between experience, information, and understanding, in which collaborative knowledge building plays a central role.

Chapter 3 continues the focus on knowing and understanding from the perspective of the role of discourse in knowledge building. The key, I suggest, is in the dual aspects of utterance: either saying to and for others and hearing and critically evaluating what is said. The emphasis in the second part of the chapter is on the creation of classroom communities of dialogic inquiry and the different kinds of meaning making that are enabled by different modes of discourse in such communities.

Part II: Discourse, Learning, and Teaching

Chapter 4 introduces the notion of the discourse tool-kit and focuses on the complementarity of talk and text in classroom activities. Taking as an example the sequence of tasks that make up one morning's work on electricity in a grade 4/5 classroom, I show how, together with practical action, these two modes of discourse function interdependently to achieve the goal of inducting students into the practice of 'doing science'. The same arguments apply equally, I suggest, to doing history, math, and so on; mastering the discourses in which knowledge is constructed, put to use, and critiqued and modified, is a central part of an apprenticeship into each of the disciplines. For this reason, I propose that schooling can usefully be seen as a semiotic apprenticeship.

The next three chapters are concerned with forms of oral discourse that mediate almost all classroom activities. Most of the time, the resource of oral discourse is taken for granted and most teachers are unaware of the uses they make of the various genres of talk that are available to them. However, as I attempt to show, it is through the discursive moves they make in eliciting and responding to student contributions that they establish the intellectual and social values that come to define the practice of education for themselves and their students.

Chapter 5 takes as its target the ubiquitous genre of triadic dialogue (Teacher Initiation, Student Response, Teacher Follow-up). However, in order to provide a basis for subsequent discussion of this genre, the first part of the chapter is devoted to an exposition of a more general framework for analyzing classroom discourse that is constructed from an articulation of Vygotsky-based activity theory with Hallidayan register and genre theory. The second part of the chapter then draws on this framework to investigate the different functions that triadic dialogue is used to perform by examining a series of episodes that occurred in small group and whole-class activities in a Grade 3 unit on the topic of time. The conclusion reached is that, in itself, triadic dialogue is neither good nor bad; its value depends on its functions in relation to the activities in which it is used.

Chapter 6 presents a case study, within the same overall framework, of the development of the genre of discussion that we refer to as "progressive discourse," as this occurred in successive lessons in a curricular unit on mass in the same inner city classroom that provided the data for the previous chapter. The focus here is on the way in which the teacher simultaneously helps the children to understand the significance of the theory-based action of predicting in carrying out practical experiments, and unobtrusively scaffolds their increasingly effective participation in collaborative knowledge building.

In Chapter 7, the framework is further developed in terms of the metaphor of the discourse tool-kit and, more specifically, of the options available to the teacher in responding to student contributions and the different opportunities for learning that choice of the different options supports. A distinction is made between two levels of teaching: the macro level of planning and initiation, and the micro level of responsive assistance and guidance, as students engage with the challenges presented at the macro level. Episodes from two inquiry-oriented activities are then analyzed in order to illustrate the utility of the scheme for teachers who wish to examine their habitual modes of following up on student contributions and, on the basis of such reflective inquiry, to extend or perhaps modify their selections from the discourse tool-kit.

In Chapter 8, the focus turns to the development of writing and its role in the construction of knowledge. I start by tracing the changing forms and functions of writing over the course of history in order to show how the emergence of different genres has been related to major changes that have occurred over the centuries in the social, economic, and intellectual practices in which writing is used. The central argument is that, as with material tools, developments in form occur in the solving of problems of function. This argument is more fully illustrated at the microgenetic level in the analysis of a single literary text. Here, I attempt to show how, in "The Inheritors," Golding invented a totally new linguistic register as a solution to the problem of representing the mental processes of the ancestors of homo sapiens. Finally, the understanding gleaned from adopting this genetic approach is brought to bear on a consideration of the conditions that might foster the development of writing at the ontogenetic level.

Part III: Learning and Teaching in the Zone of Proximal Development (zpd)

Of the four themes in Vygotsky's writings that are of particular importance for education, there can be little doubt that it is his concept of "the zone of proximal development" that has attracted most attention from educators outside Russia. Perhaps for this reason, it is also one of the aspects of his theory that has been most intensively critiqued and extended. However, as I argue, this is powerful evidence that, in the zpd, Vygotsky has gone to the heart of the relationship between learning, teaching and development, and that his ideas are still of vital relevance today.

In Chapter 9, the concept of the zpd plays a dual role in the report by two teachers and myself of a collaboratively undertaken piece of action research. The project started as an investigation of the extent to which learners in the two teachers' classroom were receiving assistance in their zones of proximal development. As we found on the basis of our video-taped observations, there were many such occasions, provided by peers as well as teachers, and in whole-class discussions as well as in one-to-one task-related interactions. But equally important, as we discovered, was the way in which, through our collaborative investigation, we teachers were also receiving assistance in our zones of proximal development – not only from each other, but also from the students. As we came to see, this mutual assistance in learning is one of the hallmarks of a classroom community of inquiry.

In the final chapter, I review current thinking about the zpd and the ways in which it continues to influence educational practice. The review is organized in terms of the steps by which the scope of the original concept, as enunciated by Vygotsky, has been progressively enlarged, so that it is now seen to illuminate almost all aspects of education, not only school-ing, but also lifelong learning, including educators' own professional and personal development. The chapter concludes with a summary of the key characteristics of learning in the zpd.

Acknowledgments

I have already mentioned the key role played by my colleagues in the Developing Inquiring Communities in Education Project, but I should particularly like to thank the teachers and students who welcomed me into their classrooms and allowed me to use video-recorded obser-vations of their activities as examples for illustration and analysis: Jackie Alspector, Gen Ling Chang, Zoe Donoahue, Karen Hume, and Mary Ann Van Tassell. I should also like to pay tribute to Myriam Shechter and Patrick Allen, who have shared the conceptualization and management of the project with me, and to those who have helped with transcrip-tion: Elizabeth Measures, Joan Howard, Lynne Nigalis, Carsten Quell, and Ann Jones. I also wish to acknowledge the generous grant from the Spencer Foundation that made this research possible and the unfailing support and gentle guidance we received from Rebecca Barr, as we took directions that were not envisaged in the original proposal.

The ideas presented here have developed through discussion with many others. I should particularly like to mention colleagues on xmca, the sociocultural listserv organized by Michael Cole; several of the following chapters have been influenced by conversations in that new medium of e-mail. Nearer home, I have been fortunate to have Carl Bereiter and David Olson as colleagues, with whom I have frequently enjoyed agreeing to disagree; their comments on early drafts have always been helpful, though I haven't always followed their advice. I should also like to thank Judy Diamondstone, Mari Haneda, Glenn Humphreys, and Neil Mercer for having taken the time to read and react to the volume as a whole; their comments and those of an anonymous reviewer have helped me greatly in making revisions, but of course I alone can be held responsible for the final text.

1. Details of publications by members of DICEP, and some of the texts, can be found on the group web page: http://www.oise.utoronto.ca/~ctd/DICEP. A collection of chapters is also to appear under the (tentative) title *Text, Talk, and Inquiry*.

Part I

Establishing the Theoretical Framework

1   The Complementary Contributions of Halliday and Vygotsky to a "Language-based Theory of Learning"

> When children learn language, they are not simply engaging in one type of learning among many; rather, they are learning the foundations of learning itself. The distinctive characteristic of human learning is that it is a process of making meaning – a semiotic process; and the prototypical form of human semiotic is language. Hence the ontogenesis of language is at the same time the ontogenesis of learning.
>
> Halliday, 1993a, p. 93

It is with this bold claim that Halliday opens the article, "Towards a language-based theory of learning" (hereafter, LTL), in which he condenses the conclusions of a lifetime's work on language and its development (Halliday, 1993a). In reading it, I was strongly reminded of Vygotsky's similar claims about the role of language and other "psychological tools" in intellectual development. In this chapter, my aim is to demonstrate the compatibility of these two language-based theories of human development as a way of creating a theoretical framework within which to consider the centrality of linguistic discourse in learning and teaching.

Long-Term Goals and the Choice of a Genetic Approach

There can be no doubt that both Vygotsky and Halliday have made major contributions to their chosen disciplines, Vygotsky in psychology and Halliday in linguistics. However, because of the breadth of their conceptions of their subjects, the impact of their work has also been felt far beyond their "home" disciplines, and perhaps nowhere more

The complementary contributions of Halliday and Vygotsky to a "Language-based Theory of Learning." *Linguistics and Education*, 6(1):41–90, 1994. Greenwich, CT: Ablex Publishing Company.

strongly than in the field of education. Indeed, both scholars devoted a considerable amount of energy to putting their theoretical ideas to practical use in attempts to improve the quality of children's educational experience. For much of his professional life, Vygotsky had a substantial involvement in the education of the mentally retarded and some of his most important ideas about the relationship between teaching and learning developed out of his research in the Laboratory of Psychology for Abnormal Childhood, which he founded in Moscow in 1925 (Vygotsky, 1978; Wertsch, 1985).

Halliday has also had an ongoing involvement in education, both in the Nuffield Programme in Linguistics and English Teaching at University College London, from 1964 to 1971, and in his many collaborations with educators in Australia (Hasan and Martin, 1989). However, in both cases, the work that has probably had the greatest long-term educational impact, through its influence on the thinking of teachers and teacher-educators, has been their developmental studies of language and learning. In both cases, too, the undertaking of this research was part of a larger program, in which the choice of a "genetic" approach was seen to be methodologically imperative.

In Vygotsky's case, his work on thinking and speech was part of a comprehensive attempt, in the years following the Russian Revolution of 1917, to establish psychology on a more adequate theoretical foundation, based in part on Marxist principles. An essential prerequisite for this enterprise was the creation of an appropriate methodology for the study of human development and, in particular, of the development of what he called "the higher mental functions." Much of this work was conducted through writings of a theoretical and somewhat polemical nature, as he took issue with what he considered to be the inadequacies of others' research. It was in this context that he formulated what he called the genetic method.

In associationistic and introspective psychology, analysis is essentially description and not explanation as we understand it. Mere description does not reveal the actual causal-dynamic relations that underlie phenomena.

K. Lewin contrasts phenomenological analysis, which is based on external features (phenotypes), with what he calls genotypic analysis, wherein a phenomenon is explained on the basis of its origin rather than its outer appearance. ... Following Lewin, we can apply this distinction between the phenotypic (descriptive) and genotypic (explanatory) viewpoints to psychology. By a developmental study of a problem, I mean the disclosure of its genesis, its causal dynamic basis. By phenotypic, I mean the analysis that begins directly with an object's current features and manifestations. (1978, p. 62)

Vygotsky's empirical study of concept development, which is reported in Chapter 5 of *Thinking and Speech* (1987), is an example of his application of the genetic method. However, the study of mental functioning over the course of individual development (ontogenesis) is not the only domain in which this approach is to be applied. In fact, Vygotsky specifies four domains in which a genetic approach is required in order to provide an adequate account of human mental processes. These are phylogenesis (development in the evolution of the human species), sociocultural history (development over time in a particular culture), ontogenesis (development over the life of an individual), and microgenesis (development over the course of, and resulting from, particular interactions in specific sociocultural settings). More recent work in the Vygotskian tradition has tackled all these domains, although the greatest emphasis has been on the ontogenetic and microgenetic analysis of development.

However, as Wertsch and Tulviste (1992) emphasize, in their overview of Vygotsky's contribution to developmental psychology, he was not arguing that development in each of these domains is simply a recapitulation of the preceding ones. Each has its own explanatory principles.

The use and "invention" of tools in humanlike apes crowns the organic devlopment of behavior in evolution and paves the way for the transition of all development to take place along new paths. It creates *the basic psychological prerequisites for the historical development of behavior*. Labor and the associated development of human speech and other psychological signs with which primitives attempt to master their behavior signify the beginning of the genuine cultural or historical development of behavior. Finally, in child development, along with processes of organic growth and maturation, a second line of development is clearly distinguished – the cultural growth of behavior. It is based on the mastery of devices and means of cultural behavior and thinking. (Vygotsky & Luria, 1930, pp. 3–4, quoted in Wertsch & Tulviste, 1992, p. 55. Emphasis in original)

Nevertheless, despite the differences of substance between these domains, the reason for adopting a genetic approach remains constant: In any domain, the present state can be understood only by studying the stages of development that preceded it. To a considerable extent, the same reasons influenced Halliday in his decision to approach his study of language development from an ontogenetic perspective. However, in terms of his overall goals as a linguist, the genetic approach serves a further purpose. One formulation of this is found in a discussion with Herman Parret (Parret, 1974):

When we investigate the nature of the linguistic system by looking at how [the] choices that the speaker makes are interrelated to each other in the system, we find that the internal structure is in its turn determined by the functions for which language is used. ... We then have to take one more step and ask how it is that the linguistic system has evolved in this way since, as we have seen, the abstract functional components are, although related to, yet different from the set of concrete uses of language that we actually find in given situations. This can best be approached through studies of language development, through the study of how it is that the child learns the linguistic system. (Reprinted in Halliday, 1978, pp. 52–3)

Halliday's interest in ontogenesis is thus motivated, in part, by the light that it can throw on the phylogenetic development of human language in general, as exemplified in the particular historical and cultural phenomenon of the English language. In this respect, he is working in the opposite direction from Vygotsky. If Vygotsky's ultimate target is an explanation of individual mental functioning, Halliday's might be said to be the nature and organization of language as a resource for human social living.

And it is this concern with the contribution of language to social living that provides the organizing principle in terms of which Halliday's larger program can best be understood. To a degree, therefore, his genetic stance is also part of his more general attempt to rectify the imbalance he sees in much recent work in linguistics, where the interest in an idealized, ahistorical and acultural "linguistic competence" has led to a disregard of what people actually say and of the uses to which language is put in actual situations. In contrast, the linguistic theory that Halliday and his colleagues have developed is inherently social and functional in orientation. Treating language as simultaneously system and resource, code and behavior, Halliday's goal is to explain, within any particular cultural and linguistic community, what people can mean, and how they use their linguistic resources to do so.

Language and Social Activity

For both Vygotsky and Halliday, then, language is a human "invention" that is used as a means of achieving the goals of social living. And the best way to understand it, they both believe, is by adopting a genetic approach to the study of the ways in which it functions as a tool in the situations in which it is used.

Vygotsky's Conception of Language as Semiotic Tool

Vygotsky develops this insight in terms of semiotic mediation, based on an analogy with the mediating function of material tools in human activity. As Cole (1993) points out, explicating Vygotsky's ideas on this subject, all tools have a dual nature as artifacts: they are simultaneously both material and ideal, and so require of their users both physical and intellectual activity.

They are ideal in that they contain in coded form the interactions of which they were previously a part and which they mediate in the present (e.g. the structure of a pencil carries within it the history of certain forms of writing). They are material in that they are embodied in material artifacts. This principle applies with equal force whether one is considering language/speech or the more usually noted forms of artifacts such as tables and knives which constitute material culture. What differentiates a word, such as "language" from, say, a table, is the relative prominence of their material and ideal aspects. No word exists apart from its material instantiation (as a configuration of sound waves, or hand movements, or as writing, or as neuronal activity), whereas every table embodies an order imposed by thinking human beings. (p. 249)

Vygotsky's interest was in the transforming effect of introducing tools into the relationship between humans and their environment and, in particular, in the effect of signs used as psychological tools to mediate mental activity: "By being included in the process of behavior, the psychological tool alters the entire flow and structure of mental functions. It does this by determining the structure of a new instrumental act, just as a technical tool alters the process of a natural adaptation by determining the form of labor operations" (1981, p. 137). Vygotsky identified a variety of sign-based tools that function in this way – various systems for counting, mnemonic techniques, works of art – but the one that he undoubtedly considered to be of greatest significance – the "tool of tools" – was language. For language not only functions as a mediator of social activity, by enabling participants to plan, coordinate and review their actions through external speech; in addition, as a medium in which those activities are symbolically represented, it also provides the tool that mediates the associated mental activities in the internal discourse of inner speech (Vygotsky, 1987).

In fact, it was inner speech that most interested Vygotsky (as we shall see below) and its origins in the social speech that accompanied problem-solving activities of various kinds in situations of face-to-face interaction. For this reason, apart from his general statements on the relation between language and culture, Vygotsky has rather little to say about the role that semiotic mediation plays, in every social encounter, in both instantiating the culture and in recreating and modifying it.

Halliday's Conception of Language as Social Semiotic

This lacuna has been amply compensated for by Halliday, who has devoted much of his career to exploring this reciprocal relationship between language and culture, although this is only hinted at in LTL. To gain a better appreciation of the scope of his work from this perspective, one needs to read some of the other articles referenced in that paper. A particularly helpful source is the collection published as *Language as Social Semiotic* (1978). The following passage, taken from his introduction to that collection will serve to give an idea of his overall conception of the field:

A social reality (or a 'culture') is itself an edifice of meanings – a semiotic construct. In this perspective, language is one of the semiotic systems that constitute a culture; one that is distinctive in that it also serves as an encoding system for many (though not all) of the others.

This in summary terms is what is intended by the formulation "language as social semiotic." It means interpreting language within a sociocultural context, in which the culture itself is interpreted in semiotic terms – as an information system, if that terminology is preferred.

At the most concrete level, this means that we take account of the elementary fact that people talk to each other. Language does not consist of sentences; it consists of text, or discourse – the exchange of meanings in interpersonal contexts of one kind or another. The contexts in which meanings are exchanged are not devoid of social value; a context of speech is itself a semiotic construct, having a form (deriving from the culture) that enables the participants to predict features of the prevailing register, and hence to understand one another as they go along.

But they do more than understand each other, in the sense of exchanging information and goods-and-services through the dynamic interplay of speech roles. By their everyday acts of meaning, people act out the social structure, affirming their own statuses and roles, and establishing and transmitting the shared systems of value and of knowledge. (p. 2)

One particularly powerful way of approaching this two-way relationship between language and social structure is through the study of variation, both the dialectal variation that expresses the diversity of social structures of a hierarchical kind and the register variation that expresses the diversity of social processes – what is being done, who is involved in doing it, and the semiotic means that they are using.

But these variations in language behavior do not simply express the social structure.

It would be nearer the point to say that language *actively symbolizes* the social system, representing metaphorically in its patterns of variation the variation that characterizes human cultures. . . . It is this same twofold function of the linguistic system, its function both as expression of and as metaphor for social processes, that lies behind the dynamics of the interrelation of language and social context; which ensures that, in the micro-encounters of everyday life where meanings are exchanged, language not only serves to facilitate and support other modes of social action that constitute its environment, but also actively creates an environment of its own, so making possible all the imaginative modes of meaning, from backyard gossip to narrative fiction and epic poetry. The context plays a part in determining what we say; and what we say plays a part in determining the context. (1978, p. 3)

This concept of the mutually constituting role of language and social context is most fully developed in Halliday's work on register and in his own and his colleagues' work on genre (see, for example, Halliday, 1978; Halliday and Hasan, 1985; Martin, 1992). All instances of language use occur – or, putting it more dynamically, all texts are created – in particular social contexts. Of course, each event is unique in its details but, for the participants to be able to co-construct the text, they have to interpret the context as an instance of a recognizable "situation-type" and to make their interpretation recognizable to their coparticipants. This they do, Halliday proposes, in terms of their knowledge of the regular patterns of co-occurrence that exist between particular semiotic properties of the situation and particular choices from the semantic resources that make up the culture's linguistic meaning potential (register) and of the way in which these choices are sequentially deployed in the staged organization of the event (genre).

Thus, one way of thinking about register is as prediction: Given a particular context of situation – a "situation-type" – certain semantic features have a much higher probability of being selected than others in the construction of the associated texts. However, only some of the features of the situation are relevant in categorizing situation-types, Halliday suggests, and these can be captured under three headings, or dimensions: "field," "tenor" and "mode." Field concerns the social action that is involved – what is going on; in the case of certain types of event, this semiotic content may be referred to as the "subject matter." Tenor is concerned with the "who" of the event – the participants and their relationship to each other, considered from the point of view of status and their roles in the event. Mode refers to the choice of channel on the spoken–written continuum and to the role assigned to language in the event. Together, these features of the situation predict the semantic configurations that are likely to occur in the text that is constructed; or, to put it differently, the participants' interpretation of the situation in terms of these dimensions predisposes them to make certain types of choices from their meaning potential in co-constructing their text.

Register thus accounts for the probabilistic relationship between particular situation-types and the meaning choices most likely to be realized in the texts that are constructed in relation to them. However, it does not account for the sequential organization of those meanings as a text that enacts a particular, culturally recognizable type of activity in that situation. For this, the concept of genre is more appropriate. Described by Martin et al. (1987) as "a staged, goal-oriented social process," a genre specifies the elements (or "significant attributes"), both obligatory and optional, that constitute the process and the sequence in which they occur. In her exposition of the concept of genre, Hasan (1985) glosses "element" as "a stage with some consequence in the progression of the text" (p. 56) and uses the text of a service encounter in a fruit and vegetable store as an illustration. Any such text, she argues, must contain the elements of "sale request," "sale compliance," "sale," "purchase," and "purchase closure," in that order. Other elements, such as "greeting," "sale initiation" or "finis" (leave-taking), are optional. However, if they do occur, their sequential position is also fairly tightly constrained.

Exactly how the relationship between register and genre should be conceptualized is still a matter of considerable debate (Hasan, 1992; Martin, 1992), but it is clear that, between them, these two concepts provide a powerful means of explaining the predictability of the texts that are produced in particular situational contexts. Conversely, they also explain how, from the text so far produced, the participants are able both to coordinate their interpretation of the situation and to determine how to proceed with the activity/text construction (Halliday, 1984).[1]

Before leaving the topic of the relationship between language and social context, it is important to emphasize that Halliday conceives the relationship as a reciprocal one: Although the way in which we interpret the context of situation largely determines what we say, it is also true that what we say plays a part in determining the situation. This is particularly significant, from an educational point of view, when we consider attempts to bring about educational change. As I point out in Chapter 5, teachers are not entirely constrained by traditional definitions of the situation-types that constitute a typical "lesson." By making different choices from their meaning potential, particularly with respect to tenor and mode, they can significantly change the register and genre that prevail and thereby create different learning opportunities for their students.

From what has been said in the preceding paragraphs, it can be seen that, although Halliday and Vygotsky are in agreement in seeing language as a cultural tool that has been developed and refined in the service of social action and interaction, the ways in which they have explored this insight have led them in different directions. While not denying the importance of an "intra-organismic" orientation, Halliday has chosen to adopt the complementary "inter-organismic" alternative, focusing on language as social behavior (1978, pp. 12–3). Vygotsky, on the other hand, as it were taking for granted the results of Halliday's research, has been concerned with the implications for individual mental development of participation in linguistically mediated social interaction. Both are united, however, in their interest in the part that language plays in the development of the individual as a member of a particular culture. And it is to this that we shall turn in the following section.

Learning Language: Appropriating Culture

With respect to their general conceptions of what is involved in learning a first language, there can be little doubt that Vygotsky and Halliday are in accord. Halliday's account of the beginning stages will serve to set the stage.

Children are predisposed, from birth, (a) to address others, and be addressed by them (that is, to interact communicatively); and (b) to construe their experiences (that is, to interpret experience by organizing it into meanings). Signs are created at the intersection of these two modes of activity. Signs evolve (a) in mediating – or, better, in enacting – interaction with others, and (b) in construing experience into meaning. (LTL, pp. 94–5)

The example that follows the above quotation also makes it clear that he considers the creation of signs to be a joint construction by infant and adult in the course of specific social interactive events:

Thus typically at 0;3—0;5 babies are "reaching and grasping," trying to get hold of objects in the exterior domain and to reconcile this with their awareness of the interior domain (they can see the objects). Such an effort provokes the use of a sign, which is then interpreted by the adult caregiver, or an older child, as a demand for explanation; the other responds in turn with an act of meaning. There has been 'conversation' before; but this is a different kind of conversation, in which both parties are acting symbolically. A typical example from my own data would be the following, with the child at just under 0;6:

> There is a sudden loud noise from pigeons scattering.
> Child [lifts head, looks around, gives high-pitched squeak]
> Mother: Yes, those are birds. Pigeons. Aren't they noisy!

(LTL, p. 95)

Vygotsky makes essentially the same point about the co-construction of meaningful signs in describing the emergence of what he calls the "indicatory gesture." In the first stage, when failing to reach an object beyond arm's length, the child's hands "stop and hover in midair. ...Here we have a child's movements that do nothing more than objectively indicate an object." However, when the mother comprehends the significance of the movement as an indicatory gesture, there is an essential change in the situation.

The indicatory gesture becomes a gesture for others. In response to the child's unsuccessful grasping movement, a response emerges not on the part of the object but on the part of another human. Thus other people introduce the primary sense into this unsuccessful grasping movement. And only afterward, owing to the fact they have already connected the unsuccessful grasping movement with the whole objective situation, do children themselves begin to use the movement as an indication. (1981, pp. 160–1)

Despite differences between the two accounts in the extent to which the child's initial behavior is seen as symbolic, the features they have in common are very striking: The child is the initiator of the event; he or she draws on his or her existing resources to make an adaptive response (vocal or gestural) to some aspect of the environment; the adult interprets this response as intended communicatively and responds accordingly; in so doing, the adult constitutes the child's action as a sign – a symbolic action with communicative value.

A further feature that is brought out explicitly by Halliday's example is that, in responding, the mother both validates the communicative significance of the child's behavior as a sign, and also makes a further contribution to the meaning that is being co-constructed in the conversational sequence that the child's behavior has initiated. She thus not only models the dialogic nature of conversation as "exchange," but also provides evidence of how other relevant features of the situation – to which she judges the child is already attending – are encoded in the adult language.

The microgenetic significance of this "contingently responsive" behavior on the part of the adult participant can be seen very clearly in an example, involving a somewhat older child, taken from my own data (Wells, 1986, pp. 46–7).

Mark (2;3) is standing by a central heating radiator and can feel the heat coming from it. He initiates the conversation by sharing this interesting information with his mother.

> *Mark:* 'Ot, Mummy?
> *Mother:* Hot? (ckecking) Yes, that's the radiator
> *Mark:* Been- burn?
> *Mother:* Burn? (checking)
> *Mark:* Yeh
> *Mother:* Yes, you know it'll burn don't you?

A few minutes later Mark is looking out of the window, where he can see a man who is burning garden waste. Mother is now busy about housework.

Mark: A man's fire, Mummy

Mother: Mm? (requesting a repetition)

Mark: A man's fire

Mother: Mummy's flower? (checking)

Mark: No... the man . fire

Mother: Man's fire? (checking)

Mark: Yeh

Mother: (coming to look) Oh, yes, the bonfire

Mark: (imitating) Bonfire

Mother: Mm

Mark: Bonfire ...
Oh, hot, Mummy. Oh hot . it hot . it hot

Mother: Mm. It will burn, won't it?

Mark: Yeh . burn . it burn.

Several points can be made about this extract as an illustration of the way in which the co-construction of meaning in particular conversations provides the basis for the child's taking over of the adult language. First, it illustrates the way in which the conversations in which the young child participates are "functionally related to observable features of the situation around him" (Halliday, 1978, p. 18). This is for both Halliday and Vygotsky a necessary precondition for communication at this stage, when the gap between the participants is so great. It is also a necessary basis for the child to be able to "break into" the adult language. Second, as I have argued elsewhere (Wells, 1985, 1986), it is for this reason that it is important for the adult to ascertain the child's meaning intention, as Mark's mother does here, before extending the conversational exchange. When the child's interlocutor makes an incorrect interpretation, his or her extension of the assumed topic risks seriously confusing the child or, at best, bringing the conversation to a halt. However, when – as here – the adult is able to follow the child's lead and make contributions that are relevant to the child's focus of interest and attention, meanings that are initially co-constructed can be taken over by the child and brought to bear in new situations in which they apply. This can clearly be seen happening in Mark's observation that, like the radiator, the bonfire is "hot" and may "burn."

On this general issue of the interactional basis of language learning, Halliday and Vygotsky are, I believe, in close agreement. However, there are points on which they apparently differ. One of these concerns the origins of the child's language.

"Talking One's Way In"

Vygotsky argues that there are two separate "roots" to what he calls "intellectual speech" (by which he may be taken to mean speech which is recognizably based on the adult language). Both a phylogenetic analysis of the behavior of anthropoids and an ontogenetic analysis of the behavior of human infants led Vygotsky to draw the following conclusions:

1. As we found in our analysis of the phylogenetic development of thinking and speech, we find that these two processes have different roots in ontogenesis.
2. Just as we can identify a "pre-speech" stage in the development of the child's thinking, we can identify a "pre-intellectual stage" in the development of his speech.
3. Up to a certain point, speech and thinking develop along different lines and independently of one another.
4. At a certain point, the two lines cross: thinking becomes verbal and speech intellectual.

(1987, p. 112)

Vygotsky fixes this point at about the age of two, following Stern, who describes it as the moment "when the child makes the greatest discovery of his life, that each thing has its name." The reaching of this milestone is manifest in "the child's sudden, active curiosity about words . . . and the resulting rapid, saccadic increases in his vocabulary" (1987, p. 82). Prior to this point, Vygotsky notes, the child does recognize a small number of words for objects, persons, actions, states, or desires, but these are words that have been supplied by other people. However, when he reaches this milestone, "The situation changes; the child feels the need for words and, through his questions, actively tries to learn the signs attached to objects. He seems to have discovered the symbolic function of language. Speech, which in the earlier stage was affective-conative, now . . . enters the intellectual phase" (1987, p. 82).

On the surface, this account seems to be very different from the one proposed by Halliday, based on his very detailed study of Nigel (1975, LTL). Before considering the disparities, though, two points should be made about the account that Vygotsky offers. First, not having access to data that he had collected himself, Vygotsky was dependent on the published work of other scholars, such as Stern and Buhler. Second, his somewhat sketchy account of language development was written in the context of his study of the relationship between thinking and speech, including the development of inner speech, and so, to a degree, was influenced by his attempt to establish his position on this subject vis-à-vis those of Piaget and other scholars with whom he disagreed. For both these reasons, Vygotsky's account should not be taken as a comprehensive theory of language development of the kind that Halliday provides.

This being said, there are still some major discrepancies that need to be considered. On closer inspection, though, it is not so much the "facts" that are in dispute as the interpretation that is put upon them. As numerous studies have now shown, it *is* the case that a recognizable milestone occurs at about the age of two and that, thereafter, the child's speech becomes intelligible to people outside the immediate family. It is also the case that, at about this age, many children engage in the naming game concurrently with a rapid increase in vocabulary (Bruner, 1983). It is also true that, prior to this point (whether it occurs at two, or somewhat earlier – or later), the child can successfully communicate with his or her immediate family using stable forms, that may be based on relevant adult words. What is more controversial, though, is Vygotsky's interpretation of these facts.

First, the separate roots of thought and speech. In the form in which Vygotsky makes this claim, many may find the distinction too schematic and symmetrical (Bates, 1976). However, it is interesting to see that, in the two predispositions that Halliday sees as setting the stage for language development – interacting communicatively and interpreting experience – there is at least a suggestion of a distinction of the kind that Vygotsky proposes. In Vygotsky's scheme, however, the predisposition to interpret experience does not initially involve speech, but is more akin to the chimpanzee's toollike manipulation of objects. Only when both preintellectual speech and prespeech thought have reached a relatively high level does language proper begin: "To 'discover' speech, the child must think" (1987, p. 112). Halliday, on the other hand, has very little to say about the intellectual development of the child prior to the emergence of language, although he does state that "the child has the ability to process certain highly abstract types of cognitive relation which underlie (among other things) the linguistic system" (1978, p. 17). However, my interpretation of his few comments on this very early stage is that he considers both language and thinking to emerge out of what might be called "protosemiotic" systems of action and gesture. On this score, then, their views are certainly not identical, but neither are they categorically opposed.

The second, and in my view more important, difference is in their characterization of the major milestone that occurs at around the age of two. Vygotsky's identification of the discovery that things have names as the chief characteristic of the breakthrough that occurs at this age is probably partly accounted for by the salience of this aspect of the child's concurrent speech behavior and by his relative ignorance of the earlier phases of language development, which have only become known since his time (Wertsch, 1985). But just as significant, I believe, is the fact that, both in his analysis of inner speech and in his study of concept formation, it was word meaning that he selected as the critical unit for making the bridge between thinking and speech.

For Halliday, on the other hand, it is the transformation of the child's protolanguage into the adult language that is the significant milestone and, as he explains in considerable detail (1975, LTL), this is dependent on the adoption of a tristratal system.

The [protolinguistic] system as a whole is now deconstructed, and reconstructed as a stratified semiotic: that is, with a *grammar* (or, better, since this concept includes vocabulary, a *lexicogrammar*) as intermediary between meaning and expression. The grammar interfaces with a semantics at one edge and with a phonetics, or phonology at the other. In other words, the protolanguage becomes a language, in the prototypical, adult sense. (LTL, p. 96)

These are certainly very different accounts, with Halliday's being both more detailed and more centrally concerned with explaining how the child constructs an "adult" language on the basis of the resources that had been developed in the preceding phases. And it is their views of the nature of these resources that constitute the third area of disagreement.

Halliday describes the construction of what he calls the protolanguage as very much the child's own invention. About the earliest phase, he observes that "there is no obvious source for the great majority of the child's [vocal] expressions, which appear simply as spontaneous creations of the glossogenic process" (1975, p. 24). Similarly, the meanings that these expressions encode are not derived from adult meanings. By contrast, Vygotsky, in the extract quoted above, seems to suggest that, prior to the two-year milestone, the child has not been actively involved in constructing a linguistic means of communicating, but is operating with "words that have been supplied by other people" (1987, p. 82).

Paradoxically, however, this marked disagreement stems from their different ways of developing what I believe to be very similar overall perspectives, which are related to their choice of a genetic explanation. In the discussion with Halliday referred to earlier, Parret asks what the study of one child's development has to offer to general linguistics. Halliday's answer is worth quoting at length.

To me there seem to be two aspects to be stressed here. One is: what is the *ontogenesis* of the system, in the initial stage before the child takes over the mother tongue? The other is: what are the strategies through which the child takes over the mother tongue and becomes linguistically adult? ... We can postulate a very small set of uses, or functions, for which the child first creates a semiotic system. I have tried this out in relation to one subject, and you can see the child creating a meaning potential from his own vocal resources in which the meanings relate quite specifically to a certain set of functions which we presume to be general to all cultures. He learns for instance that language can be used in a regulatory function, to get people to do what he wants; and within that function he learns to express a a small number of meanings, building up a system of content/expression pairs where the expression is derived entirely from his own resources. He creates a language, in functional terms. Then at a certain point he gives up this trail... [and] he switches and starts taking over the adult system. (1978, p. 53)

The critical phrase here is "functions which we presume to be general to all cultures" or, as he put it a little earlier, "creating his own language on what is presumably a phylogenetic model." What Halliday seems to be suggesting is that the protolanguage emerges from the child's "natural" adaptation to, and interaction with, a social environment. With the child's switch to the adult language, on the other hand, we see both the influence of an already existing cultural tool on the phylogenetically "natural" protolanguage, and the consequences for the child's ability to participate in social activity which result from the dramatic expansion of his meaning potential.

However, the transition is not made entirely on the child's initiative. For, as Halliday acknowledges:

the adult language does exert an influence on the child's semantic system from a very early stage, since the child's utterances are interpreted by those around him in terms of their own semantic systems. In other words, whatever the child means, the message that gets across is one which makes sense and is translatable into the terms of the adult language. It is in this interpretation that the child's linguistic efforts are reinforced, and in this way the meanings that the child starts out with gradually come to be adapted to the meanings of the adult language. (1975, p. 24)

This, I would argue, is not very different from Vygotsky's more general account of the way in which participation in cultural practices leads to modification and transformation of the individual human's "natural" functions. In the earliest stage of interaction with others, Vygotsky states, contact is established through touching, cries or gazes – forms of direct relation that are also found among anthropoids.

At a higher level of development, however, mediated relations among people emerge. The essential feature of these relations is the sign, which aids in establishing this social interaction. It goes without saying that the higher form of social interaction, mediated by the sign, grows from the natural forms of direct social interaction, yet is distinguished from it in an essential way. (1981, p. 160)

In the chapter from which it is taken, this passage is immediately followed by the account of the development of pointing as a sign, which was quoted at the beginning of this section. And, on that basis, Vygotsky goes on to draw the following conclusion: "We could therefore say that it is through others that we develop into ourselves... The individual develops into what he/she is through what he/she produces for others. This is the process of the formation of the individual" (1981, pp. 161–2). This is strikingly similar to Halliday's more specifically linguistic account of the development of "persons," which he represents in the diagram which is reproduced as Figure 1.1.

Thus, as I intimated earlier, the differences between Vygotsky and Halliday with respect to their views on language development turn out to be relatively insignificant when compared to the areas in which they are in very general agreement. Where they differ is in the rather general and schematic framework that Vygotsky sketches compared with the much more detailed account that Halliday provides of the specifically linguistic ontogenetic process.

This way of characterizing their respective contributions to a language-based theory of learning is even more true when we come to consider their accounts of how participation in conversation provides the means for taking over the more general semiotic resources of the culture, a process referred to interchangeably as "socialization" or "enculturation."

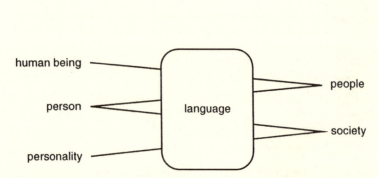

Figure 1.1 Learning Language: Becoming a Person. From Halliday, 1978, p. 15.

Appropriating the Culture

Here, we might start with the sociocultural perspective, represented by a quotation from Leont'ev, who was one of Vygotsky's colleagues and the foremost exponent of that aspect of Vygotsky's thinking that has come to be called "activity theory." As well as setting the scene for a discussion of enculturation, this quotation provides some useful background on the development of Vygotsky's ideas more generally:

The initial ideas that led Vygotsky to investigate the genesis of internal mental activity from external activity are fundamentally different from the theoretical approaches of other modern authors. These ideas came from his analysis of the features unique to human productive labor activity, which is mediated by tools. This activity is initially social in nature, that is, it is developed under the conditions of cooperation and social interaction among people. Vygotsky identified two main, interconnected features [of this activity] that are necessarily fundamental for psychology: its tool-like ('instrumental') structure, and its inclusion in a system of interrelations with other people. It is these features that define the nature of human psychological processes. The tool mediates activity and thus connects humans not only with the world of objects but also with other people. Because of this, humans' activity *assimilates the experience of humankind*. This means that humans' mental processes (their 'higher psychological functions') acquire a structure necessarily tied to the sociohistorically formed means and methods transmitted to them by others in the process of cooperative labor and social interaction. But it is impossible to transmit the means and methods needed to carry out a process in any way other than an external form – in the form of an action or external speech. In other words, higher psychological processes unique to humans can be acquired only through interaction with others, that is, through *interpsychological* processes that only later will begin to be carried out independently by the individual. (Leont'ev, 1981, pp. 55–6, emphases in the original)

In the present context, it is the two italicized passages that are most germane to the argument (although, as we shall see below, the whole quotation is crucial to an understanding of Vygotsky's contribution to a language-based theory of learning). Vygotsky's insight, Leont'ev argues, was to recognize that it is in the interpsychological processes of interaction in the context of (labor) activity that humans take over the experience of humankind, as this is encoded in the tools that are used, and particularly in the semiotic tool of external speech. Applied to the situation of the language learner, this might be restated as follows: By participating in the conversations that accompany and grow out of the everyday activities in which he or she is involved together with other members of the culture, the child learns to use the semiotic tool of language, which enables him or her to "connect" with other people; at the same time, and by virtue of the mediating role that conversation plays in these activities, the child simultaneously "assimilates the experience of humankind," as this is encoded in the semantic system of that culture's language.

Against this, let us set Halliday's account, as this is formulated in his general overview of "language and social man" (Halliday, 1978, p. 9).

In the development of the child as a social being, language has the central role. Language is the main channel through which the patterns of living are transmitted to him, through which he learns to act as a member of a 'society' – in and through the various social groups, the family, the neighbourhood, and so on – and to adopt its 'culture', its modes of thought and action, its beliefs and its values. This does not happen by instruction, at least not in the pre-school years; nobody teaches him the principles on which social groups are organized, or their systems of beliefs, nor would he understand it if they tried. It happens indirectly, through the accumulated experience of numerous small events, insignificant in themselves, in which his behavior is guided and controlled, and in the course of which he contracts and develops personal relationships of all kinds. All this takes place through the medium of language.

And, from the same source:

The child learns his mother tongue in behavioral settings where the norms of the culture are acted out and enunciated for him, settings of parental control, instruction, personal interaction and the like; and, reciprocally, he is 'socialized' into the value systems and behaviour patterns of the culture through the use of language at the same time as he is learning it. (1978, p. 23)

In order to understand in more detail what it is about language that enables this reciprocal process to function so effectively, Halliday argues, we need to explicate the relationship between culture and text, where text is understood as both the process ("texting") and the product ("text") of interaction in a specific setting. Since his proposals on this issue have already been reviewed above in the discussion of register and genre, it is not necessary to spell them out in detail here. However, it is worth considering why he believes that this aspect of his theory is of particular explanatory value in this respect.

As already noted, it is through participation in informal conversation in the context of everyday events and activities that the child's learning of and through language takes place, at least in the early years. In such settings, the meanings that are expressed relate to the events and activities that enact the social semiotic in ways that are perceptible and concrete; this is in marked contrast to settings involving more formal texts, such as literary works or lectures, where the relationship between text and social system is more complex and indirect. Informal conversation is thus much more accessible to interpretation by the child, since the various semiotic strategies and motifs that make it up are derivable from features of the social environment. But, by the same token, the features of the social environment, considered as instantiations of the social semiotic, are also derivable from the patterns of meaning and from the semantic strategies that are realized in the texts that are jointly constructed in conversation.

This is possible, Halliday suggests, because:

The linguistic system has evolved in social contexts, as (one form of) the expression of the social semiotic. We see this clearly in the organization of the semantic system, where the ideational component has evolved as the mode of reflection on the environment and the interpersonal component as the mode of action on the environment. The system is a meaning potential, which is actualized in the form of text; a text is an instance of social meaning in a particular context of situation. We shall therefore expect to find the situation embodied or enshrined in the text, not piecemeal, but in a way which reflects the systematic relation between the semantic structure and the social environment. (1978, p. 141)

It is precisely this relationship that is captured in the concept of register which, through the relationship of realization, maps situation-type, categorized in terms of field, tenor and mode, onto the meaning potential, organized in terms of the three semantic metafunctions, ideational, interpersonal and textual. Space does not permit me to include an illustration of Halliday's use of this concept to explain what he calls the "sociosemantics of language development," but an excellent example of his analysis of an extract of parent–child conversation in these terms is to be found in Chapter 6 of *Language as Social Semiotic* (Halliday, 1978); examples of language development in the school years analyzed in terms of genre are to be found in Christie (1989) and Rothery (1989).

In sum, it is abundantly clear that both Halliday and Vygotsky see the use of semiotic tools, and particularly language, as the means whereby, in the course of everyday activity and interaction, the culture is simultaneously enacted and socially 'transmitted' to succeeding generations.

Language and Intellectual Development

As has already been mentioned, Vygotsky's central preoccupation in his work as a psychologist was to construct an explanation of the development of what he called the "higher mental functions." From the outset, he assumed that such an explanation must be both historical and cultural: Fully-formed adult mental activity is not simply the outcome of maturation and individual experience, it is also profoundly enriched and transformed by the "assimilation of the experience of humankind" through the individual's engagement in social action and interaction, mediated by the use of semiotic tools.

During his brief career, Vygotsky's attempts to develop a theoretical framework adequate to this task went through a number of stages, during each of which he tended to tackle certain aspects of the framework without necessarily ensuring that he maintained consistency with respect to the whole (Minick, 1987, 1989). Nevertheless, there are two features that remain constant in all his work: first, his commitment to a "causal–genetic" analysis, and second, the central role that he assigned to speech in his explanatory efforts. Both are to the fore in *The Development of Higher Mental Functions* and *Thinking and Speech*, both of which are available in English translation (Vygotsky, 1930/1981 and 1934/1987, respectively).

In the former, Vygotsky's sociocultural theory of the development of mind is set out in broad terms. It is here that we find his "general genetic law of cultural development":

Any function in the child's cultural development appears twice, or on two planes. First it appears on the social plane, and then on the psychological plane. First it appears between people as an interpsychological category, and then within the child as an intrapsychological category. This is equally true with regard to voluntary attention, logical memory, the formation of concepts, and the development of volition. (1981, p. 163)

The connection between the two planes is found in the mediating function of signs and, in particular, of speech. Experienced first in interaction with others, the functions of speech are gradually internalized and become means for self-directed mental activity. "A sign is always originally a means used for social purposes, a means of influencing others, and only later becomes a means of influencing oneself" (1981, p. 157). This general principle was subsequently developed in more detail in *Thinking and Speech* (Vygotsky, 1987) through a number of investigations, both theoretical and empirical, into the relationship between social speech, inner speech, and thought.[2]

For Vygotsky, one of the most important prerequisites for progress in unravelling this relationship was the choice of an appropriate unit for the analysis of verbal thinking. This he found in "word meaning." Initially, his choice of this unit was motivated by the fact that it captured the characteristics of verbal thinking as a whole, rather than separating it into its separate components of speech and thinking. Word meaning, he argued, "belongs not only to the domain of thought but to the domain of speech" (1987, p. 47). However, by the time he embarked on the introductory chapter to *Thinking and Speech*, he had come to recognize that, to fulfill his overall goals, the analysis of the development of word meaning must be carried out, not only in connection with the development of individual verbal thinking, but also in connection with the function of the word in communicative interaction (Minick, 1987). This is made clear in his statement that: "it may be appropriate to view word meaning not only as *a unity of thinking and speech* but *as a unity of generalization and social interaction, a unity of thinking and communication*" (1987, p. 49, emphases in original).

However, equally important was to explain how word meanings, encountered in interaction with others, come to function as tools for internal verbal thinking. Part of his solution to this problem was developed in his critique of Piaget's (1932) account of egocentric speech. According to Vygotsky, Piaget's thesis was that, initially, the child's thought is autistic, uninfluenced by reality or the possibility that others might perceive the world differently. Development, according to Piaget, is toward rational, or directed, thinking, which is social and communicable. This progression is reflected in the child's speech. In early childhood, much of his speech, particularly in play, is egocentric, spoken to himself as if he were thinking aloud. In his social speech, on the other hand, he exchanges thoughts with others, through requests, questions and statements. However, as his thinking becomes socialized, so does his speech. By about the age of seven or eight, egocentric speech has almost disappeared; henceforth, his speech is almost entirely social.

While agreeing with the basic facts that Piaget reported, Vygotsky disagreed with his interpretation of them. Empirically, he had found that, in the case of young children, "the coefficient of egocentric speech nearly doubled when some difficulty or impediment was included in the task." By contrast, school-age children, when faced with the same task, thought in silence, and then found the solution. However, when they were asked what they had thought about, their answers "indicated a similarity between their covert behavior and the overt verbal thinking of the preschooler. Our assumption, then, is that the same operations that the preschooler carried out in overt speech are carried out by the school-age child in soundless, inner speech" (1987, p. 70).

On the basis of these results and of his own quite different interpretation of Piaget's data, Vygotsky then proposed an alternative developmental progression, based on the principle of "functional differentiation":

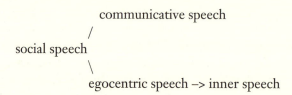

According to this view, the initial function of the child's speech is social – to interact with others. However, as the child develops, there is a differentiation of function: social speech becomes differentiated into egocentric speech and communicative speech. Then, as egocentric speech becomes further differentiated from communicative speech "through a gradual process of abbreviation," it ceases to be overt and is transformed into covert, inner speech. Egocentric speech is thus a transitional form that "develops in a social process that involves the transmission of social forms of behavior to the child. [It] develops through a movement of social forms of collaboration into the sphere of individual mental functions" (1987, p. 74).

This is not the place to go into Vygotsky's analysis of the characteristics of inner speech (for which, see Vygotsky, 1987, chapter 7), except to say that, as the syntactic and phonetic aspects of external speech are reduced to a minimum, "word meaning advances to the forefront" (1987, p. 275). Thus, with the concept of inner speech, Vygotsky was able to establish the nature of the intramental domain of verbal thinking and, at the same time, both to trace its developmental antecedents in external speech and to suggest how intramental verbal thinking could continue to be influenced by the intermental thinking that occurs in social activity. Put very simply, "the characteristics of word meaning reflect the characteristics of the communicative activity in which it develops" (Minick, 1987, p. 28).

This brings us to the third aspect of Vygotsky's thinking during the final phase – his focus on "the social situation of development" (Vygotsky, 1987). It was in this context that he developed his concept of the "zone of proximal development," to account for the role of teaching in the child's learning. Much has been written in recent years about the significance of this concept by both developmental and educational researchers (e.g., Cole, 1985; Tharp and Gallimore, 1988; and chapters in Forman et al., 1993; Moll, 1990; Rogoff and Wertsch, 1984), so I shall confine my comments to what seem to me to be the most salient features of Vygotsky's (1978, 1987) exposition for the theme of this chapter.

The first thing to note is that, although Vygotsky enunciated the concept in relation to the assessment and instruction of school-age children, it is clear that he considered the principles on which it is based to be of very general relevance. Thus, in more recent work, it has been applied both to adult learning (Tharp and Gallimore, 1988; Wells, 1993b; this volume Chapter 9) and also to children's learning before the years of schooling (Rogoff and Wertsch, 1984). In fact, in his explanation of the concept of the zpd, Vygotsky proposed that this form of assisted learning should be treated as a general developmental law: "We propose that an essential feature of learning is that it creates the zone of proximal development; that is, learning awakens a variety of internal developmental processes that are able to operate only when the child is interacting with people in his environment and in cooperation with his peers" (1978, p. 90).

A significant feature of this formulation is that it makes clear that the zone of proximal development is not an attribute of the individual learner but rather a potential for his or her intra-mental development that is created by the inter-mental interaction that occurs as the learner and other people cooperate in some activity. It is important to ask, therefore, what conditions must be met if this interaction is to enable the potential for development to be realized.

One criterion that Vygotsky emphasized was that it should take the form of assistance that enables the learner to achieve, in collaboration with another, what he or she is as yet unable to achieve alone. Hence Vygotsky's formula that "the only 'good learning' is that which is in advance of development" (1978, p. 89). But not arbitrarily so, for the upper limits are set by the learner's state of development and intellectual potential (1987, p. 209). A second criterion that Vygotsky emphasized was that the assistance should be relevant to the learner's own purposes. Taking the example of children learning to write, he argued that, if the teaching is to be effective, the activity to which it is addressed should be perceived as meaningful, satisfying an intrinsic need in the learner, and "incorporated into a task that is necessary and relevant for life" (1978, p. 118).

Taking these three aspects of Vygotsky's mature theorizing as a whole, we can see that, as Bruner (1987) remarked in his Prologue to *Thinking and Speech*, it is, at one and the same time, a theory of development, of cultural transmission, and also of education. Furthermore, far from having been superseded by more recent developments, the framework that his theory provides is still proving productive for present-day theorizing and research in all these fields.

Exactly the same could be said about Halliday's theory. One has only to look at the work of his colleagues and students to see that systemic linguistics has provided an extremely fruitful framework for work in language development (Painter, 1989), in cultural transmission (Hasan, 1986, 1992; Turner, 1973) and in the role of language in education (Christie, 1989, 1991; Lemke, 1988, 1990; Martin, 1993). It has also influenced the work of more distant scholars in all these fields – often in conjunction with ideas taken from Vygotsky and other sociocultural theorists.

With respect to their thinking about education, the closeness of fit between Halliday and Vygotsky is perhaps greatest in their views about the teaching of writing – as a comparison of Halliday's (1973 b) foreword to the American edition of *Breakthrough to Literacy* and Vygotsky's (1978) chapter on "The prehistory of written language" would show. Not only do they both see learning to write as representing a much more abstract task for the child than learning to speak, as it involves a second-order symbolic system; but they also both emphasize the need to make the tasks through which it is learned meaningful and functionally relevant for the learner. Their views about the teacher's role are also remarkably similar. Indeed, Halliday's characterization of the optimal learning environment as "a milieu that is child centred but in which the teacher functions as a guide, creating structure with the help of the students themselves" (1978, p. 210) could almost have been written by Vygotsky, if he had been formulating his concept of the zone of proximal development in the register of contemporary pedagogy.

On the other hand, Halliday differs from Vygotsky in being unwilling to theorize about thinking – at least, in so many words. However, this is consistent with his adoption of an inter-organismic orientation in his approach to language; to enter into a discussion of thinking conceived of as internal activity would be to cross the divide and to enter the domain of the intra-organismic.

At first sight, therefore, his choice of terms to describe the initial distinction that the child makes in his transition to the adult, tristratal, language system is somewhat surprising.

The transition begins with an opposition between utterance as action (doing) and utterance as reflection (understanding). ... This is transformed, in the course of the transition, into a combination whereby every utterance involves both choice of speech function (i.e. among different kinds of doing) and choice of content (i.e. among different realms of understanding). (LTL, p. 100)

On the face of it, this looks like a distinction, somewhat parallel to that between Vygotsky's communicative and egocentric functions, that will eventually become external (social) and inner speech. This interpretation receives further support when Halliday, explaining the metafunctional principle, chararacterizes the meaning of the mood system – part of the interpersonal system – as 'what relationship am I setting up between myself and the listener?,' and the meaning of the transitivity system – part of the ideational system – as 'what aspect of experience am I representing?'

Does Halliday intend this apparent parallel? At one level, the answer is very definitely that he does not. Despite its mental overtones, the term "reflection" must be understood here in the sense of "linguistically constructing the content of experience" through the experiential systems that are part of what will ultimately become the "ideational" metafunction, and the contrasting "action" as "linguistically affecting the activity of coparticipants in the situation" through the systems that make up the interpersonal function. Rather, what is significant about the child's construction of the lexicogrammatical stratum and his entry into an "adult" language is that the functions of action and reflection are now *combined* in a single utterance. This is made clear in the conclusion to the passage quoted above: "But the more significant aspect of the metafunctional principle, for learning theory, is that in language (as distinct from protolanguage) it is the *combination of the experiential and the interpersonal* that constitutes an act of meaning. All meaning – and hence all learning – is at once both action and reflection" (LTL, p. 101).

In the protolanguage stage, utterances were monofunctional. Now, with the means that the adult language makes available, the child can both establish intersubjective agreement about what aspect of experience is being referred to (reflection) and simultaneously negotiate the stance that is to be taken to that experience (action).

In using the terms action and reflection, then, Halliday is drawing attention to the two major dimensions of meaning in linguistic interaction and proposing an explanation of how the child's linguistic system becomes able to handle these two dimensions simultaneously. In his use of these terms, no distinction is intended between communicating and thinking. Both are uses that are made of language in social life and, as he observes when questioned by Parret about Chomsky's definition of language as the "expression of thought," he finds it unhelpful to isolate either thinking or communicating as fundamental (1978, p. 50).

Nevertheless, Halliday is clearly not uninterested in thinking. Indeed, in glossing the interpretation of experience associated with the ideational metafunction, he refers to it as "thinking with language" (1985, p. xix). And in describing how the child constructs the semantic system in interaction with others, he makes it clear that he is also giving an account of how she or he appropriates the culture's most powerful semiotic tool for thinking with. In the last analysis, therefore, Halliday's theory of language is also a theory about reflecting on experience and achieving understanding, as these activities are carried out with the resources of language as a tool.

We can conclude, then, that the differences between Halliday and Vygotsky in their views on the relationship between language and thinking are not as great as might at first sight appear; rather, their ways of accounting for this relationship are the result of their different overall orientation to the mediating functions that language performs in human activity. Vygotsky, as a psychologist interested in intra-organismic activity, makes appeal to the constructs 'concept' and 'thought'; however, his tool for the analysis of concepts is "word-meaning" and much of what he has to say about thinking is couched in terms of "inner" speech. Halliday, as a linguist with sociological leanings, emphasizes linguistic behavior and the purposes it serves in social life. However, as he readily recognizes, one of the most important of these purposes is the construction and manipulation of knowledge; indeed, as he states in the opening section of LTL, "language is the essential condition of knowing, the process by which experience becomes knowledge" (p. 94).

Language and Thinking in School

In our comparison so far, we have been mainly concerned with the early years – the period when the child is engaged in constructing the language system through conversation with those in his or her immediate community and, in the process, taking over their theory of experience as this is encoded in the linguistic semiotic. But neither Vygotsky nor Halliday is content to leave the matter there. Sometime in middle childhood, children in most cultures start going to school – the second of Bernstein's (1971) "critical socializing contexts" – and this initiates a new phase in their learning, which involves new ways of using language and new ways of thinking.

In chapter 6 of *Thinking and Speech*, Vygotsky addresses this transition in terms of the distinction between "everyday" and "scientific" concepts and their mutual influence on each other, arguing for the important role of instruction in helping students to appropriate the latter means of thinking. It is in this context that he most clearly explains how instruction that is in advance of development "wakens a whole series of functions that are in a stage of maturation lying in the zone of proximal development" (1987, p. 212). However, since this is by far the longest chapter in the book, I can do no more than present a very schematic account of what I see to be the most important points for the purposes of this comparison.

First, it is important to clarify what Vygotsky means by "scientific" and "everyday" concepts. By "scientific" he does not just mean concepts pertaining to the natural sciences; in fact, in his experimental research, he and his student, Shif, used material from a school social science program. Rather, "scientific" here means systematic and, for the most part, encountered in educational contexts. By contrast, "everyday" (or "spontaneous") concepts are those that are constructed in the contexts of action and interaction in the varied and naturally occurring events of everyday living.

Vygotsky proposes that these two types of concept differ in a number of ways. But, of these, the most important is that, while everyday concepts are based on direct, personal experience, involving conscious and deliberate action, the concepts themselves are not subject to conscious awareness or volitional control. Scientific concepts, by contrast, being encountered in the course of instruction, and typically through verbal definitions and explanations constructed in collaboration with the teacher, require conscious awareness and deliberate application from the outset; on the other hand, they often have little contact with direct experience.

Nevertheless, the two types of concept are not unrelated. Until everyday concepts have reached a certain level in any field, it is not possible for the child to learn the related scientific concepts. Moreover, the learning of the latter influences the continued development of the former, bringing the everyday concepts into the domain of conscious awareness and volition. "The scientific concept grows downward through the everyday concept and the everyday concept moves upward through the scientific" (1987, p. 220).

To explain this development, Vygotsky invokes two processes: generalization and systematization. All concepts involve generalization, but the earliest type of generalization is simply that which is required for the classification of objects; no hierarchical relationships exist between the resulting concepts, he claims. At the next stage, vertical, taxonomic relationships between concepts are developed, a process which involves the generalization of the generalizations achieved in the preceding stage. The next stage is characterized by the development of concept equivalence – any concept can be represented through other concepts in indefinitely many ways. Combining these two dimensions – the vertical (degree of abstractness) and the horizontal (breadth of connections with other concepts) – Vygotsky proposes that each concept can be assigned a measure of generality. And, in functional terms, "the measure of generality determines the set of possible operations of thought available for a given concept" (1987, p. 228). In addition, as progress is made towards greater generality, concepts and the operations performed on them become increasingly independent of particular forms of verbal expression.

In general, everyday concepts are relatively low on this measure of generality, while scientific concepts are higher. However, the key to the difference between the two types of concept, Vygotsky claims, is a function of the presence or absence of a system. Everyday concepts are learned "unsystematically," in the sense that it is the structure of the activities in which the child spontaneously engages that determines what concepts he or she will develop. On the other hand, nonspontaneous scientific concepts, encountered in school, are presented and learned as part of a system of concepts, which are related both horizontally and vertically. It is this that makes them conscious and deliberate from the outset. However, as systematization is introduced into the child's thinking through instruction in relation to scientific concepts, it leads to a restructuring of his or her spontaneous concepts, making them more systemic and bringing them under conscious control.

In summarizing the results of his research, Vygotsky emphasizes three points. First, although described schematically, the actual structure of a child's concepts is much more complex and uneven. Word meaning is always a generalization, but the generality of meaning of each word continues to develop, as it enters into structural relationships with other words. Second, the mode and character of thinking depends on the structure of generality of the concepts that are being operated on. As these develop, so do the types of thinking that are possible. Third, teaching plays a crucial role in this process, not only in school but also in the preschool stage. However, although the concept of the zone of proximal development applies to all teaching, the relationship between teaching and learning is different at different stages, with teaching in school being characterized by an emphasis on scientific concepts, that is to say concepts that capture relationships between other concepts and that are most readily realized through linguistic formulations.

In LTL, Halliday provides what is essentially a parallel account of intellectual – or semiotic – development. But whereas Vygotsky's account is couched in terms of the development of word meaning, Halliday's is based on progressive reconstructions of the grammar as a whole, each of which involves a new way of construing experience. Although the development of word meanings is certainly part of this process, it is the child's meaning potential as a whole that is reconstituted at each step, as new experiences of language in use lead to developments in what the child can do with language.

The first reconstruction – and the most far-reaching in terms of its social semiotic consequences – occurs when the child reconstructs his protolanguage as a meaning potential organized in terms of three strata, with a lexicogrammar functioning as intermediary between semantic content and phonological expression. As Halliday explains: "The grammar opens the way to naming and reference, and hence can function as a theory of human experience" (LTL, p. 97). Equally significantly, as a result of this reconstruction, the child's "theory of experience" can be influenced by the cultural theory that is encoded in the adult contributions to the conversations in which they construct meanings together.

At this stage, the child's symbols become "conventional" (in the sense of the relationship between meaning and phonological expression being arbitrary) and words (lexical items) become names of classes of objects, attributes, actions and so on, as it is only class names that can enter into grammatical constructions. Like Vygotsky, Halliday sees classification as generalization, though he also sees the latter as involving the development of taxonomically based systems: "Words are learnt not as in a dictionary but as in a thesaurus, each one being progressively located, in the expanding topological space, by reference to the 'others' to which it is taxonomically related" (LTL, p. 99).

Furthermore, with the adoption of the adults' linguistic semiotic system, a number of strategies for expanding the meaning potential become available. Of these, undoubtedly the most powerful is the ability to give and ask for information, where this is interpreted as "imparting meanings that are not already shared by the person addressed." "Now for the first time learning becomes a two-way semiotic process, based on the reciprocity of learning and teaching. And just as children are predisposed to learn, so parents and other 'others' are predisposed to teach" (LTL, p. 102). However, this teaching is spontaneous, arising for the most part out of the need for the establishment and negotiation of intersubjective agreement about the way in which the situations in which they are jointly engaged should be interpreted. Furthermore, the theory of experience that the child constructs on this basis is not all of a piece. As Halliday points out, "the common-sense grammars of daily life . . . embody complementarities of many kinds, contradictory interpretations of some aspect of experience, each of which illuminates one facet of it – such that the whole is construed in terms of the tension between them" (LTL, p. 108).

It is the transition to school and the demands of literacy that bring about the next reconstruction. Halliday characterizes it in terms of "abstraction" – movement from the concrete to the abstract. Because of the more abstract nature of written language, both with respect to its use of a second order symbolism and with respect to its tendency to make use of words that refer to abstract entities (i.e., "other wordings"), in learning to read and write, children have to reconstitute their meaning potential in a new, more abstract mode. A further important consequence is that, in the process, they begin to become aware of language itself as a semiotic tool that has its own structure and organization. This metalinguistic awareness is what Olson (1994b) sees as the major cognitive consequence of learning to write.

Finally, like Vygotsky, he considers that teachers have an essential role to play in helping children to reconstruct their grammars to cope with the abstractions involved in the use of grammatical metaphor and to recognize and exploit the "synoptic"/"dynamic" complementarity (see Chapter 4). In fact, I believe that it is when we recognize the importance of the teaching function performed by the child's interlocutor more generally, in helping him or her to communicate meanings of personal importance in the terms of a more "adult" grammar, that we discover the reason why "the magic gateways" through which children make the transitions to successive steps in the developmental trajectory are most strongly associated with the interpersonal metafunction (LTL, p. 103).

Once again, comparing the accounts of school learning that Halliday and Vygotsky propose, we find that there is a large degree of similarity between them, including their use of many of the same terms to refer to more or less identical phenomena. And, even when the terms are different – everyday/scientific concepts as opposed to commonsense/ educated knowledge – it is clear that it is very much the same kind of distinction that is being drawn in each case. However, it is also illuminating to look at the ways in which the two accounts differ. I should like to consider two.

Different Conceptions of the Demands of Schooling

Both Vygotsky and Halliday recognize that schooling is very much concerned with the development and reconstruction of meaning. However, they differ in the ways in which they analyze meaning and, in particular, in their choice of units of analysis. Whereas Vygotsky focuses almost exclusively on word meanings as the locus of conceptual development, for Halliday the minimum unit of analysis is a text, that is to say, an instance of language being used in discourse. In the latter's account, meaning is made in the constructing and interpreting of texts, and this involves the interplay of different components of meaning – interpersonal, textual, logical, as well as experiential.

This broader view of meaning has two consequences. First, it allows us to see more clearly that development in the functions of thinking that are possible for the child depends as much on the relationships that are made between word meanings *within the text* as on the structures of generality of the word meanings considered in isolation. In other words, the development of verbally mediated thinking depends on the stage reached in the development of the grammar as a whole. Second, when the act of meaning is seen as involving both (interpersonal) action and (ideational) understanding, as is always the case in the thinking that is embodied in discourse, there is no need to seek outside for the motivation that engenders thinking. This is something of which Vygotsky seems to have been intuitively aware when he wrote, in the final chapter of *Thinking and Speech*, "Thought has its origins in the motivating sphere of consciousness, a sphere that includes our inclinations and needs, our interests and impulses, and our affect and emotion" (1987, p. 282). By focusing on the way in which the full resources of the lexicogrammar enable all these aspects of consciousness to be integrated in the meaning construction that is required in the production of an *external* text, Halliday provides a strong clue as to how these same resources may be drawn on in the thinking of inner speech.

The second difference is in the feature of schooling that is proposed as the spur to the development of what Vygotsky calls the "higher mental functions." For Halliday, it is essentially the demands of coping with written language and its synoptic mode of meaning. For Vygotsky, it is the systemic nature of scientific concepts and their basis in school instruction. However, if we look at the underlying features of the two explanations, we find that they have much in common. Halliday characterizes written language in terms of its relative abstractness and its tendency to project a synoptic perspective on to reality. Vygotsky notes the greater degree of generality (i.e. abstraction) that characterizes scientific concepts and the fact that their relationships to objects are mediated through relationships with other concepts. For Vygotsky, the strength of the scientific concept lies in its promotion of the higher characteristics of conscious awareness and volition. For Halliday, written language encourages the development of metalinguistic awareness and children's monitoring and direction of their own learning processes. Nevertheless, they are in agreement in seeing the systematization of meaning as a central feature of this stage of development.

Interestingly, the first part of Vygotsky's chapter on the development of scientific concepts contains an analysis of learning the written language that stresses the abstract, conscious and volitional nature of the processes involved and identifies them as "the features that distinguish all the higher mental functions that develop during this period" under the influence of instruction (1987, p. 213). Although there is no mention of written language in the later part of the chapter, where the analysis of the development of scientific concepts is made in terms of their level of generality and systemic relatedness, it could be argued that the construction of scientific concepts is just one particular aspect of the "reconstrual" of both language and experience that is involved in learning to read and write. If this is so, as I have argued elsewhere (Chang-Wells and Wells, 1993), the congruence of the two accounts of the development of language-based thinking is even greater than at first sight appears.

Where does this leave the additional developmental step in Halliday's account which is associated with the reconstruction of the grammar in terms of grammatical metaphor? First, it should be stated that, with the development of the concept of grammatical metaphor, Halliday has made a major contribution to our understanding of the way in which the structure of written text influences the possibilities for using language as a semiotic tool. It also makes explicit the nature of one of the major difficulties with which students have to grapple as they begin to encounter texts written from the perspective of the disciplines that underpin the subjects of the secondary school curriculum.[3]

Vygotsky's research extended only to the equivalent of the end of the elementary stage of education and so it is impossible to say whether a continuation into the secondary stage, or the more differentiated, discipline-based analysis of scientific concepts foreshadowed at the conclusion of chapter 6 of *Thinking and Speech*, would have led him to propose a further stage of conceptual development corresponding to this feature of written language. However, it is clear that the social studies texts from which he selected the materials for his research with Shif contained this feature of discipline-based written language, for nominals such as "exploitation" and "revolution" are among the small number of cited examples of scientific concepts. It is therefore tempting to surmise that Vygotsky's failure to recognize the relationship between this feature of the structure of written text and the "higher" forms of verbal thought was due to his greater attention to inner as opposed to outer discourse and, in particular, to his choice of word meaning as the unit of anlysis. However, setting this last difference aside for the moment, it is clear that the two accounts are, overall, very similar; where they differ, the differences reflect complementary rather than contradictory perspectives.

The Complementary Nature of the Two Theories

I hope that by now it will be evident that the theories of language and learning developed by Halliday and Vygotsky are essentially compatible. This is in large part because they both subscribe to the following assumptions:

1. In order to understand any form of human behavior, it is necessary to adopt a genetic approach.
2. Both phylogenetically and ontogenetically, development is dependent on the availability of tools; for intellectual development, semiotic tools are of particular importance.
3. Language is a particularly powerful semiotic tool because its semantic structure:
   - encodes the culture's theory of experience, including the knowledge associated with the use of all other tools;
   - enables its users to interact with each other in order to coordinate their activity and simultaneously to reflect on and share their interpretations of experience.
4. In ontogenesis, development is raised to new levels by the appropriation of the tools created by previous generations. In particular, in learning their mother tongue through situationally based conversation, children also appropriate the knowledge and practices of their culture.

No doubt this list could be extended, but it will serve as a summary of much of the preceding discussion. It will also serve as a background against which the differences between them can be evaluated before going on to consider some of the ways in which treating their perspectives as complementary may lead us to a more comprehensive language-based theory of learning.

Perhaps the most significant difference – and the one that accounts for most of the others – is in the content of their research. Halliday is a linguist, and Vygotsky a psychologist. It is not surprising, therefore, that the former should study texts and the latter mental activity. Nor is it surprising that, although both have a strong interest in the functions of language, Halliday studies these functions as they are realized in external speech and writing, while Vygotsky tends to be more interested in the ways in which language influences mental functions, and in the way it functions in inner speech.

However, the choice of orientation with respect to the phenomena of language – whether external or internal – does not necessarily imply a corresponding choice of either the social or the individual as the frame of reference for interpreting the phenomena. Although Halliday deliberately and explicitly adopts an "inter-organismic" orientation, this does not mean that his social perspective is adopted at the expense of the individual. As his account of language development makes clear, and as Figure 1.1 illustrates, Halliday's conception of the relationship between the individual and the social group, in relation to which he or she simultaneously becomes a member and a person, is very similar to Vygotsky's conception of this relationship.

It is for this reason, I would argue, that we can treat these two orientations as complementary – as Halliday himself suggests (1978, 1984) – and thereby arrive at a richer interpretation of phenomena which both have studied, each from his own theoretical perspective. In the remaining sections of this chapter, therefore, I shall look at four areas in which I believe there is much to be gained by adopting this strategy.

The Educational Consequences of Sociosemantic Variation

The first area in which the complementary perspectives of Halliday and Vygotsky may combine to give a more complete account is that of enculturation and the consequences of growing up in different sociocultural milieux.

Vygotsky raises this issue most explicitly in relation to Piaget's account of intellectual development which, he argues, is seriously flawed because Piaget neglected the impact that differences in sociocultural experience may have on children's development. The developmental uniformities established by Piaget, he points out, "are not the eternal laws of nature but historical and social laws. . . . Whether the child speaks egocentrically or socially depends not only on his age but on the conditions in which he finds himself" (1987, p. 90).

However, in this context, Piaget is only a stalking horse that Vygotsky uses in order to make a more general point. Thought development, he argues, is not simply an individual process, but is contingent on the child's mastering the social means of thought through linguistic interaction with others; furthermore, children's experience of language in use varies as a result of cultural differences in the activities in which they are permitted to participate. It follows, therefore, that studying the development of the child's thinking in different social environments, especially environments where children work, "will create a potential for establishing laws relevant not only to the *here and now* but to the development of the child generally" (1987, p. 91).

More generally, in his writings on this issue, Vygotsky was concerned to establish two very important principles. The first was that the intellectual development of the individual cannot be understood without taking into account his or her interactions with other people in his or her social environment; as he put it, "the very mechanism underlying higher mental functions is a copy from social interaction; all higher mental functions are internalized social relationships" (1981, p. 164). And the second was that this social environment is itself influenced by the wider culture, which varies according to the forms and organization of labor activity that are practiced and the material and semiotic tools that are employed.

Unfortunately, Vygotsky did not himself have time to carry out empirical investigations to substantiate the second of these principles in relation to children's intellectual development, and the study of adult thinking carried out in Central Asia, in which Luria and his colleagues attempted to test the connection between cognition and socially organized modes of interaction (Luria, 1976), had serious methodological limitations (Cole, 1985). More recently, however, there have been renewed attempts to test Vygotsky's ideas through cross-cultural research, and corroborating evidence has been obtained for the two principles, particularly with respect to the cognitive effects of schooled literacy (Bruner and Greenfield, 1972; Scribner and Cole, 1981).

For Halliday, on the other hand, the relationship between the social structure and language behavior has been an abiding concern. Indeed, much of his effort has been directed toward explaining how language has come to be as it is "because of the functions it has evolved to serve in people's lives" (1978, p. 4). Furthermore, his views about the effects on intellectual development of social and cultural differences in linguistic experience are in very general agreement with those of Vygotsky. As he says, "it is not difficult to suppose an intimate connection between language on the one hand and modes of thought and behavior on the other" (1978, p. 25). However, in exploring this issue he has built on ideas derived from sociology and anthropology rather than from cross-cultural psychology, and he has pursued it with respect to differences *within* rather than between cultures, concentrating, in particular, on the role of language in the relationship between social class and educational achievement.

Here, as he is the first to acknowledge, Halliday has been strongly influenced by the work of Basil Bernstein, who was his colleague at the University of London at the time he was leading the Linguistics and English Teaching Programme. What interested Halliday in Bernstein's work was the latter's attempt to explain the relationship betweeen social class and differential educational achievement, not in terms of genetic inheritance, but in terms of the cultural transmission of educational inequality "through linguistic codes, or fashions of speaking, which arise as a consequence of the social structure and the types of social relationship associated with it" (Halliday, 1978, p. 25).

Emphasizing that it is not particular words or sentence structures, and still less pronunciation or accent, that Bernstein is referring to, Halliday explains the connection as follows:

The 'fashions of speaking' are sociosemantic in nature; they are patterns of meaning that emerge more or less strongly, in particular contexts, especially those relating to the socialization of the child in the family. Hence, although each child's language-learning environment is unique, he also shares certain common features with other children of a similar social background; not merely in the superficial sense that the material environments may well be alike – in fact they may not – but in the deeper sense that the forms of social relation and the role systems surrounding him have their effects on the kind of choices in meaning which will be highlighted and given prominence in different types of situation.[4] (1978, pp. 25–6)

Here, it seems to me, Halliday is providing an account, in sociolinguistic terms, of precisely the sorts of differences in sociocultural experience that Vygotsky considered to be critical in relation to intellectual development. What is more, he sees these experiences of linguistically mediated social interaction as constitutive of development in very much the same way as Vygotsky does – as the continuation of the above quotation makes clear: "This dependence on social structure is not merely unavoidable, it is essential to the child's development; he can develop only as *social* man, and therefore his experience must be shaped in ways which make him a member of society and his particular section of it"(1978, p. 26).

When Halliday's theoretical description of sociosemantic variation is taken in conjunction with the evidence from Hasan's (1986, 1992; Hasan and Cloran, 1990) empirical investigations based on Bernstein's theory of socialization, the result is a powerful account of the way in which certain key features of the social structure are enacted and "transmitted" through the everyday conversations experienced by children from different social classes. On the other hand, as we might expect, Halliday has little to say about the specifically intra-organismic consequences of this sociosemantic variation.

As pointed out above, Halliday's concern is with the role of language in the formation of *social man*; his interest is in language as the prototypical form of *social* semiotic and, in particular, in the way in which the semantic system of language both finds its realization in the lexicogrammar and itself realizes the larger behavioral systems which constitute the social semiotic. Vygotsky, by contrast, was concerned with the development of consciousness and the semiotically mediated mental phenomena of which it is constituted. Although emphasizing the origins of language in social action, both phylogenetically and ontogenetically, his own research concentrated on the transformation of the child's mental, that is to say internal, functioning that occurs when social, or external, language is internalized to become a more powerful means of mediating intra-mental intellectual activity.

Far from being in conflict, however, I believe these two orientations are complementary in the account they offer of the educational consequences of growing up in different cultural or subcultural environments. The explanation of intellectual development that Vygotsky offers, in terms of the internalization of the modes of discourse that mediate social action and interaction, is a major part of such an account. However, as Wertsch (1989) observes, it is far from complete. For, in concentrating almost exclusively on dyadic social interaction, Vygotsky failed to explain how the discursive means that are internalized to mediate intramental functioning are themselves influenced by sociocultural factors such as class, ethnicity and gender. However, it is just this part of the overall account that is found in Halliday's theoretical description of sociosemantic variation as it impacts on educational achievement.

Putting these two theoretical contributions together, therefore, we might propose the following account: Children's ability to engage effectively in the different tasks that they may be expected to undertake in school depends on the extent to which they have internalized the sociosemantic functions of the specific modes of discourse that mediate these tasks, both inter-mentally and intramentally; and this depends on the extent to which these functions have been highlighted in their interactions with the significant others in their immediate family environments which, in turn, varies according to the family's relationship to the larger social structure. In particular, it varies according to ethnic and social class membership.

Clearly, a key factor in the working out of the relationship between sociocultural background and school achievement is the nature of the activities in which children are expected to engage in school. In principle, there is no reason why school tasks should not be selected such that they validate and build on the sociosemantic functions that individual children have already mastered, while systematically introducing those that are as yet undeveloped (cf. Heath, 1983; Moll and Greenberg, 1990). This would certainly be in keeping with Vygotsky's conception of learning and teaching in the zone of proximal development (Tharp and Gallimore, 1988). However, in practice, the tasks and modes of discourse that tend to be privileged are precisely those that are least familiar to nonmainstream children; as a result, a situation is created in which these children become educationally disadvantaged.

Whether the modes of discourse that are privileged are really of inherently greater intellectual value is a matter of current debate (Lemke, 1988). However, as Halliday points out,

As things are, certain ways of organizing experience through language, and of participating and interacting with things, are necessary to success in school. The child who is not predisposed to this type of verbal exploration in this type of experiential and interpersonal context 'is not at home in the educational context', as Bernstein puts it. Whether a child is so predisposed or not turns out not to be any innate property of the child as an individual, an inherent limitation on his mental powers, as used to be generally assumed; it is merely the result of a mismatch between his own symbolic orders of meaning and those of the school, a mismatch that results from the different patterns of socialization that characterize different sections of society, or subcultures, and which are in turn a function of the underlying social relations in the family and elsewhere. (1978, p. 26)

Enculturation: Cultural Reproduction or Individual Empowerment?

It might be objected, however, that this theory of language-mediated enculturation, as just outlined, is heavily weighted towards the cultural determination of individual development. Indeed, a criticism that has sometimes been levelled against the work of both Halliday and Vygotsky – or at least against some of the uses that are being made of their work in education – is that it emphasizes cultural reproduction at the expense of cultural change, and conformity at the expense of individual creativity (Dixon, 1987; Engeström, 1991 b; Hatano, 1993; Sawyer and Watson, 1987). In order to evaluate this charge, we must look briefly at the ways in which the possibility of change is envisaged in the writings of the two theorists.

As might be expected, Halliday deals with cultural change through the relationship between the cultural semiotic and the particular texts that are constructed in relation to it. The social system is not static, he argues, for it is being constantly recreated in the social encounters in which it is instantiated, and these are themselves dynamic. This can be seen most clearly by looking at the discourse processes through which texts are created. As these proceed in real time, "the meaning of the text is fed back into the situation, and becomes part of it, changing it in the process; it is also fed back, through the register, into the semantic system, which it likewise affects and modifies" (1978, p. 126).

It is within this general account that we can best understand the permeability of the situation described in the previous section. There, I characterized Halliday's interpretation of the sociolinguistic codes proposed by Bernstein as involving a variation in semantic style, or meaning orientation, that is associated with the positions that different individuals and their families occupy in the social structure. However, since all conversations are dynamic, encounters involving interactions between users and uses of these different codes have the potential of bringing about change through feedback, both in the meaning orientations of the speakers and in their role relationships vis-à-vis the members of their family and other social groups.

Thus, in the course of growing up, the young child is involved in encounters with people occupying various positions in the social structure; these include encounters through reading and television viewing, as well as face-to-face encounters with family members, teachers and other people in the wider community. As a result, the meaning potential that each child constructs, and the "personality" that he or she develops, is the unique outcome of the particular interactions in which he or she has participated. Nevertheless, the degree to which these encounters extend or modify the meaning orientation initially developed within the individual child's family depends on further factors having to do with the conditions under which later encounters take place, notably the way in which she or he is welcomed into, or made to feel excluded from, the social groups to which her or his interlocutors belong.

However, the child is never simply a passive recipient of the ways of speaking that he or she encounters, but is continually constructing from them a personal meaning potential and a related perspective on experience. At every stage in his or her development, therefore – in childhood and beyond – each individual has unique contributions to make to the interactions in which he or she participates and an opportunity thereby to contribute to the modification of the social structure. For, as Halliday emphasizes, it is by individual acts of meaning in the situations in which those interactions occur, that the "social reality is created, maintained in good order, and continuously shaped and modified" (1978, p. 139). In keeping with his chosen perspective, therefore, Halliday's explanation of the possibility – indeed the inevitability – of change is inter-organismic, based in the dynamics of interaction and his conception of social man.

Vygotsky's explanation also gives a central role to language and other semiotic tools but, rather than being either inter- or intra-organismic, it is focused on the relationship between the two. In this way, it offers a psychological interpretation of the more sociologically oriented account that Halliday proposes. Briefly, Vygotsky's argument is that, in appropriating the resources of the culture through participation in social action and interaction, the individual both transforms those resources and is transformed in the process.

The first step in his argument is included, almost as an afterthought, in his exposition of the genetic law of cultural development, quoted above (p. 22). Having asserted the primacy of the *inter*-mental plane in the development of any mental function, he continues as follows: "but it goes without saying that internalization transforms the process itself and changes its structure and function" (1981, p. 163).

Although this statement is not much further developed in the chapter in question, Vygotsky's seminal remark about the constructive and creative nature of the transformations that take place in the internalization of mental processes has begun to receive sustained attention in more recent work in the sociocultural tradition (Engeström, 1991a; Gal'perin, 1969; Wertsch and Stone, 1985). As these writers emphasize, following Vygotsky, internalization does not involve a simple copying of an external intermental process, but rather an internal construction of the corresponding process, which builds upon and is shaped by what the child can already do and understand. This gives rise to the first type of transformation – a modification of the child's own mental processes, that changes the ways in which he or she perceives, interprets and organizes the world (Nikolopoulou, 1991).

However, since the prior experience on which this construction is based is inevitably different, both between individual children and from one generation to the next, the resulting constructions also differ, giving rise to transformations of the process itself. The potential significance of this can be seen in the final phase of the internalization cycle, when, in the course of further social activity, the individual externalizes the process that he or she has appropriated in behavior which is novel in the situation and which, as a result, may transform the way in which the situation is understood by other members of the culture.

For both Halliday and Vygotsky, therefore, creativity and change are inherent characteristics of all action and interaction, resulting, over time, in the transformation of the resources of the individual participants and of the sociocultural practices in relation to which they occur. As already described, the facets of this complex process of cultural and individual transformation that they have each explored are essentially complementary. By combining them, I believe, we can construct a more comprehensive explanation of cultural change and individual creativity, which shows how the two are related. This might be briefly stated as follows.

As Halliday suggests, the impetus for change is to be found in the social semiotic world, in tensions of various kinds, either within the system itself, or in relation to encounters involving individuals that arise in the course of everyday situations. An individual who is faced with a problem that he or she cannot manage alone is a particular case of such tension. In one form or another, these tensions are resolved – at least partially – in the dynamics of social action and interaction, involving the use of language and possibly other mediating tools as well; in some cases, the resolution may also result in modification of, or addition to, the culture's available repertoire of mediating tools. Furthermore, from the perspective of the individual, participation in such collaborative action and interaction provides the opportunity for him or her to appropriate the processes involved, which, when internalized and integrated with their existing resources, as Vygotsky explains, transforms the way in which they tackle similar problems in the future. However, since internalization always involves a construction based on the individual's existing resources, the process that is internalized may itself be transformed, leading to subsequent innovatory forms of externalization in contexts of social action and interaction which, in turn, may introduce change into the semiotic system.[5]

Change, creativity and diversification are thus of the essence of interaction, both between and within groups and individuals, as is clearly brought out by the genetic method of analysis. Whether these qualities are encouraged – or, alternatively, suppressed – depends on value judgments made by those with greater power in the social system. However, these too, as Lemke (1990) argues, are also ultimately open to negotiation and change.

The Intellectual Consequences
of Language-based Learning in School

A third area in which I believe the combining of the different perspectives provided by Halliday and Vygotsky can offer a more comprehensive account is in relation to the linguistic and cognitive benefits of schooling. Their individual accounts were considered comparatively in an earlier section of this chapter. An interpretation that combines them might look something like the following.

When children come to school, they have already made considerable progress in constructing a practical theory of experience, based on commonsense knowledge. This they have achieved, simultaneously with learning their mother tongue, from taking part in the activity and discourse of everyday life in and around their homes, in which that knowledge is encoded in the texts that they co-construct with significant others. The specific content of this theory, including beliefs about the goals of action and interaction, and about the particular semiotic resources that are appropriately recruited in their achievement, varies from child to child, depending on each child's unique experience, as this is mediated by the roles that he or she is called on to play by virtue of membership of a particular culture, ethnic group, social class, and gender. Furthermore, although children's behavior, both verbal and nonverbal, is for the most part fluent and purposeful, they are not yet consciously aware of the means that they employ. In particular, although they use language as a means for understanding and reflecting on their experience, they cannot yet make language itself or the meanings that it encodes the subject of deliberate attention and manipulation.

However, in the first few years of schooling, an important transformation takes place, engendered largely by the experience of learning to read and write and of using this language mode as a tool for the achievement of a wide variety of tasks. Written language requires a considerable degree of abstraction, both of the written expression from the spoken, and of the solo process from the co-constructed. This abstraction draws children's attention to the medium of language itself and also to the meanings that it encodes, thereby bringing both into the domain of conscious awareness and volition.

Through engaging with written texts in relation to the topics that they study in school, therefore, children gradually reconstitute their lexicogrammar in the more abstract written mode; at the same time, they come to reinterpret their experience according to the semantic structures that are characteristic of these written texts. Furthermore, as the content of the curriculum becomes more text-based, they begin to encounter new meanings that are more abstract and systemic in nature than those encountered in everyday speech. Thus, in learning to reconstrue experience in terms of the semantic structure of written language, children construct what Vygotsky refers to as "scientific concepts." That is to say, it is written texts – and the talk about them – that provide the discursive means for the development of the "higher mental functions," through the appropriation of the systematically related concepts that correspond to the more abstract semantic structures found in written texts.

One particular characteristic of the written texts in which discipline-based, school knowledge is presented is the prevalence of grammatical metaphor in the lexicogrammatical realization of meaning. In contrast to the dynamic interpretation of experience in terms of actions and processes that is characteristic of commonsense knowledge and everyday speech, grammatical metaphor foregrounds the synoptic interpretation of reality, which objectifies experience by encoding processes and relations in structures organized around nouns. To understand and use this mode of written language requires a further reconstruction of the grammar; however, once mastered, this written, "scientific" mode of construing experience provides a powerful complement to the narrative (dynamic) mode that is characteristic of spontaneous everyday speech.

The reorganization of the grammar and the concomitant reconstrual of experience that are required in order to use synoptic written text as a tool for thinking and communicating do not occur spontaneously for most children. In order to master this new mode, they need to perceive it as functional for them in relation to activities that they find both challenging and personally meaningful. They also need to be given guidance and assistance in carrying out those parts of these activities that they are unable to manage on their own. This is most likely to occur when activities are carried out in situations of collaboration with the teacher or other children, in which the new, synoptic mode of construing experience is related to the more familiar, dynamic mode through talk that moves back and forth between the two modes, building bridges between them.

Exactly what activities and classroom conditions are most likely to provide the necessary guidance and assistance is a question that is currently being investigated in a considerable number of classroom-based studies, many of which are inspired by one or other of the theorists whose work has been considered here. However, my belief is that such studies might have even more to gain by adopting a perspective that takes account of both.

It is with this in mind that, in the final section of this chapter, I wish briefly to consider the claims about learning to mean that Halliday makes in the stimulating, but highly condensed, article, "Towards a language-based theory of learning."

Action, Speech, and Thought

In the opening paragraph of LTL, Halliday states that "the distinctive characteristic of human learning is that it is a process of making meaning – a semiotic process." And, in the sense that all learning contributes to the individual's ability to participate in activities that take their meaning from the part they play in the lives of the sociocultural groups to which the individual belongs or aspires, this claim is undoubtedly correct. In this sense, one might agree that even learning to swim (to use his own example) is semiotic, although the physical skills that are involved can, in principle, be mastered in the absence of interaction with other human beings and are functionally equivalent to those that are part of the repertoire of mammals that are not, like humans, "quintessentially creatures who mean" (LTL, abstract).

However, the consequence of conflating all human behavior under the single rubric of 'meaning' is that one loses sight of some important distinctions that need to be made in developing a language-based theory of learning. Halliday is obviously aware of this for, in the opening chapter of the 1978 collection, he clearly distinguishes "meaning" from "doing" and "saying."

Language is being regarded as the encoding of a 'behaviour potential' into a 'meaning potential'; that is, as a means of expressing what the human organism 'can do', in interaction with other human organisms, by turning it into what he 'can mean'. What he can mean (the semantic system) is, in turn, encoded into what he 'can say' (the lexicogrammatical system, or grammar and vocabulary). (1978, p. 21)

In this definition, Halliday draws a clear distinction between doing and meaning, while seeing them both as forms of semiotic behavior, more generally conceived. Maintaining this distinction, therefore, it seems to follow that, although one can talk (i.e. can mean) about what one is doing, did or might do, the actual "doing," although a form of semiotic behavior, is not itself "meaning," except in the case where the "doing" is in language.

What I am arguing, then, is that, on the one hand, there are serious ambiguities in Halliday's use of the term "meaning" from one occasion to another, and that, on the other, in conflating the learning of all semiotic systems under the umbrella phrase "learning to mean," as he seems to do in LTL, he fails to distinguish the different roles that language plays in the development of "social man."

However, there is, in my view, a further reason for objecting to treating all doing as "meaning," in the sense in which "meaning" is defined in the above quotation. That is that this formulation fails to recognize the toollike function of language in the achievement of the goals of semiotic activity more broadly conceived. In Vygotsky's terms, meaning linguistically is one – albeit the most important – form of semiotic mediation and, to understand its significance on particular occasions, one must look at the goals of the activity it mediates. To recall Leont'ev's argument (quoted above), "The tool mediates activity and thus connects humans not only with the world of objects but also with other people." While language is certainly a powerful and versatile tool, it is the activity that it mediates that has conceptual and historical primacy, for it is through action and activities that we are related to the external world (Minick, 1987).

As set out in LTL, where the emphasis is on language learning and learning through language through the successive reorganizations of the grammar, together with the progressive reconstruing of experience that these entail, Halliday's language-based theory of learning goes a long way toward explaining how language functions to connect humans with objects and with other people. However, it has very little to say about the wide range of activities in relation to which it performs this mediating role or about the specific functions of planning, directing, interpreting, and so on, through which this role is enacted. Here, it seems to me, the extension of Vygotsky's initial insights about semiotic mediation in more recent work on the theory of activity (Leont'ev, 1978, 1981; Engeström, 1991) can provide an important complementary perspective.

On the other hand, it is important to reiterate the reciprocal nature of the complementarity I have sought to demonstrate. In suggesting that Halliday's sociolinguistic perspective will benefit from being articulated with activity theory, therefore, I wish to make clear that I equally believe that activity theory will benefit from the inclusion of Halliday's well-developed theory of language as social semiotic. As Minick (1987) points out, although Vygotsky was intellectually convinced of the importance of developing greater understanding of interpersonal and social discourse, neither he nor his colleagues and followers have pursued this program to any great extent. It is here, I believe, that Halliday has a particularly important contribution to make.

If we now combine the two perspectives, we might propose the following specification for a theory of learning: A comprehensive language-based theory of learning should not only explain how language is learned and how cultural knowledge is learned through language. It should also show how this knowledge arises out of collaborative practical and intellectual activities and, in turn, mediates the actions and operations by means of which these activities are carried out, in the light of the conditions and exigencies that obtain in particular situations. Finally, such a theory should explain how change, both individual development and social and cultural change, occurs through the individual's linguistically mediated internalization and subsequent externalization of the goals and processes of action and interaction in the course of these activities.

If we now apply this more comprehensive theory to education, we might characterize school learning rather more broadly than Halliday does in LTL. Certainly, learning is a semiotic process, for which the prototypical resource is language. But it involves learning to do as well as to mean – to expand one's action potential as well as one's potential for meaning through language. Discourse, both spoken and written, plays an essential, mediating, role in this process, together with other semiotic tools. But the object of all this learning is not just the development of the learner's meaning potential, conceived as the construction of discipline-based knowledge, but the development of the resources of action, speech, and thinking that enable the learner to participate effectively and creatively in further practical, social, and intellectual activity.

Such a theory of learning also has implications for the recommendations we might wish to make for the kinds of classroom activity through which these resources can be developed. However, in order to go beyond current practice in ways that are pedagogically feasible as well as theoretically desirable, such recommendations will need to be derived from further research. And this must not only be based on this language-based theory of learning but – equally important – carried out in collaboration with teachers in relation to issues arising from the particular historical and cultural conditions in which they work. These are issues that I shall take up in the chapters that follow.

Notes

1. In this context, it is interesting to note, as Martin (1993) does, the similarity of this Hallidayan framework to the perspective proposed by Bakhtin, who was one of Vygotsky's contemporaries. Substituting the term "text" for "utterance" throughout, Martin quotes the following extract:

> All the diverse ares of human activity involve the use of language. Quite understandably, the nature of forms of this use are just as diverse as are the areas of human activity. . . . Language is realised in the form of individual concrete texts (oral and written) by participants in the various areas of human activity. The texts reflect the specific conditions and goals of each such area not only through their content (thematic) and linguisitic style, that is the selection of the lexical, phraseological, and grammatical resources of the language, but above all through their compositional structure. All three of these aspects – thematic content, style, and compositional structure – are inseparably linked to the *whole* of the text and are equally determined by the specific nature of the particular sphere of communication. Each separate text is individual, of course, but each sphere in which language is used develops its own *relatively stable types* of these texts. These we may call *speech genres*. (Bakhtin, 1986, p. 60. Quoted in Martin, 1993, p. 2)

2. As Minick (1987) makes clear in his translator's introduction, the chapters that make up this monograph were written at different times between 1929 and 1934 and therefore, although the monograph as a whole was one of his last completed works, its separate chapters belong to more than one stage in the development of Vygotsky's thinking on the relationship between speech and thinking.

3. The following is an example from a secondary school history text about the Chinese revolution, together with one possible alternative more characteristic of speech, that I have adapted from Martin (1993).

   Written

   This most successful phase of the Long March owes a great deal to the diplomatic skills of Zhou Enlai and to the bravery of the rearguard.

   Spoken

   [Zhou Enlai was able to negotiate skillfully with Chen Jitang (1)] and [the soldiers {who were left to guard the rear (3)} were very brave (2)], so [the Red Army successfully escaped (4)]. (p. 10)

   In the "spoken" version, there are four clauses, numbered 1–4 (clause 3 is a relative clause defining which soldiers were brave). In the written version, the (approximate) meaning of each of these clauses is realized by the following correspondingly numbered nominal structures: (1) "the diplomatic *skills* of Zhou Enlai"; (2) "the *bravery* of the rearguard"; (3) "of the *rearguard*"; (4) "This most successful *phase* of the Long March." The only verb in the written clause does not realize a process at all but, in conjunction with a further nominal

structure – "a great *deal*" – is the metaphorical realization of the logical connec-
tor "so" in the "spoken" version.

For a fuller discussion of grammatical metaphor, see Chapter 8.

4. Halliday discusses Bernstein's theory of sociolinguistic codes in considerable
   detail in "Sociological aspects of semantic change," which is included as chapter
   3 of *Language as social semiotic* (1978).

5. A classroom-based example of such a transformation of a conceptual tool is
   discussed in Chapter 5.

2   In Search of Knowledge

One of the central claims put forward in the language-based theory of learning proposed by both Vygotsky and Halliday is that the very same conversations that provide the opportunity for the child to learn language also provide the opportunity to learn *through* language. That is to say, by participating in the conversations that form part of most everyday activities, the child not only appropriates the culture's chief means of interpersonal communication, but also its ways of making sense of experience, as these are encoded in the discourse contributions of the coparticipants in those activities. As Halliday puts it: "language is the essential condition of knowing, the process by which experience becomes knowledge" (1993a, p. 94).

This is a strong claim and one that is clearly relevant to the ongoing educational debate about "educational knowledge" – what should be taught and how. However, what is surprising about this debate is how little attention is given to the nature of the knowledge over which there is so much disagreement. What does it mean to talk about either the "transmission" or the "transformation" of knowledge, and how are these processes achieved in the discourse, both spoken and written, which constitute the major forms of activity in classrooms at all levels from kindergarten to university. In this and the next chapter I want to explore these issues in further detail.

As I shall argue below, knowledge construction and theory development most frequently occur in the context of a problem of some significance and take the form of a dialogue in which solutions are proposed and responded to with additions and extensions or objections and counterproposals from others. In this respect, these two chapters are no exception. The general problem that they address is the future of education in the twenty-first century and the proposal to which they react concerns the role of schooling, as this was envisaged in a report prepared by an educational association in one of Canada's largest provinces. Together, these chapters constitute my response; in them, I attempt to argue for an alternative to the traditional conception of schooling as knowledge transmission, putting in its place one based on the ideas of Vygotsky, Halliday and others working in what might be called the social constructivist tradition.

Here, in the first of these two chapters, I explore the nature of knowledge and its development – its construction, reconstruction and improvement through different modes of knowing and over different scales of time. I then apply this conception of knowing and knowledge to the classroom to explore the conditions under which students in school are best able to participate in knowledge construction. Then, in Chapter 3, I consider the central role of language in knowing and understanding, and review some of the work that has contributed to my own understanding of this issue. Needless to say, Chapters 2 and 3 are presented, not as definitive conclusions, but as contributions to an ongoing and, hopefully, progressive dialogue about the ends and means of schooling.

Prologue

In the fall of 1995, the Fédération Étudiante Unversitaire du Québec, an association representing 100,000 university students in the province, presented a brief to the Provincial Parliament setting out its aims for the future of education in Quebec. In general, the document is enlightened, particularly in its emphasis on the role of education in "developing free and responsible citizens" and in "creating a dynamic of social participation, involvement and commitment." However, when it comes to defining the way in which schools can contribute to the achievement of these aims, the stance adopted is both traditional and unequivocal. Schools, these students write, are "first and foremost responsible for the transmission of basic and general knowledge" (FEUQ 1996, p. 6).

What particularly concerns me about this formulation is, first, the limited – and limiting – nature of the goal that is proposed and of the means by which it is to be attained and, second, that it is those who will be the policy makers of tomorrow who are the ones to have proposed it. For from my social-constructivist perspective, the image of schooling that they endorse is doubly misguided. First, in its emphasis on social reproduction, it fails to recognize that society is constantly changing, as is what knowledge it is considered important to master; by the same token, it also subordinates diversity, adaptability, and creativity to a normative, backward looking conformity. Second, in its characterization of learning and teaching as "transmission," that is to say, as a unilateral process in which a closed and unquestioned body of information and routine skills is imposed on passive, but supposedly, receptive students, it flies in the face of all that has been discovered about the essentially dialogic and constructive nature of knowledge building.

On further reflection, however, this stance could perhaps be expected. Although constructivism has been accepted, in the last decade or so, by a growing proportion of those who study and theorize about learning and teaching, it has hardly influenced the practices of the majority of classroom teachers. It is thus unlikely that the schooling of those currently at university would have felt its impact. Most probably, therefore, these successful students speak out of their own experience. However, even if they had been inclined to take a more critical and metacognitive stance toward their experience of learning in school, it might still have been difficult for them to find a better way of characterizing the goals and means. For, even among those who embrace the constructivist paradigm, there has been an apparent reluctance critically to examine the nature of what is constructed or the manner in which the constructive processes in which students engage can be related to the processes through which the "advancement of knowledge" is collaboratively undertaken by communities of scholars and researchers (Bereiter and Scardamalia, 1996).

Thus if, as teachers and teacher educators, we hope to bring about significant improvements in the way in which the practice of education is enacted in school classrooms, an important first step, it seems to me, is to attempt to clarify our own understanding of what is involved in the construction and reconstruction of knowledge. There are two questions, in particular, that I believe need to be addressed: What do we mean by "knowledge"? And, in the light of our answer to this question, What are the conditions under which students in school are best able to participate in its construction?

Knowledge: What is the Nature of this Abstraction?

There seem to be two major impediments to making progress in understanding the nature of knowledge. The first is the wide range of ways in which the term "knowledge" is used (Alexander et al., 1991). On the one hand, it refers to a whole gamut from isolated bits of information, or "facts," through specific concepts of varying degrees of generality, to generally accepted explanatory theories of, for example, energy, disease, or the free market economy. This heterogeneity clearly raises questions about the scope of what is considered to be knowledge and about the extent to which knowledge must be couched in propositional form and organized in terms of systematically related concepts. On the other hand, the term is also used to refer to "skills" – actions that an individual can perform effectively – as well as to "strategies" that are used to guide task performance, and to "metaknowledge" about the deployment of conceptual and strategic knowledge and about the principles considered to underlie such skillful performance. Some relevant questions here concern the relationship between knowing how to perform some action and being able to represent that knowledge discursively, and how the one influences, or may be converted into, the other.

If the first problem can in general be characterized as one of reference – what should properly be considered to be an instance of knowledge? – the second concerns the existential status of such instances. Is knowledge always and necessarily manifested in particular activities, or does it exist in some abstract realm, independent of particular instantiations? Can it be "possessed" only by individuals, or is knowledge public, that is to say, what is taken to be commonly "known," even though by only a very few of those who make reference to it? Here again, usage is of little help, as most of us employ the term in both senses, depending on the particular context. In this respect, "knowledge" is no different from related words, such as "belief" or "thought," which are equally difficult to pin down. Thus, although there have been a number of recent attempts to bring conceptual clarity to the proliferation of knowledge terminology (Alexander et al., 1991; de Jong and Ferguson-Hessler, 1996), it seems that more is required than analysis and consolidation of contemporary usage.

An alternative approach, and one that I believe may prove more fruitful, is to focus, not on the terms, but on the different activities in which knowledge is involved and on the development of these activities. This is the 'genetic' approach suggested by Vygotsky (1978) and since developed by a wide variety of scholars within the cultural-historical tradition. As Luria, one of Vygotsky's students and colleagues, wrote about the study of all forms of mental activity, of which the construction and use of knowledge are clear examples: "In order to explain the highly complex forms of human consciousness one must go beyond the human organism. One must seek the origins of conscious activity . . . in the external processes of social life, in the social and historical forms of human existence" (1981, p. 25, quoted in Wertsch and Tulviste, 1992).

In what follows, I shall follow this advice by considering the genesis of knowledge in terms of the development of different modes of knowing in the historical development of human cultures. But first, a brief exposition of what Vygotsky meant by a genetic approach seems necessary, together with an explanation of my own reasons for adopting it.

A Genetic Approach to the Development of Knowledge

As a psychologist, Vygotsky was interested in all forms of human behavior. However, unlike many of his contemporaries, he did not believe that a descriptive analysis of current behavior, however detailed, could provide an adequate basis for an explanation of what was observed. Instead, he argued, it is necessary to study the *genesis* of behavior; hence the 'genetic' approach: "For the developmental psychologist the historical form of explanation is the highest possible. In order to answer the question of what a form of behavior represents, he/she finds it necessary to discover its origin and the history of its development up to the present. In Blonsky's words, behavior can be understood only as the history of behavior" (1981, p. 147).

When he referred to the history of behavior, however, Vygotsky did not mean only the development of a form of behavior in relation to an individual person. In fact, he proposed four levels of genetic analysis for the study of any form of development. These correspond to the developmental trajectories of: a particular event or situation, of an individual, of a culture, and of the human species as a whole. From one perspective, the four levels can be thought of hierarchically. How an event unfolds, *microgenetically*, depends on the affordances of the situation, on the way in which the participants construe it, and on the resources they can bring to bear in constructing solutions to the problems it poses. However, both construal of the situation and the resources actually employed depend upon the manner and extent to which the participants have *ontogenetically*, i.e. in their own life trajectories, appropriated the resources available in the culture of which they are members, that is to say, the practices, tools, motives, and values in terms of which cultural activities are organized. These resources, in turn, have their own developmental trajectories, which are both constitutive of, and shaped by, the *historical development of a particular culture*; and this itself is conditioned by the stage reached in the *phylogenetic* development of the human species.

The four genetic levels can thus be seen as operating on four different time scales, with the more extended developmental domains simultaneously serving as constraints on, and resources for, development on the less extended, down to the microgenetic events of lived experience (Cole and Engeström, 1993). Viewed from this past-to-present perspective, what is most salient about human behavior is its continuity over time, as solutions to past problems are reproduced and brought to bear in the present through the use of tools and practices in which those solutions are embodied. This is the perspective of cultural reproduction.

However, important though it is, this reproductive perspective reveals only one part of the picture. For, in practice, no event is exactly the same as those that have gone before and so there is never exact reproduction (Valsiner, 1994). Instead, viewed from the microgenetic perspective of the specific moment, all events can be seen to involve change, as the participants creatively exploit the total resources of the particular situation to construe and solve the problems that emerge in and through their activity. Indeed, every event results in some degree of transformation of all of its constituents. First, there is the transformation of the immediate situation that results from the participants' actions; an artifact is made or modified in some way in order to meet their needs. Second, to the extent that the situation makes new demands on the participants, it also brings about ontogenetic change in the form of a transformation of their own potential for further action; finally, in some cases, there may also be a transformation of the mediational means by which the action is performed, for example in the improvement or adaptation of an existing tool or practice. Each event thus has the potential to contribute, beyond the immediate moment, to a transformation of the wider culture. Whether or not it actually does so, however, depends on a number of factors, including the further events in which the participants are involved, the perceived applicability and utility of the new action or artifact and their dissemination through being appropriated by other participants and, not least, the openness to change on the part of the powerful "oldtimers" in the cultural community in which the new solutions emerge (Lave and Wenger, 1991).

Having presented this brief sketch of the four genetic levels and their interdependence, I now want to suggest some of the advantages of adopting the genetic approach. First, as I hope I have shown, it makes apparent the dialectical relationship that holds between continuity and change; it highlights the way in which the solving of the problems posed by any particular situation requires the participants both to construe it as being of a type to which, historically and ontogenetically, existing resources of tools and practices can be applied and, at the same time, to adapt and extend those resources to the specific and often novel demands that the situation poses. This is a principle that I believe has very general applicability.

Second, this approach helps us to resolve the vexed problem of the relationship between the individual and his or her social and cultural environment. By focusing on participation in jointly undertaken, mediated activity as the site of both continuity and change, it emphasizes the mutually constitutive relationship between the activity, on the one hand, seen as an ongoing historical-cultural system and, on the other hand, the participants, practices and artifacts through which the activity is instantiated on particular occasions. And this, in turn, allows us to see how, through participation in particular, situated enactments of a variety of cultural activities, participants develop simultaneously as individuals with unique sets of competences and unique life trajectories, and also as members of a wider cultural community who, with others, contribute both to its continuity and to its transformation.

Third – and of particular relevance in the present context – a genetic approach allows us to see that knowledge, too, has a history. And by this, I do not mean simply that what is taken to be true in particular fields has changed over time. Rather, as I shall hope to show, there has also been development in our modes of knowing and in the manner in which knowledge is constructed. Indeed, as Wartofsky (1979) has argued, "what we take knowledge to be is itself the subject of an historical evolution" (p. xiii).

When we look only at what is currently the most valued form of knowledge, we may easily be misled into thinking that knowledge is essentially abstract in nature and largely unrelated to the business of everyday living. We may, furthermore, see the advancement of knowledge as being almost exclusively the result of the contributions of uniquely creative individuals working in "splendid isolation." However, when we take a historical perspective, by contrast, it becomes apparent that, in its origins, knowledge is intimately bound up with activity and is essentially social in nature (Oatley, 1996). Indeed, this is a key theme in cultural-historical theory, where it is proposed that it is essentially in object-oriented joint activity that humans construct their knowledge of the world and, furthermore, that the value of this knowledge is that it serves to mediate their further collective activity (Leont'ev, 1981). Certainly, as Leont'ev acknowledged, both activity and the related knowledge are generated by particular, concrete individuals; however, he was equally emphatic that the individual's activity only has meaning "in the system of social relations" (p. 47). Quoting Vygotsky, he insisted that "consciousness is *co-knowledge*" (p. 56, emphasis added). In other words, knowledge only has significance and value in the context of joint action and interaction, where it is both constructed and used as a mediational means.

Interestingly, a similar view was recently expressed by the distinguished scientist, Ursula Franklin, when introducing one of the speakers at a recent symposium, entitled "Towards an Ecology of Knowledge," at the University of Toronto. As she very aptly put it, "knowledge is developed in the discourse between people doing things together" (Franklin, 1996).

This, then, is the perspective I shall adopt as, in what follows, I draw upon a variety of sources to sketch what I believe to be a plausible account of the way in which different modes of knowing emerged historically in the development of the earliest human cultures.[1]

The Emergence of Different Modes of Knowing in Human History

Although we know very little about our earliest ancestors, it is clear from archaeological and other evidence that, well before the emergence of homo sapiens some 250,000 years ago, they had already developed some degree of skill in the activities in which they engaged, including *instrumental* knowledge involved in the use of tools to mediate their activity. Had they lived as isolated individuals, each one would have had to construct that instrumental knowledge for him or herself from scratch, as is the case with contemporary higher primates (Tomasello, 1994), and there would have been no possibility of that knowledge being cumulatively improved over successive generations. By the same token, there would have been little if any call to reflect on the activities they performed and to construct some degree of self-conscious awareness of the processes involved.

However, the evidence strongly suggests that, on the contrary, even before the earliest homo sapiens, they did not live as isolates but in bands, spanning several generations, that had a well-developed social structure. Under these conditions, most activities were probably undertaken jointly and this clearly required some coordination of action and sharing of knowledge. Minimally, novices of whatever age needed to learn how to take part in these activities and to use the tools and practices that mediated them, and this, in turn, required that they come to construe the relevant situations and cultural practices in the same way as other participants. Whether by showing or telling, or by some combination, therefore, more skillful members of the group must have made their instrumental knowledge available for imitation and appropriation, and this required of them at least some degree of reflective analysis and the construction of conscious, *procedural* knowledge. In all probability, this was achieved through symbolic communication mediated by mimetic gesture and rudimentary speech (Donald, 1991).

Still further demands were made as, by the time of homo sapiens, activities had become more complex and choices had to be made between alternative means in relation to prevailing conditions. In order to decide on the actions to be taken on particular occasions and to coordinate what had been agreed, participants not only needed to be able to describe their proposals but also to explain and justify them in terms of their understanding of relations between ends and means, and causes and consequences. In other words, they needed to develop a mode of knowing that went beyond the particular situation. This we might call the beginnings of generalizable, *substantive* knowledge, and it almost certainly involved language and emerged, as Franklin put it, "in the discourse between people doing things together."

To some extent parallel with this form of collaborative reflection and imaginative projection of future practical action was the construction of myths, legends, rituals, and other modes of making sense of the group's experience through narrative, dance, song, and drama. For although not usually considered alongside substantive knowledge, such religious and artistic representations also serve a similar function, among others, of providing an explanatory framework in terms of which particular events can be interpreted, understood, and evaluated. Indeed, according to Donald (1991), it was through mythic invention that humans constructed the first conceptual models of the world. Together, these constitute the earliest forms of *aesthetic* knowing, which probably also included moral knowing. Gradually, however, these two modes have come to be seen as distinct and, more recently, as in fundamental ways opposed to each other; substantive knowing deals with matters of empirical fact, while aesthetic knowing is achieved through the creation and apprehension of works of art (Bruner, 1962).[2]

On the basis of this analysis, therefore, it would seem that, from the beginnings of human history, it is possible to distinguish four different modes of knowing that were involved in participation in the range of activities that constituted cultural life, however primitive. These I have called the instrumental, procedural, substantive, and aesthetic modes of knowing.[3] On the available evidence, they were certainly all well established at least

50,000 years ago (Donald, 1991) and perhaps even as far back as one million years ago.

In reconstructing these modes of knowing, as they can be assumed to have existed in the earliest cultures, there are several important features that need to be emphasized. First, all except perhaps the instrumental mode depended on social interaction, mediated by some form of symbolic communication (Deacon, 1997). And because it was face-to-face interaction, it was multi-modal, involving gestures and miming, intonation and facial expression, as well as lexico-grammatical meanings. This would greatly have assisted the achievement of intersubjectivity and a shared, or common, understanding. However, by the same token, this understanding was, initially, tied to a large degree to the experience of current group members. One important function of aesthetic performance, therefore, was to reenact significant events and practices and thus to provide a form of cultural memory so that the knowledge that the performance embodied would be retained from one generation to the next.

A second important feature was the central role of artifacts. As Cole (1993) points out, "Human beings live in an environment transformed by the artifacts of prior generations ... the basic function [of which] is to coordinate [them] with the physical world and each other" (p. 254). From this point of view, the tools and practices that were used in activities can be thought of as the first form of knowledge artifact and thus as another form of collective memory. Embodying the instrumental knowing of those who made and first used them, material tools carried the inventions of the past into the present so that they could be used to bring about a desired future. However, in order for them to perform this function, they had to be in the hands of one who understood their purpose and had the know-how to use them. Thus, a similar role in mediating activity was played by "the right way of doing things," that is, the procedural knowing that was enshrined in routine cultural practices and case-based stories of various kinds and passed on from one generation to the next. Together with traditional stories, songs, and dances, these too are clearly artifacts, constructed in performance and extended and improved over countless generations. Embodying the values and wisdom of the culture, they also had a toollike function in supporting the construction and reconstruction of procedural and substantive knowing in action, and in providing a point of reference for making decisions in a wide variety of activities.

The third feature that becomes apparent from viewing the various modes of knowing as situated in joint activity, mediated by artifacts and social interaction, is the extent to which they were interdependent. Complex activities might involve all four, often in a highly integrated manner, with the specific modes of instrumental and procedural knowing that were associated with particular routine practices and tool use being deployed relatively automatically, leaving attention free for conscious consideration of alternative lines of action based on appeal to the substantive and aesthetic knowledge embedded in narrative and mythic artifacts, where this was considered relevant.

What is also apparent, moreover, is the extent to which the modes of knowing I have been describing, and also the relationships between them, are similar to those in which every one of us is involved in the practical activities that make up daily living in contemporary societies. However, there is one important difference. In addition to the knowledge embodied in the participants, practices and material artifacts that together constitute our knowing in action, we also have access to other sources of information in the form of symbolic artifacts, such as maps, diagrams, instruction manuals, and other works of reference, which further serve to mediate action. Until relatively recently, by contrast, our ancestors were dependent on what people could remember, as this was elicited in praxis and interaction by the context of activity.

Nevertheless, from very early in human history, attempts were made to create external representations that preserved cultural knowledge in a more permanent, visuographic form (Donald, 1991). Such seems to have been the function of the cave paintings and religious carvings that have been found in various parts of the world and, in more recent times, such artifacts as the year records of the indigenous peoples of North America and Central America (Olson, 1994a). However, as most scholars are agreed, it was the invention of language-based writing that constituted the most significant advance in allowing knowledge to be preserved. By enabling the meanings exchanged in spoken interaction to be fixed in a form that could be recovered by readers in different times and places, writing eventually came to provide the basis for a new form of text-mediated knowledge construction that, as I shall argue below, radically changed the ways in which knowledge enters into activity.

The Development of Theoretical Knowledge

In the previous paragraphs, I have sketched a somewhat schematic account of the way in which, prior to the development of literacy, four modes of knowing emerged over the course of many millennia, from the appearance of the earliest bands of hunter-gatherers to the first civilizations based on settlement. For the relatively small, homogeneous groups that I have been envisaging, the range of activities in which they engaged was limited and individual members were probably involved in most of them, though perhaps at different stages in their life trajectories. However, what is important to emphasize is that, with respect to all four modes of knowing, knowledge was initially derived directly from living in the social-material world inhabited by the cultural group and was constructed largely through participation in the group's activities and through face-to-face interaction. In other words, the origin and function of knowledge was tied to enhancement of participation and increased understanding of the relationship between actions and the situations in which they were carried out.

By the time of the great civilizations of Egypt, Mesapotamia, China, and Greece, however, two significant developments had taken place. First, settlement had led to societies in which there was much less homogeneity; as different trades and occupations became established, each developed its own activities and associated procedural and substantive knowledge. Nevertheless, diversification of activity systems (Engeström, 1987) did not of itself lead to a change in the relationship between knowledge and activity since, for most people most of the time, the object of their activity continued to be some aspect of the material world, and the outcome of their action some transformation of that object.

However, along with diversification of activity came a more pronounced division of labor and, in all four of the major civilizations mentioned above, the emergence of a class or caste hierarchy, in which the priestly and administrative class, freed from direct involvement in material production, had time to engage in a new activity of knowledge construction that was to a much greater extent detached from the situations in which that knowledge was used. For this privileged class, or at least for those members of it with an inquiring and synthesizing bent, one might say that the object to which their activity was addressed was the procedural, substantive, and aesthetic knowledge created in other activity systems, and its intended outcome was the systematization and improvement of this knowledge, now treated as an independent object. As a result, a new mode of knowing began to emerge, as substantive knowledge embedded in practical activity became the material for a more detached, context-independent form of knowledge building, in which the knowledge artifacts created in one cycle served as "tools" to mediate the next cycle of knowledge building activity. This marked the beginning of what we might call *theoretical* knowing.

This new mode of knowing was obviously greatly facilitated by – if not actually dependent on – the second major development associated with these civilizations, namely the development of the technology of writing. Fully developed writing systems, such as those of ancient Egypt, Greece, or China, enabled the writer to represent, not simply the objects in the world – as in cave paintings – but also the way in which those objects were construed in the propositional meanings of spoken language (Olson, 1994b). Thus, for the first time, it became possible to produce permanent knowledge artifacts in the form of written documents, which could be collated, studied, and revised. Taken together with the emergence of the academy as the institution responsible for providing an apprenticeship into this mode of text-based activity, writing and the associated sytems of visual semiotic representation established the foundation for the growth of theoretical knowing.

However, the availability of a technology for the production and dissemination of knowledge artifacts was not in itself sufficient to bring about the sort of sustained theoretical knowledge building activity that is characteristic of contemporary Western cultures, particularly as it is found in the scientific disciplines. As Scribner and Cole (1981) have emphasized, use of the artifacts of literacy does not of itself cause a change in cognitive functioning; for this to happen, there must also be an ideological change that accords these artifacts a different status in the cultural practices that they mediate. In fact, when this change occurred, it was just one part of the complex ideological transformation of cultural practices that took place during the period that we refer to as the European Renaissance.

From the point of view of the development of the different modes of knowing, this period was particularly significant in a number of ways. First, it was at this time that the differentiation between substantive and aesthetic knowing referred to earlier became firmly established. And this, in turn, led to the "objectification" of the material world and the invention of the controlled experiment, in which a small part of the material world was deliberately manipulated in order to test the empirical validity of predictions based on a theoretical model (Hacking, 1990). The second ideological shift, which was crucial for the development of theoretical knowing, was the tendency toward the reification of knowledge artifacts (Ueno, 1995), which was itself associated with the creation of a new register of written language with which to represent and communicate the outcomes of experimental activity. Furthermore, all these processes of change were accelerated by technological developments such as the invention of the printing press and improvements in the design and manufacture of tools for scientific observation and measurement.

For our present purposes, though, it is the technical register of scientific writing and the genres in which it is used that are of particular interest, since it was in the creation of these tools with which to conduct the discourse of scientific inquiry that the concept of theoretical knowledge took on its present form. In his account of the development of scientific writing in English, Halliday (1988; Halliday and Martin, 1993) identifies two features of this register that are of particular importance. The first is the creation of a form of argumentation that integrates the activities of doing and thinking within the same clause. And the second, which provides the linguistic means for the first, is the progressive use of nominalization to represent, not simply the objects under investigation, but also their attributes and the processes in which they are involved and, finally, the mental processes through which the phenomena are interpreted. Together, these features create a mode of language use that projects a "world of things, symbolically fixed so that they can be observed and measured, reasoned about, and brought to order" (Halliday, 1993b p. 22). Halliday refers to this as the *synoptic* mode of construing experience, which he contrasts with the *dynamic* mode that is characteristic of everyday, informal conversation. In like vein, in tracing the history of ontogenetic development, Vygotsky (1987) makes a comparable distinction between "scientific" and "spontaneous" concepts.[4]

Theoretical knowing and the technical discourse in which it is conducted is by no means homogeneous, however. Within the domain of science, there early developed distinctions between the fields that we now recognize as the disciplines of physics, chemistry, and biology and, within these, there are now many subdisciplines and cross-disciplinary fields, such as astrophysics and biochemistry. Indeed, it appears that one of the most salient characteristics of theoretical knowing, as it has developed in Western culture, is the tendency towards ever-increasing specialization of fields of study, each distinguished as much by its dominant constructs and research procedures as by the specific aspect of the physical world with which it is concerned. Within the cultural-historical framework adopted here, the important role played by such social and political factors in the history of the diversification of scientific knowledge should not seem surprising; however, it does seem to be at odds with the ahistorical positivism that is still characteristic of much of the scientific writing in which knowledge claims are publicly presented – although not of the informal discourse in which they are constructed and debated (Latour, 1987).

Nor has theoretical knowing remained limited to the "natural" sciences. Almost all aspects of human activity have become subject to similar systematic investigation, through the development of theory and the collection and evaluation of appropriate evidence. The general ideological similarity of the different disciplines of theoretical knowledge construction is well brought out by the overarching category terms: They are all referred to as science, whether "natural," "human" or "social." Thus, as well as being organized in comparable activity systems, the various disciplines that study human activity have also taken over the generalized mode of technical scientific discourse and created their own range of discipline-based synoptic genres (Halliday and Martin, 1993). In fact, so pervasive is this mode of discourse that it characterizes almost all formal written communication, not only in academia, but also in administrative and service settings.

Historically, there can be little doubt that the development of this synoptic mode of discourse has played a critical role in the achievements of Western scientific rationalism and the technologies to which it has given rise. However, as Halliday also points out, this achievement has been bought at a considerable price. To those not involved in the activity systems in which this mode of discourse is used, it presents an unfamiliar and potentially alienating view of reality. What is more, it tends to put a wedge between decontextualized, theoretical knowing and the other forms of more "situated" knowing, by presenting the former as if it were independent of the dynamic and everyday human activities from which it has arisen. Indeed, it is this tendency, I would suggest, that is largely responsible for the problem we have in understanding what is meant by "knowledge." Because of the prestige of the empirical-analytic sciences and of the particular type of knowing that it privileges, "technical rationality," as Habermas (1983) calls it, has in many contexts come to be the only mode that counts, with other modes of knowing being discounted or at least being assigned a lower status. However, as I shall argue below, this state of affairs is both inimical to the espoused goals of democratic, transformative education and ultimately counter-productive for society as a whole.

Before turning to this issue, though, there is one further mode of knowing that needs to be considered, namely that of metaknowing.

Metaknowing

Compared with the other modes of knowing, metaknowing appears to be of very recent origin – at least, as far as its linguistic pedigree is concerned – for "metaknowing" and such related terms as "metaknowledge" have still not found their way into any but specialist texts in psychology and education. Yet metaknowing, in the sense of reflecting on the understanding developed through other modes of knowing, must surely have a history as ancient as theoretical knowing itself. Indeed, metaknowing can be seen as an important, and perhaps necessary, antecedent of the development of theoretical knowing of all kinds – a theme that will be developed in the following chapter. However, there is a second sense of metaknowing which refers to knowing about one's own knowing. And it is this second sense which has come into prominence in recent decades.

Recognition of the importance of metaknowing arose in the context of studies of cognitive development, when psychologists began to investigate, not simply how children performed on tasks, but also what they thought they were doing, and why. On the basis of Piaget's work, children were already seen as developing and using the earlier modes of knowing to construct a 'model of the world' as a basis for action and understanding. What was added by this new line of investigation was the recognition that their model of the world also included a "theory of mind," that is to say, a theory about their own and other people's minds and how they worked (Olson and Bruner, 1996).

Although essentially directed inward to intra-mental activity, metaknowing also has its developmental origins in joint activity, as participants reflect together on why they act and think as they do. Furthermore, it is by taking part in this discourse that they appropriate the cultural framework for thinking about thinking and begin to apply it to themselves (Olson and Astington, 1993). In fact, on the basis of research to date, it seems as if, for metaknowing to reach a level of coherence and conscious control at which it can be used for self-direction, this mode of reflective activity requires systematic encouragement and guidance, whether at home or in school. However, when this is provided, the evidence sugests that it can lead to more effective deployment of appropriate strategies in a wide range of activities involving knowledge building and problem solving (Brown, 1975).

At the same time, it has to be acknowledged that understanding about metaknowing is still in its infancy. While there are theories about it, actual evidence about when and how people engage in this mode of knowing is hard to come by, and most of what does exist was obtained in controlled rather than naturally occurring settings. Furthermore, although it seems appropriate to speak of metaknowledge as one outcome of metaknowing, metaknowledge rarely takes a form that is retrievable and available for subsequent investigation, except when think-aloud protocols or reflective discussions are deliberately recorded and transcribed for this purpose.[5] Nevertheless, as a result of the success of the initial educational interventions aimed at developing metaknowledge, this mode of knowing has, not surprisingly, begun to receive a considerable amount of attention in the school curriculum (Brown and Campione, 1994).[6] As Bruner observes:

Modern pedagogy is moving increasingly to the view that the child should be aware of her own thought processes, and that it is crucial for the pedagogical theorist and teacher alike to help her to become more metacognitive – to be as aware of how she goes about her learning and thinking as she is about the subject matter she is studying.... Equipping her with a good theory of mind ... is one part of helping her to do so. (Bruner, 1996, p. 64)

Knowledge as Representing

So far, in attempting to clarify the nature of knowledge, I have adopted a cultural-historical perspective, using it to describe the emergence, over long periods of time, of six different modes of knowing, each associated with different modes of participation in activity. Human activity, I have further argued, is always mediated by artifacts of various kinds and knowledge is associated in varying ways with the creation and use of such artifacts. In the case of instrumental knowing, for example, knowledge inheres in the skilful use of an artifact as tool and in the associated practices; such knowledge is in no sense detachable from the enactment of that mediated action. In the case of theoretical knowing, on the other hand, the construction of knowledge is the main motive or purpose of the activity, and the resulting knowledge artifacts, such as the theories and models that are the outcome of this mode of knowing, take on an existence that seems to be independent of the practical situations to which they might apply. Contrasting these two apparently very different modes of knowing, then, it appears that part of the difficulty in determining what is meant by "knowledge" may be located in the differing relationships between the actors, activities and artifacts associated with different modes of knowing. In this and the following sections, I shall consider a number of approaches that have been taken in exploring these relationships.

I start with the conceptualization of knowledge as representation, which has come to play a major role in cognitive scientists' theorizing about mental activity. In this discipline, by and large, knowledge representations have been treated as stable mental entities, usually propositional – or at least symbolic – in form, that correspond at some level of abstraction to aspects of the experienced world. However, the image of the mind as a container of such mental objects that is implied by this conceptualization has recently come under fire from a number of directions – neurological (Edelman, 1992), psychological (Bereiter and Scardamalia, 1996), as well as philosophical. Particularly cogent, in this latter respect, is the position advanced by the philosopher, Wartofsky, in his exploration of the role of models and representations in scientific understanding.

For Wartofsky (1979), the role of representations in cognitive activity can only be satisfactorily understood by placing the primary emphasis, not on the representation, but on the activity of representing itself. Representing, he proposes, is a fundamental human activity; it is something we do as an essential means of perceiving and of knowing, and is central to all forms of action. Representing is making or using something heuristically to "suggest how we should proceed in structuring our understanding of the world and of ourselves" (1979, p. xv). From this perspective, representations are those artifacts that are used as mediational means for the related ends of understanding and acting effectively in the world. They become representations by being so used.

A scientific model is one very clear example of an artifact that is intentionally produced and used in and for such representational activity. But, argues Wartofsky, it is not only symbolic artifacts that can function as representations. Material artifacts, such as tools and weapons, can also serve a similar function, for they "not only have a use, but are also understood as representing the mode of activity in which they are used, or the mode of their own production" (1979, p. xiii). An axe, for example, can be used to represent the action of felling lumber in the activity of home building; it can also be used to represent the actions of forging and sharpening a metal tool of a particular kind in the activity of tool making. However, unlike the case with the scientific model, to serve as a representation is not the primary purpose for which axes, or most other material artifacts, are made. Nevertheless, although different types of artifact tend to be associated with particular modes of knowing, they may also be used in a much wider range. An axe, for example, may be used to represent execution in the aesthetic mode of knowing, and a drawing of an axe may be used to represent the activity of forestry in a map showing the distribution of primary resources and industries. In other words, it seems that what makes something a representational artifact is not the nature of the artifact per se but the fact that it is being used intentionally as a representation on a particular occasion.

To distinguish the different ways in which artifacts can function in representing, Wartofsky (1979) proposed a three-way classification:

Primary artifacts are those that result from a transformation of part of the environment for the purpose of successful production and reproduction of the means of existence. In addition to material objects, such as weapons and tools, this category includes the skillful practices involved in satisfying productive or reproductive needs (1979, pp. 200–1). However, as primary artifacts, such objects and practices are representations only in the sense that they "carry" information about the mode of their own production.

Secondary artifacts are, by contrast, objects created or used for the purpose of preserving the skills and practices involved in the production and use of primary artifacts and of transmitting those skills and practices from one generation to the next. Such artifacts are reflexive representations in that they are produced intentionally as symbolic externalizations of the primary modes of action and serve an informative or pedagogic function (pp. 201–2). Examples would be instructions for sharpening an axe or an account of the kin relationships between members of an extended family and how to behave appropriately in interactions with them.

Tertiary artifacts take this process one stage further, as representing comes to constitute a relatively autonomous "off-line" world of imaginative activity, as in science or art, in which the formal properties of the representations are manipulated "playfully," without immediate concern for their direct application to the "actual" world. A model to explain the increasingly rapid disappearance of the rain forests would be an example of a tertiary artifact, which might itself include the axe to symbolize the forestry industry in a visual representation of the theory; equally, Shakespeare's *Richard III* would be an example of a dramatic tertiary artifact, and an actual production might well make use of an axe symbolically to represent an execution. As these examples make clear, the "imaginary" worlds that are created in the course of aesthetic and theoretical knowing do not exist only "in the mind"; they originate in the making of embodied representations in the form of imaginative artifacts in the actual world, and "can come to color and change our perception of the 'actual' world, as envisioning possibilities in it not presently recognized" (p. 209).

As will be apparent, this classification of artifacts in terms of the ways in which they can function as representations corresponds quite closely to one of the bases on which I have distinguished between the different modes of knowing. It also corresponds to the distinction that Halliday draws between the dynamic and the synoptic modes of construing experience. While primary and secondary artifacts are typically recruited in dynamic construals of experience, tertiary artifacts are typically used in synoptic construals, where they function as both means and outcomes. However, at this point, what I want to emphasize is the way in which Wartofsky makes the connection between artifacts, knowing, and the activity of representing. Representing, he proposes, is the *intentional use* of artifacts of different kinds to mediate knowing and to understand that which the artifact is used to represent.

This emphasis on "use" is critical, I believe, for it underpins two central claims. The first, which has already been mentioned, is that, in seeking to understand the nature of knowledge and representation, we should focus our attention on the *activity of knowing* rather than on the artifact that is made or used. Knowing, like perceiving, is a mode of action that necessarily involves representing, with different modes of knowing being mediated by different kinds of representational artifact.[7] Seen in these terms, the category "theoretical knowledge" directs us to a domain of knowing which is both temporarily detached from the primary modes of activity from which it arises and mediated by representational artifacts that, for the most part, are created specifically for this purpose. A similar argument could be made with respect to aesthetic knowing and the works of art by which it is mediated. What needs to be emphasized, however, is that the artifacts that are created in these domains, the most highly developed of which include scientific theories, systems of mathematics, and works of literature, music and visual art, both have their genesis in, and still have a purpose with respect to, the primary modes of activity. As Wartofsky puts it, all the cognitive artifacts we create "are models: representations to ourselves of what we do, of what we want, and of what we hope for. The model is not, therefore, simply a reflection or copy of some state of affairs, but beyond this, a putative mode of action, a representation of prospective practice, or of acquired modes of action" (1979, p. xv).

The second, and equally important, claim about knowing as a representational activity is that it is rooted in, and oriented to, collaborative social activity. We represent our experiences, actions and thoughts through the different kinds of artifacts we create and use in order to act, know and understand in activities jointly undertaken with others (Wertsch, 1998). Even when most alone and engaged with "internal representations," our solo activity is mediated by artifacts that we first encounter externalized in social activity; furthermore, the representations we ourselves create are given shape and definition as they are externalized in artifacts that then contribute to further social activity. In sum, although knowing

Table 2.1. *Modes of Knowing*

2 million years	Instrumental	Individual in action	Primary artifacts: material tools
1–1.5 million years	Procedural	Between individuals while engaged in action	Secondary artifacts: tools and practices; social interaction
50,000 years	Substantive	Among members of a cultural group, reflecting on action and as a basis for planning further action	Secondary artifacts: representations of tools and practices; spoken interaction
50,000 years	Aesthetic	Among members of a cultural group, making sense of the human predicament	Tertiary artifacts: artistic representations in narrative, graphic, musical, etc., modes
2,500 years	Theoretical	Among members of a specialist community, attempting to explain observations of the natural and human world	Tertiary artifacts: decontextualized representations, such as taxonomies, theories, models, etc.
?	Meta	Among members of a cultural group, also by individuals, seeking to understand and control their own mental activities	Tertiary artifacts: representations of mental and semiotic processes

is necessarily an activity carried out by particular individuals, it has its purpose and its fullest realization in the socially-oriented creation and use of artifacts in order to represent and extend our understanding with and for others.

The argument that I have developed so far can be summarized as in Table 2.1. There I list the six modes of knowing that I have distinguished, each performing a characteristic function in relation to social activity and each involving a characteristic form of artifact. However, before leaving this discussion of the development of knowledge, one caveat needs to be emphasized. While these six modes of knowing emerged successively over the course of human and cultural history, later modes should not be assumed to be inherently superior to earlier ones, either in validity or in utility (Donald, 1991). Different modes of knowing make different functional contributions to an overall activity system; each is more appropriate for some tasks and conditions than for others and none is superior in all situations. They are thus complementary rather than in competition. Similarly for the different representational artifacts that mediate knowing; as Wertsch (1991) remarks: "Some tools are more powerful and efficacious for certain activities or spheres of life, and others are more powerful and efficacious for others" (p. 102). This important point will be further developed below.

Where Is Knowledge to Be Located?

The preceding conceptualization of knowing as the construction and use of representational artifacts brings us back squarely to the second of the two issues that I raised at the beginning of this chapter: What is the ontological status of knowledge or, to put it differently, where is knowledge to be located?

At first sight, it might appear that knowledge is to be found in the artifacts that are the outcome of representational activity. Chief among these are texts and other visuographic artifacts, particularly instruction manuals, charts, and diagrams, theoretical papers, and works of reference such as textbooks and encyclopedias. To some extent it is natural that this view should be widely accepted, since it is often to such texts that one first has recourse when one is aware of one's need to know about a particular issue. However, there are several levels on which this interpretation can be shown to be untenable. First, as a printed document, a text clearly does not "contain" knowledge; unless one can read the script in which it is written, it conveys no more than the paper and ink used in its manufacture.[8] But even being able to decode the words or other symbols does not give the reader access to knowledge, unless he or she can bring to the reading of the text an interpretive framework that enables him or her to make sense of the meanings of the words in sentences. Indeed, as the transactional theory of reading (Rosenblatt, 1978) makes clear, knowledge, like meaning, cannot be "in," or taken "from," the text in any definitive form, since different readers, or the same reader on different occasions, will construct different interpretations of the text, depending on their current understanding and the purposes for which they are engaging with it (Wells, 1990).[9] Furthermore, it is perfectly reasonable to argue about a particular text that it misrepresents the knowledge it purports to embody. Knowledge must therefore be, not in the text, but in what writers or readers construct as they use texts as external tools to mediate their own mental activity of representing and knowing (Witte, 1992).

A second view, espoused by Plato, is that knowledge exists, independent of its representations, in a timeless realm of pure ideas – although there are probably few who actually hold this view today. Nevertheless, the "World 3" distinguished by Popper (1972) is somewhat similar, in that it too is populated by such immaterial objects as theories, conjectures, and arguments. However, for Popper there is an important difference: although the knowledge objects that he locates in World 3 are immaterial, they are very definitely human creations and, for that reason, open to modification and improvement. So Bereiter, for example, appealing to Popper, writes of knowledge objects such as numbers:

Numbers are not the numerals or Popsicle sticks or anything else used to represent them, nor are they the operations, such as counting, that arrive at them. There is only one number 3, and it is not any of the millions of representations of it that might be found. The same could be said of Newton's second law, Puccini's *Madame Butterfly*, and any particular proof of the Pythagorean Theorem. Yet all of these have most of the characteristics of real objects, except for being immaterial. They have origins, histories; they can be described and criticized, compared with others of their kind. They can be found to have properties that their creators or previous generations were unaware of. (1994b, p. 22)

This move certainly seems to have the advantage of avoiding the problem caused by conflating knowledge with the material artifacts in which it is represented. However, in order to avoid one set of problems, proponents of a World 3 of immaterial objects seem to me to have created others just as troublesome. For example, if such knowledge objects are completely immaterial, how are they to be apprehended by material human beings? And, equally puzzling, what is the status of such an object if all material representations of it are destroyed and all those who had engaged with it, in any mode, have gone the way of all flesh? Does Madame Butterfly continue to exist in World 3 when there is no longer any possibility of her being embodied by a human voice?

The mistake, I think, is in assuming that, because a text or musical score is a representational artifact, there must be an object that exists to be represented; and then, because this object – unlike its representation – does not exist in the material world, in arguing that it must therefore be located in a different world – a World 3 that is populated by the many "ideas" that humans have constructed through the creation of representational artifacts in order to gain an understanding of the "actual" World 1 that they experience, now conceived of in terms of independent, immaterial objects.

As Ryle (1949) pointed out, this is a "category error"; it is a result of failing to recognize the way in which the abstract generalizing propositions of theoretical, or synoptic, discourse are linguistically constructed. As discussed earlier, synoptic discourse achieves its explanatory power by reconstruing processes as nominals, which can then be treated grammatically as subjects or complements in other clauses; these clauses can then themselves be nominalized and so enter into processes and relationships in the construction of accounts, explanations, and theories. Where the error arises is in treating these linguistic nominalizations as names of entities that exist as "things" that have an independent existence. Thus, the construct of "force" that is central to Newton's second law, for example, does not refer to anything in the material world; rather, it is part of the theory, that is to say, a representational artifact, by means of which Newton explained how objects act on each other in the material world. Similarly, although we readily talk about the "values" of a culture, there are no independent "value-things" to be found, only specific actions of individuals that can be described as conforming to, or embodying, the value constructs of a particular culture.

This argument applies equally to accounts, explanations and theories. These are metalinguistic terms that provide a convenient, synoptic, way of referring to the constructive processes of accounting, explaining, and theorizing on particular occasions and, by extension, to the linguistic or other semiotic artifacts that are produced and used in the process. However, the fact that we can use the metalinguistic term "theory" as a way of referring to these processes and artifacts does not mean that there is a corresponding immaterial object that then exists, independent of the linguistic formulation and argumentation through which it was originally constructed and continues to be reconstructed.

The same is true for "knowledge." Although it may sometimes be useful to be able to refer to the object of the activity involved in understanding some phenomenon or state of affairs without specifying the occasion, participants and material artifacts involved, there is no corresponding determinate and stable knowledge object that "exists" in the usual sense of the term; it is therefore not "in" texts, or World 3, or even in the mind. Like "theory," "knowledge" is a linguistic construct that can be convenient for certain ways of talking. However, such ways of talking can all too easily mislead us into reifying knowledge and separating it from the activity of people knowing in particular situations. When Wartofsky says of representations that they are "paradigmatically intentional objects," he goes on to add: "They come to be what they are, are sustained or maintained as such, and are exhaustively describable in terms of our own intentions" (1979, p. xxi). A representation is thus the current, but temporary, focus of the mental process of making or using some form of artifact *as* a representation of something else, in the effort to understand. In other words, if knowing is conceived of as representing, knowledge does not exist as a separate object, but is simply what the activity of knowing is about or is directed to.[10]

This reconceptualization of knowledge as the object of ongoing representational activity can also be helpful, I believe, in trying to understand current discussions about the way in which knowledge – and cognition more generally – is "distributed," in any activity, over the participants, the mediating artifacts, the discourse and the situation (Bateson, 1972; Hutchins, 1995; Salomon, ed., 1993).

Insofar as the import of talking about knowledge being distributed is to emphasize that the key unit of analysis is not the particular individuals engaged in the activity, still less the representations said to be "contained" in their minds, but rather the multifaceted networks of practices that constitute the activity, in which the nonhuman "actors" are as integral as the human ones, this move constitutes an important corrective to the Cartesian view of knowledge as being located in the disembodied individual mind (Wertsch, 1998). However, I find it confusing to be told that knowledge is *in* artifacts as, for example, when Cole and Engeström write: "the cultural environment into which children are born contains the accumulated knowledge of prior generations" (1993, p. 9) – though perhaps "contains" here is intended to be taken metaphorically. However, this is not Pea's intention when he claims that "tools literally carry intelligence *in* them" and "knowledge is often carried in artifacts as diverse as physical tools and notational systems"(1993, pp. 53–4). This seems to me to be hyperbole. As argued above with respect to texts, without human actors who have the requisite know-how and purposes with respect to which these artifacts are potentially relevant, they are no different from the many other objects that are physically present – although unattended to – in the situation in which their activity takes place (Nickerson, 1993).

Nevertheless, the insistence on seeing these artifacts as an integral part of the total activity system, along with the practices in which they are used and the other human coparticipants, is definitely salutary. As Pea

(1993) rightly points out, tools in general, but particularly such tools as information processors of various kinds, were designed and made to be used in specific ways to solve specific types of problem at a particular point in the history of a culture; in that sense, they are "carriers of patterns of previous reasoning" (1993, p. 53) that provide affordances for skillful and knowledgeable action whenever they are used.[11]

At the same time, this active participation of artifacts in action is not unique to manufactured tools, since their production and use can be seen as merely the most clear-cut case of the ubiquitous human tendency to recruit all aspects of the material world as participants in conscious human activity. This is what Ilyenkov (1977) terms the "idealization" of the material world, a process whereby material objects come to have an "ideal" aspect in a way that complements the necessity for theories and other ideal representations to be embodied in material artifacts. But this does not, in my view, mean that knowledge is in a tool, any more than it is in a text, a painting or the landscape that the painter chose to represent. Rather, all these different kinds of artifact are integrated with human participants in knowing in action according to established social practices and interactional patterns that, nevertheless, change as the activity develops, both microgenetically and over ontogenetic and cultural history. It is only in this sense that knowledge can be said to be distributed over all participants, nonhuman as well as human.

The Nature of Knowledge: Some Tentative Conclusions

So where has the search for knowledge led? My major conclusion is that, as suggested earlier, in attempting to understand the nature of knowledge, attention should be redirected to the activity of knowing, as this is carried out by particular, concrete individuals. As Leont'ev (1981) acknowledged, it is only particular individuals who engage in intentional, representational activity; it is only individual humans who know. However, as he equally emphasized, knowing is not an activity that can be undertaken in isolation, either from other people or from the culturally produced artifacts that provide the mediational means. Knowing can thus be most adequately understood as *the intentional activity of individuals who, as members of a community, make use of and produce representations in the collaborative attempt to better understand and transform their shared world.*

Viewed from this perspective, with the activity of knowing made central, the status of knowledge becomes clear: it is the "object" of the activity of knowing – what it is "about," or directed to. In this, primary, sense, knowledge is always specific – strategically constructed in, and an inherent part of, the particular, current activity. It is neither timeless nor universal, but situated and emergent in the immediate here and now.

There are, however, a number of derivative usages of the term that have arisen through the operation of that engrained linguistic tendency toward reification through nominalization that is particularly characteristic of theoretical discourse. Although useful for some purposes, these usages can also be a cause of confusion unless we understand them for what they are: convenient language-created constructs. The first such potentially confusing usage is that of "knowledge" employed as a generic noun to denote the "objects" of knowing. In this usage, "knowledge" is treated as if it existed independently of the knowing activity of particular individuals on specific occasions. What is at issue here can perhaps best be understood by analogy to the use of a term like "breath" in relation to breathing. Clearly, although it may sometimes be useful to refer to breath in the abstract as the air that is taken in and let out in the process of breathing, breath is always the breath of some particular living organism. By the same token, although it may sometimes be convenient to refer generically to knowledge in the abstract, this should not lead us to forget that knowledge cannot be separated from the particular, temporally situated activity of which it is an inherent part, nor from the particular individual participants who are engaged in the activity.

A second derivative use of knowledge arises from the fact that knowing often involves the creation of material and symbolic artifacts as part of the process. These artifacts, which persist as outcomes after the event, include, but are not limited to: contributions to discussion, works of art, articles in academic journals, diagrams, and three-dimensional models.[12] An important feature of such artifacts is that they may subsequently be used as tools to mediate the achievement of further knowing, either by the original creators of the artifacts or by those who are able to use them to mediate or facilitate their own attempts. Nevertheless, for the reasons already discussed, it is important to emphasize that these artifacts, or knowledge objects, do not, in themselves, constitute knowledge. However, they do mediate the activity of knowing, when engaged with intentionally by those who are equipped to use them. In this respect, they can be evaluated as more or less effective as means for achieving the purpose for which they are used. They can also be evaluated aesthetically, in terms of their coherence, completeness, or elegance. Most importantly, like other artifacts, they are capable of being improved.

Lying somewhere between the first and second of these two derivative usages is a third, which is often glossed as "what is known" or, as Olson and Bruner put it, "the accumulated knowledge achieved by past human effort" (1996, p. 22). In suggesting that this usage, too, may be misleading, I do not intend to question the claim that knowledge building can be cumulative, nor the recommendation that a novice in any field should get to know the work of his or her predecessors and take account of knowledge claims that are generally believed to have stood the test of time. My point is that, in order to continue to be known, such knowledge must continually be actively reconstructed by particular individuals, often as members of a knowledge-building community; and that what is accumulated in texts from the past is not itself knowledge but the means for its reconstruction and transformation in the present. In fact, Olson and Bruner implicitly acknowledge the force of this argument when, in writing of conversing with dead authors through their texts, they add: "So long as the objective of the encounter is not worship but discourse, interpretation, or "going meta" on what's involved, the efforts are justified" (1996, p. 23).

The final usage to be considered, and in many ways the most problematic, is that of reference to an individual's knowledge. What is at issue here must include both what he or she knows how to do in situations where the knowing and doing are inseparable, and also what Wartofsky calls the "off-line" representations – beliefs, theories, rules, etc. – that he or she is able to access, either from internal memory in the form of images or verbal cues or, externally, in the material form of knowledge objects, such as texts. It may seem, from the previous arguments, that such representations, "possessed" by individuals, constitute the only case to which the term knowledge can appropriately be applied. And, in one sense, that is so. However, even though I concede that there are occasions when it is useful to be able to speak of an individual's knowledge in the above sense of what he or she knows, this does not require us to take the further step of conceiving of the mind in terms of a sort of internal filing cabinet in which memories of facts, procedures, theories, and so on, are stored away and available for recall in an identical, ready-to-use form on any occasion. As Bereiter and Scardamalia (1996) point out, the mind can be "knowledgeable" without "containing knowledge." Furthermore, as some of the recent work on situated memory suggests, it is "remembering" rather than memories that should be emphasized, and that how and what we remember depends upon the connections that are activated by the specifics of the situation and the purpose the remembering is to serve (Nuthall, in press). Ultimately, then, we do not possess knowledge in any literal sense; rather, we strategically reconstruct a version of it by using what we can remember to "re-know" in a manner appropriate to the current situation (cf. Bartlett, 1932).

It must also be emphasized that such acts of knowing are inherently social, and not purely individual (Lave and Wenger, 1991). They have little or no meaning outside a community of whose activities they form a part and to which they make a significant contribution. Even the solitary scholar or artist, working alone to resolve some philosophical problem or to create a work of literature or musical score, engages with the representations previously produced by others and works toward a moment when the representation that he or she is constructing will be brought forth into the arena of public performance or debate. Thus, to reiterate, to speak of an individual's knowledge is not to refer to a collection of objects – of independent things held in a mental container – but a convenient, although reified, way of referring to the relationship between the individual knower and the representations that mediate his or her knowing in concrete instances of praxis within a culturally established system of activity.

The Development of Knowing: An Ontogenetic Perspective

So far, I have focused on the large-scale developmental trajectory of the species, homo sapiens, and, in particular, on the historical development of theoretical knowing, as this has occurred in Western culture. However, as I suggested earlier in the brief explanation of Vygotsky's genetic method, this perspective needs to be complemented by an equal attention to the trajectories of individual members of society as they develop over the life-span, and to the microgenetic unfolding of the events that are formative of that development. It is these that I now wish to address through a consideration of the role of education in the development of knowledge. Given the complex interdependence of the different modes of knowing in the mediation of the diverse activities of contemporary society, the questions I shall attempt to answer are: How are these modes of knowing appropriated by each new generation and what part is, or might be, played by schools in facilitating this process?

It could be argued, following Lave and Wenger (1991), that as far as instrumental, procedural and substantive knowing are concerned, learning occurs largely as an integral aspect of participation in the primary activities that make up the child's daily experience as a member of the family and local community. This is very much the view that is taken by

Vygotsky (1987) with respect to the child's mastery of everyday concepts, and by Halliday (1993a) with respect to learning to construe experience in the dynamic mode of conversational interaction. In these activity settings, learning is rarely singled out and made an end in itself; instead, it is a concomitant of the task-oriented actions in which the child engages with parents, older siblings, and other more skilful and knowledgeable members of the immediate community. Nor is there much deliberate and systematic teaching, if by this is meant instruction that is preplanned with respect to content and occasion. Nevertheless, over the course of the first few years of the child's life, these significant others interact with him or her in ways that support and guide the child's progressive appropriation of the modes of knowing relevant to the joint activities in which they engage together (Wells, 1985, 1986).

Vygotsky (1978, 1987) characterized this particular form of support and guidance as working in the child's zone of proximal development, that is to say, in the zone of joint action that is in advance of what the child can manage alone. By organizing tasks to enable the child's progressively fuller and more autonomous participation, the other ensures that culturally valued modes of knowing are transferred from the dyad acting together to the child alone so that he or she becomes equally responsible for carrying out the task and solving whatever problems may be involved. Furthermore, as Litowitz (1993) points out, it is not just mastery of the relevant modes of knowing that is involved; together with the intra-mental construction of the culturally developed ways of acting and thinking goes the formation of personal identity, through identification with (or resistance to) the motivations that drive the joint actions and appropriation of the dialogic positions that may be taken up in the social (intermental) interaction that is involved. These issues are taken up in the last chapter of this book.

At the same time, given the very considerable diversity across communities in the forms that primary activities may take and in the manner in which children are assisted to master them (Rogoff, 1990), it goes without saying that there is substantial cultural and subcultural variation in what exactly children come to know and in the relative importance that they come to attach to the different modes of knowing; by the same token, there is also considerable variation in the types of identity that children construct for themselves in the process. From a cultural-historical perspective, such variation is inevitable and ecologically beneficial; however, in societies that are at once multicultural in membership but effectively monocultural in governance, there must be considerable concern about the consequences of this variation for children's ability to benefit from the more formal and standardized activities in which they are expected to participate in school (Bernstein, 1971; Hasan, 1989; Heath, 1983; Moll and Greenberg, 1990). Leaving the issue of variation aside, however, there are few who would disagree that, to a large extent, the instrumental, procedural and substantive modes of knowing are appropriated through the forms of "apprenticeship" that characterize participation in the activities of the local community (Lave and Wenger, 1991; Rogoff, 1990). The same could probably also be argued for aesthetic knowing, provided this forms part of the community's way of life, although this has been much less discussed.[13]

When it comes to theoretical knowing, on the other hand, and the mastery of scientific concepts (Vygotsky, 1987), together with the synoptic genres of discourse in which these concepts are used, there is rather general agreement that a different form of learning is necessary – one which requires systematic instruction, the responsibility for which appropriately rests with the school. In fact, one of the grounds on which the institution of schooling can be defended is that it provides a setting in which there is a systematic attempt to go beyond learning through "legitimate peripheral participation" (Lave and Wenger, 1991) and the modes of knowing associated with primary activities by encouraging students to adopt a reflective and "meta" stance to their participation in primary activities and, on that basis, to begin to engage in theoretical knowing.

In practice, however, the very fact that schools are cut off from the primary activities of the wider community and organized on principles that have more to do with managing age cohorts than fostering the co-construction of knowledge has led in many schools to a form of classroom practice that has the benefits of neither LPP nor a knowledge-building community. Thus, as is increasingly recognized (Bereiter and Scardamalia, 1996; Resnick, 1987), although it may have been adequate in the past, the way in which instruction has traditionally been organized is not proving very effective for a society that, more and more, requires that all its members be able to participate in activities that depend upon the ability to use and generate theoretical knowledge. What are needed, therefore, are ways of overcoming the encapsulation of schooled modes of knowing (Barnes, 1976; Engeström, 1991b) and of making the classroom activities in which students engage more relevant to the issues with which they are already, or will be, concerned. And this, in turn, means teachers finding ways of organizing these classroom activities so that theoretical knowing builds more organically on the modes of knowing that students already deploy and grows out of their attempts both to solve the problems arising from the specifics of the "primary" activities in which they engage and to create representations of the understandings that they achieve in the process.

As I suggested above, it was a developmental pattern of this kind that occurred on the much larger time-scale of cultural history, in which the emergence of theoretical knowing was dependent on three prior achievements: first, a substantial body of practical information in relation to a given activity, derived from procedural and substantive knowing; second, adequate means for creating representational artifacts that would preserve the outcomes of knowing so that understanding could be progressively improved; and third, a group of people sufficiently free from the demands of primary productive activities to have time and interest to devote to collaborative engagement in this "off-line" mode of knowing. Following Wartofsky (1979), I also argued that, although temporarily detached from primary activity, theoretical knowing was not ultimately an end in itself, but that its purpose was to create representational artifacts, such as explanations and models, that could be used to illumine and guide current and prospective practice.

I am well aware of the inappropriateness of suggesting that this parallelism calls for a straightforward recapitulation, on the ontogenetic level, of cultural-historical development. That would be impossible, first because the time scales are so radically different and, second, because the ontogenetic development of a person today takes place in a culture that already embodies the results of those historical developments. Nevertheless, given the conditions that I have argued were necessary for the historical development of theoretical knowing, it is certainly worth asking whether these same conditions may be, if not necessary for, then perhaps particularly conducive to, the comparable development on the ontogenetic level.[14]

Note, I am not arguing that an individual's theoretical knowing with respect to every topic must be rooted in the personal construction of procedural and substantive knowledge that comes from engagement in the relevant primary activities. Nor am I proposing that, on every occasion, the theoretical understanding achieved should immediately be put to productive, practical use. This would simply not be feasible. However, I am suggesting that such an organic relationship may be optimal for the initial development of this mode of knowing and that it may be highly desirable to repeat, or approximate, this situation in relation to each new domain in which students are expected to develop theoretical knowing. For it is only in this way, I believe, that it is possible to overcome the separation that has developed in schools between theoretical and other modes of knowing, and to avoid the resulting alienation of so many individual students, which is also counter-productive for society as a whole.

Such an organic relationship has certainly not been the principle on which the curriculum has typically been organized in the history of public education. But for most of that history it has not been a major aim that all students should develop the ability and disposition to engage in theoretical knowing, with the likelihood that this entails of their challenging and transforming currently accepted beliefs, practices, and values. Indeed, there have been – and still are – powerful vested interests that would maintain the traditional organization of schooling in order to avoid this possibility. However, if we accept the overall aims for education proposed by the university students of Quebec with which I introduced this chapter, it is essential that we reject the static, objectified conception of knowledge on which the curriculum is still so often based and, in its stead, explore alternatives that are more dynamic and open-ended.

As I shall suggest in the following chapter, one way to do this is to adopt an inquiry orientation to the curriculum and to ensure that the topics with which students are encouraged to become engaged, and the challenges that are presented to them, are connected with their interests, proclivities and relevant past and anticipated future experiences (Hatch and Gardner, 1993). Such an orientation also depends on the teacher making available potentially useful mediating tools and practices, and recognizing and drawing on the information and expertise that is distributed among all the different members of the community, including those who are present only through the knowledge artifacts they have created (Brown et al., 1993). Most important, it depends on creating settings in which these components come together in collaborative action and interaction that, while guided by well-considered long-term goals, is, in its moment-by-moment unfolding, both dynamic and emergent.

Knowing and Understanding

In what follows, I have tried to represent these guiding principles in terms of a model that relates four different opportunities for meaning making that individuals encounter in and outside the classroom. The model applies to all the modes of knowing previously discussed, with the exception, perhaps, of the purely instrumental, but it is particularly relevant for thinking about theoretical knowing, where this is conceptualized as a goal-oriented social process mediated by representational artifacts of various kinds.

The model consists of four quadrants, labeled "experience," "information," "knowledge building" and "understanding." Terms such as those I have chosen here are open to varying interpretations, so I shall start by explaining how I intend to use them.

By *experience* I mean an individual's culturally situated, affectively charged, participation in the multiple communities of practice that constitute his or her life-world. However experience is not what happens to a person, but the meanings that are constructed in the course of participation in the succession of events that make up his or her life trajectory, as these events are construed in terms of the individual's existing model of the world. Depending on the person's social circumstances, the basis of experience may be limited and repetitive or it may be diverse and richly varied; but, whatever, the case, participation in primary cultural activities, and in the actions and social interactions through which they are realized, constitutes the fundamental source of the meanings and representations on which all modes of knowing build.

By contrast, *information* is as it were "second hand." It consists of other people's interpretations of experience and the meanings that they have made and is encountered in many genres, from casual conversation to works of art and from brochures to authoritative printed works of reference. Information may be about specific objects, people or events, or it may be more general in scope, and deal with abstract, theoretical relationships presented in an explanatory genre. However, whether it can subsequently be remembered depends on the extent to which it can be infused with the receiver's experiential meaning and deliberately integrated into his or her model of the world.

Knowledge building also deals with meanings in the public domain but, by contrast with information, involves a much more active and integrative stance. Here, the individual is engaged in meaning making with others in an attempt to extend and transform their collective understanding with respect to some aspect of a jointly undertaken activity. Knowledge building typically involves constructing, using and progressively improving representational artifacts of various kinds with a concern for systematicity, coherence and consistency.

Finally, *understanding*, which can best be understood in terms of its relationship with knowledge building and experience. Understanding differs from knowledge building in being more personal and immediate. Whereas the latter, of necessity, requires that meaning should be made explicit, understanding is typically more holistic and intuitive; and where knowledge building is often temporarily detached from primary activity, understanding is deeply implicated in action, as it occurs, since it is in terms of our understanding of the possibilities for, and constraints on, action in a setting that we decide how to act. Put more generally, it is our understanding that constitutes the interpretive framework in terms of which we make sense of new experience and which guides effective and responsible action. Thus, although first-hand experience provides an essential basis for understanding, it needs to be extended and reinterpreted through collaborative knowing, using the informational resources and representational tools of the wider culture.

We can thus see understanding, metaphorically speaking, as the culminating moment in a cycle of knowing. Knowing starts with personal experience which, amplified by information, is transformed through knowledge building into understanding, where understanding is construed as knowing that is oriented to action of personal and social significance and to the continual enriching of the framework within which future experience will be interpreted. This experience, of course, then provides the starting point for a new cycle, so that, from the perspective of the developmental trajectory of either an individual or a community, a better metaphor would be that of a spiral. Seen in this light – as a means of continuously transforming both the self and the social environment – understanding, I would argue, should be the goal of all educational activity.

Before going on to consider the educational implications of the spiral metaphor, however, I should like to draw attention to certain additional features of the model that emerge when the four categories are arranged in the diagramatic representation seen in Figure 2.1.

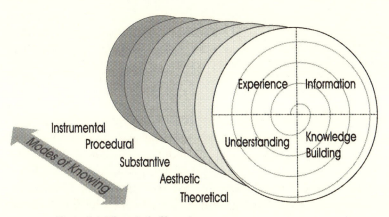

Figure 2.1 The spiral of knowing.

Emergent Features of the Model

In Figure 2.1, the four categories can be seen as resulting from the intersection of two axes. On the vertical axis, there seem to be two related dimensions; the first might be described in terms of the degree of coherence involved and the second in terms of the degree of reflectiveness and volitional control. In one sense, both experience and information can be seen as somewhat arbitrary and lacking in intentionality, in that they tend to consist of one thing after another in a sequence over which the individual exercises little control; by comparison, both knowledge building and understanding are characterized by a coherence that is the result of engagement and deliberate constructive effort.

It is the absence of such constructive effort, I would suggest, that is at the heart of the problem of "inert knowledge" (Whitehead, 1949), that is to say, of situations where what is presented as input for knowledge building is treated merely as information. As I argued earlier, the fact that one or more people have developed a coherent understanding of an issue, and have created a representation of their understanding in a knowledge artifact such as a text or blueprint, does not mean that another person will achieve a comparable understanding by simply "reading" the text. To be sure, a certain amount of active meaning making will be required to comprehend the text as information; however for the information to contribute to an increase in that person's understanding, it must be incorporated into his or her own model of the world through knowledge building and/or put to use to mediate the solving of some problem of personal significance.

This point is made very clearly by Popper with respect to theoretical knowing:

We can grasp a theory only by trying to reinvent it or to reconstruct it, and by trying out, with the help of our imagination, all the consequences of the theory which seem to us to be interesting and important . . . One could say that the process of understanding and the process of the actual production or discovery [of theories] are very much alike. (Popper and Eccles, 1977, p. 461)

In school, the contrast between information and knowledge building becomes very clear if we consider the distinction that Bereiter and Scardamalia (1987) draw between "knowledge telling" and "knowledge transformation" as strategies used in writing. As they explain, knowledge telling is essentially a strategy of moving information from one location to another without actively engaging with it. As a result, the information remains "inert" as far as the writer is concerned. However, the problem is not restricted to writing; it applies in all situations where what is recalled from memory or encountered in knowledge artifacts, such as textbooks or works of reference, is treated merely as information for reproduction rather than being transformed through purposeful knowledge building.

At the same time, the distinction between information and knowledge building should not be thought of as sharply dichotomous. Reading a written text, for example, requires some degree of constructive effort simply to construe its "literal" meaning on a sentence-by-sentence basis. The coherence of each individual reader's interpretation of the text and its significance for the development of his or her understanding increases further when they test the information constructed in transaction with the text against their personal models of the world; and this process is taken still further when personal interpretations are questioned and clarified in the forum of public discussion, and assumptions and inferences are challenged in the attempt to construct "common knowledge" (Edwards and Mercer, 1987). Finally, for many people, the transforming potential of collaborative knowledge building is most fully realized when the progressive discourse is conducted in writing, since in this mode the writer enhances his or her understanding by dialoguing with his or her emerging text as well as with the community for whom the text is intended.

Turning now to the horizontal axis, the contrast is of a quite different order; it can perhaps be most appropriately characterized in terms of direction of orientation. Information and knowledge building involve public meanings and representations mediated by culturally conventional semiotic systems; they are oriented outward, as it were, to the social world of discursive interaction. Experience and understanding, by contrast, are inner oriented; they are concerned with the individual's more direct and intuitive involvement in the world as encountered in the particularities of his or her own life trajectory. Thus, if we were to superimpose Vygotsky's distinction between "social" and "inner" speech on this model, social speech would be associated with information and knowledge building, whereas it is with experience and understanding that the idiosyncratic, sense-imbued nature of inner speech and imaging would be most closely related.

Viewing the horizontal axis in this way leads to what, for me, is a new insight about the dialectical relationship between knowledge building and understanding. On the one hand, increased personal understanding is very often achieved through engagement in collaborative knowing; that is to say, it is the outcome, on the inner, intramental plane, of the activity of engaging on the outer, intermental plane in the construction of knowledge objects with and for others. On the other hand, such collaborative knowledge building is only made possible by each of the participants bringing his or her current understanding to bear on the common problem or issue and progressively modifying it in making sense of the relevant information and in contributing to the joint activity.[15] It is this dialectic that I believe Bereiter and Scardamalia were referring to as knowledge transformation, and what Vygotsky had in mind when he wrote: "The individual develops into what he/she is through what he/she produces for others. This is the process of the formation of the individual" (1981, p. 162).[16]

As with the vertical axis, the dimension of orientation should also be thought of as a continuum. On the one hand, making a contribution to a knowledge building discussion or written interchange may, on occasion, be as much inner as outer directed. That is to say, it may be undertaken as much for the occasion it provides for clarifying and consolidating one's own understanding by trying to make it clear for others, as for the effect it may be intended to have in influencing the progress of the social discourse. And on the other hand, individual understanding is rarely entirely inner oriented, as the sense one attempts to make for oneself is nearly always embedded in some larger social activity.

There is, however, a third axis, which corresponds to the different modes of knowing.[17] Movement along this axis has, in fact, been one of the major themes of this chapter for, as I have suggested, it is in these terms that we can best understand the historical development of the different modes of knowing and, in the history of Western culture, the increasing emphasis on theoretical knowing and on the knowledge artifacts to which it gives rise. A similar progression on this dimension can also be seen to characterize ontogenetic development, at least in our culture, with the increasing emphasis on "mastering theoretical knowledge" that is typically found in the official curriculum, as children ascend the educational ladder from grade to grade. However, while I believe that the development implied by this dimension is rightly an important goal of education, I am convinced that the way in which it is generally conceptualized and enacted needs to be sustantially revised. It is to this that I now turn.

Schooling and the Construction of Knowledge and Understanding

As I explained at the outset, my purpose in writing this chapter was to challenge proposals for school reform that are couched in the simplistic terms of more effective knowledge transmission. My objection was that the conception of general, objective knowledge on which such proposals are based is seriously misleading, as is the further conception to which its apparent simplicity gives rise, namely that individual intellectual development is largely a matter of accumulating a store of such general knowledge through a process of reception and memorization.

In rejecting this view, I proposed an alternative conception, in which it is the activity of knowing that is given primacy. Distinguishing six different modes of knowing, I argued that, in every mode, knowledge does not have an independent existence, but is simply a way of referring to what is focused on in communities in which the participants, whether co-present or temporarily alone, attempt to achieve greater understanding of some aspect of an activity in which they are jointly engaged. Certainly, it is the case that material and symbolic artifacts are involved in knowing, both as mediating tools and as outcomes of the activity. However, these artifacts are not in themselves knowledge, nor do they contain knowledge in any but a metaphorical sense. Knowledge, I concluded, is not an object of any kind – material, mental, or immaterial – that exists outside particular situations of knowing; and in such situations, it does not preexist the activity but is what is recreated, modified, and extended in and through collaborative knowledge building and individual understanding.

On the face of it, this view of knowledge and knowing might seem to be in total opposition to two widely accepted assumptions, namely that knowledge consists of beliefs whose truth can be adequately justified, and that the body of such beliefs has been built up over centuries and does not depend on whether they are held by any particular individuals. However, it is not with the importance of being able to justify beliefs that I wish to take issue, nor with the claim that knowing within a community is cumulative and progressive. On the contrary, it is precisely the process of justifying beliefs through reasoning, conjecturing, evaluating evidence, considering counter-arguments, and so on, that I take to constitute the activity of knowing – at least, in the theoretical mode. Where I do disagree, however, is with the limiting of knowledge to beliefs, and with the often drawn implication that knowing can be equated with the holding, or "possession," of beliefs.

The former objection is rooted in the "genetic" approach to knowing that I have presented above; examination of the developmental trajectory of both human cultures and individual members makes it clear that the theoretical mode of knowing that is given preeminence in contemporary Western cultures has emerged from, and built upon, modes of knowing that are both integral to the practical activities necessary for everyday

living and involve a wider range of human capacities than the purely intellectual. Not only is knowing, in all its modes, ultimately inseparable from
purposeful action within a cultural framework, but it is also inherently
social in its motivation and interactional in its orientation, and therefore
involves feelings, attitudes, and values, as well as rationally justified beliefs. Both these features need to be taken into account when planning
educational opportunities for the construction of knowledge.

The second objection is more directly pedagogic in nature, and relates to the distinction drawn earlier between information and knowledge
building. Where knowledge is equated with justified true beliefs, it is too
easily assumed that, if students can be induced to memorize the beliefs that
have been justified by the knowing activities of others, they have therefore come to "possess" that knowledge. By contrast, I have argued that
such knowledge, however carefully sequenced and authoritatively presented, remains at the level of information that has little or no impact on
students' understanding until they actively engage in collaborative knowledge building to test its relevance in relation to their personal models of
the world and, where possible, its practical application in action.

Some may argue that this emphasis on knowing in action is open to
the very same objection that has been leveled against "student-centered,
activity-based learning," namely that with so much attention to process,
the acquisition and mastery of discipline-based knowledge is all too often
neglected. In response, I would draw attention to the dual-faceted nature
of knowledge building. Knowledge, in the form of jointly created knowledge artifacts and of personal understanding of the social and practical
significance of these artifacts, is very clearly a major intended outcome of
the activities I have been describing. And, engaging with such culturally
valued knowledge artifacts as textbooks and works of reference, which
represent the outcome of the knowledge building of experts in the various
disciplines in a form that is intelligible to relative novices, is an important
and necessary part of the total activity. For students to ignore what is
already taken as known in any field as they construct their own knowledge
would indeed be to their own and society's disadvantage. What is at issue,
therefore, is not whether students should engage with "what is known,"
but the manner and timing of the encounter.

This is where the "building" in knowledge building is critical. The term
is intended to capture the need for firm foundations and a design that is
oriented toward purpose and use, as well as the constructive and transformative effort that is needed in any major building project. Unfortunately,
none of these requirements is met in the library-based "research projects"

that students so often complete by transferring paragraphs from reference book to exercise book in answer to questions designed by the teacher. It is to make a clean break with this tradition of knowing as the superficial rearrangement of information that I have placed such a strong emphasis on starting with "real" questions that are generated by students' first-hand engagement with topics and problems that have become of genuine interest to them.[18] For it is when they have begun to formulate their own theories, to test them in various ways, and to submit them to critical evaluation by their peers, that they can most fully appreciate the contributions to the problems with which they are engaged that have been made by more experienced workers in the field.[19] In other words, until they have a personal stake in the knowledge under construction, they are likely to treat the published writings of others as not only authoritative but also as precluding the need for any constructive effort on their own part. By the same token, unless teachers understand the radically different relationship between knowing and knowledge artifacts that is intended by the term knowledge building and make their own understanding apparent in when and how they encourage students to make use of "what is known," it is all too easy for the advocated emphasis on inquiry that characterizes current efforts at reform to be subverted by the deep-rooted tendency to knowledge transmission that is pervasive in education (Edwards and Mercer, 1987).

To work out the pedagogical implications of this conception of knowing is obviously beyond the scope of this chapter and, in any case, it cannot be undertaken by any single individual. However, a start is being made in the collaborative classroom-based research carried out by the members of DICEP and other like-minded educators[20] and the results are encouraging. On the basis of this work, it is possible to propose some general principles to guide the changes that schools undoubtedly need to make.

First, understanding should be made the primary goal of education. That is to say, the manner in which classroom activities are selected and organized should not only lead students to construct a personal understanding of the topics involved that equips them to participate effectively and responsibly in similar and related activities beyond the classroom, but it should also encourage the development of the disposition and the necessary strategies to adopt the same stance independently in new and unfamiliar situations.

Second, it should be recognized that such understanding is achieved through engaging in joint activities with others that encourage collaborative knowledge building in response to the problems and challenges that arise in those activities.[21] Hence, it is important to reiterate that what needs to be emphasized is the *activity* of knowing through the making and using of representational artifacts as means of guiding joint action and of enhancing collective understanding. A corollary of this is that the accumulation and display of knowledge objects can no longer be seen as a worthwhile goal of education; such objects are of no value unless and until they are used as tools to mediate activity, including the activity of knowing.

Third, there should be a greater awareness that, outside the classroom, participation in an activity of any scope and complexity is likely to involve most, if not all, of the different modes of knowing in complementary relationships with each other. For this reason, and also because, genetically, theoretical knowing grows out of those modes of knowing that are directly involved in primary activities, the interdependence of the different modes should be emphasized whenever possible through the selection and organization of curricular units in which this relationship can be realistically enacted.

Finally, greater recognition should be given to the varied but critical roles that discourse plays in relation to all the modes of knowing except, perhaps, the instrumental. And here it is important to make clear that discourse is not limited to the lexicogrammatical dimensions of language that are given particular salience in writing. If, as I have argued, it is knowing with and for others that is to be given pride of place in classroom activities, then it is the dialogic potential of discourse that needs to be emphasized, and this can be achieved in a variety of modalities and often in many of them simultaneously.

Each of these recommendations has certanly been made before, although perhaps not all together and on the basis of the arguments put forward here. However, the question of importance is: How might they be realized in practice? Clearly, both the recommendations and the model from which they are derived are, themselves, highly synoptic representations. They will therefore require an imaginative process of translation into the dynamic mode if, as is my hope, they are to prove useful as tools for thinking about the practice of education in particular classroom communities. But this is precisely the purpose of collaborative action research: to enable members from different positions in the educational community to engage in knowing together, using such theoretical artifacts as this chapter, together with artifacts obtained from the classroom itself, in order progressively to improve practice and to enhance our collective understanding.

Notes

1. In the following account, I am greatly indebted to Donald's (1991) comprehensive and stimulating review and interpretation of the many sources of evidence bearing on the evolution of human cognition and to Cole's (1996a) discussion of the relationship between phylogeny and cultural history.

2. This distinction is discussed by Langer (1953), where, based on her theory of music, she proposes the following more general theory of art: "The basic concept is the articulate but non-discursive form having import without conventional reference, and therefore presenting itself not as a symbol in the ordinary sense, but as a 'significant form', in which the factor of significance is not logically discriminated, but is felt as a quality rather than recognized as a function" (p. 32).

3. I am very conscious that there are already a number of ways of referring to different kinds of knowledge and that to introduce a further set of terms may seem redundant, if not confusing. However, I believe that the distinctions I am proposing not only have an intuitive plausibility, but that they are important for the emphasis on modes of knowing that I wish to develop. As far as a correspondence can be established with exisiting terms, my instrumental knowledge seems to correspond to Piaget's sensori-motor intelligence; otherwise, both instrumental and procedural knowledge can be combined in opposition to substantive and aesthetic knowledge and the two resulting superordinate categories equated with Ryle's (1949) opposition between "knowing how" and "knowing that" or with Brown's (1975) distinction between procedural and substantive or propositional knowledge.

4. The form this historical progression has taken can be illustrated by means of the following set of sentences, adapted from an example cited by Berkenkotter (1994):

    1. The water in the ground here is flowing to the east.
    2. Ground water flows in an easterly direction.
    3. Ground water flow is in an easterly direction.
    4. Easterly ground water flow accounts for the abundant vegetation in this area.

    In these four sentences, which can be seen as representing points along a continuum from informal everyday speech to formal scientific writing, there is a parallel progression, from specific and concrete to general and abstract, in the concepts realized in the subject noun phrases: "the water (in the ground here)" –> "ground water" –> "ground water flow" –> "easterly ground water flow" (Wells, 1994a).

5. Although not explicitly described as support for metaknowing, "reciprocal teaching" with respect to reading comprehension (Palincsar and Brown, 1984) and "procedural facilitation" in writing (Bereiter and Scardamalia, 1987) certainly aim to give students greater control over processes of knowing mediated by written texts; similarly, the practice of retrospective group reflection on strategies used in inquiry and problem solving (Wells, 1995). "Think-aloud" and clinical interview techniques have also been found to promote metaknowing (Scardamalia and Bereiter, 1983) and, for this reason, although originally used as ways of eliciting data for research, they have begun to be deliberately used

as strategies for giving students insight into, and control over, their mental processes (Paulauskas, 1994; Swanson-Owens and Newell, 1994).

6. Another perspective on metaknowing is suggested by Egan (1997), who also adopts a genetic approach to human intellectual development. He proposes a developmental sequence of four kinds of understanding that are mediated by language use: mythic, romantic, philosophic, and ironic (there is also a prelinguistic kind that he calls somatic). In this scheme, ironic understanding can be seen as a form of metaknowing in that it results from self-conscious reflection about the language one uses and about the different, and sometimes mutually incompatible, ways of understanding experience that are generated by different modes of language use. However, although ironic understanding has been potentially available as long as language itself, Egan sees its current flowering as in some ways a postmodern response to our twentieth-century recognition of the ultimately uncertain and relative nature of all kinds of understanding.

Unfortunately, I only came across Egan's stimulating theory about the role of linguistic "cognitive tools" in the development of the "educated mind" as I was making the final revisions to this book and regret that, for reasons of space, I have not been able to engage with it more fully. Apart from its content, it is also innovatory in its presentation, notably in the inclusion of the address of a web page on which one may engage in discussion with the author. This can perhaps be seen as a good example of the ironic type of understanding that he champions and which I am suggesting is a form of metaknowing.

7. It might be objected that to speak of the "activity" of knowing is inappropriate: in English, "know" is a stative verb of the class "mental process: cognition" and therefore cannot be used to refer to a deliberate action. To this, I have two responses. First, although linguistic usage does indeed embody the culture's implicit theory of experience, usage does not, in itself, put the theory beyond challenge. The fact that we speak of "sunrise" and "sunset," for example, does not mean that we are still intellectually bound to a geocentric theory of the universe. So, here, it is precisely the implicit theory of the mind as a container of propositional objects that are "known" in the sense of being timelessly present that is being challenged. Moreover, as Halliday (1994) argues, the distinction between the two forms of the present tense – the simple present, as in "John knows the book," and the "present in present" form, as in "John is reading the book" – is one of temporal focus, rather than of reference to state versus process. Verbs of cognition also refer to processes, but being "in general not clearly bounded in time, [they] are associated with the less focussed tense form, the simple present" (p. 116).

Second, as should be clear, I am using "know," not to refer to a single, delimited mode of cognition, but as a cover term for a range of mental processes, such as "recognizing," "considering," "evaluating," "hypothesizing," "concluding," and so on, that are involved, together with material processes, in the construction and use of representational artifacts. Since, linguistically, they are treated as forms of (mental) action, there is no reason why the same should not hold for "knowing," when used as their superordinate.

8. Treating texts as containers of knowledge is part of the more general tendency of treating all semiotic artifacts as vehicles in which information is transported from one mind to another. Dubbed by Reddy (1979) the "conduit metaphor,"

this way of thinking is deeply rooted in Western cultures; however, according to McNeill (1992), it is not characteristic of other cultures, such as Chinese.

9. This point is more fully developed in Lotman's (1988, 1990) theory of the two functions of a text. In the univocal function, the aim is indeed to have the text act as a channel for the transfer of information from writer to reader; however, for the reasons I have suggested, this is never completely possible. In the second, dialogic, function, by contrast, the text acts as a "thinking device," provoking the reader to develop his or her own understanding of the topic. In Lotman's view, both functions are necessary; the mistake is to focus on one to the exclusion of the other. As he observes:

> We should not, however, forget that not only understanding but also misunderstanding is a necessary and useful condition in communication. A text that is absolutely comprehensible is at the same time a text that is absolutely useless. An absolutely understandable and understanding partner would be convenient but unnecessary, since he or she would be a mechanical copy of my "I" and our converse would provide us with no increase in information: just as there is no increase in money if one passes a purse from one pocket to another. A dialogue situation does not blur the distinction between the partners, but intensifies them and makes them more significant (1990, pp. 80–1).

10. The complete sentence from Wartofsky is: "Representations are nothing but what they are made to be, in and by this [representing] activity. To put this somewhat differently, representations are, paradigmatically, intentional objects" (1979, p. xxi).

    Dascal provides a helpful gloss. Reviewing the dispute on the primacy of thinking or speaking, he writes: "The term 'intention' is used by philosophers to denote both the purpose underlying an action and the fact that something is 'directed to' or 'about' something else. In this second sense, both language and thought are 'intentional'" (1995, p. 1035).

11. It is important to recognize that tools can also impose constraints on activity. Not only may the tool to hand sometimes not be the one that one would have chosen, but even an apparently appropriate one may lead one to tackle the activity in one way rather than in other, potentially equally feasible, ways. Hall (1990) extends this argument to intellectual activity when he shows that problem solving in mathematics can be constrained by the type of representation that is used as tool.

12. Interestingly, works of art are rarely treated as knowledge objects although, like written texts and diagrams, they mediate the activity of aesthetic knowing. Ths is probably because, as Langer notes, although symbolic, they have "import without conventional reference" (see note 2).

13. It seems that there may well be much greater cultural variation in the kinds of activities that involve aesthetic knowing and in the extent to which children participate in these activities. In some cultures, such activities, particularly of a religious kind, form an important part of family and community life (Heath, 1983). In highly literate homes, shared book reading, and visits to the theatre, museum, and art gallery may be a regular occurrence; in others, oral storytelling

may be the child's principal means of access to this mode of knowing. However, there also seems to be a substantial proportion of young people for whom the only experience of this mode of knowing, outside school, is via television and, as they grow older, through peer group interest in films and popular music.

14. Katherine Nelson (1996) makes a comparable suggestion in some detail with respect to the development of language in the preschool years. Basing her proposal on Donald's (1991) thesis, she writes: "potentiations of all the representational systems posited by Donald are visible in the developments taking place between 1 and 3 years of age: events, mimesis, language and categorization, with the latter containing the potential for the theoretical structures of the fourth and final stage. However, as vaguely realized potentials, the latter types do not form fully realized representational systems [in the pre-school years]; rather, they are incorporated into event and mimetic structures and processes, not as representational levels in their own right" (p. 117). One of the prime purposes of schooling, I am arguing, is to build on what Nelson calls the event-based and mimetic modes of knowing in order to realize the potential for the more advanced modes of knowing that are mediated by spoken and written language and by other symbolic modes of representation.

15. As Carol Feldman (Feldman and Kalmar,1996) points out, this dialectical relationship between understanding and knowledge building is not unimodal, but differs according to the nature of the objects or events to be explained. Starting from von Wright's (1971) distinction between causal and teleological explanation, Feldman proposes a variety of modes of teleological explanation corresponding to different narrative genres, such as autobiography and fiction. In the context of the framework developed here, these would be related to what I have called the aesthetic mode of knowing. Extending her argument, the different genres of scientific writing discussed earlier that make use of causal explanation would be related to the theoretical mode of knowing.

16. This may also be a fruitful way to interpret Vygotsky's concept of "internalization" as it applies to the appropriation of cultural knowledge (see Chapters 8 and 10).

17. I actually found the attempt to represent this third dimension appropriately to be extremely instructive, for it led to several further insights about the model as a whole. In this way, it also exemplified my argument that personal understanding develops through working to improve a knowledge artifact with the intention of making a contribution to an ongoing social dialogue. At the same time, I became very conscious of how easy it is to fall into the trap of reification and of how, as with all representations, the form chosen constrains as well as facilitates understanding. Here, the bipolar dimensions might misleadingly suggest that there are discrete and mutually exclusive categories of meaning making; yet such an implication would certainly be incorrect. Similarly, talk of a cycle – or spiral – through these categories might also be potentially misleading. Perhaps better would be to think of the four quadrants as representing different perspectives on knowing, with the choice between them being rhetorical, i.e. dependent on the immediate discursive purpose.

18. As I have emphasized elsewhere, this does not mean restricting oneself to the interests that students bring with them to school. One of the aims of a well-chosen

curricular unit is to awaken new interests; it is also to help students to see as problematic and challenging matters which they take for granted as already completely understood (Wells, 1995; Wells, Chang, and Maher, 1990).

19. Interestingly, several members of DICEP, and other teacher researchers with whom I have worked, have made the same observation about their own investigations. Reading the published work of theorists or other researchers is of much greater interest and value to them when they have already collected evidence with respect to their chosen topic and begun to work on constructing an interpretation of it (Wells, 1994b,c).

20. See, for example, the classroom-based work associated with the reforms proposed by the National Council of Teachers of Mathematics (Cobb et al., 1992; Lampert, 1990), the work of Project Zero (Gardner, 1989) and the efforts to establish classrooms that are knowledge building communities (Brown and Campione, 1994; Scardamalia, Bereiter, and Lamon, 1994).

21. In emphasizing joint activity, I do not mean to suggest that all activities should be carried out through group work. As I have argued elsewhere, there needs to be an appropriate balance struck between whole class, small group and solo formats, since each has specific benefits, and each complements the others (Wells and Chang-Wells, 1992, ch.3). What I do wish to emphasize, though, is the importance of adopting an outer, social orientation in all three formats, since I believe that it is through knowing with others that personal understanding develops most effectively.

3   Discourse and Knowing
in the Classroom

The centrality of language has run like a leitmotiv through the exploration of knowing and knowledge in the preceding chapter. Here I want
to focus on it more directly, first by setting out the arguments for treating it as the very essence of education and, second, by considering in
more detail the relationship between discourse and knowing. I shall then
consider some of the implications of the preceding arguments for the
discourse through which so many of the daily practices of learning and
teaching are enacted in the classroom. Briefly, I shall propose that classrooms should become communities of inquiry, in which the curriculum
is seen as being created emergently in the many modes of conversation
through which teacher and students dialogically make sense of topics of
individual and social significance, through action, knowledge building
and reflection.

The Role of Language in Human Development

Vygotsky's contribution to our understanding of the central role
of language in human development has already been spelled out in some
detail in Chapter 1. It rests on the fruitful analogy he drew between material artifacts and signs: both function as tools to mediate joint, productive
activity. Viewed in this way, language and other semiotic systems can be
thought of as "psychological tools" that, through their inclusion in activity, radically transform participants' orientations both to the material
situation and to their coparticipants.

From a phylogenetic perspective, we have already seen this transformative effect in the account that was offered, in Chapter 2, of the emergence
of the different modes of knowing in the evolution from primate to contemporary humans. Indeed, that account might be recast, to a considerable

extent, in terms of the development of modes of semiosis. Instrumental knowing, the first mode of knowing to emerge, involves both attention and action that are intentional (Tomasello, 1994); however, it does not require communication with other members of the species in order to be successful. For procedural knowing, on the other hand, with its goal of coordinating action and teaching it to others, communication is clearly essential. Nevertheless, this need not involve language. Indeed, as Premack (1976) observes, it is only our modern obsession with language that blinds us to the large steps in social and cognitive evolution that occurred before the emergence of speech.

Homo erectus, the immediate predecessor of homo sapiens, is known to have made shelters, manufactured a variety of tools, cooperated in seasonal hunting, used fire to cook food, and migrated from Africa to Europe and Asia. These achievements are evidence of relatively highly developed social skills, yet the evidence suggests that these skills predated the full evolution of the vocal apparatus that is necessary for human speech as we know it. On these grounds, Donald (1991) has proposed that, prior to the emergence of speech, hominid culture was based on a mode of mimetic communication, which he characterizes as "the ability to produce conscious, self-initiated, representational acts that are intentional but not linguistic" (p. 168). Combining gesture, mime, and modulated vocalization, mimesis was the mode of discourse of a culture that continued relatively unchanged for more than a million years and enabled coordination of joint activity, modeling of social structure, and effective pedagogy. Even today, moreover, the various components of mimetic communication continue to play a significant role in face-to-face interaction, although participants are for the most part unaware of them (Wells, in press).

For the next mode of knowing to emerge, however – what I have called substantive knowing – some form of linguistic communication would seem to have been essential. For, unlike the preceding two modes, substantive knowing involves not simply "intention," but also "intentionality," or what Bruner (1997) characterizes as the "aboutness" of intention. That is to say, substantive knowing is concerned not only with particular objects, actions, and events, but with the consideration of particulars as instances of general classes, and with the relationships among these classes. For these purposes, the arbitrary but conventional symbols of language represent a considerable advance on mimesis. Unlike facial expressions and gestures, lexical items and the syntactic structures into which they enter are discrete and categorical; they also enter as much into intra-linguistic relationships of sense as into those of reference. It thus seems likely that there was a strong historical interdependence between the emergence and development of spoken language and that of substantive knowing.

However, language – and particularly spoken language – should not be seen as totally distinct from mimesis, nor as replacing it. If its lexicogrammar allows for greater precision and explicitness in meaning making, speech still remains closely related in its production to the motoric behavior involved in gesture and expressive vocalization and shares their strong affective base (Deacon, 1997). It also remains strongly oriented to the negotiation of interpersonal relationships and social values. As Eggins and Slade remark of casual conversation, "in any interaction we negotiate meanings about what we think is going on in the world, how we feel about it, and how we feel about the people we interact with" (1997, p. 6). The resources of spoken language on which we draw in conversation thus represent a rich, multidimensional "meaning potential" (Halliday, 1978) that enriches rather than supersedes the potential of the prelinguistic modes of communication.

At the same time, this meaning potential can be extended to a wide variety of more specialized functions. Some of these are closely related to the modes of knowing that I have called aesthetic and theoretical, each of which involves clusters of more differentiated registers and genres that highlight and exploit some aspects of the meaning potential more than others.[1] These modes of knowing and meaning making did not emerge fully formed, however. As in the case of substantive knowing, the relationship between these latter modes of knowing and ways of using language was, and continues to be, one of developmental interdependence – as was illustrated in the account offered in Chapter 2 of the relationship between theoretical knowing in science and the (written) genres in which scientists engage in knowledge building. Furthermore, as the case of scientific knowing makes clear, language is often combined with other modes of semiosis, such as visuographic and mathematical representation, each of which makes its own distinct contribution to the kinds of meaning that are made. Seen in this light, language is not a single, undifferentiated tool, nor is it totally distinct from other modes of meaning making. Rather, together with these other modes, it forms a rich and versatile resource from which a diversity of tools is constantly being fashioned to mediate the modes of knowing that are involved in the full range of joint activities in which human beings engage.

Language as Mediator of Individual
Mental Development

What is emphasized by adopting the phylogenetic and cultural historical perspective on human intellectual development is the role that semiotic mediation plays in enabling participants to collaborate effectively in activities of increasing social and technical complexity. In particular, it provides the cultural means for the inter-mental activity of knowledge building with respect to these activities – the "discourse between people doing things together" in which knowledge is developed. This already establishes a firm basis for asserting the centrality of language and other modes of meaning making in education.

However, the particular significance of Vygotsky's theory of semiotic mediation for education lies in the connections he made, first, between the different time scales, phylogenetic, cultural historical, and ontogenetic on which development occurs, and second, between inter-mental and intra-mental sign-based mediation of activity at the ontogenetic level. Individual intellectual development, he argued, is not the result of the gradual maturation of preexisting higher mental functions that are innate, but the process of transformation of biologically given primitive functions that takes place through the individual's appropriation of the inter-mental, semiotic processes encountered in activities undertaken with others. As he puts it, "children master the social forms of behavior and transfer these forms to themselves"; and more specifically with respect to sign-mediated behavior, "a sign is always originally a means used for social purposes, a means of influencing others, and only later becomes a means of influencing oneself" (Vygotsky, 1981, p. 157).

In learning his or her first language, therefore, a child not only masters what has come to be humans' most versatile mode of social interaction, but also becomes heir to the modes of mental functioning that have emerged over human history through the progressive development of linguistic and language-related modes of meaning making. That is to say, through participation in the activities that make up everyday life and in the conversations that accompany them, the child encounters and begins to appropriate such semiotically mediated mental actions as remembering, classifying and reasoning, as these enter into the modes of knowing that are enacted in these activities. Thus, by the time they enter school, children in contemporary literate cultures will already have some familiarity with all the modes of knowing except possibly the theoretical and will have begun to recreate them on the intramental plane so that they can serve as mediators of their solo mental functioning. For example, in addition to being instructed in the use of the artifacts around the home (procedural), they will also have been involved in resolving problems of various kinds and in planning future activities (substantive). In our culture, they will amost certainly also have engaged in aesthetic knowing through the medium of television and perhaps also through shared reading of picture story books. In all these activities, it is in talk with more experienced participants, as they engage in the activities together, that the child enters into and appropriates the modes of knowing as they are practiced within his or her culture (Wells, 1990). At the same time, as Halliday (1978) points out, they will have assimilated the culture's implicit 'theory of experience', as this is encoded in the language of those with whom they interact.

Thus, in sketching the broad outlines of a theory of the development of individual mental functioning through the mastery and appropriation of intermental semiotic processes used to mediate knowing with and for others, Vygotsky provides a firm basis for a language-based theory of learning and development that is of central importance for education.

What his theory does not provide, however, is explicit guidance on the kinds of language use that would best facilitate this developmental process in the classroom. As later chapters will argue, Vygotsky's concept of the zone of proximal development suggests some general principles for the manner in which curricular activities should be organized, but about the linguistic interaction through which they are enacted he has little of significance to say. This may well be because, in his brief working life, he did not have the opportunity to gain first-hand experience of working with students and teachers in classrooms.[2] However, a more likely explanation is to be found in the rather abstract and static nature of his conception of linguistic activity that is revealed in his choice of the categories – "sign," "word," "language" – in terms of which he discusses semiotic mediation. In order to translate Vygotsky's insightful theory about the social origin of individual mental functioning into a practice-oriented theory of classroom interaction, therefore, we need to adopt a more dynamic approach to language in use. Instead of focusing on the relationship between such synoptic categories as "word" and "thought," as Vygotsky did, we need to investigate the relationship between discourse and knowing as it occurs in particular, situated activities.

Bakhtinian Perspectives on Discourse

One of the first to recognize the importance of this distinction was Bakhtin, a contemporary although not a colleague of Vygotsky.

Although concerned mainly with literary texts, it was Bakhtin who first clearly argued for the primacy of "utterance" in the consideration of linguistic communication. As he points out, "speech can exist in reality only in the form of concrete utterances of individual speaking people" (1986, p. 71). Furthermore, utterances do not occur as isolated acts, but are always contextualized both by the specific goals and conditions of the activity in which they occur and by the utterances that both precede and follow.

In emphasizing the 'situated' nature of utterance, Bakhtin drew attention to two features of linguistic communication that are, I believe, of particular significance for an understanding of discourse. The first of these he referred to as speech genres. Although imbued with the individuality and subjectivity of the speaker's current concern, he argued, every utterance is also "shaped and developed within a certain generic form" (Bakhtin, 1986 p. 78). The range of speech genres is immense, corresponding to the diversity of the social activity settings in which people communicate; nevertheless for the most part they are used effortlessly, since they are learned, together with the grammar, lexis, and phonology of the language, in everyday conversation. Furthermore, he points out, "if speech genres did not exist and we had not mastered them ... speech communication would be almost impossible" (1986, p. 79).

A concern with the generic organization of discourse has since been the focus of extensive work in a variety of intellectual traditions, not necessarily directly influenced by Bakhtin. For example, in the field of social semiotics, Halliday's development of register theory (see Chapter 1) provides a systematization of the concept of speech genres; this has been further developed in the context of education by Lemke (1990) and Christie (1993) with respect to oral discourse, and by Martin (1989) with respect to the written genres of schooling. Also focusing on the genres of written texts is the North American school that sees genre as social action (Miller, 1984; Kamberelis, 1995). And from a quite different perspective, the work of conversation analysts, from Sacks, Schegloff, and Jefferson (1974) to Goodwin and Heritage (1990), can be seen as an attempt to discover how, through participants' orientation to the generic forms of utterances, as in the organization of turn-taking, adjacency pairs, or repairs, the actual business of "talk-in-interaction" (Schegloff, 1989) is accomplished. This work, too, has a clear bearing on the way in which discourse mediates knowing in interaction.

The second important feature of utterance to which Bakhtin drew attention was that of "responsivity," which applies both in listening and in speaking. For the listener, to perceive and understand another's utterance is "to take an active, responsive attitude toward it. . . . Sooner or later what is heard and actively understood will find its response in the subsequent speech or behavior of the listener" (1986, p. 68–69). For the speaker, on the other hand, responsivity works in both directions. Not only are utterances shaped in anticipation of a response of a certain kind from the intended listener, but they are themselves responsive to preceding utterances, expressing the speaker's attitude to them as well as to the topic that the current utterance addresses. Thus, "any utterance is a link in a very complexly organized chain of other utterances" (p. 69); it is "filled with *dialogic overtones*" (p. 92).

In fact, with this notion of dialogic overtones, Bakhtin offers a valuable pointer as to how participation in discourse allows the child to appropriate or, as Vygotsky puts it, to internalize the mental functions encountered in particular instances of interaction with others. In the course of explaining the source of personal voice in the creation of a particular utterance, he writes:

the unique speech experience of each individual is shaped and developed in continuous and constant interaction with others' individual utterances. This experience can be characterized to some degree as the process of *assimilation* – more or less creative – of others' words (and not the words of a language). Our speech, that is, all our utterances (including creative works) is filled with others' words, varying degrees of otherness or varying degrees of 'our-own-ness,' varying degrees of awareness and detachment. These words of others carry with them their own expression, their own evaluative tone, which we assimilate, rework and accentuate. (1986, p. 89)

Dubbing this process of speaking through others' words "ventriloquation," Wertsch (1991) expands the notion to offer an alternative to Vygotsky's use of "internalization" in explaining the more general process whereby each individual takes over and makes his or her own the cultural array of means for mediating both material and mental action. Just as we learn to speak by ventriloquating others' words, so we also take over their ideas and values by trying them on and transforming them to suit our own needs and purposes. However, what is equally important to recognize is that this process does not apply only in childhood; it continues throughout our lives whenever we encounter fruitful new ideas in the utterances of others as we engage with them in various modes of collaborative knowledge building.

However, there is a further corollary of taking seriously the responsivity that is at the heart of dialogue, which has only recently begun to receive attention in the new field of discursive psychology (Edwards, 1997; Edwards and Potter, 1992). If, as Bakhtin claims, "every utterance must be regarded primarily as a *response* to preceding utterances" (1986, p. 91), particular utterances cannot be taken as the expression of the speaker's stable, underlying beliefs and attitudes, but rather must be understood as strategic moves tailored to the speaker's assessment of the exigencies of the immediate discursive situation. To the extent that individual understanding is mediated by social discourse, therefore, it too must be recognized to be variable over time and contingent upon the nature of the activity and of the contributions of coparticipants. Thus, no utterance is final, in the sense of providing a definitive account of the topic it addresses. However knowledgeable the speaker/writer, and however authoritative the tone, all utterances should be treated as no more – and no less – than contributions to the ongoing dialogue, and therefore open to further response.

From an educational perspective, recognition of the strong influence of the discursive context on the content and form of utterances has a number of significant implications. Some of these are demonstrated by Edwards (1993) through an analysis of several excerpts from a recording of a session in which a teacher discussed with a class of five-year-olds some things they had "learned" during an earlier trip to a greenhouse. First, as he shows, what the teacher's way of conducting the discourse elicited was, not an attempt by each child to formulate his or her conceptual understanding, but a collective exercise in remembering what the gardener had said. However, as he argues, even if the teacher had adopted strategies that facilitated the former objective, the children would still have had to draw on the discursive resources, modes of explanation and terms of reference that they had at their disposal from previous discourse experience; furthermore, they would still have had to shape their contributions to take account of what had already been said in the current session – by their peers as well as by the teacher. In other words, there is no way of using what they say to discover "what children really think."

Nevertheless, if children's contributions to educational discourse can never be treated as providing a direct "window on the mind," they can still be informative about the manner in which their conceptual development occurs. For, as Edwards points out, "the very features of discourse that render it opaque with respect to individual cognitions are just the ones that are especially revealing about the social shaping of thought and the local, situational, and pragmatic organization of conceptual thinking" (1993, p. 213). Although not directly addressed by Edwards, the demonstration his paper provides of the consequential effects of the particular discursive context on what is said – or written – should also lead us to think seriously about the way in which students' "utterances" are evaluated as evidence of what they have learned and come to understand, whether these be answers to teachers' questions, oral contributions to discussion, or sustained written responses under examination conditions.[3] Here, too, it is important to recognize that no test can tell us what children *really* think or understand.

In sum, what emerges from this brief review of the work of Vygotsky, Bakhtin, and others who have extended their initial insights is a view of the relationship between language and knowing that is much more complex than the one that has generally been taken for granted in education. While it is the case, in educational settings in particular, that language serves as the principal medium in which the understandings gained in the past are made available for uptake and use in the present, the process whereby these understandings are "shared" is very far from being one of simple transmission and reception. As we have seen, ideas do not exist independently of the semiotic processes through which they are formulated and communicated for particular purposes on particular occasions; furthermore, since communication is a dialogic process, the meanings that are made by speakers and listeners or writers and readers with respect to individual utterances are strongly influenced by the discourse context in which they occur. Knowing, then, is both situated and dialogic.

Since this conclusion is clearly very different from the generally accepted one, in the next section I shall attempt to spell out what I see to be its implications through a more detailed exploration of the relationship between discourse and knowing. For how we construe this relationship is obviously going to be crucial for the kinds of classroom activities we attempt to promote.

Progressive Discourse: The Dialogue of Knowing

As a way into this issue, we might start with the claim made by Halliday, in the introduction to his proposal for a "language-based theory of learning." Language, he states, "is the essential condition of knowing, the process by which experience becomes knowledge" (1993a, p. 94). Part of what Halliday is referring to here is the meaning-making potential of language as a system for picking out, classifying and naming elements of experience and for establishing conceptual relationships of various kinds between the categories so created. This is to focus on language as a culturally created cognitive artifact (Hutchins, 1995) – the toolkit with which we know and are able to relate our knowing to that of others. But in Halliday's sentence the emphasis is on language as *process*, on using the tool-kit in the activity of knowing through the creation of what I earlier called knowledge artifacts – *products* – in the form of spoken and written texts.

In educational politics, process and product are often treated as incompatible alternatives; an emphasis on either is thought to lead to neglect of the other. But, as my gloss of Halliday's claim makes clear, the two terms do not refer to two different "things," but to two simultaneously valid perspectives on a single event. There can be no saying without something that is said; discourse is inevitably always both process and product. Similarly for "knowing" and "knowledge"; the one is not independent of the other, for they are related in the same way as "saying" and "what is said."

However, there is more to it than that. For the utterance that is produced in the process of speaking comes to have an independent existence, both material and ideal (Cole, 1996a), that is consequential for the activity of knowing. Most obviously, it becomes a knowledge object for others, to which they can respond in various ways – by extending, questioning, or rejecting it. This is the process of knowledge building that I referred to in the previous chapter. The utterance also becomes a knowledge object for the speaker, who is thus able to contemplate his own current understanding in externalized form and to respond to it in the same way as do other participants. Although at first sight odd, there is thus real insight in the saying "How do I know what I think until I hear what I say?"

This is what I was trying to capture in the previous chapter when I suggested that knowledge building and understanding are related to each other as the outer and inner orientations that individuals adopt at different moments in the spiral of knowing. There I also suggested that, in Vygotskyan terms, this relationship could be seen as corresponding to the relationship between "communicative" and "inner" speech or, in contemporary terminology, between discourse with others and with oneself. However, in the light of the preceding discussion, I now see that this initial formulation needs to be somewhat revised.

Understanding, I would now suggest, is the sense of coherence achieved in the act of saying – the impression one has of the elements of the problem or puzzle fitting together in a meaningful pattern. This is a function of the way in which the "utterance" is actually shaped, in the moment, to fit the demands of the particular activity in which one is engaged (Britton, 1982). In order to contribute in a "progressive" manner to the ongoing dialogue, one has to interpret the preceding contribution in terms of the information it introduces as well as of the speaker's stance to that information, compare that with one's own current understanding of the issue under discussion, and then formulate a contribution that will, in some relevant way, add to the common understanding achieved in the discourse so far, by extending, questioning or qualifying what has already been said. In uttering, therefore, one's effort is directed to the saying – to producing meaning for others. Thus, as Bakhtin says, "to be means to be for the other, and through him, for oneself" (1979, quoted in Wertsch, 1998, p. 116). More specifically, by contributing to the joint meaning making with and for others, one also makes meaning for oneself and, in the process, extends one's own understanding. At the same time, the "utterance," viewed from the perspective of what is said, is a knowledge artifact that potentially contributes to the collaborative knowledge building of all those who are co-participants in the activity.

Several important implications follow from this formulation. First, understanding is not something one has – not a permanent state or an object in some mental filing cabinet. Rather, it comes into existence through participation in a particular activity and as that changes so it develops – or fades. In one sense, then, for the initial understanding to be recaptured, it must be reachieved in another utterance that is responsive to whatever demands the new activity, or later phase of the same activity, makes. And since these occasions are always different to some degree, so also is the understanding. However, this picture is incomplete, for it ignores the importance of the utterance viewed as what is said. Being the recipient – as well as the producer – of this object, one can achieve a different, but related, understanding by construing its meaning in a way comparable to that employed by other recipients. (I stress "comparable" because, as the one who produced the utterance, one has a somewhat different stance toward it than do other recipients; its sense is necessarily colored by one's unique personal experience.) As long as one can remember what was said, one can recapture at least some part of the understanding achieved in the saying.

A second implication that seems to follow from this account is that receiving and interpreting an "utterance" is very similar, in many respects, to producing one. It, too, involves a kind of saying which is, in part, a resaying of what was said by its producer. But, because the receiver's stance is inevitably different from that of the producer, this resaying creates a different "object" from what was said, which we might call "what is comprehended." At the same time, as Bakhtin points out, comprehending is also incipiently saying in response: "All real and integral understanding is actively responsive, and constitutes nothing other than the initial preparatory stage of a response (in whatever form it may be actualized)" (1986, p. 69).

Support for this view can also be found in other traditions. Recall, for example, Popper's claim (quoted above) that "we can grasp a theory only by trying to reinvent it or to reconstruct it." There are also clear affinities with reader response theory (Rosenblatt, 1978), to which I also referred in Chapter 2. For the moment, we can summarize the argument by saying that both producing and comprehending utterances involves constructive mental (and physical) effort and it is in this process that understanding is achieved.

In stating this conception of the relationship between understanding and the discourse of knowledge building above, I deliberately placed "utterance" in quotes. This was to signal a broader than usual interpretation of the term, that I now want to pursue. Although the term is most frequently used to refer to instances of speech or, as in the works of Vygotsky and Bakhtin, of writing as well as speech, it can be applied by a straightforward analogy to all instances of semiotically mediated activity and, without straining the analogy very far, to creative problem solving of all kinds. What all these have in common is: (1) a "problem" arising in the course of some kind of joint activity in which more than mere reproduction of an existing solution is required; (2) the presence in the situation of an array of cultural artifacts which may be used to mediate the making of a solution; (3) coparticipants with varying degrees of skill in their use; and (4) an "object" – that is to say, whatever artifact or practice is created or modified in the process that mediates the solution of the problem.[4]

The point of using "utterance" in this way, to refer to both perspectives on the event – the saying/making a solution, on the one hand, and what is said/the solution that is made, on the other – is that it brings out the commonality between all the modes of knowing discussed in the previous chapter, and allows us to see that, in all modes, understanding and knowledge building are related through the process–product nexus. It also highlights two further important points: First, that understanding can be achieved in doing and in comprehending what is done as well as in saying and in comprehending what is said; and second, that knowledge artifacts do not always take the form of linguistic texts.

To recall Wartofsky (above), any artifact can mediate knowing if it is intentionally used for that purpose. Recognized as the means for felling a tree, an axe or a power saw can function as a knowledge artifact, just as can a manual giving instructions on how to use the latter. This is because, as Cole (1996 a) emphasizes, all artifacts "are simultaneously *ideal* (conceptual) and *material*" (p. 117, emphases in original). To clarify this point he quotes the anthropologist, Leslie White: "An axe has a subjective component; it would be meaningless without a concept and an attitude. On the other hand, a concept or attitude would be meaningless without overt expression, in behavior or speech (which is a form of behavior)" (White, 1942, p. 372; quoted in Cole, 1996a, p. 120). This is not to deny the difference between material tools and symbolic texts in the ways in which they participate in activity, each alone or, as is more often the case, in concert, but rather to emphasize the wide range of artifacts that can mediate knowing (cf. Kress, 1997).

Nevertheless, there is no doubt that symbolic, and particularly linguistic, utterances have a special role to play in this respect. This is because, as Halliday puts it, as well as being one of the semiotic systems that make up culture, language "is distinctive in that it also serves as an encoding system for many (though not all) the others" (1978, p. 2). It thus not only mediates action, it also provides the means for reflecting on action and for constructing the descriptions and plans, narratives, and theories, by means of which we know substantively, aesthetically and theoretically. It is for this reason that Halliday claims that discourse is "the process by which experience becomes knowledge."

For "knowledge," here, we can read "what is said" – that is, what has been said in the countless discourses on particular occasions, over many centuries, through which what is known at any moment has been taken over and passed on from one generation to the next and, in the process, developed and accumulated, been questioned and revised. This is to focus on knowledge building in the discourse between people – the working on the "product" with others, without which, I have argued, there would be no personal understanding. This is to focus, too, on the actual linguistic formulations that are so constructed – "rivers always flow downhill," "two plus two equals four," "in a democracy, all citizens have the right to vote." These and countless others, both general and specific, are the artifacts created and recreated in discourse; they both embody what is known and mediate knowing in action in situations to which they are applied.

A focus on the discourse of knowledge building also enables us to see how particular instances of what is known are collaboratively constructed over many turns, as participants offer what they consider to be relevant information, propose candidate formulations, raise objections, and so on. The process is one of negotiation, involving disagreement as well as agreement; furthermore, although the object of knowledge building is a formulation to which all participants assent, this goal is not always achieved. However, this does not mean that the activity has failed. Viewed from the perspective of the process of intersubjectivity involved, disagreement is as important as agreement in keeping participants engaged in knowledge building (Smolka et al., 1995). As Matusov (1996) observes, without some disagreement there would be no need to communicate and therefore no dynamic for change.[5]

Change – or transformation, as I have called it – is, of course, the focal object of knowledge building; the goal is to improve or advance what is known. Change is also another way of talking about the learning that students are expected to gain from participation in classroom discourse: change in terms of increasing mastery of the processes of discourse, and change in their understanding of the topics and problems addressed. Rarely is it recognized, however, the extent to which the two forms of change can be essentially one and the same process, but seen from different perspectives. Yet, as I have tried to demonstrate in the preceding pages, it is through participation in the activity of knowledge building, as they work together to produce and respond to verbal (and other semiotic) utterances – constructing "what is known" in "what is said" – that students appropriate the genres of discourse and the modes of knowing that they mediate, and simultaneously transform their individual and collective understanding. As Lave and Wenger (1991) argue, learning is not separate and independent, but an integral aspect of increasingly full participation in an ongoing cultural activity.

To be sure, there will be times when students need to focus on learning to use the linguistic toolkit, in the sense of giving their attention to features such as new items of vocabulary or lexicogrammatical devices for expressing certainty, doubt and other forms of epistemic commitment. The same is true for the "skills" involved in locating and managing information or using material and technological tools safely and effectively. But these should be "practiced" in the same way that cricketers or tennis players periodically work on improving their strokes, that is to say, in order to be able to participate more effectively in the real game. I thus concur with Bereiter and Scardamalia (1996), when they argue that "knowledge building should be the principal activity in school, but some things need to be deliberately pursued as learning objectives" (p. 502). However, I should want to point out that these "things" to be learned also involve knowledge building, though not in the theoretical mode with which these authors are chiefly concerned.

Knowledge Building and Progressive Discourse

If collaborative knowledge building can simultaneously provide the context and motivation for the learning of the necessary constituent skills, as Bereiter and Scardamalia (1996) contend, it might seem surprising that it so rarely forms the focus of classroom activity. There appear to be two main reasons for this. The first is to be found in the pervasive influence of a conception of knowledge that treats it as something that is contained in minds and books and that can be transmitted from one container to another. Since I have dealt with this at length in the preceding chapter, I shall say no more about it here, except to note that this view is often as strongly held by students as it is by teachers. The second, which is somewhat related, is a general distrust in the value of encouraging students to express their beliefs and opinions in an open dialogue of which the outcome is unknown. Yet if one accepts, as most educators do, that what students currently believe will influence the sense they make of new experiences and information, it would at the least seem prudent to try to discover what those beliefs are in order to know how best to engage with them. Even better, however, would be to encourage students not only to express their individual opinions but also to comment on and question those of others in the belief that this process would also contribute to progress in both individual and collective understanding.

Trust in students' ability to take an active role in their own learning is obviously an essential prerequisite for the introduction of collaborative knowledge building. But for it to be worthwhile, the discourse must involve more than simply the "sharing" of opinions. It must also result in progress, in the sense that the sharing, questioning, and revising of opinions leads to "a new understanding that everyone involved agrees is superior to their own previous understanding" (Bereiter, 1994a, p. 6). Such *progressive discourse*, Bereiter argues, is what ideally characterizes scientific and other knowledge-building communities. It is discourse based on four commitments that all participants make[6]:

- to work toward common understanding satisfactory to all
- to frame questions and propositions in ways that allow evidence to be brought to bear on them
- to expand the body of collectively valid propositions
- to allow any belief to be subjected to criticism if it will advance the discourse

Excerpted from Bereiter, 1994a, p. 7

There is one further feature that is essential for the discourse to be progressive, and that is a knowledge artifact that participants work collaboratively to improve. This focus on an "improvable object," as Bereiter and Scardmalia (1996) term it, is exactly what one would expect, given the account of knowing developed in the preceding pages. However, while theories and models – tertiary artifacts, as Wartofsky (1979) called them – are the objects on which scientists most frequently work, there are many other kinds of improvable object that can be the focus of knowledge building. Depending on the mode of knowing concerned, the object could be, for example: a material artifact, such as a device for measuring rainfall; a procedure for controlling traffic flow or a plan for an exhibition; an oral narrative or a script for a film; a musical composition; a biography or an account of a significant historical event.

If progressive discourse is the means of knowledge building in many fields of activity in the larger world beyond the classroom, might it not be equally valid within the classroom? Might it not, in fact, provide a form of apprenticeship into those very activities that school is intended to equip students to enter? Bereiter is very clear that it can:

Classroom discussions may be thought of as part of the larger ongoing discourse, not as preparation for it or as after-the-fact examination of the results of the larger discourse. The fact that classroom discourse is unlikely to come up with ideas that advance the larger discourse in no way disqualifies it. ... The important thing is that the local discourses be progressive in the sense that understandings are being generated that are new to the local participants and that the participants recognize as superior to their previous understandings. (1994a, p. 9)

It would seem, therefore, that progressive discourse is an ideal means for knowledge building and, thus, an essential component in each "cycle" of the spiral of knowing described in the previous chapter. Furthermore, because – as I have interpreted it – progressive discourse can mediate knowledge building in any of the modes of knowing, it provides a way of overcoming the conceptual separation, as well as the separation in practice, between the learning of supposedly lower-level skills and factual information and the "content" knowledge building in the different areas of the curriculum for which mastery of those skills and facts is seen as a prerequisite preparation.[7] To be sure, the form of discourse appropriate for knowledge building will differ according to the mode of knowing involved and the larger activity in which students are engaged, but there is no reason why the aim of "progressiveness" should not characterize the discourse in which students master various kinds of procedural knowing as well as that in which they engage in aesthetic and theoretical knowing.

At the same time, I am not suggesting that all the discourse that occurs in the classroom should be of this kind. There are many other important functions that discourse serves besides knowledge building. What I am proposing, however, is that progressive discourse should, in principle, have a central role at all levels and in all areas of the curriculum. If that is accepted, a major aim of educational research should be to explore what forms that discourse might take and what conditions enable it to occur.

Modalities of Discourse for Knowledge Building

So far, the discussion of discourse and knowing has been concerned mainly with the spoken mode. And with good reason. For most of human history, speech was the only mode of linguistic discourse available, and it is still the one preferred in face-to-face interaction. One of the chief advantages of speech is that, as I emphasized earlier, it involves expressive dimensions of meaning making that enrich and complement the purely lexicogrammatical and facilitate the negotiation of participants' stances, both towards each other and to the topic of the talk. It also has the advantages of immediacy of response and of allowing coparticipants to attend simultaneously to other aspects of the situation with eyes and hands while still receiving the same message at the same time.

Not surprisingly, therefore, speech plays a significant role in life in classrooms. Both informally in the conversations among children that accompany curricular activities, as well as formally in teacher-led discussions, talk – together with nonverbal modes of communication – is extremely important in establishing the nature of the classroom community, its ground rules and norms of collaboration (or competition). At the same time, as is suggested in Engeström's (1991b) application to the classroom of his model of an activity system, the nature of the classroom discourse that occurs in the course of particular activities significantly affects the kinds of opportunities for knowing and coming to know experienced by the community as a whole as well as by individual participants (Holzman, 1995; Nystrand and Gamoran, 1991).

Speech has an equally significant role in classrooms where collaborative group work is encouraged. In talking together, children learn a great deal from each other, as they pool their ideas and explore their agreements and disagreements about the tasks in which they are engaged (Forman and McPhail, 1993; Mercer, 1995). The same is true of the whole class discussions in which, at the end of an activity, they reflect with their teacher upon the significance of what they have done and come to understand

(Wells and Chang, in press). In this sort of accepting climate, speech allows all participants to enter the dialogue at the level of which they are capable; it also enables the teacher or tutor to offer immediate support and assistance that is tailored to the needs of the individual student.

Many of the characteristics of speech noted above make it a highly appropriate medium for a variety of activities that take place in classrooms – at least, as classrooms are presently constituted. Organizational matters, such as negotiating the task to be carried out and deciding how to proceed with it, obviously benefit from the possibility of immediate feedback and clarification that speech permits; where practical activities are involved, for similar reasons, the monitoring and evaluation of each step is also most readily carried out through speech. Here talk together with gesture and the use of other semiotic artifacts mediates procedural and substantive knowing. There are also activities that depend upon the expressiveness of speech, such as drama or literature read aloud, or the launching narrative or exposition, designed to arouse enthusiasm and interest, with which a teacher introduces a new curricular topic.

Almost all the advantages of speech mentioned above also enable it to make an important contribution to knowing in the aesthetic and theoretical modes.[8] However, when it comes to attempts to engage in sustained knowledge building, spoken discourse also has some severe limitations. Chief among these is the evanescence of the understandings achieved in speech and the difficulty of pursuing any one line of thinking in a systematic manner long enough to be sure that progress has been made and to know in what that progress consists. Memory for the exact words spoken is extremely short and, without recourse to a definitive text of what was said, it is difficult to work systematically to improve it and the understanding it embodies. It is here that writing provides such a powerful mediating technology, enabling the group as well as the individual writer to make real progress in knowledge building. Because a written text, unlike the text produced in speaking, is a permanent artifact, it can be reviewed, rethought and revised through a different form of dialogue, in which the text under construction plays a central role. The same is true for a text already written, when it is approached as a writer's attempt to formulate his or her understanding in "what is said" and engaged with dialogically. Both for writers and readers, then, the text can function as the "improvable object" that provides the focus for progressive discourse and simultaneously embodies the progress made.

But there is a trade-off. For writing also has its limitations, particularly sustained writing in the essayist tradition, of which this book is an example. While it is excellent as the medium for the exposition and critique of complex ideas, it lacks the immediacy of responsive interchange that characterizes speech; it also privileges the lexicogrammatical over other dimensions of meaning and is therefore much more limited in its expressive capabilities. Finally, and most critically from the perspective of progressive discourse in the classroom, the individualistic nature of both production and reception, coupled with the great variation among students in speed and fluency, mean that sustained written text can only serve occasionally as the "improvable object."

However, there are other, more compact, genres of writing and, equally important, other kinds of "text" that can serve in this way. Indeed, all forms of meaning making that give permanence to "what is said" have this potential. Vygotsky (1981) included "algebraic symbol systems . . . schemes, diagrams, maps, and mechanical drawings" in his examples of "psychological tools"; to these must be added rough sketches, point-form notes, computer programs, and many others. In each case, it is the material permanence of the form in which the semiotic artifact is embodied that enables it to support the recursive reflection and revision that is so important a characteristic of knowledge building. But, as Lemke (1993a) points out, no semiotic modality is self-contained in use; situated communication always involves multiple dimensions and modalities of meaning making, some simultaneous and others playing complementary roles at different points in achieving the overall goals of the activity. Just as progressive discourse needs to be complemented by discourse in other modes, therefore, it also needs appropriately to exploit the full range of modalities of meaning making (Harste, 1993).

Social and Inner Speech Revisited

In concluding this exploration of the relationship between discourse and knowing, I want to reconsider Vygotsky's distinction between "inner" and "social" speech. One of its attractions was that it seemed to provide a way of explaining the social origin of individual mental functioning: "Any function in the child's cultural development appears twice, or on two planes. First it appears on the social plane, and then on the psychological plane. First it appears between people as an interpsychological category, and then within the child as an intrapsychological category" (1981, p. 163).

In the case of speech, the route from external to internal was to be seen in the phenomenon of "egocentric speech." As both Piaget and Vygotsky observed, at around the age of three or four, children often talk when playing with other children in a way that suggests that their speech is intended more for their own benefit than for that of their playmates. With increasing age, this practice ceases to be observed but, according to Vygotsky (*contra* Piaget), it does not disappear (as a result of the child becoming more social) but becomes internalized as inner speech. One of the chief functions that Vygotsky attributed to inner speech was that of mediating self-regulation; as Wertsch and Tulviste explain it, "inner speech enables humans to plan and regulate their action and *derives from* previous participation in verbal social interaction" (1992, p. xx, emphasis added). Vygotsky also proposed a similar history for the function of inner speech as a mediator of thinking; it too derives from thinking in verbal social interaction.

As several commentators have argued, however, there are problems with formulating this developmental process in terms of "internalization." First, it suggests that the function in question moves from outside to inside the skin of the learner and, second, it proposes a temporal sequence – first external and then internal – that is far too mechanical. Certainly, the cultural artifacts that mediate our actions preexist our use of them, as do the practices that they enable. The same is true of many of the ideas, encountered in the utterances of others, in terms of which we develop our own understanding. In this sense, they are first social – part of the ongoing culture – before they become part of the repertoire of any particular individual member. But the process of appropriation – of making practices and ideas our own – does not involve transfer from outside to inside, but the gradual construction on the part of the learner of actions equivalent to those manifested in the verbal and other behavior of others and an increasing ability to carry them out independently.

In Chapter 10, I use the analogy of learning to dance to make this general point. Learning to move to the rhythm of the dance in the culturally appropriate manner involves simultaneously coordinating one's bodily movements with those of more experienced dancers and at the same time constructing an inner, self-directing analogue of the external, social behavior. Certainly, with experience, the movement becomes more fluent, and action sequences that at first required deliberate control become relatively automatic operations that no longer need conscious attention. But dancing still involves both "mind" and "body," both ideational and physical activity. The same, I would argue, is true of more obviously intellectual activities, such as solving a practical problem or constructing an argument or explanation. Whether performed by novice or skilled practitioner, action always has both an outer and an inner dimension, with each informing the other. Furthermore, rather than speaking of these as occurring in a temporal sequence, it would be more appropriate to think of them as alternative perspectives on the same event.

What then is the role of inner speech in relation to knowing? An answer, I believe, can best be made in terms of a distinction between different modalities of discourse, similar to the distinction between speech and writing. What Vygotsky referred to as inner speech is certainly not the inner correlate of social speech; although they draw upon the same "meaning potential," they are clearly different in realization and typically occur under different conditions. However, like oral speech and writing, inner speech is a form of discursive action that is realized in utterance; but, whereas in speech and writing the saying is overt and what is said has a material form that is simultaneously accesssible to others as well as to the speaker, inner speech is not overt and what is said is accessible to the speaker alone. Nevertheless, with respect to knowing, inner-speech functions in very much the same way as the related overt modalities. First, it is dialogic, in the sense that each utterance is responsive to utterances that preceded and anticipates further response. And second, involving as it must both "saying" and "what is said," it contributes to both understanding and knowledge building. Certainly, the knowledge building is performed solo – at least, in the moment. But, as I have argued before, the dialogue of inner speech is only part of a larger dialogue related to joint activities in which many other people are involved; moreover, the utterances of inner speech respond to earlier utterances by others as well as self, and are often prospective rehearsals of what one intends to say (or write) on some future social occasion, or retrospective of what one did not say but now wishes that one had. On this account, therefore, there are no grounds for treating inner speech as the medium in which thinking occurs prior to its expression in overt speech. Rather, as with oral speech and writing, inner speech is a modality of meaning making in which thought is brought to completion as it is shaped and embodied in the act of utterance.[9]

Discourse and Knowledge Building in the Classroom: Some Research Perspectives

In the preceding sections, I have attempted to spell out the reasons for urging that greater recognition should be given to the central and formative role of language in education. As I hope I have made clear, what is at issue here is not simply the "subject" referred to variously as "Language Arts," "Mother Tongue," or "English," but the role of linguistic discourse in making meaning – in mediating communicating and knowing right "across the curriculum." Not all discourse is realized linguistically, of course, in the sense of being constructed from the lexicogrammatical resources of language. Nevertheless, as Halliday (1993a) emphasizes, linguistic discourse is "the prototypical form of human semiosis" (p. 93); and it is in learning and using language that we enter into and participate in the ongoing dialogue of meaning making in the communities to which we belong. With so much at stake, I would argue, we cannot afford simply to take the role of language for granted.

Fortunately, the last quarter century has seen an increasing attention to language among educators and, more significantly, a growing number of studies of life in classrooms which look at the language that actually occurs there, rather than through it to the knowledge that it purportedly conveys. Increasingly, too, the emphasis has come to be placed on discourse (rather than language, per se), and on the purposes it serves to accomplish.

Seminal in this respect was the work of Barnes (1976/1992), published under the title "From Communication to Curriculum." In the preface, Barnes stated his intention as "to illustrate some ways in which children use speech in the course of learning and to indicate how this depends upon the patterns of communication set up by teachers in their classrooms." As well as being of practical use to teachers, he claimed, this would also constitute a critical contribution to curriculum theory: "[S]ince the learners' understandings are the raison d'être of schooling, an adequate curriculum theory must utilize an interactive model of teaching and learning" (1992, p. 9).

Over the intervening years, a substantial number of studies in the same spirit has followed (for reviews of this work, see: Cazden, 1988; Edwards and Westgate, 1994; Hicks, 1995). More recently, as the crucial mediating role of discourse in knowing and understanding has come to be increasingly appreciated, and with it the significance of the Bakhtinian emphasis on dialogue, attention has turned to the larger context of the curriculum as a whole and to the critical role of the teacher in initiating and guiding this dialogue (Applebee, 1996; Mercer, 1995; Nystrand, 1997). As is becoming clear, this involves not simply the setting up of activities of the kind that Barnes describes but, more radically, the creation of the kind of classroom community in which the search for understanding, and the dialogue through which this is accomplished, pervades all areas of the curriculum and is inclusive of all students, whatever their social, ethnic, or linguistic background.

Significantly, while university-based researchers and theorists have continued to contribute to these developments, an increasing part has been played by classroom teachers researching and reporting their own practice (e.g. Donoahue et al.,1996; Gallas, 1994, 1995; Stock, 1995) or by collaborating groups of teacher-researchers drawn from both types of institution (McMahon and Raphael, 1997; Newman, 1989; Norman, 1992; Pierce and Gilles, 1993; Short and Burke, 1991). I believe these latter two categories of investigation are of particular importance for the attempt to bring about improvement in classroom practice; not only because they report ways of working that are proving successful in "real" classrooms, but because what is reported is the outcome of applying the same principles of knowledge bulding to the activities in which students engage as to the investigations through which the teacher-researchers attempt to improve them (Wells et al., 1994).

Several of the remaining chapters in this book arise from such collaborative investigations and all owe a great debt to the classroom teachers in interaction with whom I have developed the ideas about classroom discourse that are presented here. As an introduction to the more specific topics addressed in later chapters, therefore, I shall use the remainder of the present one to review some of the classroom studies that have been most influential for the course our work has taken.

I have already mentioned the pioneering work of Barnes and his colleagues in England (Barnes, 1976/1992; Barnes, Britton and Rosen, 1969; Barnes and Todd, 1977). For me, as for many others, it was they who pointed the way for future research as, influenced by their discovery of Vygotsky's ideas on thought and language[10] as well as by their work with teachers, they insisted that language was not simply a means of communicating the content of the curriculum but "the major means by which children in our schools formulate knowledge and relate it to their own purposes and view of the world" (Barnes, 1992, p. 19). What has taken us much longer to realize, however, is that it is not simply our view of the world that is constructed in the discourses in which we participate but our view of ourselves, our values and our very identities (Luke, 1995; Walkerdine, 1988). This idea was already prefigured in the theoretical writings of Bernstein (1971, 1975), but it was not until it was demonstrated in the empirical work of Michaels (1981), O'Connor and Michaels (1996), Heath (1983), Hasan and colleagues (Hasan,1986; Hasan and Cloran, 1989), and Gee (1992) on the continuities and discontinuities between talk in the home and talk in the classroom that it began to have an influence on our thinking about classroom practice.

At the same time, neither the discourse nor the curriculum exists independently of the activities in which teachers and students engage together and of the manner in which they do so (Engeström, 1991b). In other words, as Green and Dixon (1993) point out, teacher and student, knowing and doing, and what counts as knowledge are all mutually constituted over time in the discourses and practices through which the life of the classroom community is enacted.

In my own work, particularly in the research conducted in collaboration with members of DICEP, these realizations have gradually led to a focus on three levels in our investigations of classroom practice: community, activities, and modes and modalities of discourse.[11] Linking all three together is the orientation to inquiry.

Communities of Inquiry

In our way of using the term to characterize our "object in view," inquiry does not refer to a method (as in "discovery" learning), still less to a generic set of procedures for carrying out activities. Rather, it indicates a stance toward experiences and ideas – a willingness to wonder, to ask questions, and to seek to understand by collaborating with others in the attempt to make answers to them. At the same time, the aim of inquiry is not "knowledge for its own sake" but the disposition and ability to use the understandings so gained to act informedly and responsibly in the situations that may be encountered both now and in the future. As an approach to education, inquiry also gives full recognition to the mutually constitutive relationship between individual and society. On the one hand, it builds upon the first-hand experiences and interests of individual students and encourages them to be agentive in directing their own learning and, on the other, it seeks to equip them with the socially valued ways of thinking and acting – the modes of knowing and the practices and systems of concepts developed in the communities of the various disciplines – so that they may both use them and develop them further. Inquiry, then, is rooted in the understandings gained in the past as these are embodied in the culture's practices and artifacts and, at the same time, situated in the specific present of particular classrooms and oriented to the construction of new understandings.

An important feature of inquiry in practice is its active, object-oriented nature. And here, by "object," I mean both its intended outcome, or goal, in the making of answers or solutions that have significance and value in the lives of the inquirers, and also the artifacts that are worked on and improved in the process. Thus an important function of the focus on inquiry is to provide a way of overcoming the separation, in practice as well as in theory, between "school" knowledge (conceived of as acquired, but often inert, information) and "action-knowledge" (Barnes, 1976/1992), that is to say, the understanding that is constructed in action and is able to inform future action in situations beyond as well as in the classroom.

Along with this action orientation goes recognition of the strong affective charge that is involved. Of course, affectivity is an essential component of all situated knowing – even though frequently ignored in education; however, in inquiry its importance is particularly evident, both in the shaping of goals and in the ways in which inquirers work adaptively to achieve them. Seen from a related perspective, the affect involved in this voluntarily undertaken effort, and in the satisfaction felt in succeeding, also plays a significant part in the maintenance and development of identity. Affect does not only reside in the relationship between agent, object, and action, however, but also in the interpersonal relations between the coparticipants in the activity. Where everyone is involved in personally significant inquiry, there is an additional satisfaction and excitement in sharing what one is doing with others, in hearing what others are doing, and in discovering how these doings and understandings can be related. Herein lies the pleasure as well as the motive for collaboration.

Finally, a focus on inquiry emphasizes the essential continuity of education (Dewey, 1938, 1956). For the principles just described apply not only to students in K–12 classrooms, but equally to the teachers and administrators who are immediately responsible for their education, and to those who are responsible for the initial preparation and further professional development of these teachers and administrators (Wells, 1994b). However, a common focus on inquiry has the still further advantage of building bridges between these levels in the overall institution of education; for it creates a framework within which individual development and societal transformation are achieved through people working collaboratively with others, both more and less expert than themselves, on questions and problems that arise from practice and are focused on understanding and improving practice. A community of inquiry is thus a particular type of "community of practice," as this concept has been developed by Lave and Wenger (1991).

Recognizing the importance of "community" in education, others (Brown and Campione, 1994; Rogoff, 1994) have used the term "community of learners" to characterize the form that a community of practice might ideally take in schools and colleges. However, the problem with this expression, as I see it, is that it places the emphasis on *learning* as the apparent object of the community's practices. In Vygotsky's conception, however, and even more explicitly in Lave and Wenger's (1991) theory of "legitimate peripheral participation," learning is an integral aspect of participation in practices that have some other object in view. Putting it differently, the necessary skills and knowledge are learned as mediating means for and in achieving the object of the activity. This certainly does not preclude engaging in actions that directly focus on mastering such knowledge and skills, but always within the context of their functioning as means that mediate the activity as a whole.

Of course such an approach does require us to be more explicit about the nature of these activities and about the objects and practices involved. As Lave and Wenger (1991) point out, it is rarely possible in the classroom to engage in the activities of "professional communities of practice" in the same way and at the same level. But that does not mean that there are not simpler forms of such practices that are appropriate for situations in which participants, problems and resources are less sophisticated. As I have suggested earlier, ontogeny probably must recapitulate cultural-historical development to a considerable extent in relation to participation in professional communities of practice.

That being so, I believe that, in classroom activities, the object that provides the focus should be the artifacts that are made and improved through the students' and teacher's participation in the activity and, equally, the knowing that is involved in solving the problems encountered in the process. Examples of such objects that I have seen being constructed in the classrooms of teacher colleagues include:

- a building which is as tall and stable as possible, constructed with materials such as straws and paperclips, or (using Lego) a crane that will actually lift heavy loads
- a class newspaper, produced using a desk-top publishing program
- a role-play/dramatization of a historical event, or of a contemporary situation, such as an appeal to the Supreme Court with respect to the title to ownership of native people's ancestral lands
- models of vehicles designed to cope with the conditions that would be met in exploring the surface of Mars
- a multi-media representation of the class's theory about, for example, photosynthesis or mountain formation and erosion, together with the relevant evidence
- a play, scripted, performed, and produced by the class

In the making of any of these objects, participants certainly have to learn a great deal as they engage in the different modes of knowing involved. All demand the development and improvement of instrumental and pro- cedural knowing of various kinds, and most require the collection and evaluation of relevant information. But these forms of learning are not undertaken as ends in themselves; nor are they undertaken alone. Rather, they occur as part of what I called the spiral of knowing, as means to carrying out the inquiry, to collaborating with others in understanding and making the object in view and solving the problems encountered on the way.

However, there is a further feature of a community of inquiry that distinguishes it from most other communities of practice. And that is the importance attached to metaknowing through reflecting on what is being or has been constructed and on the tools and practices involved in the process. This is where the development of theoretical knowing most naturally occurs as, drawing on relevant first-hand experience, and with the aid of works of reference and teacher guidance, participants engage in the discourse of knowledge building in order to make connections among the different objects and activities with which they are involved and, in the process, to develop those systematic conceptual structures that Vygotsky (1987) called "scientific." However, as with the other forms of knowledge building involved, the ultimate purpose of this reflexive activity is to be able to extend the range and quality of what is "made." It is this object orientation, I believe, that makes inquiry so powerful and generative, both in creating a classroom community that energizes its members, and in developing the skills, knowledge, and dispositions for effective participation. (A summary of the characteristics of a classroom organized as a community of inquiry – as we currently understand it – is to be found in Appendix 1.)

In several of the following chapters, examples will be drawn from class- rooms in which the teachers are attempting to develop such communities of inquiry and simultaneously making their attempts the object of their own inquiries. For them, the classroom community and the curricular units that they and their students undertake together are the objects they are striving to understand and improve. However, in conducting their analyses, it is on particular activities that they typically focus, and the evi- dence they draw on is largely in the form of "texts" of various kinds, seen both as artifacts created in the discourse and as tools for engaging in the activities of inquiry. It is therefore from this perspective of discourse as toolkit that, in the final section, I review our approach to the modes and modalities of discourse.

Modes and Modalities of Discourse

In the classrooms I have just been describing, teacher-fronted lessons of the kind characterized as following a "recitation script" rarely, if ever, occur. However, there are certainly occasions when these teachers engage in whole-class interaction of a kind that Tharp and Gallimore (1988), by contrast, refer to as "instructional conversation":

Discourse in which expert and apprentices weave together spoken and written language with previous understandings appears in several guises. . . . Its generic name is Instructional Conversation. . . . The concept itself contains a paradox: 'instruction' and 'conversation' appear contrary, the one implying authority and planning, the other equality and responsiveness. The task of teaching is to resolve this paradox. To most truly teach, one must converse; to truly converse is to teach. (p. 111)

In an inquiry classroom, however, it is not only the designated teacher who is the expert; the role may be held at any particular moment by any one of the participants, or by a group of participants, or by an expert who is only present through the medium of a knowledge artifact that he or she has made. Nor does the choice of the term "instruction" adequately capture the recognition that the constructing of understanding is a collaborative enterprise. Nevertheless, with its emphasis on the dialogic nature of classroom discourse, the concept of instructional conversation and of the classroom as a place in which many instructional conversations are continuously ongoing, sometimes in small groups and sometimes in the whole class, constitutes a useful starting point for thinking about the various modes of discourse that occur and the functions that they serve in relation to inquiry (Nystrand, 1997).

Barnes (1976/1992) initiated consideration of alternatives to the recitation script by describing two modes of spoken discourse he had observed in some classrooms. One was what he called "final draft" talk, by analogy with the final draft of a piece of writing. This was the mode in which students presented what they believed they already understood; what they said was expected to be prepared and fluently presented. Barnes associated this kind of talk with teaching that emphasized knowledge transmission. The second mode he called "exploratory talk"; this was most frequently observed to occur when small groups of students worked at interpretive tasks that they found both interesting and challenging. In this mode, the talk did not report what was already known so much as provide the means for coming to know – for knowledge building, as I called it above.[12]

The value of "exploratory talk" and the conditions under which it is most likely to occur has been a continuing topic of research in Britain

(MacLure, Phillips, and Wilkinson, 1988; Edwards and Westgate, 1994) and, in the National Oracy Project, many classroom teachers became involved in this work (Norman, 1992). More recently, the role played by different kinds of computer-based tasks in facilitating (or inhibiting) exploratory talk has been the focus of another large-scale project (Wegerif and Scrimshaw, 1997). Here, observation and analysis of students at work has led to the distinguishing of three types of talk that are likely to arise in small-group, task-based activities: disputational talk, cumulative talk, and exploratory talk. These are described as enacting three fundamental orientations that are possible between participants in dialogue – three social modes of thinking. Combining elements of the first two, exploratory talk is argued to have a special status with respect to education in that it is "a dialogical model of reasoning. Its 'ground rules' are those which allow for different voices to inter-animate each other in a way which not only constructs shared knowledge but also critically assesses the quality of that knowledge" (Wegerif and Mercer, 1997, p. 59). Computer-based activities can facilitate this kind of talk, they find; however, what is clear is that, whether a computer is involved or not, for exploratory talk to occur there needs to be a task that is sufficiently open-ended to elicit alternative possibilities for consideration and a classroom ethos that encourages students to engage with and share the perspectives of others in order to understand them. These seem very much like the conditions that, I suggested, ideally obtain in an inquiry-oriented classroom; they are also important in providing the context for what I have referred to as "progressive discourse."

In North America, talk among students has largely been investigated in the context of response to literature (Dias and Hayhoe, 1988; McMahon and Raphael, 1997), learning to write (Dyson, 1989, 1993; Gianotti, 1994), mathematics, (Lampert, 1990; Lampert, et al., 1996; Yackel et al., 1990), and science (Roseberry et al., 1992). However, the emphasis in this work has tended to be less on categorizing the type of talk and more on investigating what is done in the talk and on relating this to the modes of participation by students from different ethnolinguistic backgrounds.

In addition to investigating talk in small groups, teachers and university researchers in most of the countries in which English is the language of instruction have investigated various modes of teacher–student talk. In particular, the IRF/E pattern (Teacher Initiate – Student Respond – Teacher Follow-Up/Evaluate), or "triadic dialogue" (Lemke, 1990), has been the subject of considerable research, which has variously found for or against this ubiquitous generic structure (see Hicks, 1995 for a recent review). In Chapters 5 and 7 of this book, I suggest that this is not one, but a cluster of genres that, while sharing a common structure, perform a range of very different functions depending on the types of activity that they are used to mediate. In different ways, this is also the direction taken by Christie (1991), who examines the teacher–student talk, including triadic dialogue, that occurs in different "curriculum genres," and by Edwards and Mercer (1987), who identify a range of teacher strategies that use triadic dialogue to build "common knowledge" out of the contributions offered by individual students.

In more recent work, Mercer and colleagues (Mercer, 1995; Mercer and Fisher, 1993; Maybin, Mercer, and Stierer, 1992) have focused, in particular, on the role of teacher interventions in "scaffolding" students' learning, seeing this – as do I – as a way of operationalizing Vygotsky's (1987) concept of "working in the zone of proximal development." Adapting the term from the work by Wood, Bruner and Ross (1976) on mother–child interaction, they also point to features of the classroom as a specifically educational setting that require some modification of the original definition. In a way similar to Halliday (1993a), they argue that one of the chief functions of the use of language in the classroom is to induct students into modes of discourse that provide them with frames of reference with which to "recontextualize" their experience, and that it is this task that gives educational scaffolding its particular character.

In schools, students are learning to take on new, educational frames of reference and to apply these frames to interpret observations, information and events. 'Scaffolding' learning in school may be a matter of helping students to apply frames of reference that they only partially grasp and which they are inexperienced in applying. And it may be a process that involves more than two people. But a crucial, essential quality of 'scaffolding' in all settings must be that it is the provision of guidance and support which is increased or withdrawn in response to the developing competence of the learner. (Mercer, 1995, p. 75)[13]

Many of these trends in recent and current research on spoken discourse in the classroom have influenced our own work, as will be seen in the chapters that follow. In particular, we are all in general agreement about the importance of three features: the essentially dialogic nature of the discourse in which knowledge is co-constructed; the significance of the kind of activity in which the knowing is embedded; and the important role played by the artifacts that mediate the knowing. This is not really surprising, since, as researchers, we all draw on common sources, particularly the work of Vygotsky, Bakhtin, and Halliday. However, what perhaps distinguishes the approach that the DICEP group has taken from the work reviewed above is, first, our attempt to forge stronger bonds between these three intellectual strands by explicitly linking the Hallidayan social semiotic theory of register and genre with the Russian theory of activity and, second, our attempt to investigate the complementary relationships between spoken discourse and other modalities of meaning making. It is to the latter that I now turn.

Several times in the preceding pages I have drawn attention to the special role played by written text in the construction of knowledge. Creating a written text is a particularly powerful way of coming to know and understand the topic that one writes about, especially if one uses the writing, not to report what one already understands, but to come to understand in and through the process (Langer and Applebee, 1987; Parker and Goodkin, 1986). The same is true of reading another's text, if one treats it dialogically as a "thinking device" and not simply as a univocal transmitter of the writer's message (Lotman, 1988).[14]

However, few students have discovered this function of writing, particularly those in elementary or middle school. For them, writing is often a difficult and lengthy process and they are generally unwilling to undertake any but minor revisions to their first drafts. Of course this does not mean that they should not be encouraged to discover the value of writing as a dialogic process of knowledge building through which one may come to a fuller understanding. However, it does mean that this may be more effectively achieved through the composition of texts other than extended essays or narratives, particularly when these are written for an unknown and often unspecified audience.

In recent years, many teachers have discovered that the practice of journal writing can foster a reflective stance to classroom activities, and the use of journals has become common in many classrooms. Gallas (1994), for example, describes how her grade one students used their science journals to extend the class's science talks as well as their individual observations, and Countryman (1992) offers suggestions, with examples, of a variety of ways of using journal writing in mathematics. Journals are also widely used as a way of encouraging students to respond to the novels and other literature that they are reading. As might be expected, journals are most likely to encourage thoughtful writing when the teacher or another person responds to some or all of the entries (D'Arcy, 1989; Staton et al., 1988); even then, however, as Swartz (1994) notes, the practice can easily become a routine carried out to please the teacher rather than in order to extend the writer's understanding.

What is missing from the journal mode, I believe – at least as it is typically practiced – is a sense of writing to and for others who have a comparable interest in the topic. Although teachers may genuinely be able to enter into their students' enthusiasms and puzzlements, they do so from a much wider and more consolidated base of experience and understanding so that, even if they carefully avoid giving the impression of already "knowing the answer," they are not easily perceived by their students as co-inquirers. For this reason, some teachers encourage students to write their reflective responses for the other members of the group who are reading the same novel or working on the same math problem or science topic.

Such innovatory ways of using writing as a tool for collaborative reflection and problem solving are often the inventions of classroom teacher-researchers, introduced and improved as part of their own inquiries (e.g. McMahon and Raphael,1997; Countryman, 1992). This is how we, in DICEP, have approached the issue, treating it as a focus for our own collaborative inquiries.

Common to many of our attempts to make writing a tool for inquiry is the idea of using some kind of visually displayed text as an "improvable object" that acts as the focus of collaborative knowledge building. The inspiration for this comes, at least in part, from our familiarity with the Computer-Supported Intentional Learning Environment (CSILE) Project, pioneered by my colleagues, Marlene Scardamalia and Carl Bereiter, in which the ideas about knowledge building discussed in this and the previous chapter are given practical realization. In CSILE classrooms, students spend part of each day at one of the fifteen or so Macintosh computers that are networked so that they have access to a central database that they themselves construct by typing in notes, visuals, and comments concerning the topics that they are investigating (Scardamalia et al., 1994). Key to the success of this implementation, in my view, is, first, that the students' contributions to the dialogue are in writing, which means that they can be (and are) reviewed and revised and, second, that they are stored and organized in a central database, which means that they can be accessed and responded to by other students. The result is a collaboratively produced knowledge artifact, the creation of which promotes progressive discourse, but in a mode that leaves a permanent record in the database which, itself, is available for further knowledge building.

Not many classrooms are so well equipped with computer hardware, however, so the question to be asked is: Can the principles underpinning

CSILE be realized without such extensive (and expensive) computer support? Several members of DICEP are currently investigating this possibility and results to date suggest that a critical feature is the ready accessibility of the knowledge object. Whether on a computer screen, a blackboard or wall, or projected on a screen, if the "text" can easily be "read" by all those engaged in the project, it is much more likely to be responded to in a dialogic, knowledge building manner. However the text does not have to be in written language. Diagrams, mechanical drawings, algebraic equations, etc. – as Vygotsky pointed out – can also function as "psychological tools" by providing a focus for knowledge building. Indeed, such objects may be superior to written texts for this purpose, at least as a way of initiating students into this practice, engagement in which is probably the key criterion of a classroom community of inquiry.

There is, however, one further feature of such classroom communities of inquiry, which is somewhat obscured by the exclusive focus on writing in CSILE. And that is the interrelatedness and complementarity of the various modes of meaning making which have been discussed. Although not so far investigated systematically, there is ample observational evidence that the reading and writing of the notes and visuals from which the CSILE database is built often gives rise to lively conversation, which may sometimes itself be a significant occasion of progressive discourse, but now in the oral mode. Conversely, in non-CSILE classrooms, it is certainly not unknown for participants in knowledge building discussions to quote from a published text or to make a sketch or diagram to clarify a point and for either of these texts to become, at least temporarily, an object that all work to understand and improve.

As Lemke (1993a) insists, all meaning making involves intertextuality; not simply between texts in the same mode but also between texts in different modes – spoken, visual–linguistic, visual–nonlinguistic – as well as between texts and actions involving material tools and artifacts of various kinds. And this is certainly true of the progressive discourse in which knowledge building and understanding are collaboratively and individually advanced. While it is knowing and understanding in the aesthetic and theoretical modes that are most highly prized in schools, we should not forget that all the modes of knowing are interrelated and that the principles of progressive discourse can appropriately be applied at all levels in the spiral of knowing. How these principles can most effectively be realized in different settings – across school subjects, across ages, and across differences in culture and in politics – must continue to be an important focus for the community of inquiry to which this book is addressed.

Notes

1. Significant in this respect is Donald's claim that the vestiges of mimetic discourse continue to play a substantial role in contemporary culture, for example in trades and crafts, in athletics, in most of the theatrical arts, and in much social ritual. Mimesis, to which must be added music and other modes of auditory but nonlinguistic representation, is thus a significant mediator of aesthetic as well as procedural knowing.

2. In his defense, it should be added that classroom observation did not become established as a mode of educational research until recording devices enabled the complex detail of classroom activity to be captured in a form that allowed for subsequent reviewing and analysis.

3. In this context, see Griffin and Mehan (1981) on the effects of the discourse situation on children's performance in the context of assessment and Nuthall's (Nuthall and Alton-Lee, 1995) study of remembering classroom lessons.

4. As will be apparent, I am using knowing and the terms associated with it to refer to acts of meaning making that constitute development of some kind for the individual(s) concerned; that is to say, there is a transformation of them and of the situation through the creation or modification of a mediating artifact. However, as I emphasized in Chapter 2, all situations are to some degree novel and, although the problems to which they give rise may be relatively trivial, they still require a degree of creativity. In other words, there does not have to be a major transformation for terms such as knowing and understanding to apply.

5. Eggins and Slade (1997) reach the same conclusion about casual conversation. It is disagreement rather than agreement that keeps a conversation going.

6. In practice, Bereiter recognizes, not all of these commitments are met, all of the time. However, as long as they are generally accepted and honored most of the time, the resulting discourse, he believes, is likely to be progressive.

7. A preferable way to think about the learning of these "instrumental" skills is in terms of knowledgeable actions that are most effective when they have reached a level of automaticity at which they function as operations which mediate the attainment of action goals of greater complexity. This issue is further discussed in Chapters 6 and 7.

8. See Bruner on narrative (1986) and art as a mode of knowing (1962).

9. This is, essentially, a paraphrase of the conclusion that Vygotsky (1987) reached in "Thought and Word," the final chapter of his last completed work. Despite the fact that it was "word" rather than "utterance" that was the unit of analysis with which he chose to explore this complex topic, it seems likely that Vygotsky would have been in agreement with the conclusion proposed here.

10. Vygotsky's work only began to be known in the English-speaking world with the translation of *Thought and Language* in 1962.

11. In subsequent chapters the relationship between these three levels will be explored using the conceptual tool of activity theory (Engeström, 1990; Leont'ev, 1981).

12. Much more recently, Crowder (1996) has investigated a similar contrast, not between the talk occurring in transmission and interpretative tasks, but between students' ways of explaining scientific phenomena. Their differential use

of gesture was one of the key means of discriminating between the modes of discourse used.

13. The value of scaffolding has also been explored by Palincsar and Brown, first in the context of the reciprocal teaching of comprehension strategies (Palincsar and Brown, 1984), and more recently as a component of the "Community of Learners" program (Brown and Campione, 1994).

14. In a work published after this book went to press, Wertsch (1998) recasts Lotman's distinction more generally in terms of "intersubjectivity" and "alterity," and uses these concepts to explore the different forms that classroom instructional discourse may take. His discussion relates both to my distinction, earlier in this chapter, between "saying" and "what is said" and to Chapters 5 and 7, in which I explore the potential as well as the limitations of "triadic dialogue." As I have done, Wertsch sees these two functions of text as complementary rather than as mutually exclusive: "The general point to be made about intersubjectivity and alterity, then, is not that communication is best understood in terms of one or the other in isolation. Indeed, virtually every text is viewed as *both* univocal, information-transmission characteristics, and hence intersubjectivity, as well as dialogic, thought-generating tendencies, and hence alterity" (p. 117).

Part II

Discourse, Learning, and Teaching

4   Text, Talk, and Inquiry: Schooling As Semiotic Apprenticeship

Many years ago, in *Education and Experience*, Dewey (1938) made a simple observation, but one whose implications for classroom practice have still to be taken seriously: Human beings learn by doing. At about the same time, but in a very different part of the world, a similar insight about learning through joint activity was being developed into a comprehensive theory of learning-and-teaching by Vygotsky and his colleagues and students (Vygotsky, 1978, 1987; Leont'ev, 1981; Luria, 1978). Having remained unknown outside the Soviet Union until their work began to be translated into English and other languages in the last couple of decades, the key ideas developed by this troika are now beginning to have a very considerable impact on education at all levels from preschool to teacher education.

Simply put, Vygotsky argued that each human being's capacities for acting, thinking, feeling and communicating, although based in his or her biological inheritance, are crucially dependent on the practices and artifacts, developed over time within particular cultures, that are appropriated in the course of goal-oriented joint activity. As Budilova puts it: "A special form of transmitting the achievements of preceding generations to the next takes place in human society; that is the achievements are embodied in the material and symbolic products of human activities, and specific human psychological abilities can be developed through the mastery of these products by each person" (1972, p. 310; translated and quoted by Amano, 1991).

Four features of this account merit further attention. First, the notion of "product," or "artifact." The importance of material artifacts for the

Text, talk, and inquiry: Schooling as semiotic apprenticeship. In N. Bird et al. (Eds.), *Language and Learning* (pp. 18–51), 1994. Hong Kong: Government Information Services.

development of culture is by now well understood; the invention of the flint knife and, later, of the wheel are recognized to have radically changed the possibilities for action of the prehistoric societies which invented them and of those that took over their inventions. In more recent times, the same sort of significance is attributed to the invention of the printing press, powered flying machines and the microchip. But Vygotsky's great contribution was to recognize that an even greater effect resulted from the development of semiotic tools based on signs, of which the most powerful and versatile is speech. For not only does speech function as a tool that mediates social action, it also provides one of the chief means – in what Vygotsky (1987) called "inner speech" – of mediating the individual mental activities of remembering, thinking, and reasoning.

The second feature of importance is the strong emphasis on activity as the site of both invention and use of all forms of artifact. Whether material or symbolic, artifacts are embedded in practices which have as their object the satisfaction of perceived needs. In this sense, an artifact has no meaning out of the context of the activity in which it is used, and to master the use of an artifact is to learn to participate in the practices in which it plays a functional mediating role. Here is Leont'ev's elaboration on this point:

> The tool mediates activity and thus connects humans not only with the world of objects but also with other people. Because of this, humans' activity *assimilates the experiences of humankind*. This means that humans' mental processes ... acquire a structure necessarily tied to the sociohistorically formed means and methods transmitted to them by others in the process of cooperative labor and social interaction. ... In other words, higher psychological processes unique to humans can be acquired only through interaction with others, that is, through *interpsychological* processes that only later will begin to be carried out independently by the individual. (Leont'ev, 1981, pp. 55–6. Emphasis in original.)

In the last sentence of this quotation Leont'ev focuses on the third and perhaps the most important feature of the sociocultural theory of intellectual development, namely that of appropriation. Simply put, all higher mental functions are dependent on semiotic artifacts and practices that are first encountered *intermentally* in purposeful joint activities, in which more expert members of the culture both demonstrate their use and assist the learner in mastering them. Through participation in which his or her performance is assisted, the learner gradually masters the practices in which these artifacts are used so that they also become a resource for *intramental* activity. As Vygotsky puts it, on its way to becoming an internal mode of activity, "any higher mental function necessarily goes through an external stage in its development because it is initially a social function" (1981, p. 162).

However, appropriation is not the end of the process, for the final stage occurs in further action, when the learner makes use of the new function to participate more effectively in similar or related social activity. Appropriation of cultural artifacts and practices thus involves a continuing three-stage cycle, to which corresponds a triple transformation. First there is the transformation of the learner – a modification of his or her own mental processes, that changes the ways in which he or she perceives, interprets and represents the world; second there is a transformation of the artifact itself, as its use is assimilated and reconstructed by the learner on the basis of the learner's existing knowledge; finally, in using the artifact to mediate further action, there is a transformation of the situation in which the learner acts which, to a greater or lesser degree, brings about change in the social practice and in the way in which the artifact is understood and used by other members of the culture.[1]

Finally, because appropriation of cultural resources takes place through the learner's participation in goal-oriented joint activities, a further key feature of learning concerns the part played by the other, more expert, participants in facilitating this process. Their role is to help the learner to understand the significance of the activity as a whole, and of the constituent actions and artifacts that mediate its performance and, while taking responsibility for the organization of the overall structure, to involve him or her as fully as possible, providing help and guidance with those parts of the activity that he or she cannot yet manage on his or her own. However, this assistance is seen as only a temporary "scaffolding" (Wood, Bruner, and Ross, 1976), the purpose of which is to enable the learner to become a fully competent, independently functioning participant. Vygotsky (1978, 1987) described this teaching role as working with the learner in his or her "zone of proximal development": "an essential feature of learning is that it creates the zone of proximal development; that is learning awakens a variety of internal developmental processes that are able to operate only when the child is interacting with people in his environment and in cooperation with his peers" (1978, p. 90).

To summarize this view of education, as it applies to schooling, therefore, we might characterize it as the creation of a collaborative community of practice, in which, through assisted participation in appropriate activities, students undertake a "semiotic apprenticeship," as they individually reconstruct the resources of the culture as tools for creative and responsible social living in this and the wider community. In this characterization, it is activity which is central, for, to rephrase Dewey's insight, what we learn is what we do.

Learning in School: A Semiotic Apprenticeship

In choosing the metaphor of semiotic apprenticeship to characterize learning in school, I wish to emphasize three important points. The first is that learning should be seen as the gradual but cumulative development of expertise through participation in the activities in which, in the various disciplines, knowledge is progressively constructed, applied and revised; the second is that, in their learning, students should be assisted and guided by others who engage with them in these activities and share their expertise. Both these points have been developed in some detail by Vygotsky and by contemporary sociocultural theorists (Chang-Wells and Wells, 1993; Cole, 1985; Lave and Wenger, 1991; Rogoff, 1990; Tharp and Gallimore, 1988; Wertsch, 1985b), so I shall not develop them further. However, my third point – the semiotic nature of learning – has received rather less attention, and so it is on this that I shall focus here.

In the preceding section, I frequently used the rather general expression "the resources of the culture" to refer to what has to be learned in the course of the semiotic apprenticeship. Without attempting to specify in detail what these resources are, I should like to suggest that they can be thought of as consisting of three broad categories: (a) attitudes and values concerning what are worthwhile activities to engage in; (b) understanding of the practices involved in these activities; and (c) mastery of the relevant artifacts and of the procedural and substantive knowledge associated with their use. In sociocultural theory, all these resources are viewed as mediational means for the achievement of collective and individual goals. In that sense, they can be thought of as "tools." But, whether material or symbolic, in order to perform their mediating function, all tools must meet two requirements: first, they must be capable of contributing to the achievement of desired effects in the world; and second, they must be in the hands of a person who understands their meaning and mode of functioning in relation to the goals of the activity they mediate (Cole, 1994).

From the learner's point of view, the first requirement is not initially in question: the efficacy of a tool is taken for granted on the basis of its continued use in the home and wider community. In the first instance, therefore, the learner's major task is to discover – in action – when, where and how to use the culture's most important tools, that is to say, to learn their semiotic significance. In this process, language provides the most important resource of all, for it is, as Cole (1994) puts it, "the master tool" – the tool that mediates the learning of all others.

In order to attempt to explicate this central role of language in learning, I should like to draw on some of the ideas contained in recent papers by Halliday (1993a, b), in which he summarizes and extends his previous work on language learning. In the introduction to the first of these, Halliday states: "the distinctive characteristic of human learning is that it is a process of making meaning – a semiotic process; and the prototypical form of human semiotic is language" (1993a, p. 93). Then, in the body of the paper, he goes on to show in detail how, in learning the language of his or her community, that is to say in constructing its lexicogrammar as a "meaning potential," the child appropriates a powerful and versatile tool for participating in and reflecting on activity, in collaboration with others. Like Dewey and Vygotsky, too, Halliday emphasizes that what children learn with respect to language depends on what they use it to do.

When we come to consider language from this latter point of view, it is clear that there are two rather different kinds of doing in which language plays a part, which we might gloss, rather generally, as "acting" and "understanding," corresponding to an emphasis on the interpersonal or the ideational metafunctions in terms of which – together with the textual metafunction – the grammar is organized (Halliday, 1978, 1993a). In the first of these, the primary function of language is to mediate action: to negotiate goals and means, to monitor other, nonverbal, forms of behavior, and to manage the interpersonal relationships involved. In the second, where the emphasis is on reflection, the function of language which is emphasized is that of "representing" objects, events and relationships – of creating "a theory of human experience" – "a semiotic world of its own: a parallel universe . . . [which serves] as model, or metaphor, for the world of action and experience" (Halliday, 1993a, p. 107).

Of course, these two forms of doing are never totally distinct and separate. In the former, language provides an important means of making reference to the other components of the activity in which the participants are engaged; and in the latter, any sustained reflection also requires the management of goals and interpersonal relationships. This is true of discourse contributions of any size: Whether the utterance is a single clause or a full-length book, choices are made with respect to both ideational and interpersonal metafunctions; in all utterances, too, choices with respect to the textual metafunction are necessary in order to make the utterance effective in its context. Nevertheless, as Britton's (1970) rather similar distinction between the "participant" and "spectator" modes suggests, there is an important difference between the two types of doing with language – acting and reflecting – and, for each, the grammar as a whole provides rather different kinds of semiotic resources.

This distinction will become clearer, I hope, as we turn to the various functions that language performs in the different activities that we might expect students to engage in in the classroom, if these activities are seen as an apprenticeship into the various modes of knowing (including knowing in action) on which the curriculum is based. For, in all the disciplines there are some activities that are more oriented to action and others that more obviously involve reflection, and each involves different choices from the semantic meaning potential.[2]

In the sciences, for example, a rather clear, although oversimple, distinction can be drawn between empirical and theoretical activities and, in each, language plays a rather different role. For example, we should expect to find that the kinds of discourse that occur in the context of planning and carrying out experiments are rather different from those that occur when predictions are considered in advance of the experiment or the significance of the results is subsequently interpreted in relation to the prevailing theory. In history, a comparable distinction can be made between the kinds of discourse involved in the obtaining and handling of the documents and other artifacts that constitute historical evidence, and those in which the significance of this evidence is evaluated and debated. Similarly, in the study of literature, there is clearly a difference between, on the one hand, reading a novel or poem and responding, as one reads, in terms of the particular thoughts and feelings evoked, and attempting, on the other hand, to explain the work's overall effect by reference to specific features of the text seen as instances of more general literary categories. In each of these cases, although the same substantive 'content' may be involved in the two situations, the activities in which this content is worked on are different, and so are the discourse genres through which these activities are enacted. In the first of the contrasted situations in each case, the discourse plays a somewhat ancillary role in relation to the activity as a whole, whereas in the second the discourse actually constitutes the activity.

The important point, however, is that, within each of these academic disciplines, both forms of semiotic activity are recognized to be important, as is mastery of the genres of discourse involved. Indeed, in achieving the overall goals of the discipline, the different discourse genres perform complementary and interdependent functions, together constituting, in large part, what it is to "do" science, history, or literature.

The same, I want to suggest, should be true in the classroom. In order for their learning to constitute a genuine apprenticeship into the different disciplines, students should have the opportunity to encounter and master the important genres of discourse in each discipline, through engaging in as wide a range as possible of the activities in which those genres are used. They should also receive assistance in their learning in the form of appropriate models and constructive feedback and guidance. Before going on to consider how such a goal might be achieved, however, I want to look more closely at the semiotic resources provided by language, starting with a consideration of some of the differences between talk and text.

The Distinguishing Features of Written Text

There are a number of ways in which spoken and written discourse can be contrasted, all of which are relevant to a consideration of the role of language in learning and teaching. However, because of limitations of space, I shall consider only three.

1. The Abstract Nature of Written Text

In the paper already referred to, Halliday focuses on the relatively greater abstractness of writing, with the concomitant demand this makes on learners to "reinterpret their experience in the new mode of written language" (1993a, p. 109). Interestingly, in *Thinking and Speech*, Vygotsky (1987) gives a very similar explanation of the intellectual development that is fostered by learning to read and write: "Written speech forces the child to act more intellectually. . . . It is a more difficult and more complex form of intentional and conscious speech activity" (p. 204).

As both these scholars point out, written language is more abstract than speech in three ways: first, it involves a "second-order symbolism," with written symbols standing for the spoken words of speech, which are themselves symbols; second, because the interlocutor is not physically present, the way in which meaning is communicated in writing is more abstract than in speech, since the message has to be realized through the lexicogrammar alone, unsupported by gesture and intonation, and without the opportunity to check understanding and supply additional information on request.

However, it is the third – the abstract nature of the meanings themselves – that is what often makes the written mode more difficult for children than speech. It is for this reason that Halliday describes the development of literacy as involving both the reorganization of the learner's grammar to handle the more abstract categories of written language and also the mastering of a new form of knowledge: "written, educational knowledge as against the spoken knowledge of common sense" (1993a. p. 109).

2. The Functions of Written Text

In order to understand why the meanings expressed in written language are frequently more abstract than those in speech we need to consider the different functions writing is used to perform. Although a written text can be read aloud and speech can be written down, the two modes are not interchangeable, nor are they typically used for the same purposes. In fact, the relationship between them is one of complementarity rather than of correspondence. To a large extent, this is because of the different media that they employ and the manner in which each is produced and received. Most importantly, compared with speech, written texts have much greater permanence; they are also much slower to produce, and, in reception, much more under the control of the receiver. For all these reasons, extended written texts are particularly suited to activities involving individual reflection whereas, in many ways, the dialogic exchange of meaning characteristic of speech is more suited to collaborative action.

It is the relative permanence of written text that explains its earliest uses some 3000 years ago. For, from the evidence that is available, amongst the first functions that writing was developed to serve was that of aide-mémoire with respect to important practical information to do with trade and taxes (Ong, 1982). And, in myriad forms, written text still performs this function in almost every sphere of contemporary life (Heap, 1989). Then, from this beginning, we can trace the emergence of two further functions: the archival and the instructional. If records are kept, they can be gathered together and collated, giving rise to bodies of information that can be consulted on future occasions (Olson, 1994b). Similarly, procedural skills required in the performance of practical activities can be described in written texts so that the passing on of craft knowledge and other similar information is not dependent on transmission by example or word of mouth.

As can be seen, all these functions are very clearly tied to action. In a very obvious sense, the written text serves in each case as a tool, making information available when it is needed in the course of some kind of practical activity. It therefore follows that, to be competent in performing the activity, one needs to know when and how to use the tools of written text, as well as the other tools that play a part in the activity.

However, the uses of written text are not confined to what Heap (1989) refers to as the "enabling" of practical activity. In every culture that has made widespread use of writing for practical purposes, two further, reflective, functions have eventually emerged. The first of these I have called the "re-creational," intending thereby to capture the dual function of literature as both the re-creation in words of the experiences of humankind, both real and imaginary, and also the re-creation of the writer or reader through engagement with such texts. Finally, there is what I have called the "epistemic" function – the use of a text as a tool for thinking and developing new understanding, through the dialogue that takes place between the reader or writer and the text, as he or she struggles to construct meaning that is clear and coherent and, at the same time, consistent with all the available evidence, both in the text and in his or her experience (Wells, 1990).

However, in distinguishing the different functions served by written texts, I do not wish to suggest that texts are strictly monofunctional. In principle, any of the above functions can be served by any text. Nevertheless, there is in practice – as with material tools, such as hammers or saws – a strong correspondence between text types, or written genres, and the uses to which they are put. And these uses, in turn, are defined by the activities in which they occur.

To return to the apprenticeship metaphor, then, it is clear that induction into the different disciplines involves learning to use the written genres, both practical and reflective, which mediate the activities that constitute those disciplines. And, as the metaphor implies, this learning must take place, not as an independent, decontextualized event, but as an integral part of carrying out those activities.

3. Dynamic and Synoptic Representations

So far, in contrasting written with spoken discourse, I have emphasized the relative abstractness of the former. I have also drawn attention to the functions that are particularly well served by the permanence which is a defining characteristic of written texts, in particular the epistemic function in which, through a dialogue with the written representation, the writer/reader can use the text as "a thinking device" for generating new meanings and refining those meanings that are already represented (Lotman, 1988).

However, there is a third way in which written discourse frequently differs from spoken discourse, particularly in expository genres. And this is in the different ways in which experience is typically constructed in the two modes. Here is how Halliday explains the distinction:

A written text is itself a static object: it is language to be processed synoptically. Hence it projects a synoptic perspective on to reality: it tells us to view experience like a text, so to speak. In this way writing changed the analogy between language and other domains of experience; it foregrounded the synoptic aspect, reality as object, rather than the dynamic aspect, reality as process, as the spoken language does. This synoptic perspective is then built in to the grammar of the written language, in the form of grammatical metaphor: processes and properties are construed as nouns, instead of as verbs and adjectives. Where the spoken language says *whenever an engine fails, because they can move very fast, ... happens if people smoke more*, the written language writes *in times of engine failure, rely on their great speed, ... is caused by increased smoking*. (Halliday, 1993a, p. 111)

The difference is not simply one of alternative modes of expression, however. As Halliday points out, corresponding to the grammatical differences are different perspectives on experience. In learning to read and write, therefore, children have to "learn to construe their experience in two complementary modes, the dynamic mode of the everyday common-sense grammar and the synoptic mode of the elaborated written grammar" (1993a, p. 112).

However, Halliday is not the only one to have made this kind of distinction. Vygotsky (1987), too, in his account of the development of verbal thought, proposes a similar progression from "spontaneous" to "scientific" concepts. Spontaneous concepts, according to Vygotsky, are encountered and learned in the spoken discourse that occurs in the varied and naturally occurring events of everyday living; the learning of scientific concepts, on the other hand, is dependent on schooling, and in particular on the use of genres of discourse – typically written – in which concepts are systematically related to each other through definition or explanation.

Yet another related distinction is that made by Bruner (1986) between the two modes of thought that he refers to as "narrative" and "paradigmatic." The narrative mode is primary and, as he points out, it underlies children's early experience of conversation. It is a discourse of doings and happenings, of actions and intentions: Agents act in the light of prevailing circumstances in order to achieve their goals. This is the dynamic perspective on experience to which Halliday refers and the basis on which Vygotsky's spontaneous concepts are constructed. It is a mode of discourse in which the grammatical organization of the clause corresponds to the "natural" relationship between the entities, actions and circumstances in terms of which we typically describe and explain behavior, our own and other people's. In fact, by analogy, even the smallest particles of inanimate matter are endowed with intentions and potential for action when viewed from this dynamic perspective.

However, the synoptic mode of written discourse – the "paradigmatic," as Bruner calls it – has its value too. By recoding almost every aspect of experience – processes, attributes and relationships, and even complete events in all their detail – as nouns or nominal structures, it provides a way of symbolically managing the complexity and variability of experience, allowing it to be reconstrued in "scientific" concepts, which can be systematically related in taxonomies; instances can then be counted, and made amenable to operations of mathematics and logic. Having its origins in the field of science and technology (Halliday, 1988), this powerful discursive tool has, not surprisingly, been appropriated by other fields of inquiry and, in different forms, has come to play a major role in the written genres of exposition and argument in almost all the disciplines. Indeed, as Halliday (1993a) observes, "it invades almost every register of adult English that is typically written rather than spoken" (p. 112).

At the same time – as is being increasingly recognized – the nominalizing tendency of these "genres of power" is proving to be a double-edged sword. While it may facilitate technological discourse, it does so by construing reality in a form that is remote from the dynamic perspective on experience that is embodied in everyday talk. And this makes these genres difficult for students to master. It also creates a division between the technocrats who control them and the uninitiated who do not – a division that, as Halliday points out, "is certainly dysfunctional in a modern democratic society" (1993b, p. 32). There are good reasons, therefore, for the attempts that are being made, in various domains, to modify these written genres in order to bring them closer to the language of common sense. However, for the foreseeable future, they are likely to remain the genres of power and, for that reason, students need to be given every assistance in appropriating them so that they can participate fully in the activities in which they are used.

The Complementary Roles of Talk and Text

In the previous section, the emphasis has been on how written text differs from spoken discourse. Now I want to consider how the differences between the two modes enable them to function in complementary ways in the performance of discipline-based activities.

If we review the contrasts that have already been discussed, together with a number that have only been implied, it can be seen that there is a considerable degree of parallelism between the relevant dimensions. This can be shown by arranging them in tabular form.

SPOKEN	WRITTEN
Action	Reflection
Dynamic	Synoptic
Concrete	Abstract
Spontaneous	Scientific
Narrative	Paradigmatic
Social	Individual
Dialogue	Monologue

Spoken discourse is, relatively speaking, more likely to occur in a social setting, in which several participants are engaged in dialogue about experience, often involving action – ongoing, or in the immediate past or future – which is viewed from a dynamic perspective. When people engage with written texts, on the other hand, they are more likely to be alone, reflecting on the matter addressed in the text through the medium of a genre which adopts a monologic and synoptic perspective on experience.

Adopting these stereotypical characterizations of the two modes, it is clear that, as tools, talk, and text are best suited to mediate different tasks within any activity.[3] Talk is likely to mediate the planning, monitoring and evaluation of the actions to be performed, while published texts may be referred to supply needed information for these tasks and written notes of various kinds made to record intentions and interim results; then, depending on the nature of the activity, it may conclude with the writing of some form of text that gives an account of what was done and why, and of what was achieved or learned. In this scenario, talk and text are complementary because they perform different functions in mediating tasks that occur at different stages in the activity.

What such a synoptic account fails to capture, however, is the more dynamic manner in which talk and text can complement and enrich each other through an exploitation of the intertextual relationships between them (Lemke, 1993a). For it is when participants move back and forth between text and talk, using each mode to contextualize the other, and both modes as tools to make sense of the activity in which they are engaged, that we see the most important form of complementarity between them. And it is here, in this interpenetration of talk, text, and action in relation to particular activities, that, I want to suggest, students are best able to undertake what I have called the semiotic apprenticeship into the various ways of knowing.

In the next two sections, I should like to explore the significance of such talk about texts from the perspective of two different, although related, kinds of learning that they facilitate. The first concerns the meanings that are being made – what Halliday calls the reconstruing of experience in the grammar of the genres of written text. In the second, it is the function of the text that is focused on – the part it plays in the larger activity, for it is in this context that issues of generic structure seem likely to be most readily understood. To illustrate the different opportunities for learning that talk about text can provide, I shall use a number of examples from work in science, recorded in one classroom over a period of two years.

Building Bridges Between Ways of Knowing

First, let us consider the ways in which talk can help with the more abstract meanings that are found in the texts that students are given to read. For example, with texts that present new information or new ways of organizing relatively familiar information, it is possible to offer glosses – paraphrases, explanations, or examples – that build bridges between the dynamic and synoptic perspectives and between the language in which each of these is expressed and the students' own experience. Here is a fairly typical example: In the course of a unit on electricity,[4] one of the nine-year-old members of the class has shown a persistent interest in electricity in the human body and has asked a number of questions about how, if electricity causes shock, it can also play a necessary part in the proper functioning of the body. To address this issue for Benjamin and the other children, the teacher reads a short passage from a book she has added to the classroom library and then provides a further gloss on the information in the text.

In this and in the following transcripts, the following conventions apply:

· = 1 sec. of pause
<> enclose segments where the transcription is in doubt
* = a word that is inaudible;
CAPS = spoken with emphasis
<u>underlining</u> = segments spoken simultaneously.

> *Teacher:* I'm going to read this part, 'Electricity in the Human Body, because I know Benjamin is still not satisfied about it (reads) "Tiny electric signals, which can be called synapses, <travel> through the heart muscles, triggering and coordinating the heartbeat.

These signals send "echoes" (T adds: They put 'echoes' in inverted commas) through the body tissues to the skin. Here, they can be detected by metal sensors and displayed as a wavy line called the electrocardiogram."
Now that is the most positive proof that the human body contains electricity. .... Have you seen pictures – movies – where people are harnessed up to- and a person had a heart attack and you see this wavy line (demonstrating).

Children: Yeah, yeah (excitedly)

Teacher: Now those wavy lines are showing the electricity going through the human body · that's called the electrocardiogram. And when a person is dead it goes 'deeeeeee'–

Child: Yeah, a straight line

Here, the teacher has enabled the students to bring their own experience, whether first-hand or tv-mediated, to contextualize the less familiar language of the written text.

Earlier in the same lesson, the reverse strategy was used. With a chart showing the different sources of energy displayed on the board, the teacher asked the children to mention the sources of energy with which they were familiar in their homes and local community. Over the course of considerable discussion, their contributions were then built with the teacher's guidance into a more comprehensive and taxonomic account, in which a major distinction was made between renewable and nonrenewable sources of energy. This co-constructed account was then used to make sense of the information presented in the text of the wall chart.

However, such discussions do not need to be restricted to occasions when the teacher interacts with the whole class. For example, in practical activities, where the students are working in groups and consulting a text that contains instructions for action, the meaning of the text is often clarified by matching the linguistic expressions with the materials available and with what the students already know about actions that may be performed on them. Similarly, in working with a historical text or a novel that a group is studying, discussion in which alternative individual interpretations are critically examined and compared can lead to a collaborative interpretation in the construction of which each participant extends his or her own personal understanding.

So far, I have considered talk about texts that are already written, where the problem is to recontextualize the meaning, often synoptically expressed, in the more familiar language of everyday speech. However, the same sort of facilitation can also occur when writers discuss the texts that they themselves are composing. For example, in negotiating what information to enter into a table showing the results of a practical activity, students are led to consider the structure of the table as a form of representation and, in the light of this, to decide what aspects of what they have done and observed it is appropriate to include.

The following example comes from the next stage of such an activity. Working in groups, students have tested a variety of materials to find out which can be used to complete a simple circuit, thereby making a bulb light up. Having returned to the whole class setting, the groups have reported their results, which have been written in a table in which a check mark has been entered either in the column for "bulb lights up" or in that for "bulb does not light." Now the teacher asks them to draw some conclusions.

> *Teacher:* Now, just from this chart, what does it tell you?
> Is something like paper a good conductor of electricity?
> (Several children shake their heads)
> So what are the materials that are poor conductors of electricity – that do not conduct electricity – where electricity cannot pass through there to get you a complete circuit?
> What sorts of materials are not good conductors of electricity? . . .
> Can you name them? Marie?
>
> *Marie:* Cotton reels
>
> *Teacher:* So what is it made of? Name the material . . . did you observe? What's the cotton reel made of?
>
> *Amy:* Plastic
>
> *Teacher:* Plastic · so plastic's not a good conductor, you see.
> What other materials?
>
> *Emily:* Um · beer bungs and . wood (almost inaudible)
>
> *Teacher:* Listen to the question . I want you to make a knowledge transformation, OK? I want you to transform what you did. I asked what MATERIALS are not good conductors · I didn't <ask about the> beer bung
>
> *Emily:* Wood
>
> *Teacher:* Wood, plastic · What else are not good conductors?
>
> *Philips:* Paper
>
> *Teacher:* Now these are NON-CONDUCTORS (writing the word above the column in the table for "bulb does not light up") Now can

you name for me the CONDUCTORS of electricity – the materials not the objects?

In this example, it is the table, as a genre of written text, that serves to focus the double reconstruing of experience, from the dynamic account of the specific objects tested to the more abstract representation in terms of materials, and then from the everyday categories of materials to the synoptic categories of conductors or non-conductors of electricity. And in this case, the teacher makes the process explicit by talking about the 'knowledge transformation' that the students need to make.

Later in the same unit on electricity, several instances of a somewhat similar process were observed among groups of students who were preparing posters to explain the functioning of various devices they had made, each involving some kind of electric circuit. Knowing that their posters would be on display at the science fair for other children in the school, they first discussed what they had done and why in everyday talk, then they decided how this should be expressed in a form suitable for display next to their working model.

My final example involves a rather different kind of dialogue, but one introduced for the same reason – to encourage the students to use their texts as "thinking devices" and, in the process, to build bridges between the two modes of representing their experience. From the beginning of the year, the students had been expected to keep a journal in which they wrote about what they had been doing and, more importantly, about what they thought they had learned in the process. In the electricity unit, a further dimension was added: Two adults undertook to be journal correspondents, reading what the students had written and writing back with reactions and comments. The hope was that this would give the journal writing a communicative function that it had lacked before. And this indeed turned out to be the case. Many students addressed their entries to the adult partner and, in several cases, designated an area on the page for answers to their questions, including an injunction to the reader to respond.

Because of limitations of space, it is not possible to do justice to the range of genres and styles that were used. Nevertheless, the following example (Figure 4.1), involving a nine-year-old Chinese-Canadian student, gives an indication of the sort of exchanges that occurred and of the way in which the written journal dialogue helped the students build bridges between the dynamic and synoptic construals of experience.

March 23, 93.

Dear Mr. Wells

First today [our teacher]gave us an idea of drawing simbles. Then everybody gone to their groups and work on the light bulb. Instead it had two bulbs and to make it difficul Mrs. ---- said if we can screw off one bulb off the bulb holder and see if the other bulb still lights up.

it was like this   it was like this
with simbles   with out simbles

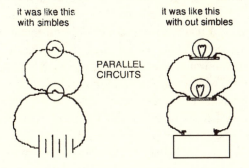

Dear Denny,

I liked the way you used symbols in your circuit diagrams.

I have a puzzle for you. Below, I have drawn two circuits. Each circuit uses a 6 volt battery and 2 volt bulbs. If you did this experiment, which bulbs would you predict would be most likely to burn out: (a), (b), both or neither?

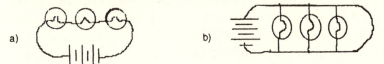

I hope you will tell me what you think next time you write. Please explain the answer you give.

Gordon Wells.

Denny's Response:

The bulbs in (b) will be burn out. because the voltage drop on eachbulb is 6 volts, but the bulb itself can only take 2 volts.

Figure 4.1 Denny's journal.

Making the Form Fit the Function

In the examples of talk about text just considered, I drew attention to the ways in which collaborative discussion helps participants to clarify and develop their understanding of the "content" of the texts they are working on and of the synoptic mode in which it is represented. However, as is clear from some of the examples, such discussion can also provide an occasion for learning about the equally important matter of 'form' and, in particular, about the structure of written genres.

As I argued earlier, an apprenticeship into the subject disciplines must include mastering the genres that are used by the members of those discipline-based communities in constructing and applying their "theories of experience," for these genres are among the essential tools of their crafts.[5] Obviously, it takes many years to develop fluent control of the more specialized genres that are used in the publications of these professional communities, and such a degree of mastery is only achieved over the course of a career in which these genres are regularly used. However, as the notion of specialization suggests, there is a much smaller set of "basic" genres, from which the more specific varieties are derived, and it is with these that the apprenticeship will naturally begin.

Considerable work has already been carried out in identifying key genres that provide an entry to the discourses of those disciplines that underpin the school curriculum (Martin, 1993) and materials have been developed as a basis for systematic instruction in their use (Christie et al., 1990; Derewianka, 1991). In this work, genre is defined as "a staged, goal-oriented social process" (Martin et al., 1987) and written genres are seen as particular instances of this more general category. In other words, written genres constitute the culturally developed ways of carrying out certain rather general communicative actions to achieve particular types of goals or purposes in the context of the relevant overarching activities. Thus, in terms of the sociocultural framework presented earlier, the different genres, such as "recount," "report," "explanation," "exposition," and so on, are best thought of as semiotic tools, whose use – as with other tools – is best learned when they are used to mediate the performance of the activity in question.

From this point of view, it may well be that materials that provide for systematic instruction in the use of particular genres can have a part to play in helping learners to understand the functional significance of their organization, particularly when the learning of the generic structure is embedded in a meaningful activity (Derewianka, 1991). However, it is important to recognize that there are many other occasions on which such learning can occur in the course of the various activities that make up a curriculum unit. Indeed, in all the cases considered above where, in the course of carrying out an activity, the shared reading or writing of a text involved the co-construction of meaning, there was equally an occasion for discussion of the generic structure, as it related to the meanings made with the text and the purpose that the text served in the activity.

Here, there is space to include only one example, which occurred in the previous year in the same classroom as the previous examples.[6] Jasmin and Alex (both Chinese-Canadian children) had been conducting an experiment to verify that, as the text that they were using informed them, light is refracted when it passes through water. Pressed by a visitor to explain how their observations provided evidence of light bending, they had in fact gone beyond the experiment suggested in the book and devised a method of convincing both themselves and the visitor that the light beams, projected through two slits in the side of a shoebox containing a jamjar, only crossed when the jar was full of water. As Jasmin triumphantly concluded at the end of the additional experiment, it was the water, not the glass, that made the light bend.

Later, the two children discussed the report they were expected to write with the visitor who had engaged in the experimental activity with them. First they considered who would read the report: people who already knew about refraction or those who didn't. Since their report was to be displayed in the classroom, they eventually decided that they would write for others who might be interested in carrying out the experiment. For this reason, they decided that they should start by "writing the question"; then they should include two "steps," one listing the materials needed and the other explaining what they did. There was considerable discussion about the ordering of these steps but Alex was finally persuaded by Jasmin's argument:

cos if you don't tell them the materials they sort of say if they want it– if THEY want to try it out um but don't know what the materials [are] they just– they sort of can't do it.

The remaining steps, it was agreed, would include what they observed and what they learned.

As these two nine-year-olds worked on their reports later in the day, there was further discussion between them about the actual layout of their report, as well as about the "steps" they needed to include. Below, I have reproduced – as accurately as possible in the medium of print – the finished version of Jasmin's report. What cannot be reproduced, unfortunately, is the series of annotated illustrations of the various stages of the experiment as it was actually carried out.

Bending Light.

Question: Can light bend?

1. Materials: One cardbord box, a glass jar filled with water (to make exprimint more clearly put food coloring in water,) sheet of white paper that can fit inside the cardbord box, scissors, ruler, pen, and a very bright flashlight.

2. <u>What we did</u>: First we drawed two nawrow slots two cm. apart each other on one side of the cardbord box. Then we cut the slots, put the sheet inside the cardbord box make sure it fits just right. Then we put the glass of water inside the cardbord box, make sure the jar of water is right beside the slots. In a very, very, very dark room (place), shine the flashlight through the two slots.

3. <u>Observations</u>: You might find out that you can only see two slots on the other side of the cardbord box but it doesn't mean that you did it wrong, if you don't belive me, try taking the flashlight and tip the back of it up (slightly) and then tip it so that it is leveled again. Repet that again and again and you will see it cross together, if you don't see it that means your either tiping it to much or you did something wrong. Now, say if you wearn't pretty sure if it's crossing together and you want to be realy sure that it's crossed, try this, use one hand to hold the flashlight and one of your finger to cover one of the slots and then lift your finger up, now look at the other side of the cardbord box where the light will apear and do it again (lift your finger up and down) and if you would notice that when you cover the right slot the left slot will disappar and when you cover the left slot the right slot dissappars, you might wonder why, Because when you cover the right slot the right slot should dissappar, not the left, so this shows you that you may not see it cross but it mabe is.

4. <u>Other questions people ask</u>: Mr. X [Teacher B] asked Alex (my partner) and me a question, "What do you think is causing the light bend?" I said it was the water but my partner said it was the glass so insded we did another exprimint what we did was take out the jar of water and put in another jar but this time without water. we did exacly the same thing, and we tested it with our finger again, but it didn't cross over together. So we new it was the water.

5. <u>Coments</u>: I must say I have to thank [my teacher] for giving me an apertunaty to do this exprimint and learning so much things and also I have to thank [Teacher B] for helping us do this exprimint, thank you both of you. Another coment from myself, the exprimint was neat.

Jasmin

Some might argue that, because Jasmin's text is still an idiosyncratic mixture of several genres, it shows the need for a much more directive form of teaching. However, I would disagree. What is important, in my view, is not whether the texts that are the outcome of such collaborative discussion conform to some abstract prescription of "report" or "explanation" – a result that could be produced by filling in spaces in a pro-forma document – but that they have the form they do because the writers have made conscious decisions to construct them in that way in order to achieve the purposes that they have set for themselves. Only when this is the case, I would argue, is it possible for them to use reader feedback as a basis for further discussion about whether the text is successful and, if it is not entirely so, about what sorts of changes could be made to improve it. Although this route to mastery may be slower, the advantage is that, at each stage, the learner is in control of the tool and can develop and adapt it to meet her expanding goals as a writer.

Talk, Text, and Activity

With the preceding examples, I have tried to give an idea of some of the different ways in which talk about texts provides the occasion for simultaneously learning the new mode of written language and also the "written, educational knowledge" that is encoded in written texts. In concluding this section, I review the points I have made from the perspective of the apprenticeship metaphor that I introduced earlier.

In sociocultural theory, as I explained above, learning is seen very generally in terms of appropriation. That is to say, learning is the taking over and mastering of cultural artifacts and practices in the course of engaging in joint activities, in which the functional significance of these artifacts and practices is modelled and the learner receives assistance in their use. Talk almost always plays a part in this process, as participants discuss what they are doing and why. In the case of the appropriation of symbolic artifacts and practices, however, talk is absolutely essential (Wells, 1990), since the way in which texts perform their mediating function is not as evident as in the case of the artifacts and practices that are used in such traditional, material activities as weaving (Rogoff, 1990) or tailoring (Lave, 1977).

This is now well understood in the field of emergent literacy, where the wide-spread occurrence of collaborative talk about books and other texts in the preschool years has been well documented, as have the benefits to be gained from these practices by young literacy apprentices (Crain-Thoreson, 1993; Heath, 1983; Teale and Sulzby, 1986; Wells, 1986). In the early school years, similar practices are found in the Reading Recovery program developed by Clay (Clay and Cazden, 1990) and in the "instructional conversations" that are at the heart of the programs for minority students pioneered by Tharp and Gallimore (1988).

What needs to be emphasized, though, is that it is not only in the early years that learners benefit from working together to make sense of the texts they are reading and writing. The teacher members of my graduate classes have also found that they understand the readings better if they have the opportunity to discuss them in small groups (Wells, 1994c). And the same is undoubtedly true for young adolescents in school, as they grapple with the unfamiliar forms and meanings of the synoptic genres of the subject disciplines in which they are expected to reconstrue their experience. However, as I hope to show below, it is possible to organize almost any curriculum unit in such a way that it provides multiple opportunities for the joint activities in which this sort of collaborative learning can occur.

Before leaving the topic of the complementary relationship between talk and text, however, there is one further point that needs to be made. And that is that, despite the characteristic differences between these two modes of discourse in both form and function, there are also many intermediate forms that combine some of the features of each. Perhaps most important, in the present context, is the extended turn in dialogue, in which the speaker develops a topic in a systematic way, whether in narrating an event, describing a situation or process, or in stating and justifying a point of view. The oral expositions of new material that figure in many lessons – and which for many teachers are the prototypical form of teaching behavior – are particularly clear examples of such intermediate modes. Their value is that they provide models of "talking science" (Lemke, 1990) – or mathematics (Forman, 1996) or literature (Chambers, 1993) – which introduce many of the features of the more formal written genres employed in these subjects, but in contexts in which the formal language is interspersed with the "everyday language of common sense."

Such models are undoubtedly important. But, as the main form of assistance, they are certainly not sufficient. Craft apprentices do not develop the skills they need simply by observing the artifacts produced by master craftsmen or even from watching the craftsmen at work. Certainly, the role of the master includes that of modelling the activity and explaining the principles and practices involved. But these contributions are of greatest value, not in the form of abstract precepts, but when offered as guidance and assistance as the apprentice is actually engaged in performing the activity (Collins et al., 1989). Similarly, in order to develop and hone their skills, semiotic apprentices also need guidance and assistance. But for them, too, this help is of greatest value when it is offered while they are at work on challenging projects that make constant demands on them to master the use of further tools and practices and even to invent new ones of their own.

It is important, therefore, that extended turns should not be the sole prerogative of the teacher. Indeed, as Lemke (1990) emphasizes, if students are to learn the genres in which scientists talk and write about the phenomena of interest to them, they need opportunities to do more than listen to teacher expositions or read what the textbook writers have written. They also need opportunities to talk and write science themselves, to others who are interested in, and responsive to, their contributions.

The same is equally true of other subjects, as is argued by Lampert about teaching mathematics to ten- and eleven-year-olds:

> This means we do not proceed as if whatever the teacher says, or whatever is in the book, is what is assumed to be true. It also means that lessons must be structured to pursue the mathematical questions that have meaning for students in the context of the problems they are trying to solve. And this means that lessons are more like messy conversations than like synoptic presentations of conclusions. (1992, p. 307)

In fact, "messy conversations" seems a very good way of describing those instances of talk about texts which, because directly related to problems with which students are grappling, are most productive for learning how both talk and text are used to make meaning and develop understanding. And when these conversations occur in the context of activities which the students have made their own, we have come close to optimizing, in school, the conditions under which these tools can be mastered. In the final section of this chapter, therefore, I want to consider one way in which these conditions might be created.

Inquiry and Education

In my own learning as a teacher, one of the ways in which sociocultural theory has most helped me is in offering a way of reconciling the opposition that is often perceived to exist between the two overriding goals of education. These are, on the one hand, to ensure that the young are socialized into the values, knowledge, and practices of the culture so that they grow up to be responsible and productive citizens and, on the other, to nurture the originality and creativity of individual students so that each is enabled to fulfill his or her unique potential. As teachers, we often find that, while believing in the second goal, the pressure to fulfill the first is so overwhelming that, in practice, there is little time or opportunity left to attend to the second. It is in this professional impasse that I have found the sociocultural metaphor of apprenticeship to be particularly helpful.

Two features of this metaphor, in particular, are worth exploring further. The first is the object of an apprenticeship. Certainly, it includes the passing on of the knowledge and skills of the craft, with an emphasis on application. This is the outcome that is emphasized in much of the current debate about accountability: What is learned in school should enable students to function effectively in the social and economic world beyond; theoretical knowledge is of value to the extent that it has implications for action. And there is much to be said for the argument that knowledge should be for effective action rather than simply for show under examination conditions.

However, there is more to apprenticeship than reproducing the achievements of the past. For the ultimate object is that the apprentice should become an independent master craftsman, who creates new artifacts and adds to the cultural resources. In fact, all of the inventions that we now take for granted grew out of past experimentation with the resources then currently available, as they were put to novel uses or adapted to deal with new problems in need of solution. In other words, creativity and originality are as much the object of education as is the reproduction of the existing order. Indeed, in the light of the problems facing humankind, they may be of even greater importance.

The second feature that needs to be explored is the means by which these twin objects are achieved. And here, unfortunately, the actual practices of trade guilds in the past leave much to be desired for, by all accounts, the young apprentice's life was very often one of drudgery and exploitation. These are not necessary conditions, however, and were probably as counter-productive in the past as they would be in any school or classroom today. On the other hand, the emphasis on learning through engaging in purposeful activity is as valid today as it ever was. And so is the principle of teaching by proposing challenging goals to be achieved, and providing assistance in meeting them in a form that is appropriate to the learner's needs and with the intention of enabling him or her to appropriate the practices that are enacted jointly, along with the responsibility for learning to manage them on his or her own.

This understanding of the teacher's role in assisting learning was expressed by Vygotsky (1978), somewhat aphoristically, as "what a child can do with assistance today she will be able to do by herself tomorrow" (p. 87). The passage occurs in the exposition of his conceptualization of teaching-and-learning as working with the learner in her "zone of proximal development," that is to say, in the zone between what she can do alone and the upper limit of what she can do with appropriate help. What this means, in practice, is: engaging with learners in activities to which they are committed, observing what they can already do unaided; then providing assistance and guidance that helps them to identify the nature of their problems and to find solutions that enable them to bring the activity to a satisfactory completion. It is in this guiding role that the teacher can most effectively pass on the artifacts and skills developed in the past, for it is under these conditions that their utility is most evident and their mode of functioning most readily understood and mastered.

One way of organizing the curriculum to make this possible is by working with broad, open-ended thematic units, within which individuals or – even better – groups of students choose and plan their own topics of inquiry in consultation with the teacher. By selecting themes that both meet the requirements of the mandated curriculum and match the known or anticipated interests of the majority of the students, and by then sharing with them the responsibility for deciding on specific topics and how they should be investigated, the teacher maximizes the chances of achieving the first requirement – that the students should be engaged in challenging activities that they find personally significant. Under these conditions, student motivation is high and so is their ability to work independently, without the need for constant supervision and control. As a result, this mode of organization also meets the second requirement – that of freeing the teacher to spend time with individuals or groups, observing their progress and providing appropriate assistance when it is needed.

The first two requirements are concerned with ensuring that students' learning, and the provision of assistance, are embedded in a broader context of purposeful joint activity which, itself, involves a variety of constituent activities. However, there are two further, equally important requirements. The first is that, as well as being personally significant, the activities in which students engage should, over the unit as a whole, provide opportunities for them to make systematic progress toward mastery of the tools and practices of the discipline. This requirement can be met through the introduction of teacher-selected activities for the whole class, interspersed with the students' self-selected activities, and through the specification of genres to be included in students' presentations of their research. It can also be linked with the final requirement, which is that learning through action should be complemented by regular opportunities for learning through reflection. Whether undertaken individually or by the class as a whole, this will need to address both what has been achieved and discovered and the new questions that have arisen as a result, and also the means – the artifacts and practices – that have been employed in the process, as well as the problems encountered, whether solved or still in search of a solution. Whole-class reflective discussion is particularly important here for, as well as fostering the development of the collaborative ethos of a community of inquiry, such discussion provides the setting, par excellence, in which knowledge is co-constructed, as students and teacher together make meaning on the basis of each other's experiences, supplemented by information from other sources beyond the classroom.

The overall structure of this inquiry-oriented approach to curriculum can be represented schematically as in Figure 4.2. I must emphasize, however, that this is a "tool" to be used for thinking and planning, not a prescription to be followed on every – or even any – particular occasion. Such decisions will always need to be made in the light of the curricular topic, the availability of resources of different kinds and, most importantly, the interests and capabilities of the particular class of students. (For further discussion of the model and its various components, see Appendix I and Wells (1995).)[7]

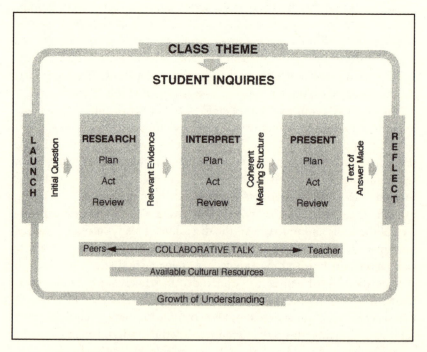

Figure 4.2 A model of inquiry.

In the unit on electricity from which the earlier examples were taken, the *Launch* took the form of a brainstorming session in which each child first wrote down what he or she knew about electricity and their ideas were then discussed in a whole-class session and written on a single large display, together with a list of questions to which students wanted to find answers (Scardamalia and Bereiter, 1992). Then, following the viewing of a video-taped program which provided an age-appropriate introduction to the topic of electricity, the teacher introduced the idea of a science fair, for which groups would construct working models that involved some application of electrical circuits. The models that groups elected to make included a robot with flashing eyes, a truck-mounted electromagnet and two morse code signaling stations connected by a length of wire.

While work proceeded on these artifacts, the teacher presented a series of challenges of increasing difficulty, starting with designing a simple circuit and continuing through parallel circuits with each bulb controlled by its own switch, to an experiment to discover the variables that determined the strength of an electro-magnet. Each of these activities was followed by a review session, in which the whole class *interpreted* the results of the *research* they had just done and *reflected* on what they had learned, both about the principles of electricity and about strategies, social as well as practical and intellectual, for successfully solving problems of the kinds encountered. There were also whole class discussions, such as the one from which I quoted above, in which questions raised by the children were considered in relation to what was learned from the practical work as well as from consulting reference material of various kinds.[8]

By the end of the unit, then, the children had worked to find solutions to the problems encountered in constructing their chosen models and, through the teacher-posed challenges, had systematically learned about some of the basic principles of electrical circuits, conductivity and electromagnetism. All this work culminated in a very successful science fair (*presentation*), in which the groups' working models were complemented by displays of various kinds which, in every case, included posters providing explanations of the principles involved, as well as other information which group members thought would be of interest to the children from other classes who came to visit their fair.

As will be apparent, such an inquiry-oriented approach to curriculum creates opportunities for students to engage in many modes of discourse, both spoken and written. Earlier, I referred to several that I observed in the course of the curricular unit on electricity that I have just described. In Table 4.1, I have also drawn on my observations of thematic units based in different areas of the curriculum to present a more comprehensive

Table 4.1. *Genres of Discourse as Tools for Inquiry*

	Oral Discourse	Written Discourse
Response to the launch event	Drama, exploratory discussion, brainstorming, formulating questions, hypothesizing, etc.	Poem, journal entry; Statement of inquiry, Initial theory, etc.
Research	Planning, negotiating, coordinating and monitoring action; observing, interviewing, consulting reference books	Plan, list of instructions; letters requesting information; notes, tables of results, protocols, diagrams
Interpretation	Interpreting evidence, debating alternative interpretations, or drawing warranted conclusions	Concept maps or webs, lists of arguments for and against alternative interpretations
Presentation	Planning, negotiating, coordinating and monitoring action; drama, report, video/audio program; commentary, panel, etc.	Plan, outline, narrative of events, procedural description, illustration, report, explanation
Review	Reflecting, theorizing, evaluating	Summary, reflection, evaluation

account of the range of genres that might play a part as tools in mediating students' inquiries.

In presenting this summary, I have generalized across different patterns of participation. For example, in suggesting the genres of spoken discourse that might occur, I have not indicated the size of group that might be involved, as this might vary from a couple of students working together to the whole class. In the case of presentations, on the other hand, the audience might involve another class or parents and other adults invited for the occasion. Similarly, with respect to written texts: these might be produced by individual students or by collaborating groups and, where appropriate, addressed to a wider audience than the teacher alone through the use of class bulletin boards, or a class or school newspaper. In several cases that I have known, the final products of groups' inquiries, usually involving a variety of genres, were published in book form and added to the resources in the school library. Finally, although I have only included journal entries once, students might be encouraged to make regular entries in their journals or learning logs at all stages in their inquiries.

Looked at from the perspective of semiotic apprenticeship, Table 4.1 lists some of the more important discursive tools and practices that are utilized in carrying out an inquiry and indicates the tasks for which they are particularly useful. No doubt there are others that could or should be included, depending on the nature of the inquiry.

Whether spoken or written, however, the genres included in this table emphasize the social functions of discourse. Together, they make up a tool-kit for coordinating action and for negotiating and communicating participants' understanding with respect to their joint activities. However, they can also be seen as providing a similar resource for the intrapersonal actions that participants carry on when they are alone, in what Vygotsky (1987) called the discourse of inner speech. From this perspective, participation in the genres of social discourse not only provides the means for the co-construction of knowledge; it also enables learners to appropriate the practices and artifacts which they can use to mediate the solo mental actions of thinking, imagining, and reasoning. It goes without saying, of course, that these two broad functions – the interpersonal and the intrapersonal – are interdependent and complementary, since they both mediate activities which, because they involve meaning, are inherently social and cultural. They are thus perhaps best seen as different phases of the continuing apprenticeship. As new genres of discourse are encountered and progressively mastered in interpersonal activity, they extend and transform the individual's intrapersonal activity, and this, in turn, enables him or her to participate more fully and effectively in further interpersonal activity, in a never-ending spiral.[9]

Conclusion

In this chapter, I have outlined a conception of education in terms of semiotic apprenticeship – an opportunity, through guided participation in discipline-based forms of inquiry, to appropriate the cultural tools and practices for meaning making in the construction and application of knowledge in all areas of human activity. In this enterprise I have accorded a special place to language, seeing in the various genres of spoken and written discourse a kit of tools that performs a dual function, both mediating participation in activity and simultaneously providing a medium in which activity is represented and thus made available to be reflected upon.

In this conception – as befits the central metaphor – the emphasis is on the learner and on the conditions that enable him or her to master the means for full participation in the activity of inquiry, both alone and in collaboration with others. As a consequence, it may appear that my intention has also been to deemphasize the importance of teaching. This is certainly not the case. However, an acceptance of this view of the classroom as a community of inquiry, in which learners share with the teacher the responsibility for deciding on the topics and on the means for their investigation, may indeed call for a reexamination of the ways in which the teacher's role might best be enacted (see Chapter 9).

However, in suggesting that we need to reexamine our conception of teaching, I am not arguing for the supplanting of one set of practices by a different set that is already fully worked out and waiting to be applied. On the contrary: Every school and every classroom presents its own set of opportunities and constraints, and there is no set of practices that is guaranteed of universal success. Models, such as the one that I presented above, are no more than tools to be adapted in use to fit the prevailing conditions; it is to be expected, therefore, that they will be transformed by those who use them. The version represented in the examples quoted in this paper was developed to meet the needs of a culturally and socioeconomically diverse class of nine- and ten-year-olds in Toronto. In other places, or with other grade levels, a different version might be more appropriate.

In other words, what I am suggesting is that teaching, like learning, is an ongoing process of inquiry, in which the knowledge that is constructed about learners and learning, as these are encountered in particular situations, continuously transforms the teacher's way of understanding and acting in the classroom. However, the practices of inquiry are not learned in isolation, nor do the various genres of discourse that mediate those practices take on their full value outside a context of joint activity. Like students in the classroom, therefore, teachers need to be participants in communities of colleagues who use the tools of inquiry to learn the craft of teaching (Wells, 1994a). Furthermore, it is when we are ourselves intentional learners and inquirers that we most effectively model the practices that we wish our students to learn. For if what we learn is what we do – to rephrase Dewey's maxim – then what we do depends on the practices that are available for us to appropriate from the communities in which we participate.

Notes

1. This triple transformation, as it applies in the appropriation and use of language as tool for both social and individual activity, is further discussed in Wells (1994c). As Halliday (1978) points out, each instance of language in use transforms the situation in which it occurs and either confirms or modifies the participants' view of the world, as this is construed in terms of the cultural categories encoded in language; by the same token, the language code is itself gradually transformed over time by the novel uses that speakers and writers make of it (Halliday, 1993b).
2. See Chapters 1 and 5 for a much more detailed exposition; see also Halliday and Hasan, 1985.
3. In Halliday's terms, all purposeful uses of language, whether spoken or written, involve the construction of text – discourse that is "functional in some context or situation" (1993a, p. 107). This is an important point that should not be forgotten. However, in popular usage, the term "text" is usually restricted to written discourse, which is distinguishable from spoken discourse in a number of ways, and not least – as I have suggested – by its relative permanence. Since this difference is particularly consequential for my argument, I shall stay with popular usage, referring to the two modes as "talk" and "text."
4. This unit occurred in a Grade 4 and 5 class in an inner-city school in Toronto. Because of its location, the school serves a very diverse community; many of the children come from nearby Chinatown, but some are brought in from suburban homes by parents who work in professional occupations in the adjacent hospitals and offices. The majority of children in this class spoke a language other than English at home and a few, being recent arrivals in Canada, were still in the early stages of learning the language of the classroom. As well as containing a number of children designated "gifted," the class also included several children who were receiving help in part-time withdrawal programs for literacy learning and behavioral difficulties.

   As this study of electricity took place in March and April, the children had already had some experience of engaging in sustained inquiry, both in science and social studies. From the work on display in the classroom, it was clear that, wherever possible, connections were made between the topics chosen for inquiry and the children's activities in mathematics, literature, art and drama. The study of electricity should be seen, therefore, as one theme within a curriculum that was both integrated and challenging.
5. While writing this paper, I came across the following paragraph, written by a professional scientist:

> Another problem with this ['scientific method'] paradigm is that it focuses only on the performance of experiments and overlooks that science is a social effort requiring communication. Because advances in science are interdependent, all the arts of communication are essential to science. Scientists visit one another's labs, travel to conferences, speak by telephone, hold advisory committee meetings, teach, argue, and write papers together, often using electronic mail. (Tinker, 1993, p. 2)

6. This example was the subject of a symposium at AERA, Chicago, March 1997. A fuller account appears in Wells, G. "Modes of meaning in a science activity," which is to appear in a forthcoming issue of *Linguistics and Education*.

7. Not all applications of the apprenticeship model of learning provide so much scope for student initiative and creativity. Examples of more narrowly focused approaches are Brown and Palincsar's "Reciprocal Teaching" (Palincsar and Brown, 1984; Brown and Palincsar, 1989) and Cole and Engestrom's (1993) "Question-Asking-Reading." An approach more like the inquiry model presented here is described in Gamberg et al. (1988), with many examples of themes that have proved successful with elementary age children. See also Kierstead (1985) for an overview of a similar approach to curriculum planning.

8. Benjamin, for example, searched among his father's books at home, consulted his uncle, a doctor, and accessed – with his teacher's help – the relevant entries in the CD-ROM Grolier Encyclopedia, in order to find out more about the role played by electricity in the human body.

9. There is one further feature of this table that only struck me after I had completed it: Quite unintentionally, I had for the most part chosen process terms to describe the genres of oral discourse, but product terms to describe the written genres. Whether or not this is appropriate, it does reinforce Halliday's point, quoted above, about the more synoptic, objectlike nature of written text as compared to the dynamic, in-process nature of talk.

5   Putting a Tool to Different Uses:

A Reevaluation of the IRF Sequence

If there is one finding on which students of classroom discourse are agreed, it must be the ubiquity of the three-part exchange structure that Lemke (1985, 1990) calls "triadic dialogue." In its prototypical form, this discourse format consists of three moves: an *initiation*, usually in the form of a teacher question, a *response*, in which a student attempts to answer the question, and a *follow-up* move, in which the teacher provides some form of feedback to the student's response. Actual frequencies of occurrence vary considerably, of course, but in many secondary classrooms it is estimated that this format accounts for some 70 percent of all the discourse that takes place between teacher and students, and even in some primary classrooms it has been found to be the dominant mode in which the teacher converses, even when talking with individual students.

When it comes to evaluating the educational significance of this mode of classroom discourse, on the other hand, there is much less agreement. Sinclair and Coulthard (1975), for example, seem to assume that triadic dialogue simply *is* the unmarked mode of classroom interaction: Unless there is a good reason to behave otherwise, teachers adopt this mode by default. Not surprisingly, therefore, they offer no evaluation of its educational effectiveness. Others, by contrast, while accepting its pervasiveness, claim that it is, in fact, functionally effective. Mercer (1992), for example, argues that triadic dialogue is justified as an effective means of: "monitoring children's knowledge and understanding," "guiding their learning," and "marking knowledge and experience which is considered educationally significant or valuable." Somewhat similarly, Newman, Griffin, and

Reevaluating the IRF sequence: A proposal for the articulation of theories of activity and discourse for the analysis of learning and teaching in the classroom. *Linguistics and Education* 5 (1): 1–37, 1993. Greenwich, CT: Ablex Publishing Corporation.

Cole (1989), claim that the three-part structure of triadic dialogue is "quite nicely designed" to achieve the goals of education. While the exchange as a whole is "collaboratively constructed," they argue, it has the particular merit of having "a built-in repair structure in the teacher's last turn so that incorrect information can be replaced with the right answers" (p. 127).

By contrast, a number of writers have been much more critical of teachers' ubiquitous use of this discourse format. Wood (1992), for example, accuses teachers of asking too many questions, particularly of the known answer variety, and suggests that, if they really want to hear what pupils think and if they genuinely want to encourage pupils to ask questions of their own, they should use a less controlling type of discourse, which would give students a greater chance to take on the initiating role. For similar reasons, Lemke (1990) also urges teachers to make less use of triadic dialogue, arguing that it is "overused in most classrooms because of a mistaken belief that it encourages maximum student participation" (p. 168).

Such disagreement would be less surprising if the opposing evaluations were made by proponents of radically different theories about the goals of education and the means by which they can best be achieved. However, this is not the case. All the writers quoted above (with the exception of Sinclair and Coulthard, who are agnostic in this matter) appeal to the principles of sociocultural theory, either in the texts quoted or in contemporaneous publications, to justify their evaluations.

Two reasons can be advanced, I believe, for this state of affairs. The first has to do with a tension within sociocultural theory itself, between the two prime goals of education, which might be described as cultural reproduction and individual development. Strong endorsements of triadic dialogue seem to occur in texts which are primarily concerned with the responsibility of educational institutions for cultural reproduction and for ensuring that students appropriate the artifacts and practices that embody the solutions to problems encountered in the past. Indictments of the pervasiveness of triadic dialogue, on the other hand, tend to occur in texts that are more concerned with the responsibility of educational institutions for cultural renewal and for the formation and empowerment of its individual members to deal effectively with future problems (Engeström, 1991b).

The second reason has to do with the somewhat undifferentiated manner in which triadic dialogue has typically been treated, as if all the occasions on which it occurs are essentially similar. Yet, as all the writers referred to above would almost certainly agree, in the hands of different teachers, the same basic discourse format can lead to very different levels of student participation and engagement (Nystrand and Gamoran, 1991). It can also be used by the same teacher, in different contexts, to achieve very different purposes – as I hope to show below, through a detailed examination of two episodes from a study of time in a grade three classroom. My intention will be to argue that, in itself, triadic dialogue is neither good nor bad; rather, its merits – or demerits – depend upon the purposes it is used to serve on particular occasions, and upon the larger goals by which those purposes are informed. In order to develop these arguments, however, I first need to situate the discourse that occurs in the classroom within a larger framework of analysis, in which the classroom is seen as a site of human activity more generally conceived.

The Organization of Classroom Activity

The concept of activity as an organizing principle of human behavior has been central to sociocultural theory for much of this century (Wertsch, 1981) and probably no one has contributed more to what is now referred to as "activity theory" than Leont'ev. In one of the most important of his works to be translated into English (Leont'ev, 1981), he offers a tristratal account of activity in terms of activity, action, and operation. From one perspective, these categories can be treated as a hierarchy, or rank scale, with an activity being carried out through the performance of one or more actions and these, in turn, consisting of one or more operations (Zinchenko and Gordon, 1981).

However, Leont'ev's formulation of the relationship between the three strata makes it clear that, while they may be treated as hierarchically related, they also represent different perspectives on the same event, those respectively of motive, goal and conditions: "When a concrete process – external or internal – unfolds before us, from the point of view of its motive, it is human activity, but in terms of subordination to a goal, it is an action or chain of actions" (1981, p. 61). And, a little later, when distinguishing between action and operation, he writes: "the action has special qualities, its own special "components," especially the means by which it is carried out . . . actions are concerned with goals and operations with conditions" (p. 63).

As Leont'ev recognizes, there is nothing in these statements to delimit the scope of the various categories nor to determine, in the abstract, which of the three perspectives should be adopted with respect to any type of event. An event that, on one occasion, may be considered from the perspective of its motive, and thus constitute an activity, may on another, when considered from the perspective of its goal, be treated as an action; or, if considered as selected in response to the prevailing conditions, it may even be treated as an operation in relation to some superordinate action or activity. More recently, however, it has been proposed that what distinguishes the three categories is the degree to which they involve conscious attention. Operations are actions that have become routinized; used as means in the achievement of the goal of action, they no longer require to be consciously attended to. Activities, by contrast, involve patterns of action that we may have grown into as members of the culture; they provide the motive and context for action but may also not be attended to directly. Actions, on the other hand, always involve a conscious attention to the means–end relationship. For the purposes of analyzing particular events, therefore, it seems that it is the goal-oriented action which is central; this may be interpreted with respect to the activity which provides its motivation and with respect to the operations through which it is realized, in the light of that motivation and the conditions obtaining in the situation.

A study carried out by Wertsch and his colleagues (1984) within an activity theoretic framework may be instructive in this respect. They investigated the different patterns of interaction that occurred when Brazilian children carried out the task of constructing an array in accordance with a model, either with their mother or with a teacher. The investigators' purpose was to compare the ways in which the two categories of adults regulated the children's behavior, either encouraging the child to be autonomous or perpetuating dependence on adult control.

In conducting their analysis, Wertsch et al. treated the completion of the array as a whole as a goal-directed action. This required a number of episodes, in each of which a single piece was placed. Each episode, in turn, involved a number of subactions or "strategic steps": looking to the model, picking up a required piece, and placing the piece in the copy. The category of action thus consisted of what Leont'ev called a chain of actions organized in a hierarchy of episodes and strategic steps.

The category of operation was employed for the analysis of the manner in which the strategic steps were carried out, in particular to account for the distribution of responsibility between adult and child. The results at this level showed that the mothers were, in general, more directive than the teachers.

Finally, to account for these results, the authors invoked the highest level category, activity. Although undertaking the same actions in working with the child to complete the array, the two sets of adults were engaged in two different activities: the teachers were engaged in the activity of education and the mothers in the activity of efficient task completion.

Although conducted outside a school setting, there are two ways in which this study's application of the categories of activity theory are relevant to the analysis of classroom activities. First, the majority of classroom activities can be seen as goal-directed actions, often involving a chain of subordinate actions with some hierarchical organization. Furthermore, the performance of these actions typically involves interaction as a central component, both between more and less competent participants and among the participants in relation to the various texts and artifacts that are utilized in carrying out the action. Indeed, it is quite largely through their participation in the interaction that constitutes or accompanies the action that the students are expected to learn (Heap, 1985). Precisely what form this interaction takes, however, is at the discretion of the teacher. In encouraging or restricting certain kinds of behavior, both verbal and nonverbal, therefore, the teacher – like the adults in the Wertsch et al. study – is operationalizing his or her theory of education.

In analyzing the events that take place in classrooms, therefore, it seems that Leont'ev's tristratal theory of activity will best be honored as follows: His category of "activity" will be used to characterize curricular events from the perspective of the teacher's (implicit) theory of education, as he or she plans what learning opportunities to provide and how the students are to engage with them (this will henceforth be referred to as the Practice of Education). The category of "action" will be used to characterize these events in terms of their immediate goals and the sequence of subactions needed to perform them. Finally, the category of "operation" will be reserved for characterizing the actual unfolding of these events, with particular emphasis on the interaction that occurs, both among the participants and between the participants and the various artifacts that are involved in performing the "action(s)."[1]

As with the picture-matching task, many classroom events have a hierarchical organizational structure. This can best be handled, as in the Wertsch et al. study, by recognizing several levels within the category of "action." How many levels are required may depend on the curricular event in question but, as a working hypothesis, I propose a minimum set of four: curricular unit, activity, task, and step (see Table 5.1).

In principle, the category of "operation" can apply at any level in the hierarchy of "action," as decisions are made as to how to achieve the chosen goal under the conditions that obtain in the situation. Whatever the level, however, there are three dimensions that need to be distinguished:

Table 5.1. *Hierarchy of Action Categories*

Curricular Unit	(CU) A thematic unit, such as "Time" in the science curriculum, or "Countries of the World" in social studies, which is the organizing concept for work carried out over an extended period of time
Activity	A relatively self-contained, goal-oriented unit of activity, such as carrying out an experiment or writing a story
Task	A relatively well-defined component of an activity, which is recognized as such by the participants
Step	The smallest recognizable component of a task

the participants that are involved and the manner in which they relate to each other; the nonverbal behavior in which the participants are engaged; and the semiotic tools, including talk, that the participants utilize to mediate the achievement of their goal. It is the choices made on these three dimensions and the relationship between them, it can be hypothesized, that best characterizes the nature of the educational "activity," in the theoretical sense, that the teacher intends the students to experience.

Within such a framework, as can be seen, spoken discourse is seen as one, but only one, of the semiotic tools that participants use to achieve the goals of action. This is not to diminish the importance that is accorded to it, but simply to emphasize its mediating role in the performance of activities, the goals of which may or may not involve talk. Nevertheless, in practice, discourse is involved in almost all classroom events, in either a constitutive or ancillary mode. In the next section, therefore, I shall attempt to show how a theory of discourse can be articulated with the interpretation of activity theory that has just been sketched.

The Organization of Classroom Discourse

As already mentioned, one of the most fully worked out models of discourse is to be found in Sinclair and Coulthard's (1975) book, subtitled "The English used by teachers and pupils," and in the work that has followed from it. From the beginning, this work owed much to the linguistic theory developed by Halliday under the rubric of "systemic linguistics" (Halliday 1970, 1975, 1978). Emphasizing the dual nature of language as code and as behavior (Halliday 1984), Halliday has constantly sought to show the relationship between the form of the language system and the uses to which it is put. As a formal system, it functions as the specifically linguistic component of the culture's semiotic resources – its "meaning potential"; in linguistic behavior, on the other hand, elements of this potential are drawn upon according to the situational context to actualize that cultural potential in the creation of spoken or written texts, which are themselves a form of situated social action.

For our present purposes, there are two aspects of Halliday's work that are of particular importance. The first is the emphasis on language use as a form of social activity and the recognition of the exchange, rather than the individual utterance, as the basic unit of communication (Halliday, 1984). Whether the commodity involved concerns "goods and services" or "information," an exchange necessarily consists of at least one move by both the primary and the secondary actor or knower, and as many further moves as are required to confirm or clarify the proposal or proposition that is under negotiation (Berry, 1981). The IRF structure, identified in so many studies of classroom interaction, is a particular variant of exchange structure, in which the teacher, by virtue of his or her status as primary actor or knower, both initiates the exchange and provides evaluation or follow-up to the student's medial responding move. The student's response is essential, however, for without it there is no exchange. In descriptive schemes that have been developed to study classroom discourse, larger structures above the level of the exchange have also been proposed, variously referred to as transactions (Sinclair and Coulthard 1975), topically related sequences (Mehan, 1979) or topic sequences (Poole, 1990), which, as these labels imply, consist of a number of exchanges of topically related material, frequently opened and closed by some form of boundary marking.

If the exchange accounts for the *internal* organization of discourse in terms, primarily, of the reciprocal relationship of predicting and predicted between adjacent moves (see Chapter 7), Halliday's second major contribution to the study of discourse concerns the *external* relationship between the discourse and the context in which it occurs. To account for this relationship, he introduces the concept of *register*, which is "a particular configuration of meanings that is associated with a particular situation.... Considered in terms of the notion of meaning potential, the register is the range of meaning potential that is activated by the semiotic properties of the situation" (1975, p. 126). To give greater precision to this concept, Halliday introduces a threefold analysis of situation-type in terms of the dimensions of field, tenor and mode, each dimension relating simultaneously to the semiotic structure of the situation and to the way in which the language system is itself organized in terms of three metafunctions: ideational, interpersonal, and textual. Register thus looks in two directions: to the situation, and to language as a resource for acting in the situation.

From the perspective of the situation, field accounts for what is going on: the nature of the social activity, its goals, materials, and processes. Tenor accounts for the participants in the activity, their roles and status, and the degree of social distance between them. Mode accounts for the role of language in the activity, whether ancillary or constitutive, whether primarily spoken or written, and for the extent to which all participants share in the linguistic process. Viewed from the perspective of the linguistic semiotic, on the other hand, the dimension of field maps on to the ideational metafunction, tenor on to the interpersonal metafunction, and mode on to the textual metafunction (Halliday and Hasan, 1985).

Bringing these two seminal ideas together, we can characterize discourse as the collaborative behavior of two or more participants as they use the meaning potential of a shared language to mediate the establishment and achievement of their goals in social action. In order to be successful in this endeavor, they must negotiate a common interpretation of the situation in terms of field, tenor and mode and, in the successive moves through which they complete the exchange of goods and services or information, they must make appropriate choices from their meaning potential in terms of the ideational, interpersonal, and textual metafunctions.

Applications of Hallidayan Theory to the Classroom

Halliday himself has never specifically investigated the role of discourse in classroom activities. However, there have been a number of recent studies of classroom language in which his ideas have been applied and developed within a more general social semiotic framework (Christie, 1991; Hasan and Martin, 1989; Lemke, 1985, 1990).

Lemke (1985), for example, makes use of the concept of register to differentiate classroom situations and the activities that go on within them. Starting with "activity-type" as the basic unit of semiotic analysis, he suggests that the events that make up classroom life can be seen as constituting a specific, linguistic, subset of activity-types and, drawing on his data-base from science lessons, he describes some of those that most frequently occur, which include Going Over Homework, Seatwork, Copying Notes, as well as Triadic Dialogue. As can be seen, however, not all of these activity-types necessarily involve spoken discourse in their actual realization. They therefore correspond most closely to what were referred to above as activities and tasks. Nevertheless, most activity-types in the classroom do indeed involve linguistic interaction, and Lemke proposes two dimensions for their analysis. The first concerns the structure of the activity in terms of the functions performed by the successive moves in the exchange(s) through which the activity is realized. The second is concerned with what can be loosely called the subject content, through the construction of what he calls "thematic systems," i.e. the interrelationships of meaning between the terms that are used in the talk. As Lemke clearly demonstrates, an adequate account of an episode of classroom interaction must pay attention to the thematic content that is being developed in the discourse, as well as to the activity structures through which this development takes place.

Interestingly, a somewhat similar distinction between content and pedagogy is handled by Christie (1991) using a different arrangement of Halliday's theoretical categories. She proposes that two different registers are involved: first, the pedagogical register, which carries forward the learning–teaching activity (the activity-type in Lemke's terms) and second, the content register, which is "projected" by the first in the sense of being embedded within it. However, in Christie's model, the organizing structure that drives the lesson as a whole is the superordinate category of "genre."

Taking its origin as a term for distinguishing functionally different types of written text, such as novels, memos, letters to the editor, and so on, the concept of genre has recently been extended in usage to describe any text, whether spoken or written. What gives a text its generic pattern of organization, it is argued, is the fact that it results from a "staged, goal-oriented, social process" (Martin, Christie, and Rothery, 1987). One of the clearest expositions of this extended use of the concept of genre is to be found in Hasan's (1985) account of a service encounter in a local fruit and vegetable store. Setting up such "elements" as greeting, sale initiation, purchase, etc., she shows how a service encounter in this genre has a schematic structure consisting of certain obligatory elements, some of which may be recursive, together with further optional elements, with all elements normally occurring in a fixed order.

What Christie has done is to apply this extended concept of genre to the different sorts of linguistic activity that occur in the classroom, arguing that, like the service encounter described by Hasan, "they represent goal-directed, purposive ways of doing things in a culture, and in that sense they may be thought of as artifacts of the culture" (Christie, 1991 p. 205). Texts created in the course of different classroom activities can thus be thought of as belonging to different genres, depending on the goals and social processes involved. In the paper from which the above quotation is taken, Christie describes the curriculum genre of planning writing, in which a teacher leads a whole-class activity. There is no reason, however, why the concept of curriculum genre cannot also be applied to activities in which a small group is involved or only a teacher with an individual student. Indeed, there is no reason, in principle, why the concept could not also be applied to any social activity that has a recognizable organizational structure.

In developing the concept of genre in this way, its proponents have made two important further distinctions. First, as Martin (1985) argues, the identification of the elements that constitute a genre, together with their sequential organization, gives rise to a specification of its schematic structure which is essentially static. This sort of specification is what Hasan provides with the genre of shopping in the fruit and vegetable store. However, alongside this "synoptic," account, there must also be a dynamic decision-making process which might be modeled, for example, in the form of a flow chart (Ventola, 1987). The actual speech that occurs in the realization of any particular instance of a genre is thus the product of the dynamic application of the synoptic specifications for engaging in that genre, jointly constructed by all the participants involved; it is also a record which retains in its organization as a text the traces of the stages of its production and the elements from which it is constituted. This leads naturally to the second of the two distinctions, namely, that between text seen as the product or record of the discourse, and text as the actual discursive processes by means of which that product was generated.

Articulating the Relationship between Activity and Discourse

Despite the obvious similarities in orientation between this work on discourse from a social semiotic perspective and work carried out under the rubric of activity theory, neither Halliday nor those who have applied his theory to the description of classroom interaction explicitly refer to the work that has been done in activity theory. Nevertheless, it is clear that, in very general terms, the two approaches to the study of social activity and the role of language in mediating that activity are compatible. For example, there is a considerable degree of similarity between the category of "action" in activity theory and "curriculum genre" as used in Christie's application of systemic linguistics to the analysis of classroom interaction. There also seems to be a close match between both these categories and "activity-type," as used by Lemke (1985). Indeed, in his more recent work, Lemke explicitly states "a synonym for activity structure [activity-type] might be 'action genre'" (1990, p. 199). It seems, then, that the concept of genre may provide a useful bridging category that permits the two theoretical domains of activity and discourse to be articulated.

One possibility would be to follow the suggestion implicit in Lemke's account, namely that of treating linguistic activity-types, or genres, as simply a subcategory of the more general category of "action" genres. In the terms proposed in Table 5.1 above, then, there would be discourse genres corresponding to the levels of activity, task and step. What would distinguish these discourse genres from the more general category of "action" genres would be the specifically linguistic nature of the social behavior involved.

This approach, in fact, seems to be what is implied in Christie's discussion of curriculum genres. Her example of the writing planning genre, for instance, corresponds to an activity, which has its own internal structure. The elements that she proposes as the constituents of this curriculum genre – Task Orientation, Task Specification, and Task – are equivalent to the tasks that, together and in sequence, make up a classroom activity. However, as her analysis shows, each of these constituent tasks also has its own generic organization, distinguishable in terms of the different types of goal that are involved and also of the characteristic patterns of discourse through which they are realized. There thus seem to be a number of different curriculum genres involved, with more microgenres corresponding to the constituent tasks nested within the superordinate curriculum genre corresponding to activity.

If the aim were to describe and account only for the specifically linguistic aspects of classroom life, this approach might have much to recommend it. However, from the wider perspective being adopted here, it has some serious limitations. In particular, it offers no principled account of events that are not linguistic in nature – or at least not centrally so – and it provides no way of relating linguistic and nonlinguistic modes of behavior. Furthermore, it fails to recognize the fact that a given curriculum genre can be realized by means of a variety of discourse genres and thus makes it impossible to compare the ways in which different teachers implement the same activity.

However, a solution that does better justice to these distinctions may perhaps be found by appealing to activity theory. Activity theory, it will be recalled, proposes three major categories of analysis: "activity," "action," and "operation." Analysis of classroom discourse in terms of curriculum genres conflates these latter two categories and therefore fails to recognize the distinction between an "action" and the "operation" by means of which it is actually implemented in the light of the prevailing situation. Discourse, I would argue, falls into the latter category, since it is one of the semiotic tools that participants may make use of to achieve the intended goal of the chosen "action."

What I am proposing, therefore, is to make a distinction between action genres – of which curriculum genres are a subcategory, specific to educational settings – and discourse genres, which along with genres of nonlinguistic semiotic behavior, are drawn upon in the "operationalization" of an action genre. To use the concept of genre in both these cases would seem to be justified, since the criteria proposed for the definition of genre are that the behavior involved in any particular case should be the result of the dynamic application by all the participants of the synoptic specifications for engaging in the relevant staged, goal-oriented, social process (Martin, Christie, and Rothery, 1987; Martin, 1985). These criteria, I would claim, are equally well met by the activities, with their constituent tasks and steps, that make up a curriculum unit, as by the patterns of specifically linguistic behavior that generate spoken or written texts. However, rather than use the same term for both levels, I shall refer to the different genres of action as activity-types, with their constituent "task-types" and possibly also "step-types," and I shall reserve the use of the term genre for discourse at the level of operation. Here, since the operations through which almost all classroom activities are realized make some use of discourse, I shall make a further distinction between discourse constitutive genres (i.e. those in which the operation is fully realized in the discourse) and discourse ancillary genres (i.e those in which the discourse is ancillary to some other form of behavior).

In terms of this latter distinction, the discourse genres identified by those working in the Hallidayan tradition would for the most part be characterized as discourse constitutive. Indeed, in some of these cases, such as whole-class instruction or teacher-led class discussion, the activity is fully operationalized through the discourse genre. However, there are other types of activity and task in which discourse plays only an ancillary role, such as in relation to dance, model making, or practical activities in science. To date, the discourse that accompanies the realization of these activities has received much less attention (but cf. Barnes, 1976; Barnes et al., 1969). One of our aims will therefore be to discover the similarities and differences between these discourse ancillary genres and the better understood discourse constitutive genres. It may still be the case, for example, that some of the discourse microgenres that have already been identified, such as triadic dialogue, are also recruited in the achievement of the tasks and steps through which these more practical activities are operationalized.

Having taken the concept of genre, originally developed to describe the organization of specifically linguistic activity, and extended it to the description of activity more generally, it is worth asking whether the same step can be taken with respect to the concept of register. Here, too, the answer seems to be in the affirmative, for there appears to be a very close fit between the three dimensions of register – field, tenor, and mode – and the three dimensions that were proposed for the analysis of operations. This is perhaps not surprising, since Halliday sees these dimensions as activated by the semiotic properties of the situations that predict the linguistic features of the texts that are generated within them. And since the generation of text is a form of social action, it seems plausible that the same categories should also apply to the situational conditions that determine the form in which 'action' more generally is operationalized. In other words, the manner in which an action is operationalized will depend upon the participants' evaluation of what type of behavior and interpersonal interaction and what semiotic tools, including genres of discourse, are appropriate for achieving the goal of the action in the light of the affordances and constraints of the situation.

In expounding the concept of register, Halliday has a tendency to characterize the relationship between a situation-type and the texts that are generated within it as a unilateral one, with situation-type determining text-type. However, he also emphasizes the two-faced nature of the concept. In exercising choices with respect to what they make the focus of joint attention (field), how they relate to each other (tenor), and the role of language in their interaction (mode), the participants are not bound by a preexisting situation-type but can, within certain limits set by the physical conditions and the social conventions to which they subscribe, define the situation-type by means of the type of text they jointly create. That is to say, within the limits set by the affordances and constraints of the situation, participants are able to enact the beliefs and values they espouse by choosing to interact in one way rather than another – by minimizing social distance rather than maximizing it, for example, or by sharing equally in the process of text-production rather than allowing it to be a monologic process (Hasan, 1985).

Similarly, by extension, if the three dimensions of register govern the manner in which action is operationalized, the choices that are made are not entirely situation-determined, for by choosing to operationalize action in one way rather than another, the participants are able, within limits, to modify the situation in which they act. By the same token, the choices that are made reveal the participants' beliefs about the nature and value of the activity in which they are involved.

This extension of the scope of register beyond the purely linguistic to the domain of social action in general is compatible, I would argue, with the way in which the category of activity was interpreted in the study referred to earlier by Wertsch et al. (1984). Although the two sets of adults performed the same action with the children, the manner in which they operationalized the action of completing the puzzle array led the authors to describe them as engaging in different activities. In choosing to encourage the children's independent problem solving by exercising low control over their actions, the teachers were seen to be engaging in the activity of education; by contrast, the mothers' choice of a more controlling style of interaction was seen to be the realization of the different activity of completing the task as efficiently as possible. In terms of the concept of register, therefore, the two sets of adults selected different values on the dimensions of tenor and mode and thus employed different registers in their interactions with the children. In so doing, they constituted the action of completing the puzzle array as instances of different types of activity and, in the process, they created somewhat different situations for the children to work within.

It could be argued that the activity that all teachers are engaged in is, by definition, the Practice of Education. However, differences somewhat similar to those observed by Wertsch et al. can be observed between individual teachers in the ways in which they actually set up and perform the actions that constitute that activity. By the choice of topics to focus on and activities to engage in, by the manner in which they relate to their students, and by the roles that they arrange for semiotic tools to play in the tasks that the students are required to carry out, teachers create different situation-types within which the texts of action are generated. And the choices that they make are governed, not only by the situations in which they work, but also by their differing beliefs about the goals of education and about the nature of the learning–teaching relationship that were discussed in the opening section of this chapter. Register is thus a potentially powerful concept for exploring the relationship between teachers' conceptualizations of the Practice of Education and the actions and operations through which they are realized, as these are observed in actual classroom practice.

To summarize these proposals, then, I am suggesting that the categories of genre and register, which were originally developed to account for variations in the patterns of linguistic behavior that occur in situations in which discourse is the primary mode of social action, can be extended, in principle, to account for the patterns of behavior through which all forms of social action are realized. Register, I suggest, provides a way of accounting for the choices that participants make in deciding what forms of action to engage in and the manner in which to operationalize these actions according to the prevailing situational conditions. These choices, it can be hypothesized, will be influenced by their interpretation of the sort of activity in which they wish to engage. Furthermore, they will determine the choices participants make from their repertoires of linguistic and nonlinguistic behavioral resources. Genre, on the other hand, provides a way of characterizing the organization of the chosen actions and operations in terms of socially shared specifications of the constituent elements and their sequential arrangement. Activity-types characterize the generic organization of the activities that make up a curricular unit, while constitutive and ancillary discourse genres and microgenres characterize the organization of the actual linguistic behavior by means of which these activities are operationalized. Figure 5.1 provides a schematic representation of the relationships between these various categories.

Applying the Model: Co-constructing the Meaning of Time

Having sketched this tentative proposal for an integrated theory of discourse and activity, I intend to devote the second part of this chapter to an attempt to apply this synoptic model in a more dynamic (partial) analysis of selected episodes from one curricular unit. In particular, my aim will be to utilize the model to explore the different roles played by the microgenre of triadic dialogue in some of the activities and tasks through which the goals of the curricular unit were achieved.

The unit that I wish to examine took place in a combined grade three and four class in a downtown school in Toronto which serves a population that is both multilingual and mixed in terms of social class background.[2] The data are drawn from video-recorded observations and from informal

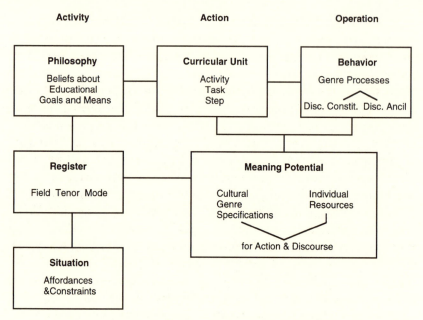

Figure 5.1 Framework for the Articulation of Activity and Discourse.

interviews with the teacher and students concerned (Wells and Chang, 1997). Only the fifteen grade three students were involved in this unit on time, as the grade four students were engaged in a unit on forensic science. The teacher, on the other hand, was responsible for both these science units simultaneously. Within the integrated program that characterized this classroom, work on the science unit was typically scheduled for the first half of the morning on two days each week, although on several occasions the period was extended to the whole morning. The unit as a whole extended over approximately six weeks.

In planning this unit, the teacher had several objectives in mind. These included making provision for activities that allowed the students, working in groups, to gain first-hand experience of trying to solve practical problems of measuring time. She was equally concerned, however, that the "hands-on" work should be complemented by "minds-on" work (Driver, 1983) and, to this end, she created a stimulating environment in which, in addition to the necessary materials for the hands-on activities, reference books and writing materials were also freely available. She also required the students to keep a science journal, in which they recorded their experiments and observations and also their thoughts about them.

In addition to conferences with small groups about work in progress, she also intended to have meetings with the whole group in order to plan and review the work they were doing and to relate what they were discovering to their existing knowledge and experience.

Looked at in the light of the theoretical model, this account of the teacher's intentions can be seen as both an indication of her philosophy of education and a specification of the register to be adopted, which, in turn, predicts the sorts of activities that will be likely to occur and the manner in which they will be operationalized. In line with the sociocultural theory of learning and teaching that she espouses, she intends to present the students with a variety of challenges in relation to the theme of time and, in the light of their responses, to engage with them in interaction about the tasks they will be tackling, in order to provide guidance and support that will enable each of them to extend their knowledge and skills in their zones of proximal development. In terms of register, the field with which they will be concerned involves concepts related to time and activities that allow experimentation and group problem solving, using the materials made available; there will also be discussion as well as instruction in relation to these activities. With respect to tenor, the students will be expected to work collaboratively in groups, with the teacher available to provide support and guidance when necessary; they will also be expected to participate actively in whole group sessions in which the teacher takes a leading role. With respect to mode, personal experience will be treated as of equal importance with the culturally approved account of the phenomena to be investigated; language will be involved in almost all activities, sometimes in a constitutive role and sometimes as an ancillary to the achievement of the goal of the extralinguistic activity; both spoken and written texts will be generated and all students will be expected to be actively involved in these processes.

With this overview of the teacher's intentions in mind, let us now consider one of the constituent activities (or curriculum genres, as Christie [1991] would call them) through which this curricular unit was realized. It occurred early on and was one in which the students could choose from several alternative topics, all of which were designed to render problematic their taken-for-granted notions of the measurement of time. The goal of the particular activity I observed, as communicated to the students by the teacher, was to imagine that they lived in a world without clocks and watches and to invent a method of timing how long it took to empty a bottle of water. The group of three girls that I observed – Emily, Veronica

Table 5.2. *Tasks and Steps Involved in the Measuring Time Activity*

Activity: Inventing a method of Time Measurement

Tasks:

1. *Preparation*, which consisted of (a) collecting the materials they thought were needed, (b) taking them to a suitable location, (c) filling the bottles with water, and (d) discussing what exactly they were going to do.

2. *Experiment (Part One)*, which involved (a) a first trial, which was marked by some confusion about what exactly they were trying to do, and (b) a decision to seek advice from the teacher.

3. *Conference*, a discussion with the teacher, which the teacher used to go over with them again (a) the purpose of the activity, (b) the alternative means they might use, and (c) the 'problems' she wanted them to address.

4. *Experiment (Part Two)*, which consisted of (a) filling their identical bottles with water, (b) taking turns to empty their bottles into a plastic basin while a designated group member rhythmically clapped two plastic cups together and counted the number of claps until the bottle was empty, (c) a brief discussion of why Lily was slower than the other two, in order to decide how to proceed; (d) at this point, Emily went to fetch everybody's science logs so that they could record their results.

5. *Group Writing Conference*, initiated by Emily: (a) she announces the three questions they are to answer, then, after (b) a brief interruption caused by the proximity of another group, (c) she initiates a discussion of why it took Lily longer to empty her bottle than it took the others. This was interrupted by the teacher joining the group.

6. *Conference with Teacher*, consisting of (a) reporting progress to date, including the preceding discussion of reasons for Lily being slower, (b) planning how to do the experiment again with the angle of pouring held constant across all three children.

7. *Experiment (Part Three)*, consisting of a number of further trials similar to Task 4, in which 'winning' gradually comes to be as important a goal as the 'official' goal of inventing and perfecting a method of measuring time.

8. *Clearing Up* (not observed).

9. *Report Writing* (not observed).

and Lily[3] – spent about an hour in total on this activity, including writing a report of what they had done in their science journals. As can be seen from Table 5.2, the activity quite spontaneously broke into a number of relatively distinct tasks.

As the titles indicate, the major elements in the realization of this activity involve fairly easily recognizable tasks. For some of the constituent steps, too, it is relatively easy to imagine what took place. (Unfortunately, I was not able to stay until the end of the morning and so am unable to document the steps involved in the last two tasks.) To that extent, we can recognize the event as an activity-type which consists of a number of different task-types nested within it. It is also apparent that, at this level of delicacy, these task-types can be seen as predicted by the teacher's choice of register, discussed above.

Of course, the segmentation of an activity into constituent tasks and steps is necessarily somewhat arbitrary and is, in any case, performed by the analyst, post hoc, on the basis of reviewing the video recording and the resulting transcript. For the participants, on the other hand, the boundaries may be less clear-cut and occur at different points for different individuals, according to the nature of their involvement. In a few cases, the structure of the activity may itself impose the boundary between tasks as, for example when a period of waiting is brought to an end by the occurrence of the anticipated event (e.g. the return of Emily at the beginning of Task 5). But usually the transition is brought about by the attempt of one of the participants to shift to a new task and, since the proposal has to be accepted by the other participants in order to become a reality, there may be a protracted period during which the change is negotiated.

Another way of looking at these boundaries between tasks is in terms of a change on one or more of the dimensions of their operationalization. The change of semiotic tools when Emily initiates the writing up of the experiment so far marks a clear boundary between Tasks 4 and 5. In the present case, too, several boundaries were created by a change in the participants, this being most sharply marked when the teacher joined or left the group. From viewing the video-tape, it is very apparent that the children oriented differently to each other depending on whether the teacher was a member of the group or not. When one of the dimensions of register changes, there is a concomitant change in the operation. And this holds even when, as in the case of the boundary between Tasks 5 and 6, the goal of the task remains very largely unchanged.

The presence or absence of the teacher was also associated with differences on the other two dimensions associated with operation: the nature of the nonverbal behavior in which the participants were engaged and the semiotic tools, including talk, that the participants utilized to mediate the achievement of their goal. In most of the tasks that the girls performed when alone, their goal was focally concerned with the actions required to time the emptying of the bottles, and bottles, basin and pail of water were all mediating artifacts that they recruited to the achievement of their goal. In these tasks, discourse was an additional artifact, but with an ancillary role with respect to the physical activity; the girls used it largely as a means of coordinating and commenting on their actions with the material artifacts.

The two tasks performed with the teacher, as well as the group writing conference, on the other hand, were quite different in this respect. Here the goal was either problem formulation and consideration of potential solutions, or retrospective review of actions performed in order to evaluate their significance with respect to the problem to be solved. In these tasks, discourse was the dominant artifact, while the bottles and cups, etc. were now cast in the ancillary role of being used occasionally to demonstrate, as opposed to perform, the actions in question. In other words, whereas the presence of the material artifacts was essential for the performance of the practical tasks, it was entirely optional in the conference tasks. In the latter, on the other hand, it was the artifact of discourse that was essential for, by exploiting the symbolic potential of language, they were able to free themselves to some extent from the tyranny of actuality and to operate in the hypothetical mode. This activity thus shows very clearly a major difference between discourse genres that are constitutive and those that are ancillary.

If we now turn to a transcript of the discourse itself, we can see correlates of these differences in the content and organization of the discourse that occurred. For reasons of space, however, only representative episodes from the two types of task are included in the following transcript.

Task 3: Conference with Teacher

Immediately before this episode, the teacher and students have been looking at the textbook they are using,[4] in which instructions are given for performing the activity.

> *1 T:* Here the picture (a cartoon of children doing the activity) suggests that you can clap, but are there other ways that you can use to figure out how . long it takes for the bottle to empty?
>
> *2 E:* Stamp your feet
>
> *3 T:* Stamp your feet, good . another way?
>
> *4 E:* Er snap
>
> *5 T:* Snap . .
> OK, besides using your hands and feet, what other methods could you think of ?

6 L: <Stop-watch>

7 T: No, you're not supposed to use a clock and a watch

8 V: * * * *

9 T: OK, so I put the problem to you: think of as many ways as you can . to figure out the time it takes . for you (= E) to empty the bottle compared to her (= L), compared to . er Veronica
Now the next problem I would like you to think about is . . what are- what the three of you are doing . is it a fair test?
The meaning of 'fair test' is if you empty a bottle- say if you (= E) fill the bottle half . and Veronica fills her bottle full . would it be a fair test?

10 V: No

11 E: No . you have to- if I filled my bottle half and to make that a fair test she would fill her bottle half

12 T: That's right . and what about Lily's bottle?

13 E: She would fill her bottle <u>half</u>

14 T: <u>half</u>

So all your three bottles must have the same amount of water
Now how do you ensure the same amount of water?

15 E: Well .

16 T: Do you just estimate?

17 E,V: No

18 T: Ah-ha!
Do we have measuring jugs?

19 E,V: (nod)

20 T: Ah-ha!

So maybe you need to use a measuring jug and say- use the measuring jug, you're going to fill each bottle two hundred and fifty milliliters of water . so then you all have the same amount of water
What's the second fair test?
If you use a pop bottle (to E) and you use a milk bottle (to V) and she (= L) uses a pop can, would it be a fair test?

21 E,V,L: No

22 T: No, why? because <u>the-</u>

23 E: <u>the</u> * of the pop bottle may be bigger <u>than</u> my bottle or the milk bottle

24 V: - <u>hers</u>

25 T: That's right . that might not be a fair test either

Not so much that the bottle is bigger but–
Let's take the three things and have a look
[The girls each pick up the bottle they have chosen]

26 T: Are they the same size? (indicating the bottle mouths)

27 V: No

28 T: Are they the same size? (to Emily)

29 E: No

30 T: Would water fall– flow– How would water flow through these two?

31 E: * * *

32 T: What would you predict? Which would be faster?

33 V: That one would be faster (pointing to one of the bottles)

34 T: Right

35 E: * * * * *

36 T: So for a fair test for the three of you you must make sure . that even if the bottles are different shapes that they have the same– they look– they release the water at the same . time . . the mouth of the bottle must be more or less the same size
So it would be good if the three of you take Fivealive bottles or the three of you take pop bottles

37 E: OK

38 T: OK, so you think about what counts as a fair test

In Task 3, in which the children have approached the teacher to ask for advice, the teacher uses the occasion to achieve her own additional goal – that of ensuring the children understand the purpose of the activity. This leads naturally into a consideration of possible strategies. Here, the discourse genre is that of triadic dialogue, with the teacher asking for suggestions and then evaluating and extending them. She also takes the opportunity to pose a number of challenges, which she calls "problems." The moves in which these are presented do not require an immediate response; instead, they project to a later discussion, following the experimental task, when the children will have constructed a solution which they will be expected to report. Here, therefore, we see the discourse performing a further function – that of creating the larger framework of the activity as a whole.

As far as the content of the discourse is concerned, there are references to a number of actions and objects that might be included in the experiment though, as noted above, these are generally considered in the hypothetical mode. This is signaled by the choice of modal auxiliaries, as in turns 5, 9, 11, 13, 20, and 23 and by the use of "maybe" in 20. There are also a number of "thematic patterns" (Lemke, 1990) associated with the processes of doing an experiment. Of these, the importance of carrying out "a fair test" is the most salient (9, 11, 20) as it is exemplified in relation to a number of possibly relevant variables. But there is also passing reference to such other operations as comparison, as indicated by "comparing" (9), "same" (14, 20), estimation (16) and measuring (18). Here we see the teacher deliberately introducing the children to the discipline-based register of science by talking science with them as, together, they consider the about-to-be-performed experimental task.

Task 4: Experiment (Part Two)

After some further discussion with the teacher, the girls return to their corner of the room and carry out the first trial. They then decide that, on the next trial, they will use a different way of measuring the amount of water in their identical Fivealive bottles.

56 V: Yeh, let's fill them up to the top

57 E: OK . to the brim

58 V: Yeh

59 E: Bring mine too
[They return to the bucket, where some other children are also filling containers with water]

60 E: Can we have the measuring cup please? (to one of Cs)
[C gives E the cup and she starts to fill the bottles. Some inaudible conversation accompanies the filling. They then return to their area and prepare to start the trial]

61 E: OK, one . two, get ready, pour! (said like the official starting a race)

62 L: [empties her bottle, holding it almost horizontally]

63 E: One, two, three, four (clapping the cups and counting the claps) Finish? (to L)

64 L: Yes

65 E: Four, OK, four (i.e. L's turn lasted for a count of 4 claps) . .

66 V: ***

67 E: Yeh, you can pour (to V)
Lily, you take <the cups> and go over <there> . .
One . two . three . go! (starting V's turn)

68 V: [empties her bottle, holding it nearly vertical]

69 E: One, two, three (clapping the cups while V empties the bottle)
Three, good!
Take my cups here (giving cups to L) . .
You *** to Lily (instructing V on her role in the next turn)

70 V: I didn't

71 E: No, Lily, go 'one, two', OK? (demonstrating how to clap the
cups) One . two . *** (said softly, as she is starting herself)
Ready . go!
[empties her bottle, holding it vertically. L claps]

72 V: One, two, three

73 E: (laughs)

74 V: Tied with me <u>*</u> (= E's and V's turns both took 3 claps)

75 E: <u>So</u> me and– we tied
And d'you know wh– (to L)

76 V: So I <tied with you>

77 E: I know, me and Veronica are tied
Do you know why you were slow? (to L)

78 L: * . . .

79 E: OK now um– . <u>what we did–</u>

80 V: <u>****</u>

81 E: What we did– . what we did was we . did a method by timing
Now, d'you guys think it was a fair match?

82 V: Yeh

83 E: Do you? (doubtfully)

84 V: Cos we each used the same . <thing>

85 E: Yeh, let's do the SAME thing– no, let's– .
I'll go get your books . and you guys just . fill them back (referring to
the bottles)

By contrast with the previous task, the focus here is on the doing of
the experiment, and the dominant discourse genre is one in which one
of the moves in each exchange is realized by action. Emily requests the
measuring cup from another child (60) and it is handed over; she permits
Veronica to take her turn at emptying her bottle (67) and Veronica does

so; she instructs Lily on how to clap the cups (71) and Lily follows the instructions. Another interesting structure is that of counting, in which the uttering of successive digits co-occurs with the regular repetition of a non-verbal event as a way of publicly marking and measuring the passage of time; in this case, the verbal move, along with its nonverbal counterpart, can be seen as a kind of response to the action of the pourer. In content, the emphasis is on physical process verbs and on the associated agents and affected objects; but as they are co-present in the situation, they ar' often referred to by exophoric pronouns and pro-forms such as "do" and "thing." There is, however, a partial carry-over from the previous task of the thematic pattern of fair test, although, significantly, in the excitement of doing the task, it is conflated with the more familiar thematic pattern of competition.

Task 5: Group Writing Conference

A few minutes later, Emily returns with the books. When they are all seated, she announces the questions they should use to organize their recording.

86 E: OK now . I want you guys to write down– . ooh!
Now I want you guys to write down what you did . and write down d'you think it's a fair match and write down . who . did it fastest

87 V: Yes . **

88 E: Yes, but that's OK
[There is an interruption of about ten seconds while they watch other children who are moving close to them]

89 E: I want to ask you some questions before we do something

90 V: What?

91 E: Why do you think it was a fair match?

92 V: *

93 E: Lily . your back is to the camera (telling L to move)
Why?

94 V: Cos the bottles were filled to the exact same amount . because exactly the same *

95 E: Yeh, like we counted EXACTLY . *

96 V: <u>Yeh</u> like I ****

97 E: Now . why d'you think . she lost? (referring to L)
Why?

98 V: Cos she was .

99 E: Probably she poured it– probably she poured it slow

100 V: Like she goes like this (demonstrating) and then she–

Task 6: Conference with Teacher

Before Veronica can complete her explanation, the teacher joins the group and initiates discussion by asking for a report on their progress.

101 T: So how are you all doing?

102 E: Fine

103 T: What did you all do?

104 E: Well, what we did was we used cups and then we started um- I start clapping when we <got back> and we counted the exact with the cups–

105 V: Like whenever <u>anyone–</u>

106 E: <u>and then</u> we started pouring the bottles
We (= E and V) were about the same * three and she (= L) had four .
And right now we're wondering why she had four because probably she um . poured out slowly . or- . and probably we poured it out real fast

107 T: You used these containers? (pointing to plastic cups)

108 E: No, we used the Fivealive–

109 T: The Fivealive bottles?

110 E: Yeh, these (= cups) are to keep the beat

111 T: OK, so you– so that is a good observation– you observed . that Lily's count . was much . less– more or less?

112 E: More

113 T: – more . than both of you . and you figure that it's because of the way she poured it
Now, how can you make sure . that it's a fair test between all three of you?

114 E: Well, because <u>we used–</u>

115 T: <u>How can you–</u>

116 E: Well . a fair test– well I don't really think it's fair now because . it was fair we put it the same size of the cup by the measuring cup, but I don't think it was fair because WE poured it– we turned it right over . and LILY just poured it like this, kind of (demonstrating)
So I don't think it was fair . (T: uh-huh) I that– I think that's why she um .. <u>was slow</u>

117 T: *******

118 E: Yeh

119 T: Because she tilted . her bottle–

120 E: **** but** we–

121 T: – a different angle from you ******

122 E: But we just went like that (demonstrating) yeh

123 T: So what– would you re– would you redo the test again? Just to see whether the count is the same?

124 E: OK

125 V: Yeh

Task 5 begins when Emily returns with the science logs and hands them out. When they are all seated, Emily, as group leader, announces the questions they are to use to organize their writing. At this point, the task seems to be one of individual writing, in obedience to Emily's teacherlike indirect command. However, little writing takes place, as another group of children, who are carrying their materials to a table nearby, causes a distraction. When they are settled again, Emily makes a bid to change to a conference task with a further teacherlike move, announcing that she wants to ask some questions. Two sequences follow, in which Emily and Veronica collaborate in constructing an explanation.

Task 6, which starts when the teacher joins the group, is essentially a continuation of Task 5, but with the teacher now directing the discussion. On this occasion, however, not having been present during the experiment, the teacher treats the children as the experts, allowing them to take several long turns to describe what they did and to offer a tentative explanation of their discrepant results; only at the end of this long sequence does she offer an evaluation. The more equal status of the participants in the construction of the text in this episode can also be seen in the number of occasions on which they interrupt each other. In turn 123 the teacher takes over the initiating role again and, at this point, the discourse reverts to a pattern similar to that seen in the latter part of Task 3, when she was instructing them on what they had to do.

In both Tasks 5 and 6, the thematic patterns highlight reflection rather than action. Although many of the same lexical items are used as in the experimental task, there are two significant differences. First, the use of past tense signals that the participants are reporting events that have already taken place rather than negotiating or directing ongoing action. Second, several of the clauses describing physical processes are embedded in clauses that contain metadiscoursal verbs, such as "ask," "think," and "wonder." The overall concern is thus with explanation of action rather than with the action itself.

Looking back over the activity as a whole, we can see that, in general, the discourse is ancillary to the achievement of the goal, which is, officially – that is to say, by the teacher's definition – to invent a method of measuring time and to record the results of the experiment. At this macro level, the activity-type determines how the participants relate to each other and how they orient to the material objects and processes that constitute the content of the activity. However, when we look at the constituent tasks, the picture can be seen to be more complex. First, the definition of the goal of each task is negotiated in the course of pursuing it and this leads, over the activity as a whole, to the emergence of an alternative goal for the activity, namely to see who can win the pouring match. Second, at the level of the constituent tasks, the relationship between action and discourse varies, with some tasks involving a constitutive discourse genre rather than an ancillary one. In these cases, it is as if a discourse genre, that could, under other circumstances, function as the operationalization of an activity in its own right, has been embedded as the operationalization of a unit at a lower level on the action rank-scale. Overall, however, it is clear that both the nature of the tasks and the transitions between them are co-constructed through the discourse that operationalizes the superordinate action-oriented goal of the activity as a whole.

There is clearly a great deal more that could be said about the detail of this token of the activity-type of experiment and about the different discourse genres that occur in the performance of the constituent tasks. However, I wish to turn now to a different sort of activity, one in which the teacher led a review of the work they had done with the whole group.

Reviewing the Unit: What Have We Learned?

Over the weeks following the events just described, the students engaged in a variety of practical activities, including investigating the factors that determine a pendulum's rate of swing and designing their own timing device. Running throughout the unit as a subtext to the main theme of time was the issue of experimental methodology: the need to control all but the experimental variable in order that the experiment should be a fair test. This thematic formation, as Lemke (1985, 1990) terms it, constantly recurred, both in the teacher's talk and in that of the students (cf. Tasks 4 and 5 above), although, as Lemke notes, this is no guarantee that it was understood in the same way by all the participants. This is apparent in the episode transcribed below.

As the unit was drawing to a close, the teacher called the class together to review the work they had been doing. Her intention was to consolidate the learning that had been taking place in the different groups by talking it over in the group as a whole, thereby making it common knowledge (Edwards and Mercer, 1987). She also wanted the students to make connections among the various different activities in which they had engaged and to move towards a more principled understanding of some of the key ideas that they had encountered. At the same time, however, she wanted to hear and validate the students' opinions, both because she considered them to be important in their own right and because she wanted the common knowledge that was constructed to develop from the sense that *they* had made as well as from the conventionally accepted beliefs of the scientific community. These, then, were some of the choices with respect to field, tenor, and mode that she intended should govern the situation and shape the text to be constructed in the activity.

When the students were quietly assembled in a semicircle on the rug, the teacher started the review by asking "What have you learned about time?" This opening question established the field for the discussion and immediately elicited several replies, each of which offered a personal experience relevant to the general theme, which was accepted and briefly commented on by the teacher in a way that drew out its more general significance. In this way the teacher established the tenor of the discussion by validating the student responses, thereby indicating that the topics to be discussed were to come from them. At the same time, however, she was on the lookout for contributions from the students that she judged to have the potential for further development. The first of these was offered by Auritro.

> *07 A:* Counting isn't always accurate
>
> *08 T:* Counting is not accurate, so there are certain pa– ways of .
> timing that some are more accurate and some are less accurate, for example like counting
> What is more accurate than counting?

In her follow-up to Auritro's introduction of the topic of accuracy of measurement, the teacher makes explicit his tacit comparison with other possible methods by putting his observation back to the group in the form of a question. This enables other children to bring in their expertise and, over the next twenty turns, they recall the various devices that they have experimented with. Then, in turn 31, the teacher asks them to think about which methods are *least* accurate. This elicits two answers, the second of which, from Bianca, acts as the bridge to the second main topic of the discussion.

> *34 Bi:* If you <use> your heart-beat sometimes your heart-beat gets faster, like fai– um– like you've– like you've been– you've got um so many– like a lot of energy and then <you're trained> to get your heart-beat and then because you've got a lot of energy you feel like running around and then you start running around your heart-beat's going to get faster
> <so it changes>
>
> *35 T:* And I think er Bianca is bringing things to another part of this science unit <that you have> . the processes of science (writing on board) .

The development of this topic is worth looking at in more detail, as it relates to the issue of experimental methodology that we already saw being discussed in the first activity. Here it is in relation to the work on pendulums that this thematic pattern is taken up and developed.

> *41 T:* OK . why must we control our variables?
>
> *42 Te:* Because if we don't, the time won't be accurate and so you won't get the correct timing
>
> *43 T:* Not so much the time is not accurate, what is not accurate?
>
> *44 Bi:* It's not a fair test
>
> *45 T:* It's not a fair test . a fair test. . . (writing)
> Your experiments are your tests . the fair test– or your science experiment . . . . (writing) or what you call your science testing– your testing– all your various methods would not be . fair, 'fair' here meaning . . (writing) consistent, right? . .
> Remember when you did the pendulum, when one group did the bob . changing the weight of the bob, one group changing the type of bob, one group changing the release height . and all of us did changing the length . that– what– when you want to change the release height what was constant?
> What was the variable we held constant?
> Your group? (to Tema)

46 Te: Our group . we um . had to change it and we kept on skipping the same amount

47 T: No, you're not listening to my question, Tema .
I said when we were testing– finding out whether . the release height made a difference, what was– what were the variables you kept constant? . .

48 Te What we kept constant was the same– the same length of string, the same um amount of bob ***

49 T: That's right, the same bob, and the same length of string . and what you would change was your . release height
In your group, what was- what was the one you did?
Veronica?

50 V: Um we did er the same thing and we had to add them on

51 T: Mm?

52 E: Add the–

53 V: Add the er washers on

54 T: So, the weight of the bob
So what did you keep constant? What were the variables you kept constant so that it was a fair test every time?

55 E: We kept the same bob . like *

56 X: *

57 T: No, you were testing–

58 Bi: It was the– it– we– the same type of bob

59 T: The same type of bob, washer
What else did you keep constant?

60 J: Um the height–

61 T: The height . the release height–

62 J: –the release-

63 T: What else did you keep constant

64 E: The length of the string

65 T: The length of the pendulum . just to find out whether the weight of the bob makes a difference

There is no doubt that, in these exchanges, the teacher knows what information she is trying to elicit. She had, after all, been present during the experiments and discussed what they were doing with each group. However, this is not a quiz. She is not testing the students to see whether they can give the correct answer. Rather, the purpose is to establish an agreed account of what they did that will serve as an instantiation of the practice of controlling the independent variables to ensure that it is "a fair test." This is brought out very clearly in the exchange which concludes this episode:

> 73 *T:* So that is an example of what we mean by 'a fair test'
> And that– do you . think about variables and fair tests not just in pendulums, but in everything you do? . .
> Yes or no?
>
> 74 *Ch:* Yes
>
> 75 *T:* Yes, it's very important in science
> Those are some of the science processes you have to think about . OK?

After some further discussion of the timers that the students themselves had invented, the teacher returns to the opening question and a new topic is initiated, again on the basis of a student's response.

> 91 *T:* What else did we learn . in the total of this unit– What did YOU learn? you tell me what you learned
>
> 92 *Te:* I learned that time may not only be in seconds, you may . see it as a minute, a second and a second is made up of . quite a few fast counts
>
> 93 *T:* That's right, a second–
> OK, how many children know how many seconds make up a minute?
> [several children indicate they want to answer]
>
> 94 *T:* Lily
>
> 95 *L:* Sixty (very softly)
>
> 96 *T:* Sixty . and how many minutes make up an hour?

As can be seen from these opening exchanges, this topic is developed in a very different manner. Here the teacher is very definitely checking to ensure that the students know this basic information, and the structural pattern of the exchanges is the familiar three-part one, with teacher evaluation as the third move. From seconds, they proceed through minutes, hours, and days, to end with a more extensive discussion of the basis for the extra day in leap years.

After some fifty turns, there is another natural closure and, without prompting, Tema introduces a new topic by referring to what she discovered when she experimented with pendulums the previous year

(141). This is followed by another student initiation on the topic of different sources of power for clocks and watches (151). Then at 161, the teacher makes her only explicit topic initiation by picking up the previous topic of days, months, and years as units of time and asking how each is related to the different movements of the earth. This topic continues for some forty-six turns until, in a brief pause while two students go to fetch the globe, Bianca raises her hand and, being given permission to speak, she introduces what is to be the final topic, that of time zones and time differences between different places.

> Bi: Well, um, you know last night I was going to bed something like um I think nineish (T: Uh-huh) like quarter to ten- I can't exactly remember but um my sister said that um- I asked her um 'Guess how lo- guess what time it is in Scotland' (Bianca had recently arrived in Toronto from Scotland, where she had lived previously) and she goes 'I think it's um about ten o'clock' and I go 'But it's only ten o'clock here, it can't be ten o'clock over there'

In fact, this proves to be the most extended of all the topics, as many of the students have relatives in other parts of the world and several take quite extended turns to recount experiences similar to Bianca's.

Finally, with the ringing of the school bell, the discussion comes to a close. It had lasted approximately forty-five minutes and, during that time, eight different topics had been discussed, several at considerable length. As the following summary shows (Table 5.3), all but one of them was introduced by one or other of the students. In total, there were one hundred and ten exchanges, distributed as shown in the final column. Of these, all but twenty-six started with a teacher question and almost all contained a final move in which the teacher followed up on the preceding student contribution.

These rather crude statistics raise a number of interesting questions about the function(s) of the IRF exchange in teacher–student interaction.

A Reevaluation of the IRF Exchange

As I have just indicated, the dominant discourse genre throughout the review discussion was what Lemke (1990) calls "triadic dialogue," that is to say, a sequence of IRF exchanges. This, as many observers have pointed out, is ubiquitous in classroom interactions in which the teacher

Table 5.3. *An Overview of the Review Discussion*

	Topic	Initiator	No. of Exchanges
Episode 1	Introduction: Personal experiences	Teacher	3
Episode 2	Accuracy: Need for standard measurement – comparing various methods used by groups	Auritro	10
Episode 3	"Processes of science": Fair test, variables – reviewing experiments on pendulums	Bianca	20
Episode 4	Checking knowledge of units of time	Tema	16
Episode 5	Previous work with pendulums – personal recollection	Tema	4
Episode 6	Sources of power for clocks and timers – students' personal experiences	Bianca	4
Episode 7	Basis for units of time in earth's movement – demonstration using various artifacts	Teacher	13
Episode 8	Time differences between time zones – exploring personal anecdotes, using globe	Bianca	40

is one of the participants. However, to suggest, on that basis, that the complete activity was all of a piece would be seriously misleading.

One of the distinctions that needs to be made is hinted at by the difference between the two terms that have been used to describe the third move in the three-part exchange. Sinclair and Coulthard (1975) refer to it as Follow-up, while Mehan (1979) and others refer to it as Evaluate. Evaluation is certainly the dominant function of the third move in the exchanges in Episode 4, in which the teacher checked the students' knowledge of the "consists of" relationship between seconds, minutes, hours, and so on. However, in dealing with the other topics, the third move functions much more as an opportunity to extend the student's answer, to draw out its significance, or to make connections with other parts of the students' total experience during the unit. (A similar distinction is made between "low" level and "high" level evaluation in the paper already cited by Nystrand and Gamoran (1991).) These are clearly quite distinct functions, stemming from quite different choices with respect to the tenor dimension of register, that is to say the interpersonal relations between the participants. As Barnes (1976) has argued, these different functions also have markedly different contributions to make to the students' learning.

A second significant feature of this discussion is the way in which the different topics are established. With the exception of Episode 7, the topic of each episode is co-constructed by teacher and students together, rather than being preselected by the teacher. Even here, however, there are some interesting differences. In Episodes 1, 2, and 3, the student contribution that was taken up by the teacher and developed into the topic occurred as a response to a teacher question (cf. the discussion of "uptake" by Collins (1982)). From Episode 4 onward, however, (with the exception of Episode 7) the topic results from a volunteered initiation by one of the students. Furthermore, it is almost exclusively in these later episodes that exchanges not in the triadic dialogue mode are found, as students offer quite lengthy contributions and the teacher makes similarly lengthy informing moves. What is at issue here is differences in the extent of equality of participation in the process of text construction, that is to say, differences with respect to the mode dimension of register.

A final difference between the different episodes that is of relevance here is the status of the information under discussion. In the introductory episode (turns 1–6), as already mentioned, the student contributions are somewhat narrowly based in their personal experience. The same is true of the topics proposed in Episodes 5 and 6. However, in Episodes 2 and 3, there is a common point of reference in the various experiments that the groups have been conducting. Everybody can be assumed to have relevant personal experience of the shared activities from which to construct common knowledge. Episode 4, by contrast, is concerned with more general knowledge, not tied to this particular unit of study. With the final two topics, however, the discussion moves beyond immediately shared experience; much of the information is therefore offered as "new" rather than as previously "given." It is this that accounts for the much higher proportion of informing moves in exchange-initial position in these episodes. It is also significant that it is only in relation to these two topics that use is made of other semiotic artifacts to illustrate the concepts under consideration. From the point of view of register, then, these differences can be accounted for in terms of the dimensions of field and mode, respectively.

Thus, one way of capturing these various differences between the different episodes that make up the overall discussion would be to see them as resulting from different choices in relation to one or more of the three register dimensions of the category of operation. In other words, the different episodes can be seen as the discourse realization of different tasks within the overall activity, each having its own specific goal and mode of operationalization. And, indeed, the nature of these different tasks is to some extent indicated by the glosses put on the Episodes in the summary (Table 5.3) above. Viewed in this light, then, the fact that the genre of triadic dialogue was employed in each task would be only part of a complete description of how each task was operationalized in the interaction between teacher and students.

Such a conclusion, however, poses a question about the relationship between the various episodes and the discussion as a whole. Should it be treated as a single instantiation of one discourse genre? At one level, the eight task-related episodes very obviously form one continuous activity, so the term "discussion" seems both to describe this activity and to suggest the genre of discourse that is involved. Each of the episodes is realized through what students of classroom discourse have referred to as a single topically related sequence of exchanges (or topic sequence) and, as could readily be demonstrated, there is both continuity and comparability between them on several important linguistic dimensions. On the other hand, as has been argued above, there are also important differences between these episodes, corresponding to the goals of the different tasks that they serve to operationalize.

The solution that I wish to propose to this dilemma is one that was prefigured above in the discussion of the experimental activity of inventing a method of timing the emptying of a bottle. There, it will be recalled, it was suggested that the primary analysis of classroom events should be based on the categories derived from activity theory, with the discourse being seen as one of the semiotic tools used to mediate the achievement of the goal of an activity or of one of its constituent tasks. In discussing the bottle-emptying experimental activity, a number of distinct tasks was identified, each of which was operationalized in a manner which utilized discourse as either ancillary or constitutive, depending on the goal of the particular task. To evaluate the genre of discourse employed, therefore, it would also be necessary to consider the task involved and its relation to the overall activity.

The same approach is proposed in the present case. Here the activity-type, which we might term a review, is operationalized through what might be called a teacher-led discussion. However, this activity consists of a number of distinguishable tasks, each of which has its own distinct goal, realized through its own particular use of the basic discourse genre of triadic dialogue. The similarity between the successive episodes of triadic dialogue that make up the discussion as a whole can, I believe, be attributed, first, to the fact that, unlike in the experimental activity, there is continuity of participants across all the tasks and, second, to the constitutive role that the discourse plays in each. The differences, on the other hand, can be attributed to the different goals of the various tasks and to the different choices of field, tenor, and mode in the use of the same basic discourse genre to achieve those goals.

What this suggests is that the notion of discourse genre can only be applied very loosely in the characterization of the discourse through which an activity as a whole is operationalized. Where the activity consists of a number of distinct tasks, the discourse genre selected is likely to vary according to the goal of each task, as in the case of the experimental activity that was discussed earlier. And even when the same basic discourse genre is used in successive tasks, as in the case of the review activity, the function it performs is likely to vary depending on the goal of each particular task, and possibly also on the position of the task in relation to the evolving goal of the activity as a whole, which is being jointly constructed by students and teacher together. To characterize the discourse genre of the review activity as a whole as "discussion using triadic dialogue" would thus be to suggest a homogeneity that does not exist.

On the basis of this, admittedly, small corpus of classroom data, therefore, I should like to suggest that, in order to achieve a more adequate understanding of classroom discourse, it will be helpful to place it in the larger context of the theory of activity developed by Leont'ev (1981) and others. More specifically, I am proposing that both its internal characteristics and its relation to accompanying nonverbal behavior will best be understood by treating discourse as just one of the semiotic tools that may be utilized in the operationalization of action, that is to say in the enactment of a negotiated or teacher-selected activity. Furthermore, since an activity may consist of a number of constituent or related tasks – each having its own goal, and perhaps involving different choices on one or more of the dimensions of register, including different uses of the available semiotic tools – I suggest that the selection and deployment of discourse genres will best be understood if genres are seen as being recruited by tasks rather than by activities.[5]

Conclusion

From its inception, one of the central concerns of sociocultural theory has been to gain a greater understanding of the Practice of Education with its two interrelated goals. These are, first, to ensure cultural continuity through the transmission to each new generation of the artifacts which embody the achievements of the past; and, second, to enable individual students to appropriate these artifacts and to transform the associated knowledge and practices into a resource that both empowers them personally and enables them to contribute to the solution of problems facing the larger culture in innovative ways. These goals are preeminently achieved, it has been argued, through problem-solving social activity, mediated by linguistic interaction with teachers and peers (Wells and Chang-Wells, 1992).

However, in order to study particular instances of educational activity, both to understand why they are as they are and to help those involved to act more effectively, it is necessary to have a framework of description that articulates the relationship between the overarching goals and the actual behavior of learners and teachers in the succession of events that constitute the activities, lessons and curricular units in particular classrooms.

In this chapter, I have tried to take a first step in this direction by bringing together the insights of leading contributors in the two fields of activity theory and systemic discourse theory and showing their essential compatibility. On this basis, I have sketched an approach to the analysis of classroom events that integrates these two theories to provide a principled way of accounting for the different patterns of discourse that play a part in almost every type of learning-and-teaching activity. Although still to be tested on a larger and more heterogeneous corpus of data, this approach, I believe, will also provide a method for looking at discourse as one of the modes of action through which the Practice of Education is differentially operationalized, depending on the underlying theories about learning and teaching to which different teachers subscribe.

However, the framework proposed is clearly incomplete, leaving unspecified, as it does, the particular activity-types and discourse genres that need to be distinguished and defined, and the relationships between these and the choices that are made on the three dimensions of register. It also leaves for further investigation the assumption underlying the concept of genre – namely, that the synoptic specifications of particular genres of

activity and discourse, conceived in terms of obligatory and optional elements and their sequential organization, are actually realized in the texts
that are created in the dynamics of classroom interaction. On the basis of
the small amount of evidence considered here, it appears that, the greater
the equality of participation by teachers and students in the processes of
text creation, the more varied and idiosyncratic are likely to be the resulting texts. However, although likely to have far-reaching consequences if
correct, this conjecture must be considered purely hypothetical until it
has been subjected to further empirical investigation.

A further, and perhaps more serious, limitation of this chapter is that,
throughout, the perspective adopted is predominantly that of the teacher.
In practice, of course, students also have 'theories of education' as well
as goals for the activities in which they engage, and these may not be
– indeed, probably are not – congruent with those of the teacher.[6] In
fact, this covert lack of conguence is made overt in the experimental
activity discussed above, where Emily introduces her goal of making the
experiment "a fair match" (81).

Two reasons can be given in defense of the teacher-oriented perspective
adopted here. First, although it is certainly the case that the situated,
dynamic construction of activity, task, and discourse genre on any occasion
is the outcome of negotiation among all the participants, it is also the case
that the teacher's "intentions" play a substantially greater role than the
students' on most occasions, particularly in relation to the superordinate
categories. As Dewey puts it:

> The plan, in other words, is a cooperative enterprise, not a dictation. The teacher's
> suggestion is not a mold for a cast-iron result but is a starting point to be developed
> into a plan through contributions from the experience of all engaged in the learning
> process. . . . The essential point is that the purpose grow and take shape through
> the process of social intelligence. (1938 p. 72) [7]

At the present time, however, it is an almost insuperable problem to
bring the perspectives of all the participants to bear in an analysis of the
moment-by-moment unfolding of events, and to do so in a manner that
can be reported in a paper of this length. The second reason for the stance
adopted in this paper is therefore strategic: my prime intention has been
to sketch a proposal for the articulation of discourse and activity in rather
general terms. However, in further work, I hope to develop this model in
the direction of a more adequate account of the multiple perspectives that
need to be taken into consideration, and of ways in which the participants'
different activities can be brought into greater convergence, leading to a

common goal – a *shared* learning-and-teaching activity-type – which is, presumably, what the teacher, at least, would hope to achieve.

Despite its present limitations, however, I believe the model outlined here has a certain value. For, on this occasion, the results of applying it to the recorded observations made over the course of one unit of science in one classroom, have provided a basis for calling into question the oversimplified account of the three-part IRF sequence – which was the point of departure for this chapter. As I hope to have shown, when viewed within an integrated theory of discourse and activity, episodes of this discourse genre which are similar in the sequential structure of moves making up their constituent exchanges are seen to operationalize quite different actions. Recruited in the realization of different task goals, they thus have quite different contributions to make to the enactment of the teaching-learning relationship.

Three particular instances are worth recalling. Most stereotypical is Episode 4 in the review activity, in which the teacher checks on and consolidates the students' knowledge of the constitutive relationship between standard units of time. Contrasted with this is Task 3 in the experimental activity, in which the teacher employs the triadic dialogue genre to help Emily and her friends envisage the problems to be solved in their experiment and the conditions that will have to be met in order to make their experiment a fair test. Finally, we might consider Episode 3 of the review activity, in which the same basic discourse genre is used to help the students to reenvision the activities in which they have engaged as particular instances of the application of this scientific principle and, thereby, to construct it as part of the group's common knowledge.

If the triadic dialogue genre – and the succession of IRF exchanges, of which it consists – were always used to achieve goals similar to those of the first of these examples, there would be good reason to join with Wood (1992) in calling for its demise. However, as the second and third examples clearly show, this genre can also be used to achieve other, and more productive, goals, including the co-construction of knowledge on the basis of ideas and experiences contributed by the students as well as the teacher.

Finally, when the third part of this structure is characterized as follow-up, rather than more narrowly as evaluation, there are compelling reasons for seeing the IRF sequence as the prototypical action structure for the achievement of the overarching goals of education, as these were defined above. As teachers, our task is to present our students with challenging activities of various kinds, including thought-provoking questions, that initiate new cycles of knowing. Our hope is that, if our challenges are well chosen, they will engage the students' interest and stimulate them to respond by making their own sense of the problem and by constructing a personal solution to it with the resources, both personal and cultural, that they have at their disposal. This response then provides the basis for us to follow up with teaching that is tailored to their particular needs and informed by the wider cultural context. And, as happens in the third move of the IRF exchange – when this discourse genre is used effectively – it is in this third step in the co-construction of meaning that the next cycle of the learning-and-teaching spiral has its point of departure.

Notes

1. The naming of these levels presents some problems of nomenclature, as "activity" rather than "action" is the term most readily used in school settings to refer to the major components of a unit of curricular study. In the remainder of this chapter, therefore, I shall use the term "activity" to refer to such major curricular components. When referring to the categories of "activity," "action" and "operation" within activity theory, on the other hand, I shall adopt the convention of enclosing them in double quotes.
2. In many respects, the children in this combined grade 3 and grade 4 class are fairly typical of those in Toronto schools in general, in being drawn from a wide social and cultural background. Some live in the area, which borders on the city's Chinatown; others live in more distant parts of Metropolitan Toronto and travel to school each day with a parent who works in one of the nearby hospitals or office complexes. Parental occupations range from laboring and service jobs to the professions of medicine and law. Some of the children are members of large extended families; others live with a single parent. Some have several siblings; others have none. The majority of them are bilingual; most were born in Canada but a small number are recent arrivals in Canada and are still in the early stages of learning English. Almost all these children speak a language other than English at home and some are literate in that language. A small number have learning difficulties of various kinds and are withdrawn for special help on a daily basis; others are designated "gifted," and spend one day a week in a special program in another school. In short, in this class of thirty children there is a very wide range in the current level of their academic performance and in their command of spoken and written English and, in this, they are fairly typical of classes in inner-city schools.
3. Emily and Lily are both Chinese-Canadian children, Veronica is a Caucasian-Canadian. Lily is a recent arrival in Canada, having come from mainland China some fifteen months previously.
4. Peturson, R., Johns, M., and Mutton, R., *Innovations in Science, Level 3*. Toronto: Holt, Rinehart and Winston of Canada, 1990.
5. In the case of single-task activities, of course, the genre selected for the task will apply to the whole activity.

6. This point was justly made by Ellen Ansell, in a contribution to a discussion of the present paper on the xlchc e-mail network (23 Nov. 1992). Her comment initiated a valuable exchange on this subject, which I have drawn on in revising the paper for publication.
7. Quoted by Michael Cole in the e-mail discussion referred to above (xlchc), 24 Nov. 1992.

6   From Guessing to Predicting:

Progressive Discourse in the Learning and Teaching of Science

In the preceding chapter, I argued that triadic dialogue is not necessarily incompatible with a mode of classroom interaction in which students play a part in proposing topics for discussion. The next question to be addressed is whether such collaborative discussion can become progressive; that is to say, can students contribute in such a way that they build on their peers' earlier contributions in a manner that advances the collective understanding of the topic under discussion?

The two episodes to be discussed in this chapter are taken from a curricular unit on mass which took place in the same classroom early in the following school year. Several of the children have continued with the same teacher into what is now a Grade 4/5 class and, as will be seen, a collaborative community of inquiry is becoming quite well established.

The Importance of Predicting When Carrying Out an Experiment

The first activity occurred in the second lesson in this curricular unit and was part of a series devoted to answering the question: "Does mass change when matter changes state?" In the previous lesson, the class had carried out a number of teacher-planned experiments, which involved massing the relevant materials before and after the change of state (e.g. melting a block of ice, dissolving sugar cubes in water) in order to discover whether there had been any change in mass. Today's

From guessing to predicting: Progressive discourse in the learning and teaching of science. In C. Coll and D. Edwards (Eds.), *Teaching, learning and classroom discourse: Approaches to the study of educational discourse* (pp. 67–88). Madrid: Infancia y Aprendizaje, 1997.

lesson is going to be devoted to continuing the experiments, with attention to the procedures necessary to ensure that the experiments are fair tests.

Before starting on the practical work, however, the teacher and students briefly review the previous day's activity and the teacher asks them to recall the predictions they made *prior* to carrying out the experiments. Did they predict that the mass would remain the same, increase or decrease? Starting with the experiment involving the sugar solution, she elicits the answers of those groups that performed this experiment, and writes them on the blackboard. Then, having recorded the predictions for the first experiment, the teacher moves on to the experiment involving melting ice and, turning to John, she asks for his group's predictions.[1]

11 T: Did your group predict before you massed?

12 Jo: Yes . we estimated how much it would–

13 T: I'm not talking about the estimation . .
So you did not do predictions?
(turning to Jessica) What about your group?

14 Je: Um four people said it would decrease –

15 T: (writing) Four people say 'decrease' –

16 Je: – and one person said it was the same

17 T: – one person says 'the same'
What about your group, Tracy? You did the ice too

18 Tr: Yes, but we didn't predict

19 T: You didn't predict . .
Please, guys, it's very important that you do some prediction . .
Now, those people who say 'decrease,' why do you think it decreased? . .
Philips, that day you offered some reasons . Why do you think it would decrease . when it changes state from solid to liquid – the ice?

20 P: Um . because like when it's– ice has some air in it and when it's melted the air will go so it's . um <lighter>

21 T: Uh-huh . so the air– there's air that's trapped in the block of ice will escape as the ice melts and therefore you think the mass will decrease, right?

22 P: Mm

23 T: Any other reasons behind those who say it will decrease?
Yes, Benjamin?

24 B: I said that it would decrease because there was a little bit of air inside the ice and it would um– um it would melt so the <more than . * greater than air> . .

25 T: You say it would decrease but then it would mass MORE? . . I didn't follow, can you repeat what you said, Benjamin?

26 B: Um . when– . it decreases because the air comes out and that means it would . weigh less (softly). mass less

27 T: Are you agreeing with Philips or disagreeing with Philips?

28 B: Agreeing

29 T: You're agreeing with Philips that it would decrease? Now Mr Wells also raised the point– now, when the ice melts Say we froze that water again, what would you predict?

30 An: I have two things to say . The first thing is, if you left it long enough <while> it was melted, some of the water could evaporate . and then, when you froze it, it would add um– it would probably have more air left <then> it might be slightly different or it might be– er or it might increase . depends if you left it <long enough> for the water to evaporate

31 T: Uh-huh . good point! Very good point!

32 Je: I think that if– if the ice melted and then we froze it again, the mass would increase because of the dust and particles in the air, that might like get captured * um onto the ice or into the ice that might–

33 T: into the water

34 Je: Yeh, so it might um– the mass might increase

A few turns later, Benjamin offers a different prediction: if the melted ice were refrozen, he thinks, there would be no change in mass. The teacher is puzzled by the apparent inconsistency between this and his earlier prediction and presses him to be more explicit.

51 T: So you agree that . from ice to melted water . it will decrease because air escapes, but yet from melted water back to ice you don't agree that air will get in and therefore it would increase?

52 B: Cos there's not– there's not as much wind as outside and the air doesn't get pushed around as much

53 T: WIND! . . . There's no wind in this room

54 B: I know! That's what I'm saying, there's wind outside and the air– the air would get in

55 T: Why are you talking about outside? . . We brought in the block of ice . we melt it in the room temperature . and then Philips says it will decrease because of air escaping .
We take the same water . we take it to the staffroom, put it in the freezer and freeze it again, and you say– . where's the wind you're talking about?

56 B: There IS no wind . I'm saying there's no . wind in there compared to outside, so I . I say * * *

57 T: What if you took it outside and let the cold air freeze it, do you think it would increase?

58 B: Yes

59 T: Because you think air would get in?

60 B: Yes

So what is happening here? In what terms should we characterize this episode of classroom discourse? There are clearly many educational issues that could be illuminated by a careful analysis of the event which is (partially) represented in the preceding transcription. However, in the context of the present discussion, the following seem to me to be among those most worthy of attention:

- What is the purpose of this discussion and how does it contribute to the larger goals of the activity and of the curriculum unit as a whole?
- How does the discourse both signal and mediate the achievement of these goals?
- What are the students learning from participating in this discussion – about science? – and about classroom discourse?
- What resources are the participants drawing on to enable them to contribute so productively?

Setting the Activity in its Curricular Context

"Please, guys, it's very important that you do some prediction."

To ask about the purpose of any classroom event is to enter immediately into an area of considerable complexity. Most classroom events can simultaneously serve a variety of purposes – organizational and social, as well as intellectual – and so there may not be one single, overriding purpose. And even when the teacher's principal purpose in initiating the event is relatively straightforward, this may well be superseded by others that emerge as the event proceeds. This seems to have been the case in the present instance.

The teacher's goal for the activity as a whole was for the different groups to carry out the experiments that they had not had time to complete in the previous session and thereby to contribute replications of the individual experiments. In this context, the request to groups who had already carried out each experiment to recall their earlier predictions was initially intended as part of the constituent task of preparing to continue with the experiments. This activity structure was frequently observed in this classroom, the teacher starting by talking with the whole class about the goal of the activity, and about the various tasks they would need to perform.

However, to understand what happened as the activity proceeded, it is necessary to know more about the teacher's beliefs concerning the purpose of studying science in school and about her goals for this unit as a whole. As she explained when we discussed this lesson, one of her overriding intentions is that the students should learn that science is a form of inquiry, that is to say, an active construction of understanding about the material world, and not just the memorization of information that has been accumulated through the inquiries of others. In starting the present unit on mass, therefore, the teacher had posed a problem and selected experiments that she believed could contribute to its solution – a solution that is already part of the knowledge of the scientific community, and one that the students, too, will eventually reach as a result of their own inquiries. However, just as important as coming to know the accepted solution, the teacher believes, is learning to engage in the practices through which solutions to scientific problems in general are progressively constructed, through a dialectical interplay between theory and the evidence obtained through experimentation. From this perspective, then, each curriculum unit is part of a continuing apprenticeship into the practices of doing science, enacted through guided participation in appropriate activities.

With this in mind, the teacher tries to ensure that, in each activity, the "hands-on," practical work is complemented by an equal attention to what Driver (1983) refers to as "minds-on" work. In the previous lesson, the emphasis had been on the former, and the students had learned how to obtain accurate measurements when using pan balances and how to enter these measurements into tables of results. They were also reminded of the importance of ensuring that their experiment constituted a fair test – a principle that had been the focus of attention in a previous unit (see previous chapter). However, what is important in the present context is that the emphasis on the procedures to be carried out had also included instructions to estimate the mass of the materials to be used and to predict what would happen to their combined mass as a result of the change of state. Not surprisingly, therefore, when it becomes apparent that two groups have failed to make predictions, this emerges as a matter which, in the teacher's judgment, requires immediate attention.

However, before going on to examine the way in which this topic is developed, it is worth looking more closely at the reasons for the teacher's emphasis on the importance of this step in the conduct of an experiment. One of these has to do with her responsibility for ensuring that, as far as possible, the purposes that motivate the students' engagement in the activity are closely matched to her own or, to put it differently, that the students are coming to share her definition of the Practice of Education.

When science is approached through hands-on work, there is always a danger that, in the actual process of performing the experiments, the students will lose sight of the goals of the activity, as these are defined by the teacher. This is all the more likely when students are working in groups, since it is impossible for the teacher to attend to all groups simultaneously. Under these conditions, students may develop alternative goals, ranging from conducting what they consider to be more interesting experiments, to merely going through the motions necessary to arrive at some result, or even to engaging in a whole variety of forms of time-wasting or disruptive behavior. From one point of view, then, the teacher's emphasis on making a prediction about the outcome of an experiment prior to actually carrying it out can be seen as an attempt on her part to co-opt the students' purposes to her goal for doing science in school – that is to say, to get them to see the experiment as an occasion for confirming or disconfirming their current understanding – rather than allowing such purposes as simply "doing school" or "fooling around" to direct the students' behavior.

When questioned, it becomes apparent that John's group had at least not been fooling around, although it is not clear from his answer whether they had simply forgotten to make a prediction or had been confused about the difference between estimating and predicting. Nevertheless, what is clear is that, for this group, making a considered prediction has not yet reached the stage of being a routine operation mediating the achievement of the goal of an experiment. This and the similar failure of the next group questioned is the immediate reason for the teacher's decision to spend more time on the issue of making a prediction.

However, while the teacher's intention is that the making of a prediction should become a routine part of the students' conduct of any experiment, it is the "minds-on" function of the prediction rather than the act itself that leads her to give it such importance. For, in making a prediction, one is involved in a form of theorizing, as one examines one's beliefs about the phenomenon in question and relates them to any other knowledge one has that is relevant to the possible outcomes of the experiment. As important as the actual predictions that students make, therefore, are the reasoning processes that lead to them. And so it is natural that, having emphasized the importance of making predictions, the teacher should turn to the more theory-oriented matter of the basis of the predictions in the students' beliefs.

Emerging Goals and Their Operationalization in Discourse

"Now those people who say 'decrease,' why do you think it decreased?"

As already suggested, the topic of predictions arose initially in the context of the task of preparing to continue the experiments. The teacher's goal was to record the frequency with which each prediction – increase, decrease, remain unchanged – had been made in relation to each of the different experiments, and the genre through which this was operationalized was basically that of providing information on request. In practice, this turned out to involve what might be called a composite genre, in which providing the information involved referring to another semiotic artifact – the tables in which the groups had recorded their predictions in writing. (It was this latter operation – that of interpreting the written table – that John found difficult, causing him to be unable to supply the requested information.)

However, the decision to make the predictions themselves the focus of attention involves a new departure. What had been simply a part of the preparatory task is "stepped up" to become an activity in its own right. In Saxe's (1992) terms, this is an *emergent goal*, which arises as the teacher's response to what some students have revealed about their level of competence in predicting. For these students, and probably for others as well, this step in the experimental procedure has not yet become sufficiently routine to function as an operation; it still needs to be treated as an action, requiring both attention and further practice.

This problem could have been dealt with in a variety of ways, including simple exhortation. However, for the reasons already discussed, the teacher chooses to emphasize the thinking involved in making a prediction rather than simply the act itself, and so she invites the students to explain why they made the predictions that they did.

With the emergence of this new goal, there occurs a concomitant shift in the type of discourse. From now on, the genre is one in which students are called on to explain their predictions in terms of their beliefs about the factors likely to be responsible for the predicted effect. Because the teacher's goal is now to encourage as many students as possible to contribute their ideas, she changes her own role in the discussion, adopting an encouraging stance and only intervening to facilitate the turn-taking and, when she judges it necessary, to clarify particular contributions.

The Learning Opportunities Provided by the Discourse

1. Learning About Science

"What was the reason behind saying it would decrease?"

Although the importance of making a prediction must by now be clear to everybody, some students may still have only a rather vague idea about what this involves. In particular, they may not understand that a prediction is not just a guess about what will happen, but an opinion supported by relevant reasons. In turn 19, therefore, the teacher initiates the new activity as follows:

Now, those people who say 'decrease', why do you think it decreased?
What was the reason behind saying it would decrease?

Even this may not be sufficient, however; some children may not know what counts as a reason. So she calls on Philips, who, at the end of the previous lesson, had offered an opinion on the subject of the melting ice.

Philips, that day you offered some reasons . Why do you think it would decrease . when it changes state from solid to liquid – the ice?

Now, the restating of his opinion will instantiate for the rest of the class what it is to give "a reason." Philips duly obliges, and the discussion spontaneously gets under way, as this and alternative reasons are offered and critically examined.

As can be seen, some of the students have very plausible reasons for their predictions. Philips' suggestion that the lump of ice contained air that would escape as it melted was very much to the point. The "ice" did indeed contain air, as the lump that had been brought in from the yard was not frozen water but a piece of compacted snow. In pointing out that this air would escape, he was introducing a very relevant consideration. Angeline's explanation that, if left long enough, some of the water from the melted ice might evaporate (34) was an equally good reason for predicting a decrease in mass, as her teacher recognizes: "Uh-huh . good point! Very good point!" (35). Jessica (36) also makes a significant contribution. But perhaps most impressive of all is Benjamin, who, despite the difficulty he has in making his meaning understood, persists in his attempt to distinguish between what he would predict if the water were refrozen in the refrigerator and his prediction if the water were refrozen in the windy, sub-zero conditions in the school yard (52–62).

After the predictions concerning the melting ice have been considered, attention turns to the other experiments. So, when the discussion comes to an end, all the students – not only those who have spoken – will embark on the second round of experiments with a much clearer idea of reasons for expecting one or other of the possible outcomes and be better able to interpret the significance of whatever results are obtained.

The discussion also provides for the learning of a more specifically linguistic aspect of doing science. All the students' explanations are based on rudimentary theories that make connections with other phenomena in addition to the melting ice. However, they vary in the language which is used. Philips states his explanation in everyday terms: "– ice has some air in it and when it's melted the air will go so it's . um <lighter>." Both Angeline and Jessica, on the other hand, use a number of technical scientific terms, such as "evaporate," "mass" and "particle," which they have appropriated from participation in previous discussions. The children thus vary in the extent of the register-appropriate resources that they can bring to bear in participating in this activity. Another advantage of this sort of discussion, therefore, is that, by listening to their peers and their teacher, those who have little command of this more technical register hear it used interchangeably with the everyday register and thus have the opportunity to become familiar with it and gradually to make it their own.

However, even more important than the use of the scientific register is the quality of the explanation itself, as is seen in the teacher's response to Benjamin (25). Benjamin's contribution is certainly far from clear and, in restating what she understands him to have said, the teacher draws attention to an apparent contradiction and adds: "I didn't follow. Can you repeat what you said, Benjamin?"

The same problem arises later, when he struggles to explain his prediction with respect to refreezing the melted ice (52–62). Although not stated explicitly, the teacher's message in each case is clear: to be acceptable, a prediction must be supported by reasons and those reasons must be logically consistent and coherently expressed.

Finally, two further lessons of a more general kind are being taught – though by example rather than by direct instruction. By taking time to consider the various reasons that the students offer in support of their predictions, the teacher is showing that discourse is just as important as experimental action in the practice of doing science. Both are essential and, as here, they perform complementary functions. And second, by inviting and accepting a variety of suggested explanations, the teacher is making it clear that there is not one "right" answer, known in advance; in developing their understanding of the world, scientists consider and evaluate a range of possible explanations for the phenomena that they observe.

2. Learning about Discourse

"Are you agreeing with Philips or disagreeing with Philips?"

Of course, there are few classroom activities – in science or any other subject – in which discourse does not play an integral part. However, what is noteworthy here is the goal that the discourse is mediating. In most classrooms, as Lemke (1990) found in his study of high school science lessons, a variety of discourse genres can be observed, including "going over homework," "teacher–student debate" and "admonition sequences," as well as the ubiquitous "triadic dialogue." But only extremely rarely did he observe the genre of discourse we see here, in which the students are encouraged to formulate coherent and logically consistent grounds for predicting the outcome of an experiment. Yet, along with the similar genre of arguing for a particular interpretation of the results obtained, this genre is an essential tool of scientific inquiry and one which is to be heard in any scientific community; its written counterpart also figures prominently in scientific publications. Clearly, therefore, it is one that is important for students to master. In fact, as I suggested in the previous section, several of the students have already achieved some facility in engaging in this genre of discourse and they are able to offer very relevant contributions. On the other hand, there are even more students who do not contribute at all on this particular occasion. Some of them, no doubt, are silent because they do not have anything further to add at this point; but there are certainly others who are silent because of their unfamiliarity with the genre itself. However, this does not mean that they are excluded from participation in the activity.

As Lave and Wenger (1991) argue, much of our learning takes place through what they call "legitimate peripheral participation." This frequently involves more observation than action until the novice reaches a level of understanding of the activity in question at which he or she is able to play a more central role.[2] One important reason for the success that people experience with this mode of learning, I believe, is that they are able to make sense of what is going on because they obtain a general grasp of the goal of the activity from other cues in the situation. In the present case, the fact that all the children had already carried out either the melting ice experiment or one of the other experiments in which matter changed state gave them a basis for following the arguments of their more vocal peers. As a result, as we shall see below, several additional children were able to join in the discussion that took place on the following day.

However, there is one very important aspect of this discourse genre that none of them has yet mastered, and it is to this that I now wish to turn. When the discussion starts, the children's contributions are offered simply as individual opinions, which are addressed to the teacher for her approval. However, in turn 31, the teacher asks Benjamin to consider how his suggestion relates to what Philips has already said:

> *31 T:* Are you agreeing with Philips or disagreeing with Philips?
>
> *32 B:* Agreeing.
>
> *33 T:* You're agreeing with Philips that it would decrease?

In so doing, the teacher introduces a further essential feature. In this genre of scientific discourse, contributions build on what has gone before, either agreeing or disagreeing, or connecting in some other way that rationally extends the debate. As Bereiter (1994 a) argues, in an age in which belief in objective truth has been replaced by a recognition of the cultural and historical situatedness of all human knowledge, the only basis on which the scientific endeavor can continue is that of "progressive discourse." One way of interpreting what is happening here, therefore, is that the students are experiencing an apprenticeship into this genre of discourse, moving from peripheral to more skillful and central participation.

What Resources Are the Participants Drawing on to Enable Them to Contribute so Productively?

Part of the answer to this question has already been touched on in passing and so I will not develop it at length. Put very briefly, they are drawing on the understanding they have constructed in the course of relevant past experiences and, in particular, the experiments conducted in the previous lesson and other observations they have made. They are also drawing on what they have gleaned from looking at the books on the topic that the teacher has added to the classroom library; on the talk in their groups while they were conducting the experiments, whether they remembered to make predictions or not; and on their linguistic resources more generally, as these are activated by their understanding of what is called for by the present situation.

However, there is a further resource that needs to be mentioned, which is of rather a different kind. What I am referring to here is the spirit of collaborative inquiry which clearly motivates this and most other activities in which these children engage. The emphasis on inquiry has already been mentioned as being in keeping both with the practices of professional scientists and with the way in which knowledge is constructed by people more generally. But the importance of collaboration in inquiry, and of the social and affective dimensions of classroom life, are, as yet, less clearly recognized. Yet they are not just a pleasant addition – a sort of icing on the cognitive cake – but, as recent work clearly shows, an integral part of learning in both group and whole class situations (Chang-Wells and Wells, 1993; Litowitz, 1993).

All too often, a teacher's sensitivity to the need to build students' self-esteem can lead to an unwillingness to challenge them intellectually. However, it is by having high expectations of what their students can achieve, and by helping them to meet them, that teachers can best give students a firm basis for believing in their ability to learn. So, in the present case, although it might initially seem unreasonable for a teacher to expect nine- and ten-year-olds to be able to engage in this sort of explanatory discourse, her expectation is shown to be well-founded. This is in part because the discourse grows out of first-hand experience and occurs in a social context in which collaboration is encouraged and meaning is recognized to be co-constructed. But it is equally because the teacher herself genuinely wants to know what the students think. Because she takes their contributions seriously, the students feel able to risk offering opinions instead of being concerned only with giving the "right" answer. Together, these features create a social–intellectual climate that is both supportive and challenging, and it is this, I would argue, that enables *all* of them to take part in the activity at *some* level – even if only that of active listener – and, as a result, to learn something from their participation.

In recent research, this sort of learning through participation in a culturally meaningful intellectual activity has been referred to as a "cognitive apprenticeship" (Rogoff, 1990, 1994; Chapter 4 this book). And as a description of the way in which, on the present occasion, the teacher inducts the children into the use of this new genre of discourse, this term is very apt. For here there is no separation of learning from doing; rather, the children learn as they do (Dewey, 1938), with the teacher "scaffolding" their efforts to participate in the expectation that, with her help, they will soon be able to manage on their own (Bruner, 1983; Cazden, 1988).

In fact, it is the transfer of responsibility for the task to the students, Mercer and Fisher (1993) argue, that should be one of the major goals of this sort of teaching. And so, in order to qualify as scaffolding, they propose, a teaching and learning event should: (A) enable the learners to carry out a task that they would not have been able to manage on their own; (B) be intended to bring the learners to a state of competence which will enable them eventually to complete such a task on their own; and (C) be followed by evidence of the learners having achieved some greater level of independent competence as a result of the scaffolding experience (adapted from Mercer and Fisher, 1993, p. 343).

As they admit, from a research perspective, the third criterion is often difficult to satisfy, since an occasion on which the students engage in a similar activity may not occur while they are being observed. In this unit on mass, however, a closely related activity was observed just a few days later and, as will be seen, there is clear evidence of several children having achieved a greater level of competence.

On Guessing, Estimating, and Predicting

After the lesson just discussed, the teacher and I spent some time talking about the value of making and justifying predictions as an integral part of science work in the classroom. Since at least two groups had failed to make their predictions prior to carrying out their experiments on the previous occasion, I asked whether it might be appropriate for her to spend some time making explicit the reasons for asking them to do so.

The following day, the lesson started with a review of the results from all the experiments to date which, in addition to those already mentioned, had included dissolving antacid tablets in a weak solution of vinegar under two conditions, first, allowing the resulting gas to escape, and then repeating the experiment but corking the bottle immediately after the tablets were dropped into the acid. Then, on the basis of a discussion of all the results, the teacher helped the children to arrive at a conclusion, which was stated in the form of a "rule." Emily's version was expressed as follows: "The mass of the matter will not change if you can capture every part of the matter, but if you cannot catch like just one part of the matter it will change."

Then, having concluded the first main phase of the curricular unit, the teacher initiated a new activity – not, the mini-lecture that I had suggested, but a much more interactive event. Writing the two words on the blackboard, she asked: "When I say 'estimate' and 'predict' . . . Are they two different activities?"

Once again, Philips is the first to offer an opinion. As far as he is concerned, they are the same; they are both just forms of guessing. Immediately, several children indicate that they wish to speak. The following is a verbatim record of the ensuing few minutes in the discussion, which continued for almost forty minutes.

> *07 T:* What do YOU think, Emily?
>
> *08 E:* I think that– well I don't agree with Philips because I think that they are two different things . because 'predict' is sort of like guess what will happen . and then 'estimate' is like you estimate the mass . using a form of weight, or centimeters . and it's not just with mass, you estimate other things
>
> *09 T:* OK
>
> *10 A:* I don't agree with Philips either because 'predict' sort of means like what WILL happen and 'estimate' is the er– do it– estimating something that's already there, but taking it further
>
> *11 T:* Now, listen to these answers . None of the answers are right or wrong . Will someone make a distinction?
>
> *12 Je:* I don't agree with Philips (laughs) because he said that 'estimate' is guessing . and 'predicting' is ALSO guessing but . um– actually guessing is also different from those two because when you guess you don't have very much information about the object or the thing (T: uh-huh) and so you're just making a– like a wild guess . but when you predict you're– you're actually you're maybe doing an experiment . and you are trying– using the information, you are trying to find out what would happen . . and estimating is um different from guess because . you have um certain information, for instance if you estimate the mass, you get the object in your hand and you . and you have the weights in the other hand and you can sort of . like estimate the . mass, so it's not guessing

As becomes clear, the majority of the class disagree with Philips. Not only are predicting and estimating different activities from guessing, in that they are only possible if one has relevant information – as Jessica explains (12) – but they differ from each other in being used under different conditions. As Auritro points out (10), predicting involves the consideration of a future state, which will occur as the outcome of an action still to be performed, whereas estimating involves the consideration of some aspect of an existing state of affairs.

As the discussion proceeds, further possible distinctions are suggested, and revisions are proposed to those already expressed as, for example, when Emily attempts to clarify the distinction proposed by Auritro. This starts a further line of thinking, which draws in several children who have not spoken before.

> *27 T:* OK . Wilson?
>
> *28 W:* I don't agree with um . Philips because . um in our math book it says 'estimate to the nearest tenth' but it didn't– it doesn't say 'PREDICT to the nearest tenth'.
>
> *29 T:* That's right . so what's the distinction?
> Good, you're using– <you're> using experience in math . to help you make a distinction . and do you ever see in your science that I ask you to predict? ...
> [Several children nod in agreement]

After a few more turns in which the connection between math and science is developed, the teacher turns to Philips to ask him if he wants to reply to those who disagree with him. However, he still stands by his earlier opinion:

> *34 P:* OK, for example I have a tennis ball and I estimate there's twenty grams so it's– when I say I predict – like what's the weight of a . tennis ball and I say twenty grams, it's more or less the same thing and 'estimate' is seeing like how much it weighs and 'predict' is . sort of . go- . . (shaking his head from side to side)
>
> *35 T:* What do YOU think, Jessica?
>
> *36 Je:* Well, um– Philips' answer is um– in a way it's right but maybe I want to change it . um . the 'estimate' 'predict' and 'guess' um . are RELATED but they're not the same
>
> *37 T:* OK, they're related but they're not the same
> Benjamin? (who has his hand up)
>
> *38 B:* I think the same thing as Jessica adding on to it . I– I think that whe– what Philips said– I <see that> estimating um . estimating- like if you . estimate . what a– what a ball weighs . (T: uh-huh) what a ball weighs– what a tennis ball's weight would be– or the amount would be, um . it would not be the same as predict because predict . would be what would HAPPEN . You could use it in the same form but not the same question

The example of the tennis ball is pursued over several more turns, as various children attempt to clarify the distinction for themselves and for others. Benjamin, in particular, struggles with his idea of changing the mass of the tennis ball by adding something to it and other children comment on his proposal.

54 E: You know . when . Benjamin said like . it will be 'predict' . what the weight is if you added feathers, I sort of agree and sort of don't . because . it's also um . estimating the weight or the mass because . you're <just adding> something, but you still have to estimate the mass, you're not really predicting what
<u>will</u> happen.

55 T: <u>Yes</u> (to B) . she picked– <u>your example is not a very good example–</u>

56 B: <u>Um . I– . . I–</u>

57 T: – because she says it's still ABOUT the tennis ball, it's not about what will HAPPEN to the tennis ball

58 B: Yes, but I'm saying that 'predicting' is not predicting the MASS that it will be, I'm saying it'll predict . whether it will be the same . mass, or will it change?

59 T: OK . right . any more comments on this issue?
Yes (to Emily)

60 E: Well, yes, he is right if you say predict if it will be same or different or, for example, will the mass increase, decrease or be the same . . but then if– yeah that's right – but then if you add– like estimate the weight after you add those things you're still using 'estimate'.

61 T: OK

62 Je: And my answer is sort of like Emily's but um . if she– she– Benjamin said that it was um asking a question um er he said he'd add two feathers . on to a tennis ball and predict what the mass will be . um . well it would the– um– if you were to predict if the mass would be the same, increase or <decrease>**, you would ask it in a different way though, you'd ask . 'What . d'you think will happen . to the mass?'

The teacher was right: The lecture was not necessary. As these excerpts show, several of the children had already developed quite a sophisticated understanding of the activity of predicting, and those who understood less well probably gained more from listening to the discussion among their peers than they would have from a monologue delivered by the teacher. As she commented later, there was really nothing further for her to add; between them, the children had made all the distinctions that we found when we subsequently consulted the *Concise Oxford Dictionary* and *Webster's New World Dictionary*.

Nevertheless it could be argued that this second discussion is not about science at all, but about epistemology and the appropriate use of epistemic verbs.[3] Certainly, the distinction that Jessica makes between "guess," on the one hand, and "estimate" and "predict," on the other (12), is concerned with the presence or absence of information as a basis for judgment; similarly, Auritro's distinction between judging a measurable attribute of an entity ("estimate") and judging the outcome of a change in an entity ("predict") is concerned with the metalinguistic issue of how the terms are used. However, this does not make the discussion any the less relevant to the practice of science. Both the context in which the discussion arose and the form in which the initial question was posed make it clear that the teacher's concern was as much with the intellectual activities that are performed in making these speech acts as with the terms that are used to label them. Thus, in clarifying the conditions under which the terms are used, the discussion also served to emphasize the fact that the discourse in which these speech acts are performed is an essential part of the practice of doing science.

But, in the context of this chapter, what is just as impressive as the metalinguistic and epistemological distinctions that the children are able to make is the increased skill they demonstrate in using this genre of "progressive discourse" to construct a solution to the problem that the teacher has posed. At no point does she need to remind them to listen to each other; the scaffolding that she provided on the previous occasion is no longer necessary. As can be seen, they spontaneously refer to previous contributions – agreeing, disagreeing, adding, revising and clarifying – in their collective attempt to work towards a consensual understanding of the distinction between the terms and the contexts in which they are used.

Such confidence and skill in whole-class discussion is rarely seen in children of this age – or at least not in the studies of classroom discourse that have been published in recent years (e.g. Cazden, 1988; Edwards and Mercer, 1987; Newman, 1989). And even among high school students, it is the exception rather than the rule (Nystrand and Gamoran, 1991). However, this is almost certainly not because of a lack of competence on the part of the students, but because of their lack of opportunity to exploit the competence they have. Under similar conditions, I am convinced, the same sort of purposeful and collaborative talk could occur in every classroom. It is worth asking, therefore, what it is about *this* classroom that has made possible the realization of these children's potential.

The answer, I believe, is to be found in the ways in which talk is here related to action. First, both the episodes that I have quoted arose from activities that involved the children in practical observation and experimental manipulation of real-world material phenomena. In this sense, they spoke of what they knew from first-hand experience, gained both in the classroom and in the wider community. Second, as Hatano and Inagaki (1991) argue in relation to a somewhat similar approach to science teaching in Japan, the effectiveness of this form of progressive discourse owes much to the collaborative nature of the knowledge building activity it serves – which is not without an element of competitiveness, as students take up a position or argue against positions adopted by others. In such a setting, the sharing of cognition is, as they put it, "energized by social (partisan) motivation" (p. 345).[4]

But perhaps the most important point is that the activities from which I have quoted were not isolated events, but part of a larger undertaking – the curricular unit as a whole – the goal of which was to arrive at a shared understanding of the principles underlying the phenomena they had been investigating, where "understanding" means knowledge that has a bearing on action (Barnes, 1976; Wells, 1995). In fact, after some further activities in which the relationship between mass and volume was explored, the curriculum unit concluded with a *very* practical activity, that of using their understanding of these principles, as they apply to flotation, to design, construct and test wooden boats in order to discover which group's design of boat could carry the greatest load at the greatest speed. And, in the course of this activity, a less purely verbal form of prediction was observed in action, as children considered and tested the probable effects on stability of adding a keel, or of decreasing resistance by making a V-shaped bow or sanding the hull and superstructure.[5]

However, although open-ended and to some extent emergent in the situation, these sorts of learning opportunities do not occur by chance, but are deliberately planned for and nurtured by the teacher, in this as in all areas of the curriculum. In effect, they are the realization of a particular vision of the Practice of Education that she is attempting to enact, based on her understanding of ideas appropriated from sociocultural theory, as she has tempered and refined them in the crucible of situated practice. And it is to a brief discussion of this conception of the Practice of Education that I should like to turn in the concluding section of this chapter.

Toward a Dialogic Conception of Education

There is general agreement that the practice of education has two main objects. The first of these is cultural reproduction – the transmission to successive generations of the accumulated resources of the culture so that they will be able to contribute productively and responsibly, in their turn, as members of the workforce and of the larger society. The second object is the development of individual students, in such a way that they are enabled to achieve their full potential as human beings and to develop original, and possibly divergent, skills and ideas. Unfortunately, these two objects are frequently treated as if they were in conflict, as is seen in the arguments between proponents of traditional as opposed to progressive education.

The nub of the problem is that those who place the emphasis on cultural reproduction seem to believe that this requires uniform, teacher-directed instruction, according to a curriculum that is centrally mandated, based on authoritative textbooks, and monitored by frequent standardized testing. According to this view, creativity and originality based on individual interest and initiative are only possible when students have acquired a firm grasp of the basic skills and the canon of knowledge that is handed on from the past. Those who place the emphasis on individual development, on the other hand, argue that, since knowledge is individually constructed on the basis of what the learner brings to the task by way of prior knowledge, interest and motivation, learning should be student-centered, with the teacher's role being limited to that of supporting and facilitating individual interest and initiative. Characterized in these terms, it is not surprising that traditional and progressive education should be seen as polar opposites, nor that educational debate conducted from these positions should resemble a perpetual swinging of the pendulum from one side to the other.

A vision of education derived from sociocultural theory, by contrast, recognizes the partial validity of both these positions, but proposes a dialogic conceptualization of learning-and-teaching in which knowledge is *co-constructed* by teacher and students together as they engage in *joint activities*, which are negotiated rather than imposed. According to this conception, the primary object of education is growth in understanding on the part of *all* concerned, through the appropriation and exploitation of the culture's resources as tools for engaging in inquiries which are of both individual and social significance, and which have implications for action beyond the classroom (Engeström, 1991b). Furthermore, just as the artifacts and practices which are appropriated in such activities are dual in nature, being both conceptual and material (Cole, 1996), so, in the appropriation of these cultural resources, there is a dual transformation: the individual is transformed in terms of his or her understanding and potential for action and, in putting these resources to use, he or she transforms the situation in which they are used.

In planning a unit of study, in science or any other subject in the curriculum, a teacher is guided, whether consciously or unconsciously, by her or his beliefs about the Practice of Education. In choosing and organizing the actions to be engaged in – the activities and tasks, with their hierarchy of goals, social, conceptual and material – and in deciding on the operational means by which these goals are to be achieved, the teacher enacts these beliefs and attempts to get the students to adopt them too.

In the classroom I have described, the teacher is guided quite consciously by what I have called a sociocultural conception of the Practice of Education. And it is this that largely determines the activities that she selects and the ways in which they are operationalized. Some of the most important characteristics of this approach, I believe, are the following:

- the activities undertaken are such that, although chosen by the teacher for their cumulative contribution to an understanding of the central theme, they allow for groups of students to make them their own and progressively to exercise more choice over how they are conducted
- they involve a combination of action and reflection, and of group work, individual reading and writing, and whole-class discussion
- goals are made explicit, and the relationship between these goals and the operations by means of which they are to be achieved is made the subject of discussion
- perhaps most important, there are frequent opportunities for students to express their beliefs and opinions, to calibrate them with those of their peers, and to change them in the light of persuasive argument or of further information

It is these last two characteristics that I have focused on in this chapter, showing how, with the teacher's initial scaffolding and continuing support, and with an increasing grasp of its function in knowledge building arrived at through participation, the children begin to appropriate the form of the genre of progressive discourse as a means of sharing and refining their understanding of the topics they are investigating. At the same time, the episodes discussed provide a good example of teaching that is responsive to students' current abilities and pitched within their zone of proximal development (Vygotsky, 1978). In particular, in the first episode, I have tried to show how this is achieved through the technique of 'stepping up' an operation that is causing difficulty and treating it as an action that warrants attention in its own right.

Elsewhere I have characterized this dialogic interpretation of the Practice of Education as having as its object the creation and sustaining of a community of inquiry in which knowledge is co-constructed (Wells and Chang-Wells, 1992; Chapters 3 and 4 this book). However, in the current climate, this is not easy to achieve. In terms of Halliday's concept of register, the situation in most educational institutions does not readily "activate" these particular types of activity or discourse. Nevertheless, because the relationship of activation between situation and meaning potential is reciprocal, a teacher who is motivated by this vision of education can do much to make it a reality by the choices she or he makes with respect to the activities to pursue and the operations that are used in the process – of which the genres of discourse are among the most important.

Thus, to the extent that a classroom does indeed become a community of inquiry, both of the objects of education will be achieved. Not only will the students be empowered by taking over the achievements of the past but, by transforming them to solve the problems that they encounter in the present, they will also ensure both the continuing existence of our culture and its ability to adapt creatively to the demands of the future.

Notes

1. I am indebted to Giyoo Hatano for this way of describing what happens here and in other situations in which a problem encountered in passing is "stepped up" to become the focus of attention.
2. This is a phenomenon very familiar to teachers who receive into their classrooms students who, because they have newly arrived from outside Canada, do not yet speak English, the language of the classroom. By listening to their peers and using whatever resources they have to make sense of what is going on, these children gradually become able to take a more active part in the conversation and, through participation, eventually master the linguistic system and the conventions for using it. Several members of this classroom community are, in fact, learning English in exactly this way (see Allen, 1993).
3. This point was made by David Olson. In his own work he had noted how rarely epistemic verbs are used in the classroom, either by teachers or by students, even at the high school level.
4. One important difference between the classroom I am describing and the Hypothesize–Experiment–Instruction (HEI) method developed by Itakura (1967) has

to do with the role of the teacher. In the HEI method, once the teacher has presented the problem, he or she is expected to stand back, leaving the debate to the students. In the present classroom, on the other hand, because the discussion is organically related to previous activities in which the teacher has been a coparticipant, she plays a rather more active role, both in facilitating the turn taking and in highlighting particularly important contributions or pressing for necessary clarification.

5. As can be seen, this unit was a very clear example of several cycles through the spiral of knowing, involving multiple modes of knowing.

7   Using the Tool-kit of Discourse in the Activity of Learning and Teaching

Schooling, as a form of socialization through culture transmission, has been part of our culture for so long that we take for granted its encapsulated nature and its almost total dependence on oral and written discourse. Add to this an uncritical acceptance by many educators of the conduit metaphor of communication, in which utterances carry thoughts as trucks carry coal (Reddy, 1979), and it is perhaps not surprising that many attempts to understand the role of language in learning and teaching have treated the verbal component of classroom events as self-sufficient, and analyzed the talk as if, like a window, it gave direct access to what was going on in the learners' minds (Edwards, 1993).

But what if this view of learning as the increasing ability to send and receive verbal messages containing more, and more complex and abstract, information about non-present objects and events is an aberration – a byproduct of the form that schooling has happened to take in Western culture? In many other cultures, learning is not treated as a separate activity; and, even in our own culture, this is rarely the case outside the classroom. Instead, it is recognized to be a concomitant of engagement in joint activity with help from other people. Nor, outside the classroom, is learning conceived of as a purely verbal affair. For simply being able to talk or write about a practice is no substitute for being able to engage in it effectively. Discourse is a means, not an end in itself, and verbal information is valued not for the correctness of the way in which it is formulated but for its use as a means towards the achievement of some larger purpose. What we need to attend to, therefore, in order to understand the role of talk in the classroom, is not so much the talk per se, as the contribution

Using the tool-kit of discourse in the activity of learning and teaching. *Mind, Culture, and Activity*, 3(2):74–101, 1996, Mahwah, NJ: Lawrence Erlbaum Associates.

it makes to the activities in which students engage in the "lived-in world" of the classroom, the actual structures of participation, and the functions that talk performs – along with other semiotic systems – in mediating the goals of these activities.

This is the approach that our research group of teachers and teacher educators has been taking as, through collaborative action research, we attempt to improve students' opportunities for learning through the development of classroom communities of inquiry. However, in order to analyze the videorecorded observations that provide the primary data for our research, we found we first had to devise a more adequate analytic framework: one that focuses not only on the turn-by-turn organizational structure of talk described by conversational analysts (Sacks, Schegloff, and Jefferson, 1974) and discourse analysts (Sinclair and Coulthard, 1975), but also on the different functions that talk performs in enabling, interpreting, and evaluating the joint activities of which it is a part. Only when conceptualized in this sort of way, we believe, can the study of classroom interaction make a significant contribution to our understanding of learning and teaching in schools and other educational institutions, and help teachers to use the discourse tool-kit most effectively to facilitate their students' learning.

Briefly, the framework we have developed is based on an articulation of activity theory and systemic linguistics, which will be explained in the first part of this chapter. Then, in the second part, through the examination of two particular episodes, I shall try to show how the framework can be used to arrive at a fuller understanding of the role of discourse in the practice of education, and to identify points of leverage for those teachers who wish to find ways of changing their practice in the interests of bringing it into closer touch with the world of relevant social action (Bruner, 1990).

I

Developing the Framework: The Primacy of Activity

Our starting point is the tristratal analysis of joint activity developed by Leont'ev (1981) on the basis of ideas initially proposed by Vygotsky. The three strata are those of *activity, action, and operation*, each of which provides a different perspective on the organization of events. In any event-in-a-setting, the *activity* that is being undertaken can be identified according to its motive – the "object" in view that provides its driving force. In the classroom, the predominant activity is that of education, although, in practice, the object of this activity takes a range of varied, and sometimes mutually incompatible, forms. In educational discourse, however, the term "activity" is typically used in a nontechnical sense to refer to a relatively self-contained curricular event, often occupying one time-tabled lesson; so, in order to avoid terminological confusion, I shall from here on refer to the stratum of "activity," as it applies to education, as the Practice of Education.[1]

The second stratum is that of "*action*," which is the perspective on an event which is afforded by considering the goal to be achieved. It is only in "action" that an "activity" is "translated into reality." But even the stratum of "action" is not directly tied to actual behavior. For that, we must invoke the third stratum, that of "*operation*," where the focus is on the particular means that participants use to achieve the goal of the "action" in view, under the conditions that prevail in the situation.

In distinguishing between the strata of "action" and "operation," Leont'ev also introduces a second criterion. An "action," by virtue of being goal-directed, requires that the actors give it their conscious attention. One of the defining features of an "operation," by contrast, is that, as a means for achieving the goal of "action," it is likely to be a well-practiced routine, and therefore no longer in need of conscious attention. A corollary of this second distinction is that a pattern of behavior that starts as an "action" may, over time, become so routinized that it becomes an "operation," to be deployed, when appropriate, in the achievement of a more molar "action." However, the reverse movement can also occur. When difficulty is encountered in performing an "operation," it may be necessary to refocus on the "operation" and attend to it once more as an "action," until it again becomes automatic. In the classroom, such a "stepping up" may be instigated quite deliberately when the teacher recognizes that an "operation" is not being carried out appropriately (see previous chapter).

In sum, then, what I am suggesting is that classroom events are best understood as "actions" which, organized as structured sequences of activities and tasks, enact the Practice of Education. However, while "action" provides the organizing structure for classroom events and for the goals and outcomes in terms of which they are planned, directed, and evaluated, it is the stratum of "operations" that accounts for the means by which these goals are attained. That is to say, at a level below full conscious attention, participants select from their repertoire of routinized behaviors the ones that, in the light of the prevailing conditions, they judge appropriate for the activity or task in hand and deploy them relatively automatically towards the achievement of that end.[2]

Activity Systems and Communities of Practice

In the foregoing account, I have emphasized the realization relationship between the three strata but, like Leont'ev, have said little about the ways in which an "activity," and the "actions" through which it is realized, is embedded in the cultural context in which it occurs. In the last decade, however, there have been a number of important proposals which situate "activity" more dynamically in a world of interacting, self-renewing communities of practice (e.g. Lave and Wenger, 1991). For our purposes here, perhaps the most important is the construct of an *activity system* developed by Engeström (1990).

Following Leont'ev, Engeström takes as his point of departure the basic mediational triangle, in which the incorporation of the tool as mediational means radically transforms the relation between a subject and the object of his or her "action." However, this model needs to be expanded, he argues, in order to understand the relationship between such isolated "actions" and the ongoing cultural "activities" in which they are embedded. This enlarged model he represents as in Figure 7.1.

In this expanded model, the individual "action," represented by the top portion of the diagram, is related to the larger cultural and historical context by the relationships represented by the other triangles. For example, the subject–object relationship – that is to say, the subject's goal orientation – is modified by the cultural rules that apply to this relationship

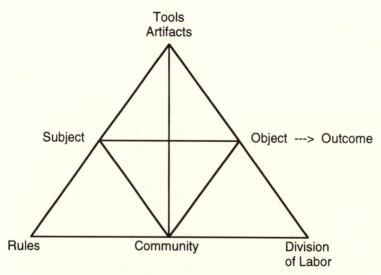

Figure 7.1 Engeström's (1990) Model of an Activity System.

and by the division of labor in which it is embedded. These rules, or norms, might well include the tools considered appropriate to use, and the way in which control of their use is distributed among the different categories of community members who are regularly involved in this and related "actions." However, these relationships are not static; they are continuously being constructed and reformulated in the course of their deployment in particular, situated "actions."[3]

In the present context, one of the particular virtues of this model, as I hope to show below, is that it enables comparisons to be made between quite different ways of enacting the Practice of Education and encourages a critical and innovative approach to teaching (Engeström, 1991b). It also draws attention to possible points of leverage in the attempt to overcome the encapsulated nature of schooling. For example, changing the nature of the rules that prescribe the sorts of "actions" that participants engage in and their intended outcomes, modifying the division of labor, or valuing other semiotic tools in addition to written texts, all create quite different "activity systems," and ones that may encourage rather than resist student initiative and creativity.

Discourse as Semiotic Tool

Within this "activity" framework, discourse is seen as a tool-kit that is drawn on in achieving the goals of "actions" and "sub-actions" (or, in classroom terms, the goals of activities and their constituent tasks) (Cole, 1996a; Wertsch, 1991). This perspective is quite similar to that found in Halliday's systemic functional theory of language (Halliday, 1978, 1984) and, for this reason, our approach to the analysis of discourse draws heavily on his writings. As Leont'ev argues, tools have a central role in the theory of "activity," for "the tool mediates activity and thus connects humans not only with the world of objects but also with other people", (1981, p. 55). And as Halliday (1993a) points out, as a semiotic tool, language is admirably organized for this purpose, for any individual act of meaning simultaneously performs two functions. First, a speaker's choices with respect to what he calls the "ideational" metafunction encode the aspect of experience (including the "world of objects") that she or he is representing and, second, choices with respect to the "interpersonal" metafunction encode the speaker's relation to his or her interlocutors.

Acts of meaning do not occur in isolation, however, but as dialogic contributions to discourse – or "text," in Halliday's terms. That is to say, they occur in the course of an exchange of meanings between participants in order to perform some action(s) in a specific situation. It is thus texts rather than individual acts of meaning that constitute the tools that are used in mediating "activity." In order to articulate this functional theory of discourse with the theory of "activity," therefore, it is necessary to specify briefly how texts are constructed and then to consider the relationship between the analytic categories of the two theories. In the present context, I shall focus only on spoken texts. But the same general arguments also apply to written texts; as Bakhtin (1981) emphasizes, they too mediate "activity" and they are also dialogic.

Categories for the Analysis of the Sequential Organization of Discourse

In the co-construction of a text, the smallest building block is the *move*, for example a "question" or an "answer." However, it is the *exchange* – in which such reciprocally related moves combine – that constitutes the most appropriate unit for the analysis of spoken discourse. Every exchange consists of an *initiating* move and a *response* move (either of which may on occasion be nonverbal); under certain conditions, there may also be a third, *follow-up*, move. Exchanges are of two types: *nuclear* exchanges, which can stand alone, independently contributing new content to the discourse, and *bound* exchanges, which – as the label implies – are not freestanding, but depend on the nuclear exchange in some way. The most important of these is the *dependent* exchange, in which some aspect of the nuclear exchange is developed through further specification, exemplification, justification, and so on. A second category of bound exchange is the *embedded* exchange, which deals with problems in the uptake of a move in the current exchange, for example, a need for repetition or identification of a referent. (These are what Jefferson (1972) refers to as "side sequences.") A further bound category is the *preparatory* exchange, such as the bid-nomination exchange in whole-class question-and-answer sessions.

The unit that includes a single nuclear exchange and any exchanges that are bound to it is called a *sequence*. In understanding the role of talk in joint activity, it is this unit which is of greatest functional significance. For it is in the succession of moves that occurs in following through on the expectations set up by the initiating move in a nuclear exchange that the "commodity" being exchanged – some form of goods or services, or some form of information (Halliday, 1984) – is introduced, negotiated and brought to completion.[4]

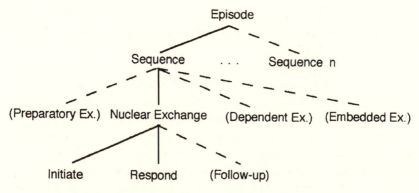

Figure 7.2 Sequential Organization of Spoken Discourse.

Above Sequence is the level of *episode*, that is to say, all the talk that occurs in the performance of an activity or – more probably – one of its constituent tasks. It seems quite likely that it will eventually be possible to distinguish different subcategories of sequence according to their functions within an episode (Coulthard, 1977) but, as yet, we have no firm proposals to make on this issue. The relationship between the four levels can be shown schematically as in Figure 7.2, where dotted lines and parentheses indicate a category that is not obligatory.

The constituent structure described above is only one part of what is involved in giving a text its unity and coherence. Other important resources include cohesion (Halliday and Hasan, 1976) and what Lemke (1990) calls thematic patterning. Because of space limitations, these systems will not be further described here. However, a detailed account of their interrelationship in the creation of textual coherence can be found in Martin (1992).

It is important to emphasize, furthermore, that the account of the organization of discourse just presented is both schematic and idealized. Actual examples of discourse are often much less tidy: Participants may be involved in more than one conversation simultaneously; responses do not always immediately follow initiations, and in multiparty talk there may be more than one response; and moves and sequences may – and usually do – perform more than a single function (cf. Labov and Fanshel, 1977). Furthermore, not all meaning is expressed lexicogrammatically – intonation, gesture, etc. also contribute to the meanings exchanged. It seems, nevertheless, that this scheme – or something like it – has a normative function; as with Grice's (1975) "cooperative principle," it is because all the members of a speech community share very similar expectations about the ways in which conversation typically proceeds that they are able to make sense of what actually occurs. (For a fuller discussion, see Wells, 1981, Chapter 1.)

As well as expectations concerning the general sequential organization of discourse, participants also have more specific expectations that are related to the situation in which the discourse occurs. In systemic theory, these relationships between text and situation are conceptualized in terms of "register" and "genre" (see Chapter 5 for an explanation). Briefly, register accounts for the sorts of things that are likely to be said in particular types of situation, and genre accounts for the sequential organization of what is said in order to achieve the goal of the "action" in the situation. Together, they define what things can be done in a culture, and how, with the use of the semiotic tool-kit of language. At present, however, these perspectives are still somewhat programmatic in nature. They provide a way of thinking about the relationship between texts and situations, but not yet a taxonomy that is ready-made for use in the analysis of naturally occurring data (but cf. Lemke, 1990; Martin, 1992).

Describing Discourse in the Classroom: Relating Action and Genre

Having introduced the two theories individually, the next step is to articulate the systemic linguistics approach to the analysis of discourse with the categories proposed by "activity" theory in order to construct an analytic tool for the description of classroom events that is more powerful and comprehensive than that provided by either theory alone.

The most obvious point of intersection between the two theories is to be found in the notion of goal-oriented social process. As we have seen, this is the way in which both "action" and genre are conceptualized. Both are concerned with patterned ways of doing things that are culturally recognized; both are structured in terms of the goal in view; and both require for their realization the strategic deployment of relatively routinized forms of behavior that are appropriate to the prevailing conditions. In fact, the two categories seem to be almost identical, differing only in the extent to which the focus is specifically on the linguistic processes involved. This is the perspective adopted in Lemke's (1990) study of science classrooms, where he uses the term "genre" more or less interchangeably with the term "activity" in describing such recurring constituents of lessons as "seatwork," "going over homework," "teacher exposition," or "teacher–student debate."

This naturally raises the question as to how these two categories of 'action' and genre should be related. The answer we have adopted is suggested by focusing on the toollike nature of discourse. As Cole (1994) puts it, drawing on a strong tradition in sociocultural theory, language is the "tool of tools." It allows us both to intervene in social action to shape and direct it, and also linguistically to represent that action and the world in which it occurs in a "theory of human experience" (Halliday, 1993a, p. 97). On this basis, I shall propose that a genre is best thought of as a type of "action," but one that is viewed from the perspective of its linguistic realization. Or, to put it differently, genres are items in the linguistic tool-kit; they constitute the range of linguistic means whereby different kinds of "action" are "operationalized."

In attempting to further categorize genres as different types of "operation," a useful initial distinction to make is that between events in which the discourse plays a role that is ancillary to the "action" goal to be achieved and those in which the discourse is itself constitutive of the "action." An example of the former would be the talk that accompanies and monitors the preparation of a meal or the carrying out of the practical part of a science experiment; in both these cases, it is the goal of the material action that is the focus of attention and the function of the discourse is to facilitate the achievement of this goal. By contrast, in events such as a committee meeting or a discussion in which the results of an experiment are interpreted and evaluated, it is the talk that is primary, and the goal is both established and achieved chiefly through the medium of the appropriate discourse. In this latter situation, the distinction between "action" and "operation" is more difficult to draw. However, even here, it is useful to think of "action" as focusing on the outcome to be achieved, and of "operation" as focusing on the situation-specific ways in which the discourse is co-constructed as a means of achieving that outcome.

Although currently invoked to explain the functional-sequential organization of any kind of linguistic text, the concept of genre was first used by rhetoricians to categorize written texts. And certainly, the interpretation of genres as the means by which "action" is discursively "operationalized" seems particularly appropriate when thinking about written genres. As Bazerman (1994) shows, in his study of the different genres that are involved in the "activity" of obtaining a patent, it is through the appropriate use of the relevant written genres that the constituent "actions" are performed and the overall outcome achieved. However, oral genres may also function in similar fashion in certain activities that involve face-to-face interaction. For example, in the formal setting of a trial, there are such clearly defined genres as cross-examination of witnesses, the defence counsel's closing speech to the jury, and the judge's summing up of the evidence. In such cases, as Hasan (1985) suggests, there is a culturally recognized pattern to be followed, involving obligatory elements which must occur in a certain order.

In most face-to-face interactions, however, this sort of conformity to preexisting generic patterns of discourse organization is the exception rather than the rule – at least at the level of "action" comparable to the written genres in the "activity" of patent granting. For example, the deliberations whereby the jury arrives at a verdict constitute a recognizable "action" in the overall "activity" of trial by jury, but the cases must be rare in which these deliberations follow a prescripted pattern. The same is true of most classroom interaction. Recognizable "actions" – what I earlier referred to as classroom activities – such as reviewing work done on a topic to date, or carrying out an experiment, occur with considerable frequency, but the discourse through which they are 'operationalized' does not follow the same pattern from one occasion to another; there are few, if any, obligatory elements, and a minimal degree of order in which occurring elements must be arranged. (But, for an alternative view, cf. Christie's (1993) description of classroom activities in terms of "curriculum genres.")

Yet this does not mean that oral discourse is usually random and disorganized. If it were, it would be ineffective in enabling the goals of collaborative action to be achieved. Rather, the organizational structures to which participants orient operate at a lower level, corresponding to the tasks and steps that make up the superordinate 'action'. In other words, where 'action' is realized through oral discourse of an informal kind, the generic patterns through which it is 'operationalized' are most frequently to be found at the levels of sequence, rather than at the superordinate level of episode.

What the choice of sequence as the unit of analysis brings out is the essentially collaborative nature of oral text construction, in contrast with the more individually controlled creation or reception of a written text. For, although the point of the sequence is typically proposed in the initiating move of the nuclear exchange (e.g. the offering of an interesting piece of information, a request for explanation, or the elicitation of suggestions), its satisfactory completion requires contributions by at least one other participant that appropriately meet the expectations set up by the initiating move. Furthermore, since there are many appropriate ways in which to respond to the initiating move – not all of them anticipated or anticipatable by the initiator – the precise meaning that is made in a sequence can never be determined until the sequence is concluded. And, since it is this meaning that typically forms the point of departure for the sequence that follows, no single participant – except when constructing an extended monologue – can ever predict or control how an episode of discourse will develop beyond the current move. Thus, dialogic discourse – even when one participant has unequal topic control – is co-constructed sequence by sequence; it both depends on, and further develops, the intersubjective agreement between the participants about the interactional goal to which they are orienting.[5]

Nevertheless, the very fact that sequences are for the most part smoothly negotiated to a conclusion provides strong evidence for the existence of generic structures at this level, to which participants orient in making their sucessive moves. The one that has received the most attention in educational research to date is the teacher-directed three-part structure that Lemke (1990) refers to as "triadic dialogue." As its name implies, this structure consists of three obligatory moves, *initiation*, *response* and *follow-up*, which must occur in this order. However, this is by no means the only generic structure to occur in classroom interaction, particularly if task-oriented talk between students is also taken into account (Forman and McPhail, 1993; Phillips, 1988). And as I have shown in Chapter 5 and will further argue below, even this basic IRF structure can be used by a teacher to achieve quite different goals.

In the present context, however, what needs to be emphasized is that the generic organization of these different sequence-types is readily recognized by members of a discourse community in which they frequently occur.[6] And so, by orienting to the sequence-type's organizational structure, participants are able to determine what sorts of moves are permitted or required at each stage and so to contribute appropriately to the meaning that is being jointly constructed. Thus, whether we refer to them as "microgenres," or by some other term, it is clear that, as with the more familiar genres of written discourse, the culturally recognized patterns in terms of which they are organized enable them to function as tools in the jointly organized "operationalization" of "action."

Discourse in the Classroom: Exploring the Significance of Follow-up

In the discussion so far, I have been concerned to show, in general terms, how different modes of discourse can be conceptualized, within an "activity theory" framework, as a tool-kit that is utilized to perform the "operations" through which the goals of "action" are achieved.[7] However, although my purpose is to bring this descriptive apparatus to bear on particular episodes of classroom interaction, I have not as yet explicitly addressed the ways in which discourse is organized to serve a specifically teaching function. This will be my focus in the second part of the chapter. But first I must situate my conception of the teacher's role in the context of my understanding of the Practice of Education.

The Two Levels of Teaching

In the ongoing debate about the goals of education, there are two main contending points of view. One puts the main emphasis on "cultural reproduction," while the other emphasizes individual development, creativity, and diversity. However, as I argued in the previous chapter, from a sociocultural perspective these two goals, far from being in conflict, are seen to be both equally necessary and dialectically interrelated. In this view, individual development is only possible through increasingly full participation in ongoing communities of practice (Lave and Wenger, 1991) and this, in turn, involves the appropriation of the cultural resources by means of which those practices are mediated (Rogoff, 1990). However, appropriation is not a matter of simple internalized reproduction. On the contrary, it is essentially transformative in its effects (Engeström, 1991a). As newcomers engage in joint activities with other members of the culture, they are transformed in terms of their understanding and mastery of the community's practices and in their ability to participate in them; and this, in turn, transforms the community into which they are being inducted. Furthermore, as newcomers become progressively more able to engage in solving the problems that the community faces, they may contribute to a transformation of the practices and artifacts that are employed, and this, in turn, transforms the community's relationship with the larger social and material environment.

Within such a transformational framework, my conceptualizion of the teacher's role is based on two assumptions: that schooling should provide an apprenticeship into the semiotic practices – the ways of making meaning – that that are valued in the culture; and that teaching-and-learning involves an essentially dialogic relationship. However, this is not a dialogue between equals. Both by virtue of his or her status as an employed representative of the community, and as a result of personal experience and education, the teacher must play a different role from that of the students in the classroom community (Rogoff, 1994). As leader and guide, it is the teacher's responsibility to ensure that the student members engage with the mandated curriculum and that they are assisted to appropriate it as effectively as possible, both as a personal resource for their own current and future purposes, and so that they may be productive members of the society in which they are growing up. How this dual responsibility is re-alized in practice can be conceptualized as involving two levels of activity, the "macro" and the "micro" (Wells, 1995).

At the macro level, the teacher is the chief initiator and is responsible, among other things, for selecting the themes for curricular units and the activities through which they are to be addressed. These decisions should be based both on knowledge of the students' interests and current levels of participation and on expectations concerning the semiotic resources that such themes and activities are likely to call into play. In this initiating role, the teacher is also responsible for leading whole class sessions, in which theme and activities are introduced, students presented with appro-priately pitched challenges, expectations made clear and, in due course, both processes and outcomes evaluated and reflected upon.

At the micro level, by contrast, teaching can be characterized much more in terms of response. Having created the setting and provided the challenge, the teacher observes how students take it up, both individually and collectively, and acts to assist them in whatever ways seem most ap-propriate to enable them to achieve the goals that have been negotiated. It is thus at the micro level of teaching, when working with individuals or small groups of students, that the teacher is best able to practice the sort of teaching that Vygotsky (1978) characterized as "working in the student's zone of proximal development."

These are the requirements, I would suggest, that all teachers have to meet. However, in deciding on the manner in which they meet them, they have a considerable amount of discretion. For, although the teacher must act as leader, leadership does not *have* to be exercised in a directive manner; and although the teacher is ultimately responsible for the goals to which "action" is directed, and for monitoring the outcomes in terms of students' increasing mastery of valued cultural tools and practices, it is still possible for students to have a significant part in negotiating both these processes. Here, then, is the teacher's opportunity for professional growth and creativity – in constantly trying to find more effective ways of fulfilling her or his responsibilities both to the wider society and to the diversity of individual students who constitute the community of the classroom.

A major part of this responsibility is to engage the students in a semiotic apprenticeship into the "actions" and discourse genres that constitute the ways of making meaning in the different disciplines (see Chapter 4). In fact, it is this intended outcome that should guide the choice of activities within curricular units, as it is only when students engage in activities in which these "actions" and genres constitute the appropriate tools for mediating the achievement of the activity goals, that they will have the opportunity to master them through genuine participation. Ensuring that such opportunities occur clearly constitutes a central component of what I earlier called the macro level of teaching.

At the micro level, it is in the moment-by-moment co-construction of meaning, in the sequences and episodes of discourse through which these activities are realized, that the craft of teaching is found. In particular, I would suggest, it is through the strategic use that the teacher makes of opportunities to follow up on students' contributions that he or she most effectively facilitates their entry into the relevant discourse communities. And so it is to a consideration of this aspect of teacher–student discourse that I now wish to turn in order to illustrate the application of the framework presented in the first part of this chapter.

II

The Follow-up: Teaching as Responsive Intervention

Some years ago, when I was trying to develop the thesis that children's increasing mastery of their first language occurs as a result of their participation in conversations about the events that constitute their everyday experience, I became interested in the conversational strategies that parents employ to extend the conversational topic beyond one single-exchange sequence (Wells, 1981). One group of strategies, in particular, caught my attention. Simply put, these strategies involve making the response move in the first exchange act as a pivot for the introduction of a further, bound exchange.

Typically, in the early stages, it is the child's initiating move which is responded to in such a way that it calls for a further response. In the following sequence, recorded when Mark was twenty-three months old, his mother uses three variants of this strategy. [Note: The coding categories will be described more fully later; a full listing is included in Appendix 2.

For the moment, it is sufficient to know that 'I' and 'R' in the second column stand for *initiate* and *respond*, respectively.]

		Exch	Move	Prosp	Function
1. Mark:	Jubs (= birds)	Nuc.	I	G	Inform
2. Mother:	What are they doing?	Nuc.	R	(A)	
		Dep.	I	D	Req. inform
3. Mark:	Jubs bread (= birds eat bread)	Dep.	R	G	Inform
4. Mother:	Oh look they're eating the berries, aren't they?	Dep.	I	G+	Reformulate + Req. confirm
5. Mark:	Yeh	Dep.	R	G	Confirm
6. Mother:	That's their food . they have berries for dinner	Dep.	I	G	Extend
7. Mark:	Oh	Dep.	R	A	Acknowledge

(adapted from Wells, 1981, p. 102)

In this conversational sequence, Mark's mother extends the topic he initiated at three points: in (2), she implicitly acknowledges Mark's topic-initiating informing move by asking a dependent question; in (4), she offers an alternative interpretation of what the birds are doing and invites Mark to confirm it; and in (6), she extends the agreed upon proposition about the birds eating the berries.

What I soon realized, however, was that these strategies for sustaining the conversation can equally well be seen as a form of teaching, in which the adult encourages the child to add more information and clarifies and extends his or her attempts. And, because it is the child who has initiated the topic, the adult can be reasonably certain that there is intersubjective agreement about the current focus of attention and that, as a result, the new information will be (at least partially) understood.

In the classroom, where there are thirty children for the teacher to interact with, it is impossible to adopt the same strategies – at least when interacting with all of them simultaneously. In this context, an alternative is for the teacher to initiate the sequence with a move that simultaneously specifies the topic and invites one of the students to contribute further information; then, following the student response, the teacher can add a further move to confirm, clarify or extend the proposition that has been co-constructed in the nuclear exchange. Sequence 3 in Episode 1, quoted below, (see p. 254) is a very clear example of this strategy. In response to the teacher's request, Salina offers a relevant suggestion and the teacher extends that suggestion by proposing practical ways in which it could be put into effect.

As can be seen, from a functional and pedagogic perspective, there is considerable similarity between this sequence and the one in which Mark and his mother talked about the birds. Although they differ in who initiates the topic that forms the point of departure for the adult question, in both cases the child's response is further responded to in the following adult move(s). Yet, despite this similarity, the two sequence types would, in most work on classroom discourse, be analyzed very differently. The former – if it was discussed at all – would be treated as a succession of topically related exchanges, whereas the latter would be treated as a single instance of a triadic dialogue exchange, with the structure: *initiate – response – follow-up*. There is, however, an alternative analysis, which allows the two sequence types to be treated as variants of a single more generic discourse structure.

It is a very general principle of conversation that, within an exchange, moves decrease in "prospectiveness" (Wells, 1981; Brazil, 1981). The most strongly prospective move is a *demand*, which requires a *give* in response. A *give* is less prospective: it expects but does not require a response. Least prospective is an *acknowledge*, which always occurs in response to a more prospective move but itself expects no further response. The scale is thus ordered D>G>A and there are two basic exchange types, depending on whether the initiating move is *demand* or *give*:

(i) D–G–A
D: Did you hear the forecast for today?
G: They said there'd be snow later
A: Ugh!

(ii) G–A
G: The forecast says there'll be snow today
A: Oh

Conversation that was made up only of such sequences, each consisting of a single nuclear exchange, would perhaps be efficient, but it would not be very interesting. Nor would it provide a very rich opportunity for learning about the ways in which community members conceive of objects and events being related to each other – i.e. the community's "theory of experience" (Halliday, 1993a). In "normal" conversation, however, such minimal sequences are the exception rather than the rule. For there is a second principle to the effect that, at any point after the initiating move in an exchange, a participant can, while still minimally or implicitly fulfilling the expectations of the preceding move, step up the prospectiveness of the current move so that it, in turn, requires or expects a response. In effect, what this does is to initiate a further, dependent exchange, in which some aspect of the preceding exchange is extended or qualified in some way.

Adopting this analysis, we can now see the similarity between the two examples considered above. In both cases, the adult uses this "follow-up" strategy to involve the child(ren) in an extension of the "content" that has been co-constructed up to that point. In the first example, this strategy is used three times. In (2), the mother makes a D move where only A is expected, thereby requiring Mark to extend his own initial observation. In (4), she makes a G move in place of the expected A and offers a more accurate formulation of the birds' activity; she also adds a tag, which has the effect of making her move more strongly prospective (G+), thus requiring Mark to confirm her formulation. And in (6), she once more substitutes a G for the barely expected A in order to add information which relates the observed event to a cultural pattern more familiar to the child. And, since her G move expects an A in response, Mark duly obliges with a minimal "Oh," which brings the sequence to a close.

In the classroom example (pp. 253–5), the strategy is used only once. The expected structure of the nuclear exchange is I–R–F, with the teacher contributing a D in the first move and an A in the third. However, in the second part of the third move, the teacher steps up the prospectiveness by making a G move (lines 54–58), in which she extends the student's response by adding a further, related suggestion of her own. In this case, however, the dependent exchange that she initiates does not close with an overt A move from the student(s) – and it rarely does in triadic dialogue – as she herself concludes the sequence by returning to the nuclear exchange and giving a fuller realization of her earlier evaluation and, without pausing, goes on to initiate a new sequence, and the episode continues in similar format, with the students contributing suggestions and the teacher extending them.

The point of introducing this comparative analysis of the two examples, then, has been to show how, in very different contexts, the use of the same basic strategy of exploiting the possibility for follow-up within a sequence in progress allows a more knowledgeable participant to contribute to the learning of the less knowledgeable in ways which nevertheless incorporate and build on the latter's contributions. This is one important form that responsive teaching can take at what I earlier described as the micro level of teaching. However, as we shall see below, there are other, significantly different ways in which the follow-up move can be used to perform this teaching function.

In their pioneering scheme of analysis for classroom discourse, Sinclair and Coulthard (1975) propose three categories of "act" that can occur in the follow-up move of a triadic dialogue exchange: "accept" (including reject), "evaluate" and "comment." This latter category includes the more delicate subcategories of "exemplify," "expand" and "justify," each of which, according to the reanalysis proposed here, is realized through the initiation of a dependent exchange, by the teacher making a G move where only an A is expected. Put in different terms, by exploiting the scale of prospectiveness, a dependent exchange can be added on to the nuclear exchange in the follow-up and one of the various subcategories of comment used to relate the current sequence to the personal experience of one or more of the participants or to some more systematic knowledge structure which has been built up within the classroom community or is imported from the relevant discipline.

In the North American tradition (e.g. Mehan, 1979), by contrast, "Evaluate" is the term used to designate the third move of every triadic dialogue exchange (I–R–E), and not just one of its functions – no doubt because this is the function that the third move is most frequently observed to perform. However, this functional category, too, consists of more delicate subcategories; in addition to "accept" and "reject," the teacher may "reformulate" (by restating a student's response in a clearer or more accurate form) or "correct" (by providing an alternative response that is to be heard as more appropriate than the one supplied by the student).

Newman et al. (1989) describe these follow-up interventions in terms of "gatekeeping":

Rather than seeing it primarily as an evaluation of the child speaker, [Griffin and Humphrey] demonstrated that the third part of the sequence acts as a gatekeeper for the content of the lesson. Unless a teacher goes into a lecture format, this gatekeeping turn is about the only thing that a teacher can use to make sure that the proper information is available for learning and that improper content is removed from consideration by the lesson participants. In essence, the three parts can be seen as one assertion that is *collaboratively constructed* by the teacher and the children. (p. 125)

A very similar argument is made by Edwards and Mercer (1987) for the use of moves with these functions in the interest of jointly constructing what they call "common knowledge."

One feature shared by all the functions of follow-up moves so far discussed is that it is the teacher who, in the dependent exchange, does the work of supplying the proper information or of making connections to other bodies of knowledge – albeit in a responsive manner that takes account of the student's contribution. However, there is another group of follow-up interventions that offers this role to the student. These typically occur in dependent exchanges initiated by a D move in which a student is requested to perform the very same functions that are typically performed by the teacher in the third move of triadic dialogue. Thus, the request may be to "clarify," "exemplify," "expand" or "explain," or it may take the form of a challenge to the speaker to "justify" a proposal (or a proposition presupposed by that proposal). Instances of some of these functions can be seen in Episode 2 (below). The final outcome of such a sequence – an increment in the group's common knowledge – is often similar to that arrived at by means of teacher-dominated triadic dialogue, but the distribution of responsibility for achieving it is very different. For here it is the student, rather than the teacher, who does most of the work involved in producing the acceptable formulation.

In focusing on the various ways in which a teacher can initiate a dependent exchange to follow up on a student move, I have, in effect, been developing an account of an important set of discourse "operations" that she or he may use, both strategically and responsively, to mediate the "action" of teaching at what I earlier called the micro level. In order to understand better when and why the different alternatives are selected, however, we need to return to the "activity system" as a whole and, in particular, to a consideration of the nature of the goals which direct the participants' "actions."

Determining the Goals of Classroom Activities

Let me start by attempting to bring together the various strands of the foregoing discussion in a synoptic representation of the overall descriptive framework that is being proposed. This is set out in Table 7.1. The two dimensions of the table correspond to two different ways of conceiving of "enactment" of the Practice of Education. On the horizontal dimension, the relationship is that of realization, as proposed in Leont'ev's tristratal theory of "activity." On the vertical dimension, by contrast, the relationship is that of constituency: Units at higher levels consist of one or more units at the level next below. Inevitably, this representation is extremely schematic and nonspecific, as it is intended,

Table 7.1. *The Enactment of the Practice of Education*

Activity	(Motive)	Action	(Goal)	Operation
Practice of Education	(a) cultural reproduction (b) development of individual potential (c) fostering of communities of inquiry	Curricular Unit	Increasing mastery of: (a) content knowledge (b) discipline-based practices (c) tools & artifacts (d) metacognition (e) collaboration	
		Curricular Activity	Outcomes related to (a)–(e) above	Use of semiotic tools, including spoken discourse, e.g. curriculum genres (cf. Christie,1993)
		Task	Completion of a component of an activity outcome	e.g. Co-construction of episode of discourse
		Step	Contribution to outcome of task	e.g. Co-construction of sequence of discourse, using a microgenre e.g. triadic dialogue

in principle, to account for the full range of variability that occurs across classroom events as a result of differences in: age of the students, curricular area being addressed, resources available, as well as the teacher's philosophy of education. Furthermore, it makes no attempt to represent the *dynamic* dimension of "enactment," as events are co-constructed over time. Despite these limitations, however, it does provide a useful summary of the main categories previously discussed and of the relationships between them.

The next step toward filling out the framework is to incorporate the model of an "activity system" proposed by Engeström (1990), which was presented in Figure 7.1. However, since an expanded triangle of mediated action applies at every level in the hierarchy of "action," I will not attempt to represent the resulting framework here. Nevertheless, that model does supplement Table 7.1 in a number of important ways, notably by introducing the influence of the contextual categories of "rules," "community" and "division of labor" into the relationships of realization, and by making clear that there are different perspectives on the enactment of the "activity system" depending on who is in the "subject" position. This is nowhere more apparent than with respect to the goals and mediating artifacts that are associated with the different levels of "action."[8]

As I pointed out in the previous chapter, there is no guarantee that, even in a classroom organized to foster collaboration, there will be agreement about the goals that are being pursued at any time. There are two major reasons for this. First, the goal may not have been made (sufficiently) explicit, and participants' individual construals of the situation may result in a diversity of interpretations. This is particularly likely to take the form of mismatch between the teacher's goals and those constructed by the students, as for example, when the class is dispersed to carry out practical work in groups or individually. The second major cause of goal mismatch arises from conflicting agendas. Such conflict may well occur when the teacher's goals do not engage the students' commitment to the task in hand; however, it can also occur within a student group that is fully engaged in the task but where individual members have different ideas about how the task might best be carried out. Any of these forms of goal mismatch inevitably impact on the smooth running of the "operations" through which the "action" is realized and can frequently be detected in the discourse, as goals are renegotiated or participants draw attention to the mismatch.

However, there is another way in which Table 7.1 oversimplifies the status of goal in relation to "action," for it seems to suggest that, at every level, the goal is both determined in advance and constant throughout the "operationalization" of the "action." However, as Lemke (1993b) has pointed out, the notion of a stable goal is incompatible with the reality of the move-by-move co-construction of discourse, in which each move is strategically made in the light of what has preceded. The goal which is the current focus of attention cannot, therefore, be prescribed in advance of the moment of utterance. In fact, the same is true of any form of *joint* activity, if the participants are responsive to each other's contributions and to the constantly changing situation which results from these contributions. Thus, whether the goal is operationalized through discourse or through some other form of semiotic mediation, new possibilities are constantly being opened up at each step in the action and, in responding to these, the participants necessarily modify the goal to which they are orienting to a greater or lesser degree. Lemke, in fact, suggests that the goal can only be determined in retrospect, once it has been achieved. And Leont'ev also points to the emergent nature of goals when he observes: "selection and conscious perception of goals are by no means automatic or instantaneous acts. Rather, they are a relatively long process of *testing goals through action* and, so to speak, fleshing them out. As Hegel correctly noted, an individual 'cannot define the *goal* of his action until he has acted'." (1981, p. 62).

Nevertheless, while recognizing the force of this argument, I do not think it should lead us to abandon the concept of "goal." Instead, we should recognize that the goals to which participants are orienting are always to some extent emergent, and that this tendency increases the lower one goes down the scale of "action." In fact, just as there is a hierarchy of "action," so too there is a hierarchy of associated goals, with those at lower levels being increasingly sensitive to the specifics of the unfolding situation. Particularly in classrooms where the students work for much of the time in groups and in which they are encouraged to share in the planning and execution of the tasks that they undertake, therefore, we should expect to find that, at the level of task and step, goals are emergent and negotiated. On the other hand, this does not preclude the appropriateness of relatively stable goals at the higher levels of curricular activity and of the curricular unit as a whole, that is to say, goals which are selected by the teacher, perhaps after some degree of negotiation with the students, and then announced in the expectation that they will serve as a basis for the formulation, evaluation and modification of lower-level goals as the "action" progresses. Indeed, without some organizing goal structure of this kind, to which all participants orient in general terms, it is difficult to see how the thirty or so members of the classroom community could work together productively within the constraints of limited space, time and resources. Nevertheless, these goals, too, are subject to change if the situation demands it – as in stepping up an operation for deliberate attention (see Chapter 6) – or if new opportunities emerge that were not initially foreseen.[9]

Thus, when the emergent nature of goals – particularly at the lower level – *is* taken into account, it is easy to understand why participants may sometimes have different ideas about the current goal – leading to uncoordinated, or even conflictual, "operations." It also explains the difficulties that are frequently experienced by analysts as they attempt to segment the transcribed stream of discourse into episodes and sequences. For, when goals are progressively negotiated as events unfold, boundaries are not clear-cut, and the transition to a new "action" unit may only be recognized, by participants as well as by analysts, as having occurred some moments after it was initiated by those who were most responsible for bringing it about.

Finally, in attempting to explain the overall orderliness that characterizes life in most classrooms, we should not ignore the coherence that is given to joint activity by the participants' orientation to a variety of other features of their shared situation – the objects that are being acted upon and the relations among persons and objects that are familiar from previous occasions. As various writers have pointed out, while the co-construction of meaning is always newly enacted, its achievement is dependent on the cultural continuity provided by the social–material environment.

A Comparison of Two Episodes of Classroom Discourse

At this point I should like to introduce two episodes of discourse from science activities in elementary classrooms. The first occurred in a Grade 4/5 class, at the beginning of an early lesson in a unit on weather. The teacher is conducting a discussion with the whole class and starts by referring to written questions on the topic that the students have already generated.

	Exch	Move	Prosp	Function
Episode 1				
Sequence 1				
6 T: Here are all your ideas about how we can learn about weather, the different things that we can do . . What I'm wondering about is how should we go about this, like if we're having a weather time to work on weather, what should we be doing during that time?				
How should we go about learning using all these different things?	Nuc.	I	D	Req. suggest
[Several hands go up, including Jenny's]	Emb.	I	D	Bid
7 T: Jenny?	Emb.	R	G	Nominate

		Exch	Move	Prosp	Function
8 J:	We should make a few groups and then one group does weather from books using those little fact sheets and then say the other group gets it from um a movie or from film– from like film slides or from all different places, from experimenting, so there's several groups doing things and then we trade	Nuc.	R	G	Suggest
9 T:	OK	Nuc.	F	A	Acknowledge
	Sequence 2				
10 T:	Another idea?	Nuc.	I	D	Req. suggest
	[Several hands up, including Lyndsey's]	Emb.	I	D	Bid
11 T:	Lyndsey?	Emb.	R	G	Nominate
12 L:	Maybe you could have games ** (inaudible)	Nuc.	R	G	Suggest
13 T:	OK	Nuc.	F	A	Acknowledge
	Maybe some people would like to make up some games about the weather that would allow you to learn				Reformulate
	Uhhuh				Acknowledge
	Sequence 3				
14 T:	Other ideas about how we can go about this?	Nuc.	I	D	Req. suggest
15 S:	We can like look in newspapers and stuff ** –	Nuc.	R	G	Suggest
16 T:	OK				(backchannel)[10]
17 S:	– see if we can find articles or something like magazines or something				
18 T:	Great	Nuc.	F	A	Acknowledge/ Evaluate
	So I'd like you to start looking in the newspaper and when you find articles about weather you could cut them out and bring them in . .	Dep.	I	G	Extend

	Exch	Move	Prosp	Function
Ask first to make sure that whoever at home reads the paper is finished with it.				
But that's a great idea, Salina	Nuc.	F	G	Evaluate

After several more sequences of this kind, the class moves on to a consideration of possible participant structures, and there is some debate about whether it would be good or bad to work in friendship groups. The whole discussion, which lasted for some twenty minutes, continued in this mode throughout.

The second episode occurred in a Grade 6 class, as a visiting teacher (T) joined three students, Nir, Vi-Hung and Ian, who were formulating questions for the next stage of their inquiry into the metamorphosis of some painted lady caterpillars. In the first sequence, they propose a candidate question: "What happens inside the chrysalis?" This leads quite naturally to the second, which this time they treat as a "real" question and immediately begin to search for an answer.

		Exch	Move	Prosp	Function
Episode 2					
		Sequence 2			
74 I:	How do they eat?	Nuc.	I	D	Req. inform
75 N:	Well they can go out through their *	Nuc.	R	G	Inform
76 T:	Well, when you say "how do they eat" you're making an assumption that they DO eat	Dep.	I	G+	Indirect challenge
77 I:	I know they eat when they're not in the chrysalis	Dep.	R	G	Qualify
78 T:	HOW do you know?	Dep.	I	D	Req. justif.
79 I:	Well, ** food	Dep.	R	G	Justif.

		Exch	Move	Prosp	Function
80 T:	What did you see that makes you think they eat when they're in the chrysalis?	Dep.	I	D	Req. justif.
81 I:	**	Dep.	R	(not heard)	
82 T:	Pardon? Sorry, I didn't hear . say it again	Emb.	I	D	Req. repeat
83 I:	Do they eat?	Emb.	R	(G)	Repetition
		Dep.	I	D	Req. inform
84 T:	Do they?	Emb.	I	D	Check
85 I:	Yeah,	Emb.	R	G	Confirm
	like is there food for them in the chrysalis?	Dep.	I	D	Reformulate Req. inform
86 T:	Well, wait a minute, there are two ways you can think about this: does the chrysalis go to its– the chrysalis make contact with food	Dep.	R	G	Clarify
	outside itself ?	Dep.	I	D	Req. pos/neg
87 I:	No	Dep.	R	G	Neg
89 T:	Okay	Dep.	F	A	Acknowledge
	So . so if the chrysalis feeds inside the chrysalis, what would the food be? Where does it come from?	Dep.	I	D	Req. inform
90 I:	**	Dep.	R1 (not heard)		
91 N:	I think that they like ate, they ate a lot to get energy to change inside the chrysalis . . so I think they were eating the– like * for seven days and they almost ate the food you see there's almost none left . .	Dep.	R2	G	Inform

		Exch	Move	Prosp	Function
92 T:	Uhhuh			(backchannel)	
93 N:	and– and now it's got like a lot of energy to change and it's changing inside . . That's what I think				
94 T:	So you're- you think it doesn't need food	Dep.	I	A	Reformulate
	during THIS stage because it's already stored a lot?			D	Req. Confirm
95 N:	Yeah	Dep.	R	G	Confirm
96 T:	Yeah	Dep.	F	A	Acknowledge
97 N:	What do YOU think?	Dep.	I	D	Req. Opinion
98 T:	What do I think?	Emb.	I	D	Check
	I think I agree with you	Dep.	R1	G	Opinion
99 I:	I think I agree with you too	Dep.	R2	G	Opinion

Several more sequences of a similar kind follow, culminating in a sequence in which the appropriateness of a proposal by Nir is discussed: He suggests that the best way to answer the question about what is happening inside the cocoons would be to dissect one every other day until the butterflies begin to emerge. At this point, the teacher calls the students back into the classroom and the episode comes to an end. However, there the suggestion is taken up by the whole class and, after a lengthy discussion in which everyone participates, it is finally decided that Nir should be allowed to carry out a dissection of a cocoon that seems to have died and, the next day, with help from some of his peers, Nir goes ahead with the autopsy. (This whole unit is described in more detail in Wells, 1993b.)

In what follows, I shall attempt to relate these two episodes of discourse to the "activity systems" in which they occurred. By so doing, I hope to be able to provide a plausible, although tentative and incomplete, explanation of the differences between them with respect to the discourse microgenres that were deployed. For purposes of comparison, I present the most relevant information in tabular form (see Table 7.2).

Table 7.2. *Discourse Episodes in Activity Systems in Two Classrooms*

	Example 1	Example 2
Curricular Unit (C.U.)		
Topic	Understanding the Weather	Life Cycle of Butterfly
Teacher's Dominant goals	(a) Content knowledge (b) Practices of inquiry (c) Collaboration	(a) Practices of inquiry (b) Collaboration (c) Self-evaluation (d) Content knowledge
Activity		
Stage in C.U.	Early: before starting inquiry	Late: after observing caterpillars
Teacher's goal	Plan organization of C.U.	Continue self-selected inquiries
Object	Not yet decided	Chrysalis
Mediating tools	Spoken discourse, lists of individually generated questions	Magnifying glass, etc.; reference books; spoken discourse
Task		
Preceding task	None	T's directions to generate questions
Teacher's goals	Generate suggestions for planning C.U.	Students generate questions for study of chrysalis
Students' goal	Generate suggestions for planning C.U.	Generate questions for group's further inquiry
Mediating tools	Spoken discourse	Spoken discourse
Community	Teacher with whole class	3 students with visiting teacher
Rules	Wait to be nominated	Any participant may initiate
Division of labor	T. controls topic and turns	Shared control of topic and turns

Despite the one to two year's gap in age between the two groups of students and the difference in the topics under investigation, there are considerable similarities between these two classrooms, as compared, say, with the science classrooms reported in Edwards and Mercer's (1987) study. For in both these classrooms a dominant goal on the part of the teacher is for the students to master practices of inquiry and, to this end, they are encouraged to contribute to the formulation of the goals and procedures that will guide their activities. Nevertheless, although student suggestions are taken into account, it is the teacher who ultimately controls the timing of curricular activities and sets and announces the goals for each lesson period. Student initiative in goal-setting and in choice of means to be used (e.g. the balance between obtaining observational as opposed to library-based evidence) is thus largely exercised within a common superordinate goal structure, which remains relatively stable, at least for the duration of individual lessons.

If the "activity system" as a whole is broadly similar in the two classrooms, what might account for the difference in the very different microgenres deployed in the sequences contained in the two episodes? Here, it seems to me, there are a number of factors, none of which is uniquely responsible, but which, taken in conjunction, provide a plausible explanation. First, there is the task itself and its timing in relation to previous activities undertaken. In the Grade 6 class, the study of the developmental cycle of the painted lady caterpillars occurred towards the end of a year in which the students had gained considerable experience in conducting inquiries into topics of their own choosing within an overall theme. Furthermore, they had already spent a considerable amount of time formulating questions and collecting observational evidence concerning development at the earlier, caterpillar stage. They therefore had relevant knowledge and experience to draw on in carrying out the task set by the teacher, the goal of which was to formulate further questions for their group's investigation of the current chrysalis stage of development. By contrast, the students in the Grade 4/5 class had had little previous experience of inquiry learning, except through library-based research. Additionally, the activity in question occurred early in the curricular unit and was concerned with developing an overall plan for the unit; furthermore, the task of generating suggestions concerning relevant parameters itself occurred at the beginning of the planning activity.

A second group of factors of considerable importance was the size and constitution of the "community" immediately involved in each event and the "division of labor" among the members. In the Grade 4/5 activity, all the students in the class were gathered in a circle on the carpet, with the teacher as leader and animator. Her goal, which she announced to the group, was to elicit suggestions, on the basis of which they would collectively develop a plan to which all students would then be expected to orient in the subsequent lesson periods devoted to the unit. There was thus a clear outcome in view for the teacher which, although unknown in its specific details, involved the class working toward consensus both about what was to be done and about the reasons for the decisions to be made. The main goals of the discussion task, from her perspective, therefore, were to elicit specific suggestions that could contribute to this outcome, and to establish a forum of collaborative discussion appropriate for the joint inquiry about weather by actually engaging with them in its "operationalization." In terms of the task goals, then, and of the division of labor, while the goal of engaging in collaborative exploratory discussion was set and maintained by the teacher, the actual outcomes were recognized to be emergent, depending on the specific suggestions made by the students.

In the Grade 6 episode, on the other hand, the class teacher had already set the goal for the task, and the group of three boys was engaged in working toward it when they were joined by the visiting teacher. Both as visitor to the class and as temporary member of this small community, the teacher did not have the same authority as the class teacher would have had, if she had been present; he also had no preconceived outcome in mind in joining the group. There was thus no status-based division of labor, although, as a teacher, the visitor was prepared to intervene if he thought he could assist the group in achieving their goal(s).

With these differences in mind, we can now turn to some of the features of the microgenres that were deployed, with a view to explaining the types of follow-up that occurred and their role in the development of the episode/task. As already pointed out, the episodes differed with respect to the parameter of "topic control." In the weather unit planning episode, for reasons discussed above, the teacher chose to engage the students in "unequal dialogue," in which she controlled both the topic and the turn taking. Her selection, at sequence level, of the triadic dialogue microgenre thus set up the expectation that the teacher, who initiated each sequence, would also make a contribution in the third, follow-up move. However, since she wished the discourse to be exploratory at this stage, it was important not to use the evaluative option. She therefore exploited the follow-up move in ways that extended the student suggestions in order to make clear that all suggestions would be given positive consideration, but at the same time to indicate her own evaluation of what was suggested.

In the caterpillar episode, by contrast, it was natural that, among this small group of students, topic control should be relatively equally distributed and, when the visiting teacher joined them, he tried to participate in a manner that would maintain this mode of equal dialogue. This is seen in the fact that, in both this and the preceding sequence, it was a student who was the initiator and another student who was the first to respond. With respect to "topic focus," although the overall mode was exploratory, once a candidate question had been accepted, the microgenre selected – for which we have, as yet, no label – was a form of collaborative debate in which an attempt was made to construct a warrantable answer that all would accept, at least as a working hypothesis. It was in this context that the visitor intervened to clarify the argument so far and to challenge his coparticipants to justify their proposals. And in so doing, he clearly acted as a teacher, attempting to assist his fellow participants to use the microgenre effectively to construct an answer to their question and, at the same time, providing an opportunity for them to recognize and appropriate this discourse tool.

There is, however, a further difference between the two episodes that may well be of significance for the types of follow-up that occurred. As has already been noted, the sequences in each episode involved proposals for consideration that were contributed by one or more of the students. However, although the proposals in each case shared the feature of tentativeness, they concerned different perspectives on reality. In the weather unit, the proposals were suggestions concerning future activity on the part of the community; in terms of the ancillary-constitutive parameter discussed above, they were thus action-oriented, falling into the category of "planning action." By contrast, in the caterpillar unit, under consideration were proposals about the way the world is, put forward in the form of questions; although answering the questions might subsequently involve action on the part of group members, the actual consideration of the questions themselves constituted a mode of discourse that could be categorized as incipient theorizing.

Do these two modes of construing experience through discourse, that Halliday (1993a) dubs dynamic and synoptic, tend to elicit different types of follow-up? Certainly, one of the most important lessons that students must learn in studying science is that theories about the material world need to be grounded in evidence from observation, and so the teacher's strategic challenging of the theory–evidence connections that were implicit in their proposals about the chrysalis can be seen as part of a microgenre that is central to the synoptically based discourse of science. The suggestions offered for the organization of the weather unit, on the other hand, belong more naturally to the domain of interpersonal negotiation of action, where differences in personal preference are to be expected; here, it is more appropriate to listen to each suggestion and explore its possibilities rather than immediately challenge its feasibility. These different stances toward experience suggest another possible reason for the teachers' different choices of follow-up move: A request to justify the grounds for a move just made is much more challenging than an extending or exemplifying comment, and may be more readily accepted in relation to a synoptic proposal in which one is not personally involved than in relation to a dynamic suggestion in which one is. Or perhaps they are equally acceptable in either mode – provided that other conditions are met, such as the addressee not being made to look stupid in front of his or her peers. From this point of view, a challenging follow-up is not as face-threatening in a small group setting as it is when the whole class is involved.

While these explanations must be treated as no more than speculations in the absence of corroboration from the participants involved, what they do make clear is that the choice of the sort of follow-up move to make is a highly strategic one. For it must simultaneously both respond to the ideational and interpersonal dimensions of the sequence in progress and also steer the ongoing episode in the direction required to achieve the goal of the "action" that the discourse is mediating. At the same time, given the real-time pace of spoken discourse, it is clear that teachers do not have time to consider all the implications of the options available to them at each point at which a follow-up move might be made. Rather, the selection of a particular option is an "operation" in exactly the sense intended by Leont'ev: it is both below the level of conscious attention and also strategically directed towards the goal of the current "action" in the conditions that are perceived to prevail.

If this is the case with the follow-up move, it is equally true of any other move that is made in the ongoing co-construction of discourse, including student responses. Although both purposeful and consequential with respect to the emerging goal of the "action" they are operationalizing, discourse moves are rarely independent, consciously chosen acts. Rather, they are produced in the moment, in response to the current state of the "action-in-progress," as this is construed by the participants in relation to the "activity-system" as a whole and to the "action-types" and discourse genres that have become established as the habitually used tools for pursuing the Practice of Education in their particular classroom community. In order to understand why a teacher selects one follow-up option rather than another, therefore – or, indeed, one microgenre, task or activity – it is ultimately necessary to understand both the history and sociocultural ecology of the classroom community in its wider context and also the individual teacher's conception of teaching and learning that guides his or her behavior at every level.

Conclusion: Education as Transformation

One way of thinking about the effects, in practice, of different conceptions of learning and teaching is in terms of the "rules" that figure in Engeström's model of an "activity system." As he points out: "In traditional school learning," these rules include "those that sanction behavior and regulate grading" (1991b, p. 249). They also include "rules" that concern such matters as the degree to which curricular subjects are integrated or kept firmly separated, the relationship between the macro and micro levels of teaching and, more generally, whether the pedagogy is "visible" or "invisible" (Bernstein, 1975).

To adopt the "rule" perspective on such differences between classrooms seems to carry with it an implication of external constraint. And, indeed, in some schools, teachers do work under quite severe constraints of curricular content, programming, norms of movement and noise level, and so on. However, in most jurisdictions – and certainly in the schools in which we have worked – teachers have considerable discretion in deciding how to enact the Practice of Education in the day-by-day events that make up their programs. Although suggestions or recommendations may be made by administrators at various removes from the classroom, it is the teacher who, in the last resort, decides whether to have students working collaboratively in groups or to "teach" them from the front of the class; whether to value conjectures, supported by argument, or "correct answers," as defined by the textbook; whether to attempt to get all students to achieve the same outcomes at the same time, or to recognize the various forms of diversity in the student community and to tailor expectations to take account of these differences, by negotiating appropriate challenges for each individual and providing the assistance that each needs in order to meet them.

An alternative way to think of such differences in teaching style – which gives greater recognition to the teacher as agentive decision maker – is to combine the notion of rules with Halliday's concept of register. Register, it will be recalled, accounts for the reciprocal relationship between situation-type and the choices that are made from the total linguistic meaning potential. As I argued earlier in Chapter 5, the value of this concept for thinking about educational change is that it provides a way of understanding how, through semiotic choices made in terms of the "actions" and "operations" that are selected, the teacher can change the larger situation, or, in the terms of activity theory, can instantiate a particular version of the Practice of Education.

Take, for example, the set of follow-up options that are available to the teacher when responding to a student contribution. Continually to choose the "evaluate" option - whether accepting *or* rejecting – does much to create a situational context in which right answers will be given priority by students. By contrast, frequently to choose the "extend" option creates a different context – one which emphasizes the collaborative construction of meaning, both in the setting of goals to be aimed for and in the construction of "common knowledge." And the choice of the options which call upon students to justify, explain and exemplify creates yet another context – one which encourages students critically to examine and evaluate the answers that they make to the questions that interest them and which simultaneously provides an opportunity for their apprenticeship into these "genres of power" (Lemke, 1988).

However, to suggest that teachers should deliberately change the type of feedback options they use may, at first sight, appear to involve a contradiction. Earlier I argued that, although strategic, the selection of follow-up move was made below the level of conscious attention. However, while I believe this to be generally the case, it is possible, as Leont'ev (1981) indicates, deliberately to step up an operation to the level of action for a while in order to make it a matter of conscious attention. This is what a teacher, alerted to his or her habitual behavior, might choose to do and, in this way, develop a changed stance, that makes the deployment of the more empowering options his or her "preferred" response at critical points in the unfolding discourse. In fact, investigating one's practice in order to make such improvements for the benefit of one's students is a major part of what is involved in being a "thoughtful practitioner" (Atwell, 1991).

In much of the research in the human sciences, the emphasis has been on investigating how "activity systems" determine the ways in which "actions" are "operationalized." The concept of register, by contrast, invites us to consider the converse relationship – how changing the "operations" by means of which an "action" is carried out can ultimately change the "activity system" in which the "action" is embedded. Of course I am not suggesting that the teacher's use of the more empowering types of follow-up can alone create an alternative realization of the Practice of Education. But when these options are deliberately but responsively deployed in the context of congruent choices with respect to options at other levels in the hierarchies of genre and "action," they can indeed create different "activity systems," with different "rules" and "division of labor."

It is in this way, I believe, that teachers have the power to transform the Practice of Education. If they choose to, they *can* make of their classrooms, communities in which members engage collaboratively in actions which they find personally meaningful and socially relevant; in which students are assisted to appropriate the valued resources of the culture, including artifacts and skills that are not purely linguistic; and in which individual creativity and diversity of culture, class, and gender are also recognized and valued. But, to make these transformations, as Tharp and Gallimore (1988) so cogently argue, they need assistance in exactly the same way as their students do.

For those responsible for the education of teachers, therefore, there are similar choices to be made. If we wish to see more classroom communities of the kind just described, we must create similar communities of inquiry in which teachers and researchers collaborate in investigating ways of improving practice. Both the teachers whose classrooms have provided the episodes discussed in this chapter have been involved in this sort of collaborative inquiry. By selecting which aspects of their practice they wish to problematize, and by critically examining recorded observational data, together with other evidence that their students provide, they are taking charge of their own professional development and using the resources of these different communities to achieve the goals that they consider important. And, because their inquiries, and ours as researchers, intersect with those of their students, overlapping communities of inquiry are formed, in which everyone is able to learn and, at the same time, to assist others to learn.

Notes

1. As in previous chapters, I shall refer to the stratum of "activity" as the Practice of Education and signal through the use of double quotes when I use "activity," "action," and "operation" to refer to the strata within Leont'ev's model. When the terms are used without quotes, on the other hand, I intend them to be understood as they are used in nontechnical discourse about classroom events and about human behavior more generally.

2. An important qualification must be added to this statement. Any "act" (to choose a term which is neutral with respect to the theory under discussion) can, on different occasions, be viewed as "action" or "operation." Which stratum it is assigned to depends on the focus of attention. For example, in the case of someone driving a car, the driving may function as an "operation" if the driver's attention is focused on the "action" to be carried out on arrival at the destination, or as an "action" while negotiating a tricky highway intersection. Similarly, from the analyst's perspective, the driving will be treated as an "operation"

when it is the subject's work patterns that are under investigation, and as an "action" when the focus is on the driver's coordination of multiple sources of information. Put more generally, most "acts" of any complexity cannot be treated as unequivocally "actions" *or* "operations" independently of the larger frame of reference. Furthermore, any "action" may simultaneously realize more than one "activity," and an "operation" more than one "action."

3. Kuutti (1996) provides a much fuller exposition of activity theory in his chapter in Nardi's (1996) edited collection on the use of activity theory in research on human–computer interaction.

4. Others, for example Stubbs (1983) and Eggins and Slade (1997), use the single term "exchange" for all sequential structures that range in scope from what I have called "nuclear exchange" up to "sequence." This is largely a terminological difference, since the definitions of their (expanded) "exchange" and my "sequence" are functionally equivalent (cf. Eggins and Slade, 1997, p. 222). The advantage of making the distinction that I propose is that it allows for sequences to be compared with respect to the ways in which they are built up from different types of exchange – nuclear, dependent, etc.

5. Intersubjectivity does not necessitate agreement of perspective or point of view, as Matusov (1996) makes clear. However, for the sequence to proceed, there must be an orientation toward intersubjective agreement about "what is going on," even if that is disagreeing.

6. See Bakhtin's (1986) concept of speech genres, discussed in Chapter 3.

7. Although using somewhat different terminology to refer to the units in terms of which the discourse is analyzed, Pontecorvo et al. (1990) have developed a somewhat similar framework to investigate the forms of reasoning that occur in group discussion.

8. See, for example, Engeström's discussion of the different roles in the mediation of action performed by the same tool when seen from the perspective of different subjects in "When is a tool? Multiple meanings of artifacts in human activity" (1990, chapter 8).

9. The nature and status of goals has been discussed on several occasions on xlchc/xmca, most notably in October–November 1993. In the light of the fact that there seems to be general agreement that, for an "action" in progress, the goals of the constituent sub-actions are always and inevitably emergent, it might be less confusing if a new term were found to refer to the sort of goal plan that is established in advance of an event, as for example in the agenda for a meeting or the teacher's instructions for the tasks to be carried out in a curricular activity.

10. "Backchannel" is the term used for a contribution made by listener in the course of a speaker's turn in order to signal that he or she is following the speaker's drift; such contributions do not constitute "moves," in the sense intended here, as they occur within, rather than after, the move to which they are related (cf. Coulthard, 1977, p. 62).

8   Making Meaning with Text:

A Genetic Approach to the Mediating Role of Writing

There can be little doubt that Vygotsky had a keen interest in the development of writing. As we shall see below, he saw mastering written language as playing a critical role in the development of "the higher psychological functions." However, apart from his chapter entitled "The Prehistory of Written Language" (1978), and one section of his chapter on the development of scientific concepts (1987), there is little in his translated works that addresses the subject of writing directly. Nevertheless, each of the main themes in his theory of learning and development provides a perspective on this topic and, in this chapter, I shall make reference to all of them. I shall start by considering the historical relationship between writing and speech.

Speech and the Development of Writing

Although the use of writing – as far as can be ascertained – is much more recent, in phylogenetic terms, than the use of speech, its origins are also shrouded in the mists of prehistory. However, the content and context of the earliest known written artifacts, which can be dated to some five thousand years ago, strongly suggest that the invention of writing followed the shift to a pastoral and agriculturally-based way of life and co-occurred with the development of large urban centers (Halliday, 1993b; Nicolopoulou, 1989). For in the more complex economy that resulted from settlement, a separation began to emerge between the processes of labor and the disposition of the products that were created and this, in turn, gave rise to the need to keep track of the type, quantity, and whereabouts of the products and also of those who produced them. In this context, it seems, the primary function of writing was initially to create a permanent record of information for economic purposes (Goody, 1987; Nicolopoulou, 1989).

Once invented, however, writing created possibilities for new activities that were previously unimaginable or, at least, barely feasible without its mediating role. For with the aid of writing, information that had been represented in a permanent form could also be collected, compared and codified. Thus there gradually developed new functions for writing. On the one hand, it began to play an important regulative role in the political administration of centralized states and, in religion, in the preservation of sacred texts in canonical form; on the other hand, in its archival function, it enabled the compilation of bodies of "facts" that, in due course, were to serve as the foundations for the disciplines of history, geography, natural science, medicine and so on. Finally, in the recording of oral literature, a third major function of writing emerged, although it was not until literary works began to be composed directly in the written mode that literature became a function in its own right, clearly distinguishable from the other two.

If we then ask what is the historical relationship between speech and writing, the answer would seem to be that they are alternative modes of representing the same underlying meaning potential that have been developed to serve very different functions. The primary purpose for which writing was invented was to preserve meaning so that it could be recovered in another time or place – a function for which, by its very nature, speech is quite unsuitable. In speech, meaning is typically constructed in the course of action; its primary function is to mediate interaction in the interests of getting things done. But spoken meaning fades with the utterance that brings it into being and – at least without the aid of mechanical recorders – disappears without leaving a permanent trace. Thus, although speech, whether in conversation with others or with oneself, is undoubtedly an invaluable tool for the generation of interesting and novel ideas, it is quite inadequate as a means of preserving them. By contrast, ideas that are fixed in a written text remain available as long as do the materials on which the text is inscribed, and as long as there are people who can decode it. As a result, a written text can be reread, silently or aloud, and, either by the writer or by subsequent readers, reconsidered and revised, with each successive version of the text providing the basis for further reflection and reformulation. Put very simply, then, it could be said that the primary function of speech is to mediate action whereas the primary function of writing is to mediate recall and reflection. It is this function of writing that Olson highlights when he writes: "What literacy contributes to thought is that it turns the thoughts themselves into worthy objects of contemplation" (1994b, p. 277).

This has not always been the way in which the relationship between speech and writing has been conceived, however. Because speech predates writing, both phylogenetically and ontogenetically, it was until quite recently assumed that, in inventing writing, the aim was to devise a means of giving an accurate visual representation of speech – a view that was supported by the systematic relationship between the phonemic and graphemic means of expression to be found in European, alphabetic scripts. However, since a wider range of scripts has been taken into account, this belief has been recognized to be mistaken.

Because speech and writing express the same underlying meanings, it is to be expected that there would be ways of establishing correspondence between the different means of expression. However, it is by no means the case that writing is simply transcription, based on a prior analysis of speech. Indeed, as Olson (1994b) argues, the reverse is more probably the case. For it is precisely the attempt to create a visual representation of the meanings communicated in speech that brings the spoken form in which those meanings are realized to conscious attention (see also Vygotsky, 1987, chap. 6) and, in the process, leads to the construction of an implicit theory of what is represented in speech, and how. Markedly different writing systems, as for example Chinese, English, and Vai (Scribner and Cole, 1981), render different aspects of speech salient and lead different cultures to construct different folk theories of the relationship between speech and writing.

However, no orthography represents all aspects of the meanings that are communicated in speech. For example, while an alphabetic script may seem to represent the "sounds" of speech, it becomes apparent when one attempts to transcribe a recorded conversation that the orthography ignores completely the intonational and paralinguistic features that convey the speaker's attitude, both to the topic and to his or her interlocutors. What *is* represented is the "proposition," as realized in the lexicogrammar; largely missing, on the other hand, is a representation of how the proposition is to be "taken," or interpreted. To compensate for the lack of a direct representation of these non-lexicogrammatical features in speech, written English and other alphabetically based writing systems make use of a sparse collection of punctuation marks, a more complex sentence-internal syntax, and a variety of metadiscursive terms, such as illocutionary verbs (e.g. stated, hypothesized, concluded, etc.) and manner adverbials (e.g. confidently, hesitantly, with a smile, etc.). Thus, where these affective and attitudinal aspects of meaning are enacted as an integral but largely unconscious part of speech, they are included in a written text in a much more conscious and descriptive manner in order to construct and manage the relationship between writer, reader, and the topic of the discourse.

In emphasizing the function of writing as preeminently a tool for recall and reflection, however, I do not want to imply that, by comparison with speech, the action involved in writing is a purely individual one. Like speech, writing is very much a social mode of communicating and thinking (Bakhtin, 1981), and the activities it typically mediates are collaborative endeavours, even though the participants may not be co-present in time and space. Nevertheless, as a mode of meaning making, its manner of material production, as well as the permanence of the artifacts that result, give it a range of roles in activity that complement rather than duplicate those of speech.

The Development of Writing:
An Ontogenetic Perspective

Vygotsky's interest in writing was with writing as a psychological tool rather than as an activity in its own right. In *Thinking and Speech* (1987, chap. 6), he focused on the part that mastery of the tool of writing plays in the development of mental activity, arguing that learning to write requires the child to develop a more conscious and intentional stance with respect to the realization of meaning which, in turn, promotes the development of deliberate, systematic thinking, mediated by scientific concepts. Because of its more abstract nature as compared with speech, "written speech forces the child to act more intellectually" (p. 204).

Here, Vygotsky is advancing an argument on the ontogenetic level that is somewhat comparable to that advanced by Olson in his account of the prehistory of writing (see above). Learning to write brings speech to the level of conscious awareness:

Instruction in written speech and grammar play a fundamental role in this process. ... When learning to spell words that are spelled phonetically, the child gains conscious awareness that a word such as "fast" contains the sounds F-A-S-T, that is, he gains conscious awareness of his own activity in the production of sound; he learns to pronounce each separate element of the sound structure voluntarily. In the same way, when the child learns to write, he begins to do with volition what he has previously done without volition in the domain of oral speech. Thus, both grammar and writing provide the child with the potential of moving to a higher level in speech development. (Vygotsky, 1987, p. 206)

Nevertheless, as an account of what is involved in learning to write, this passage seems curiously limited in its focus on what would now be called "phonemic awareness." First, in representing written language as essentially speech written down, it ignores the systematic and functionally based differences between the linguistic registers that are drawn upon in speaking and writing (Halliday, 1985). Learning these new registers, and when and how to deploy them, is a very important part of the apprenticeship into literacy that children undertake at school. Furthermore, the development of scientific concepts, in particular, is inseparable from children's mastery of the – typically written – language in which these concepts are encountered and used. Also in need of further emphasis is the important role that engagement with particular written texts can play, both intermentally and intramentally, in the development of understanding and in the systematic construction of knowledge. To understand this, it is helpful to look in more detail at the historical development of writing in relation to the activity systems in which it plays a significant shaping role. Key to this are the concepts of register and genre.

The Development of Writing: A Historical Perspective

In any activity system, there are certain practices, participant roles and tools that are of central importance (Engeström, 1990). Taken together, these define the most frequently occurring situation-types associated with the activity. Language is almost always one of these tools, but particular situation-types tend to draw differently on the meaning potential that it provides. It is this relationship between situation-type and selection from the total resources of the language that is referred to as register. Register thus looks in two directions. On the one hand, it looks to the situation, categorizing it with respect to three dimensions: field (what is going on), tenor (who is taking part), and mode (what role is assigned to language). And, on the other hand, it maps on to the three metafunctional components of the language's semantic system, respectively the experiential, the interpersonal and the textual. Thus, as Halliday puts it, a register is "a configuration of meanings that are typically associated with a particular configuration of field, tenor and mode" (Halliday and

Hasan, 1989, pp. 38–9). The relationship is only probabilistic, of course, but the more narrowly the situation-type is defined, the more predictable will be the selections that are made from the semantic systems, and from the lexicogrammatical resources through which the semantic systems are realized.

If we think of a register as those parts of the language's meaning potential that are most likely to be drawn on in the situations associated with a particular activity system, a genre can be thought of as the characteristic manner in which these resources are selected and deployed in order to achieve the goal of a particular action. And, since this process eventuates in particular texts which have relevant features in common, genre also refers to the characteristic text-types associated with this action. Thus, within the language as a whole, each genre can be thought of as a different tool, and the range of different genres that are available within a culture as, together, making up a literacy tool-kit. In order to function effectively as a writer or reader, therefore, one needs to be able to select the appropriate tool from the tool-kit and use it for the action and activity system in which one is involved.

One particular advantage of thinking of the different registers and genres of text as tools, I would suggest, is that it makes clear that they are neither arbitrary nor fixed. As with other tools, they are functional in origin and continually being developed and refined over time to meet the demands of the tasks they are required to perform (Miller, 1984). At the same time, their development makes possible new forms of activity and new ways of representing and thinking about experience. In what follows, I shall try to support this claim by considering the role of writing in the development of one particular cluster of activity systems – that of Western science.

The Development of Scientific English

Already in the ancient civilizations of Greece, Rome, and China, writing had begun to play a significant role in the cultural construction of knowledge in different fields, as specialized lexicons and genres were developed for classifying and organizing information that had been recorded, and for constructing and debating theories that attempted to provide explanations for the phenomena of experience. Nevertheless, it was not until the European Renaissance, with the invention of the printing press and the establishment of institutions such as the British Royal

Society, that the written text became the key tool for the advancement of knowledge, as scholars presented their ideas and critiqued those of others, in an ongoing written dialogue. As Faraday is reputed to have said in the early part of the nineteenth century, when this practice had become well established, science consists of "making experiments and publishing them."

However, the genre of the scientific report did not appear overnight. In fact, it took several centuries to reach its present form, as is clearly brought out in Halliday's study of the development of scientific written English (Halliday, 1988; Halliday and Martin, 1993). As he shows by means of detailed linguistic analysis of texts from Chaucer's *Treatise on the Astrolabe*, written in the fourteenth century, to an article from a contemporary issue of *Scientific American*, the technical register common to all the genres in which the results of scientific research are presented and debated has gradually taken on its current form as successive writers have shaped it to better perform the function of formulating scientific knowledge, as this has come to be practiced within Western culture.

Earlier, I suggested that speech and writing were generally used to perform different functions, speech being predominantly for engagement in action and writing for reflection and interpretation. Of course, each mode was also used for the less dominant function, but in neither mode were the two functions systematically related. In order to communicate with other practicing scientists, however, a new mode of discourse was found to be necessary, one that would enable the practical activities of observation and experimentation to be articulated with the mental activities of explanation and theorizing. It was this need that led to the development that Halliday documents.

As his linguistic analysis demonstrates, the evolution of this new mode took place incrementally, largely through an increasing use of nominalization. In describing the working of the astrolabe, Chaucer already used a variety of Greek- and Latin-derived nouns as technical terms (e.g. "altitude," "declination"); he also used complex nominal groups, in which the head noun is further specified by qualifying phrases. However, it is in Newton's *Treatise on Opticks* that Halliday situates the birth of scientific written English, for it is here that we first find the discourse of experimentation. From this point of view, one key feature of Newton's text is that, in it, the scope of nominals has been extended to include nominalizations of processes and attributes: e.g. "Now those Colours argue a diverging and separation of the heterogeneous Rays from one another by means of their unequal Refractions" (quoted in Halliday, 1988, p. 168). And by 1987, when the article in *Scientific American* was written, the process has been extended still further, to include nominalized processes qualified by further nominalizations. Here is the passage Halliday quotes as example: "The rate of crack growth depends not only on the chemical environment but also on the magnitude of the stress. The development of a complete model of the kinetics of fracture requires an understanding of how stress accelerates the bond-rupture reaction" (quoted in Halliday, 1988, p. 163).

This use of nominalization has two important functions with respect to the creation of a discourse appropriate for the communication of scientific activity. First, by allowing a complex process to be represented as a single clause element, it enables the relevant information to be packaged in a "given-new" structure that facilitates the development of the exposition. Second, since processes, both material and mental, are realized in nominal structures, the main verb of the clause can now be used to signal the relationship either between the processes themselves or between the processes and the interpretation that the writer puts upon them. The result is a mode of text construction "that moves forward by logical and coherent steps, each building on what has gone before" (Halliday, 1988, p. 164).[1]

That the development of Western science proceeded in an interdependent relationship with the development of this new register of written prose (here illustrated with respect to English) is quite easily understood when seen in terms of the functional requirements of the activity system. First, the members of the scientific community were widely dispersed and rarely met together, so it was necessary to communicate in writing. Second, the genres of scientific exposition required extended turns in which to develop what was often a complex argument, and this form of dialogue fitted uneasily with the norms of spoken interaction. But, most importantly, because the arguments were complex, the permanence of the written text and the unpressured pace of its production were more appropriate than speech to a solo mode of meaning construction that advances slowly, in fits and starts, and involves multiple rephrasings and revisions. Furthermore, the visual mode of writing allowed for the easy incorporation of pictorial and diagrammatic modes of representation, which further clarified the communication. For all these reasons, then, the technical register of scientific prose was the tool preeminently suited to the systematic construction and communication of this new form of knowledge.

Writing and the Development of Higher Mental Functions

In considering the role of written discourse in the development of Western science, I have so far focused on the evolution of the tools. But as Vygotsky made clear, the relationship between activity, tools and participants is one of interdependence. As one part of the system is transformed, a related transformation occurs in each of the others. In the present case, this can be seen very clearly by looking at the practices that constitute the activity of science. Among these, the publishing of written reports and of responses to those of others has come to be constitutive of the object of science, for it is in written communication that the progressive construction of knowledge is most effectively achieved. Just as important, though perhaps less obvious, is the fact that the conceptualization and organization of empirical investigation, whether laboratory or field-based, also has the register of scientific writing as its point of reference. The community of scientists has thus become an activity system that is organized around the genres of written scientific discourse. However, most important of all is the manner in which the gradually emerging register of science has come to have a shaping influence on the way in which we all – "lay" people as well as scientists – make sense of the phenomena of experience, at least for certain purposes. For it is in the gradual evolution of this mode of scientific written discourse, and its spread to other disciplines, that we can trace the construction of the concepts and ways of relating them that are characteristic of Western science, and of "rational" thinking more generally. Furthermore, from its origins in the physical sciences, this technical mode of discourse has, over the last century or so, become so widely pervasive that, as Halliday (1993 a) observes, it now "invades almost every register of adult English that is typically written rather than spoken, especially the institutionalized registers of government, industry, finance, commerce and the like" (p. 112).

The significance of the impact that written scientific discourse has had on our ways of thinking can be seen most clearly if we start with the common-sense view of experience that is taken for granted in everyday, casual conversation. This is what Bruner (1986) calls the narrative mode of thinking; it concerns a world of doings and happenings, of actions and intentions – agents acting in the light of prevailing circumstances in order to achieve their goals. Linguistically, the typical realization of this world-view is through material and mental process clauses, in which the grammatical organization corresponds to the "natural" relationship between the entities, actions, and circumstances in terms of which we typically describe and explain behavior, our own and other people's. This is what Halliday (1993 a) refers to as the *dynamic* mode of construing experience and what Vygotsky (1987) had in mind in his discussion of spontaneous, or everyday, concepts. It is also the mode of speaking and thinking in which, in interaction with others, children construct their first understanding of the world.

Against this, we can set the way of thinking which is realized in the technical written discourse of the natural and human sciences, and of most kinds of official communication. In this *synoptic* mode (or "paradigmatic," as Bruner (1986) calls it), experience is construed from a much more abstract, analytical perspective. By recoding almost every aspect of experience – processes, attributes, and relationships, and even complete events in all their detail – as nouns or nominal structures, the synoptic mode provides a way of symbolically managing the complexity and variability of experience, by allowing it to be reconstrued in the categories defined by "scientific" concepts; these categories can then be systematically related in taxonomies, and instances counted and made amenable to operations of mathematics and logic.

Key to the development of this synoptic perspective on experience is the tendency towards "thingification" – a process which is the corollary of the linguistic process that Halliday (1993 a) calls "grammatical metaphor." Here is how he explains the historical evolution of these two related processes:

A written text is itself a static object: it is language to be processed synoptically. Hence it projects a synoptic perspective on to reality: it tells us to view experience like a text, so to speak. In this way writing changed the analogy between language and other domains of experience; it foregrounded the synoptic aspect, reality as object, rather than the dynamic aspect, reality as process, as the spoken language does. This synoptic perspective is then built in to the grammar of the written language, in the form of grammatical metaphor: processes and properties are construed as nouns, instead of as verbs and adjectives. ... And so the metaphor brings about a reconstrual of experience, in which reality comes to consist of things rather than doings and happenings. (p. 111)

In this account of the evolution of written, and particularly scientific and technical, discourse, I would suggest, is the key to an explanation of the development of scientific concepts, viewed from a historical–cultural perspective. In their linguistic realization as nominal forms, scientific concepts are artifacts that have been created through the application of grammatical metaphor in the writing of particular expository texts in order to explain new observations and interpretations to others, as for example in Newton's *Treatise on Opticks*. However, as these texts have entered into the ongoing discourse that is a constitutive practice of a knowledge-building community, these same forms have come to be used more generally as tools for construing the phenomena under investigation and for attempting to understand them and to communicate that understanding to others. In other words, scientific concepts, and the written discourse in which they are used, have come to constitute key cultural resources that mediate the collaborative construction of systematic scientific knowledge.

However, it is not only the synoptic register and genres of scientific writing that have extended our culture's resources for making sense of experience. Similar arguments could be made for other domains of cultural activity, such as religion and law, in which quite different genres of writing play an equally significant role. In each domain, the characteristic registers and genres constitute culturally developed ways of construing the indeterminateness of raw experience and interpreting it in terms of recognizable situation-types, in which certain forms of action, both physical and mental, are appropriate (Miller, 1984). By the same token, the written texts that are produced in this process both instantiate the genres that shape them and provide continuity in the ways of thinking that they embody.

From a Vygotskyan perspective, however, this is only half of the story. For the cultural resource that has been developed and used in the social activity of collaborative knowledge construction becomes, when mastered, the semiotic means that mediates the mental activity of individual knowers. In other words, it is by engaging with others in the social practices of interpreting and creating texts in relation to the material actions that the texts construe, that the individual is able to appropriate these cultural resources and use them for the construction of personal understanding. As Wartofsky (1979) explains:

Our own perceptual and cognitive understanding of the world is in large part shaped and changed by the representational artifacts we ourselves create. We are, in effect, the products of our own activity, in this way; we transform our own perceptual and cognitive modes, our ways of seeing and of understanding, by means of the representations we make. (p. xxiii)

In sum, it is against the background provided by the preceding cultural–historical account of the development of the registers of scientific and technical writing that we can best understand Vygotsky's emphasis on the dual roles of writing and scientific concepts in the development of what he called the higher mental functions. As he makes clear in his formulation of the "general genetic law of cultural development," it is by appropriating and mastering the cultural tools that mediate social, inter-mental, activity that the individual constructs the psychological tools for intra-mental activity. And clearly both writing and scientific concepts are particularly powerful tools for the abstract, rational mode of thinking that he considered to be the endpoint of mental development.

However, because Vygotsky concentrated almost exclusively on the ontogenetic level in his study of intellectual development, he tended to treat both writing and scientific concepts ahistorically, as relatively fixed and independent of each other, and so he did not make the connection between them that I have attempted to develop above. That is to say, he did not fully recognize the extent to which, as cultural artifacts, they are the products of a specific cultural–historical tradition (Scribner, 1985). And because he focused on learning in elementary school – where writing and scientific concepts have traditionally been treated as quite separate areas of instruction – he did not see that learning to read and write the synoptic genres is the mode in which scientific concepts are most naturally encountered and mastered. Nor, I think, did he fully appreciate the role that the construction of "public" knowledge through the composing of a written text can play in the development of understanding of a topic, both for the author and for other readers. It is to this that we shall turn in the next section, as we consider the microgenetic level in the development of writing.

Writing a Text: The Microgenetic Level

In considering the development of writing so far, we have been looking at changes that take place over time in the historical development of a culture or in the life trajectory of one of its individual members, as he or she learns and uses written language. One way of interpreting the micrognetic level of analysis, therefore, might be to examine in fine detail the mastery of some aspect of the literacy tool-kit. But there is another form of microgenetic development that I believe is equally important – that of the composition of a particular text. For, as Halliday's (1988) study shows, it is in meeting the functional demands of some particular situ-ation in which a written text is critical in the mediation of the activity that writers introduce changes which have the potential to transform all components of the activity system.

In adopting this interpretation of the microgenetic level of writing development, I should like to focus on a literary text: William Golding's novel, *The Inheritors* (1955). I have two reasons for choosing a literary, as opposed to a scientific, text at this stage in the development of my argument. First, I want to dispel any suggestion that it is only in the scientific genres that writing is a tool for the development of understanding through the representation of experience. And second, by choosing this particular text, I hope to be able to show how Golding's solution of a particular problem of representation casts light on the general theme of this chapter.

At first sight, it might appear that the composition of a literary work, such as a novel, is very different from a work in which scientific, historical, or psychological research is reported. This is certainly the view presented in most studies of writing that adopt a genre-based approach. And at one level it is true that literary and scientific texts tend to differ with respect to all three of the major parameters: topic, audience, and purpose. In terms of the distinction introduced earlier, literary texts invite us to construe a particular experience dynamically, frequently in the narrative mode, whereas scientific texts invoke a synoptic perspective, an abstracting away from particularities towards timeless, generalized relationships. Nevertheless, as Wartofsky (1979), from whom I quoted above, makes clear, both types of text are "representational artifacts we ourselves create" and, as such – albeit in different modes – both contribute to our understanding of the world.[2]

It is also at this level of the creation of a representational artifact that the essential similarity between literary and scientific writing can be most clearly seen. In both cases, and indeed in all writing that involves the creation of a new structure of meaning, writing can be thought of as a form of problem solving (Flower and Hayes, 1980). In fact, writing involves solving problems at many levels, from selecting the genre most appropriate to the topic, audience and purpose that the writer "has in mind," to the choice between alternative phrasings in order to make a particular point most effectively. One helpful way of conceptualizing what is involved when writing is viewed from this perspective is that suggested by Bereiter and Scardamalia (1987). They propose that the composition of any text involves two problem spaces: the content space, which is concerned with beliefs about the world, and the rhetorical space, which is concerned specifically with "mental representations of actual or intended text . . . at various levels of abstraction" (p. 302). However, rather than conceiving of composition as unidirectional, with the output from the content space serving as the input which is processed in the rhetorical space, they argue that, ideally, the interaction between the two spaces should be bidirectional and recursive. Indeed, it is this bidirectionality that makes the process of writing such a powerful tool for knowledge construction.

Our contention is that this interaction between the two problem spaces constitutes the essence of reflection in writing. There may, of course, be reflective thought that goes on wholly within the content space or within the rhetorical space. . . . But the peculiar value that many have claimed for writing as a way of developing one's understanding (Murray, 1978) cannot inhere in either of these problem spaces separately. Thought carried out solely within the content space is not distinctive to writing, and thought carried out solely within the rhetorical space would be expected to develop craft but not wisdom or world knowledge. (pp. 302–3)

In tracing the development of scientific writing earlier, we saw an illustration of this claim on a very large scale. For it was the continuing efforts of many writers to solve the pervasive rhetorical problem of relating what was done to what was thought within a single clause, and then organizing those clauses as a cumulative argument, that shaped the synoptic genres in which most academic writing is now done. But even more important was the effect of this on the "content space," for the synoptic mode of construing experience came to form the organizing basis for what we think of as scientific knowledge.

Clearly, in most cases, the problem solving in which the writer has engaged is not easily detected by the reader. Except where a new and unfamiliar solution has been adopted, the proof that a problem has been solved is that it is no longer apparent. However, some problems, such as the one discussed above, by their very nature require a solution that is new for both writer and reader. This is also the case with *The Inheritors*.

Creating a New Register: Representing the Speech of the Neanderthals

In this novel, Golding imaginatively recreates the world of Neanderthal Man, in a story in which a family group of these protohuman people encounters, and is destroyed by, a tribe of more advanced humans. On their own, the People have been able to survive; over countless generations, they have maintained a culture that is well adapted to their environment. However, in the face of the much more sophisticated practices of the New Men, who raid their encampment and carry off the two young ones, it is the limitations of their ability to use language to interpret and plan events that is chiefly responsible for the People's ultimate defeat.

In choosing this evolutionary theme, Golding has set himself a major rhetorical problem – that of presenting the world of the People, not only as seen by an omniscient narrator, but also experienced as it were from behind the eyes of the characters themselves. But this, in turn, creates an equally substantial problem of a different kind: What exactly was the nature of Neanderthal Man's experience? How did they construe the material and social world with which they interacted, and how did they communicate their understanding of it? Since there are no extant records, nor even evidence of an indirect kind, the answer has to be imagined and, with it, a linguistic form that will effectively enact it. However, herein lies another problem. Although the language that represents the People's way of being in the world must be such as to cause the reader to register and explore its strangeness, it must not be so far removed from what the reader expects as to defeat its own purpose. It must be different, but not different in a way that cannot be interpreted.

Not surprisingly, Golding's solution involves many levels. At the plot level, the novel starts quite traditionally, with the narrator's description of the People's reaction to the disappearance of the log on which, each year, they have crossed the river on their journey to their summer camp. However, the manner in which the log has disappeared, which is perceived but not understood by the People, already alerts the reader to something problematic but as yet undefined. Also familiar are the many domestic practices in which the People engage, such as fire making, food gathering, child care and story telling. In addition, by referring to the members of the group, from the beginning, as, for example, "the old woman," as well as by their proper names, Golding invites the reader to think of them as "normal" human beings. At the same time, on the other hand, in the abundance of sensory detail with which the People's environment is described and in other ways, such as the frequent references to "pictures in the head," there are features that suggest, but do not spell out, what is essentially different about them.

However, as the story progresses and, although still unseen, the presence of "the Other" (the New Men) becomes more palpable to the ears and noses of the People, so too does the reader become more aware of the extreme acuity of their physical senses. Then Ha, one of the young males in the group, unaccountably disappears. Lok sets out to find him and, in his search, picks up the scent of the Other, which he follows until he comes to the river. Here the scent stops, but a series of rocks between Lok and the island on the other side begins to evoke in him a picture of the Other leaping from rock to rock all the way across.

At this point, the text continues as follows: "As he watched, one of the farther rocks began to change shape. At one side a small bump elongated then disappeared quickly. The top of the rock swelled, the hump fined off at the base and elongated again then halved its height. Then it was gone." This is what Lok sees. And because Golding here, for the first time, places us, as it were, behind Lok's eyes, we experience his seeing as he does – as perception without interpretation. As a result, after the initial bewilderment we share with Lok, we finally begin to understand what it is about the People that puts them at risk as they come up against the New Men. They do indeed live through their senses, and insofar as they can think, their thinking is limited to what they can infer from their own experience. But they cannot understand the Other because they can neither deduce nor reason.

This may seem something of a paradox. The People certainly have language, which they use to communicate about the activities in which they engage. They also have "pictures" in which they sometimes recall past experiences or prevision their own future. Yet they are unable to use language to externalize or coordinate these pictures; they cannot use language as a tool for thinking. Why should this be so?

Golding offers us a clue when he says of Lok, "He had no words to formulate these thoughts." Is the problem, then, to be attributed to their limited vocabulary? Briefly, the answer is "yes," but it is essentially a semantic limitation that has syntactic as well as lexical implications. As in the passage quoted above, in which Lok watches what is happening on the rock, almost all their conversational utterances consist of intransitive clauses, typically movement in space, or of clauses of mental process, in which the two noun phrases refer to the person who sees or feels and to the object of perception. What is noticeable by its absence, on the other hand, is any expression of agentive action. The People do not deliberately act on the world around them to bring about events, nor can they conceive of the Other as being able to do so. Not surprisingly, therefore, with no way of expressing or conceiving of cause and effect, they are unable to survive the confrontation with the New Men, who are at a more advanced stage of linguistic, and therefore of mental, development.[3]

As I suggested earlier, the problem Golding set himself in this novel was to find a way of conveying the lived experience of Neanderthal Man by enacting as well as describing it. And the way in which he solved it, I have suggested, was by selectively drawing on the existing resources of the English language to create a new register that is as different from the dynamic mode of normal conversational speech in one direction as is the synoptic mode of scientific writing in the other. Yet, as with the latter, its very strangeness forces the reader to engage in a new way of knowing. Here, however, the response that the writing demands is imaginative rather than rational. Far from requiring us to analyze their world – a feat which the People themselves are totally incapable of performing – the register that Golding has created invites us to discover what it is like "to look through eyes empty of thought and as innocent of judgement as of hatred, suspicion and fear" (Kinkead-Weekes and Gregor, 1967, p. 68).

Nevertheless, as I hope to have shown, the novel certainly repays analysis, and particularly from a linguistic point of view. For by paying close attention to the register to which the People are confined, we understand both how Golding solved his problem as a writer and what Vygotsky could have meant when he characterized the very early stage of mental development in terms of "preintellectual speech" (1987, p. 243). Of equal importance, perhaps, as Kinkead-Weekes and Gregor point out, is that: "By the end, we have been forced to make real to ourselves the dimensions, and the costs, of our linguistic inheritance" (1967, p. 73).

The Interdependence of the Four Genetic Levels

However, this is not all that is to be gained from viewing Golding's text through the lenses of Vygotskyan theory. As I have already suggested, when seen from the perspective of the confrontation between the People and the New Men who destroy them, the story can serve as an exemplification of the role of language in activity at the phylogenetic level. What is most apparent from this perspective is the limitations of the tool and the way in which this limits the possibilities for adaptive action. At the same time, if we attend to the People's use of language, as this is manifested in the dialogue and in the way in which their construal of experience is portrayed in the text, we can see this stage in the evolution of the species as a historical culture in its own right. While being constrained by the current state of the psychological tool of language, the People have nevertheless used it to fashion a way of life that – up until the arrival of the New Men – has allowed them to survive in their environment, and to make some sense of the phenomena of their experience. As Halliday notes, "Lok has a theory – as he must have because he has language" (1973a, p. 124).

The story can also be seen from the perspective of the ontogenetic development of Lok and the woman, Fa. Over the course of their fateful encounter with the New Men, the People are forced to modify their traditional patterns of behavior in their attempt to survive as a group. Trapped in a situation where they have to observe and attempt to interpret the intruders' initially unintelligible behavior, they begin to think differently and more agentively. To a considerable extent, this takes the form of putting their existing language resources to a new use.

The first of a number of such occasions occurs when, after several members of the group have already been killed and their young ones have been carried off to the island, Fa and Lok have to invent a way of recovering them. Here is how Golding describes this moment:

> The moon had risen when they moved. Fa stood up and squinted at it then looked at the island. She went down to the river and drank and stayed there, kneeling. Lok stood by her.
> "Fa."
> She made a motion with her hand of not to be disturbed and went on looking at the water. Then she was up and running along the terrace.
> "The log! The log!"
> Lok ran after her but could not understand. She was pointing at a slim trunk that was sliding towards them and turning as it went. . . . . . Fa spoke over her back.
> "I have a picture of us crossing to the island on the log."
> Lok's hair bristled.
> "But men cannot go over the fall like a log!"
> "Be silent!"
> She puffed for a while and got her breath back.
> "Up at the other end of the terrace we can rest the log across to the rock." She blew her breath out hugely.
> "The people cross the water on the trail by running along a log."
> Then Lok was frightened.
> "We cannot go over the fall."
> Fa explained again, patiently.

Note that what Golding is describing here is also an example of development at the microgenetic level – a unique moment in which a specific challenge elicits a new form of mediated action. It is the uttering of the words "the log" that enables Fa, in externalizing her "pictures," to make connections between them and to use them to direct her own and Lok's behavior. It is through verbal thought that she invents a solution to the problem of getting to the island – a problem that had never arisen before, either in her own life or in the history of the group.

This episode also very clearly exemplifies the significance Vygotsky attached to the mediating function of psychological tools: "By being included in the process of behavior, the psychological tool alters the entire flow and structure of mental functions. It does this by determining the structure of a new instrumental act, just as a technical tool alters the process of a natural adaptation by determining the form of labor operations" (1981, p. 137).

In Golding's skillful written evocation of this critical scene, we can clearly see an example of the interdependency of all four levels in Vygotsky's genetic conceptualization of development. Changes in the actions through which the object of an activity is realized always occur on unique, specific occasions. And the possibility and manner of their occurrence depends on the interaction between the problems posed by the particular situation and the creativity with which the existing resources of the culture – as these are embodied in the learned repertoire of the particular participants – are brought to bear in solving these problems. However, the outcome is not tied to the particular occasion. In inventing a new mode of action through a development of the mediational means, the participants themselves are changed; and as they perform the new action on subsequent occasions with other participants, and they with still others, the new mode of action enters into, and transforms the cultural repertoire as a whole, so that what is learned by new members incorporates the developments that took place in previous generations.

Finally, Golding's depiction of Fa and Lok's first steps towards a language-mediated mode of problem solving can also help us to understand the third of the key themes in Vygotsky's theory: the social origin of individual mental functions. Several features of the events leading to their crossing to the island are worth noting in this respect. First, it is their fundamental and unreflective commitment to the People, with its requirement that they act to get back the young ones, that pushes them to take a more agentive stance in relation to the New Men. And this, in turn, requires them to collaborate in inventing and carrying out an appropriate goal-directed action. The motivation is thus clearly social. Second, when Fa tells Lok "I have a picture of us crossing to the island on a log," she is not so much reporting an earlier "thought," already individually achieved, as using the words to bring the thought into existence between them. And a moment later, in explaining again to counter Lok's objections, she is further clarifying the plan of action in interaction with him. It is only later, after further problems have been tackled jointly, that Fa and Lok begin to be able to function in this way alone, although their problem solving remains group oriented; indeed, it is partly because they cannot adopt the individualistic ethic of the New Men that, both individually and as a group, the People are doomed to be superseded.

A third way in which the development of the new mental function is social in origin is to be seen in its basis in the activities of the New Men. In the earlier part of the chapter in which the crossing occurs, both Fa and Lok had spent a considerable time observing the comings and go-ings of Men from the island, and their behavior, which at first had been incomprehensible to them, had gradually been becoming interpretable in terms of deliberate actions, even if the meaning of those actions re-mained impossible for them to understand. As Fa said after watching two men paddle their canoe to the island shore, "The new people have many pictures. And I have many pictures too." It is one of these pictures, ex-pressed in words to Lok, "The people cross the water on the trail by running along a log," that enables them to "see" how to use one of the logs floating down the river as a bridge that will enable them to cross to the island.[4]

In several ways, then, the first occasion of language-mediated problem solving by Fa and Lok is very clearly social. It is strongly group oriented and it occurs in the context of joint activity. It is also dependent on assis-tance from others. In their case, on the other hand, there is no "adult" or "more competent peer" to demonstrate and to guide their participation, as there is in most cases of ontogenetic development in childhood. How-ever, this must always be the case with radically new types of mediated action since, by definition, they are not yet part of the cultural repertoire. Nevertheless, even in such situations, the need to advance the joint activ-ity and, with it, the need to communicate with coparticipants, can create a "zone of proximal development" in which a new form of action is jointly constructed.

Both as a work of imaginative fiction and as the solution to a rhetorical problem, *The Inheritors* is undoubtedly a brilliant literary achievement. By now it will be equally apparent that, in my view, it also deserves to be recommended reading for all those interested in Vygotsky's genetic theory of human development.

Writing and Learning to Write: An Expanded Vygotskyan Perspective

Golding would no doubt be surprised to see his literary text used as a tool for the exploration and further development of sociocultural the-ory. Yet, as I hope to have shown, it is not only texts written in the technical, synoptic genres of the natural and human sciences that can mediate the construction of knowledge and the development of personal understand-ing. Nor, in principle, should it matter whether one's encounter with the text occurs as reader or writer. Much more important than either genre of text or mode of encounter is the manner and conditions of engaging with it (Wells, 1990).

Nevertheless, there are good reasons for arguing that, in practice, it is in writing rather than in reading that the power of written language to create new meaning is most fully exploited. Indeed, from a historical and cultural perspective this is fairly self-evident. Although progressive discourse necessarily involves the participant members of an activity system in reading as well as in writing, it is in writing that new ideas are brought into the ongoing dialogue, and it is the resulting written texts that preserve those ideas and make them available for critique and further development. As we have seen, it is also in writing that new registers and genres of discourse are developed and, with them, new ways of engaging in the activities that they mediate and new ways of construing the situations involved. Looked at through the telescope of history, it is clear that it is in this way that both new knowledge and new ways of knowing have been added to the culture's resources for, in creating particular texts for others, their authors were both learning to write and writing to learn.

Similar arguments can also be advanced for the leading role of writing at the ontogenetic level, even though the writer may be in the early stages of mastering the writing tool-kit and have a limited grasp of the topic being addressed. For it is in solving the problems of meaning making that occur in creating a written text for others that writers of all ages and stages of development both develop their mastery of the craft and extend and deepen their individual understanding. In Vygotsky's words, "The individual develops into what he/she is through what he/she produces for others" (1981, p. 162).

A major reason for this, I believe, is to be found in the artifactual nature of the written text. Before it can function as a resource to mediate further activity (for example, by being read as a source of information), it must first be made and, as with most hand-made artifacts, the making typically evokes much greater engagement and commitment than the subsequent use. Furthermore, to invoke the arguments of Bereiter and Scardamalia (1987) cited earlier, the extent to which the individual engages in the transformation of existing knowledge and available information is likely to be considerably greater in the problem solving that occurs when writing than in that which occurs when reading; this is because a new and independent material and semiotic artifact is created as the outcome of writing, but not in the case of reading. Put more simply, what I am suggesting is that, because it makes greater creative demands on the individual, writing is more engaging than reading and, to the extent that the intended outcome is of concern to the writer, it is therefore both more motivating and more rewarding. And this, I think, would be true at any stage of ontogenetic development, once the individual has begun to master the written medium.[5]

However, in arguing for the greater potential of writing as a mediator of knowledge building, both intermentally and intramentally, I do not intend to decry the importance of reading. On the contrary, I take it for granted that in the course of creating a written text, a writer needs to read, both in order to take account of, and respond to, what other participants in the dialogue have to say (Bakhtin, 1986) and in order to obtain needed information. Reading also provides models from which the writer gains familiarity with the registers and genres that are culturally available for his or her purposes in writing. It is also in reading, rather than in writing, that one encounters new and engaging ideas.

Nor do I wish to oppose writing to the composition and construction of semiotic artifacts in media such as graphic art, film, music, dance, and so on. To a considerable extent, the arguments I have developed here could apply to each of these media. On the other hand, there are many situations in which their relationship to writing is one of functional complementarity, and the optimal text is a multimodal one in which different kinds of meaning are realized through different media (Kress, 1997).

But most of all I want to make it clear that I am not setting up writing as an alternative that is superior on all occasions to speaking. On the contrary, as I said in the opening section of this chapter, spoken and written discourse serve different but interdependent functions, as they relate to action within an activity system. This is particularly true in educational settings, where work on written texts is often at or beyond the individual student's level of solo ability, yet is frequently undertaken alone. In such cases, talk plays an extremely important role in establishing and maintaining the community and in providing an informal network of mutual support and assistance; it is also the medium in which the teacher can help to build bridges of understanding between the students' spontaneous, dynamic mode of construing their new experiences and the more difficult, because less familiar, modes of the literary and synoptic texts they are learning to read and write (see Chapter 4).

In arguing for the leading role of writing, I have several times added the qualification: provided the appropriate conditions are met. What these conditions are can be deduced from much of the preceding discussion. Rather than attempt to spell them out in detail, therefore, I shall propose four very general requirements, which, I suggest, apply to all occasions of making meaning with text, if the activity of writing is to be developmental on at least the microgenetic and ontogenetic levels.

First, there must be an activity system and associated community within which the writing plays a significant role. For the writing to engage the commitment of the writer, the resulting text must be functional with respect to the joint activity in which the writer is involved with at least some other members. Second, it must concern a topic in which the writer is interested and about which he or she believes there is more to discover. And third, the writer must care sufficiently about the aesthetic quality of the textual artifact that he or she is creating to engage with, and find solutions to, the problems that arise in the process of its creation.[6] Finally, the writer must be able to count on the community to give help in accessing textual and other relevant resources and in providing support and guidance as this is felt to be necessary.

These are not very different from the conditions that Vygotsky himself proposed: "Teaching should be organized in such a way that reading and writing are necessary for something. ... Writing should be meaningful for children ... Writing should be incorporated into a task that is necessary and relevant for life" (1978, p. 117–18). Although written more than half a century ago, this message still needs to be heard.

Notes

1. A further consequence of this nominalizing tendency was the displacement of the agent – both the experimenter and the author – with the resulting impression of increased objectivity (cf. Latour and Woolgar (1986)). It was these features, in particular, that created an apparently "autonomous text" (Olson, 1977).
2. Vygotsky would certainly corroborate this view. Significantly, his early research in *The Psychology of Art* (1925/1971) explored the way in which literature achieves its effects and, in *Thinking and Speech* (1987), he draws several of his examples from literary works.
3. In offering this explanation, I am greatly indebted to Halliday's (1973a) very detailed analysis of Golding's way of representing the People through what they say and through the language in which their experience is portrayed. In fact, it was my recollection of this work that led me to reread *The Inheritors* while I was preparing to write this chapter.
4. Cf. Vygotsky's observation: "The very essence of cultural development is in the collision of mature cultural forms of behavior with the primitive forms that characterize the child's behavior" (1981, p. 151).
5. Interestingly, Clay and Cazden (1990) make a similar claim about the leading role of writing in the early stages of literacy development.
6. "Aesthetic quality" is necessarily vague, since what counts as aesthetically satisfying will depend on the values of the community for which the text is intended and on the genre that the writer works with.

Part III

Learning and Teaching in the ZPD

9   On Learning With and From
       Our Students

The Authors

Barbara Galbraith teaches a Grade 2 class and Mary Ann Van Tassell a combined class of Grade 1 and Grade 2 children. Through creative time tabling, we have arranged, each Wednesday afternoon, to work together on science with a group of some twenty Grade 2 children drawn from both our classrooms. Although we have been team teaching together for several years, and have progressively modified our teaching strategies in order to allow opportunities for the children to engage in hands-on investigations, we were still dissatisfied, when we reviewed our program at the beginning of this year, with the relationship between the questions that the children generated in the course of these investigations and our own teacherly agenda. Specifically, we noticed that, although we encouraged and noted their questions, we did not give them a central place in planning subsequent activities; in a sense, their questions were more an outcome of the topics we tackled rather than a point of departure for their organization. Our own question, then, was how could we arrange for the children's questions to play a more generative role in the planning of the science curriculum?

This question was also of interest to Gordon Wells, a researcher and teacher educator at the university, who, with Mary Ann, is a member of an action research project which is exploring ways to give a greater emphasis to inquiry in the curriculum. With this common interest, we

This chapter was prepared with the assistance of my colleagues, Barbara Galbraith and Mary Ann Van Tassell.
Aprendizaje y ensenanza en la zona de desarrollo proximo. By Barbara Galbraith and Mary Ann Van Tassell, and Gordon Wells. In A. Alvarez (Ed.) *Hacia un curriculum cultural: La vigencia de Vygotski en educación*, pp. 55–76. Madrid:Fundación Infancia y Aprendizaje.

293

decided to make the Grade 2 science program the basis for a collaborative investigation in which we would try to give a greater role to the children's questions and simultaneously to develop our own understanding of the conditions that made this possible. To this end, we selected one particular unit, which will be described in detail below, and made two changes to the normal classroom arrangements: First, all three of us took part in every lesson – Barbara and Mary Ann as teachers and Gordon as participant observer – and met periodically to reflect on the way in which the unit was progressing; second, we arranged for each lesson to be recorded on audio or video tape, both to aid us in our reflections and also to provide evidence for more systematic evaluation later. We also decided to draw on sociocultural theory to provide a perspective from which to make sense of our observations and reflections.

A Sociocultural Framework for Learning and Teaching

As teachers, all three of us have had a continuing interest in language, and it was this that initially drew us to the work of Vygotsky and his colleagues and followers. Observing children learning to talk, we had been struck by the social and interactive nature of this process – by the child's need for interested and collaborative, conversational partners and by the importance of there being a shared purpose for engaging in conversation (Wells, 1986). We had also seen similar principles at work in the early stages of learning to read and write (Gianotti, 1994). Vygotsky's theory of learning and development provided a framework within which these observations of children's language development took on a broader significance. In particular, it helped us to understand more clearly the role of a "teacher" in guiding and supporting the child's innate desire to learn.

For Vygotsky, and for those who have extended and developed his ideas, learning is not a separate activity undertaken for its own sake, but an integral aspect of engaging in the ongoing activities of one's community and, in the process, gradually mastering the purposes of those activities and the means by which they are achieved (Lave and Wenger, 1991). This does not mean that a child will never independently attempt to learn and practice a particular skill or acquire certain items of information, but this will always occur in a larger context within which what is learned has a functional significance for the child in enabling him or her to achieve some goal which is personally meaningful and also socially valued.

As we have already noted, this account very obviously describes the learning of language; but, as Vygotsky (1978, 1981) makes clear, it is equally applicable to almost every other form of cultural knowledge, from mastering the physical skills needed to participate in games and organized sports, or acquiring the knowledge to design and build houses or navigate ships and aircraft, to bringing up children or running a complex organization. However, in this process of taking over the accumulated resources of the culture, language – and other systems of representation, such as drawing, drama and model making – have a particularly important role. For not only do they enable people to coordinate their activities in the here and now, and to share their feelings and intentions, but they also allow those activities, feelings and intentions to be referred to independently of the situations in which they occur so that they can become the subject of reflection, explanation and, where appropriate, instruction.

However, these social means of meaning making and communication play an equally important role in individual intellectual development. Initially encountered in the course of interaction with others as the means of achieving shared goals, they become, when mastered, a resource for individual thinking – a set of "semiotic," or meaning-making, tools and practices which mediate such intellectual actions as remembering, reasoning and problem solving, in the course of activities carried out alone or in collaboration with others. From this perspective, then, learning to use these tools and practices through participation in jointly undertaken activity can be seen to involve a triple transformation: first, a transformation of the individual's intellectual functioning and of his or her capacity for effective participation in the activity; second, a transformation of the situation brought about by the participants' actions; and, third, a transformation of the tools and practices as they are creatively adapted to suit the particular situation and activity in which they are used.

In the light of this social conception of learning and of its contribution to development, it is clear that development cannot be thought of as an individual accomplishment (Cole, 1985). On the contrary, Vygotsky stressed the crucial role of more expert members of the culture in providing the guidance and assistance that enables the learner to become an increasingly competent and autonomous participant in the activities in which he or she engages. In recent years, this conception of the relationship between learning and teaching has been described in terms of apprenticeship (Lave and Wenger, 1991) in the purposeful use of semiotic tools that takes place through guided participation in shared, culturally valued endeavors (Mercer, 1995; Rogoff, 1990).

Exactly what form such guidance should take was a matter to which Vygotsky returned several times in his later published work (1978,1987) and it was in this context that he formulated his now well-known construct of the "zone of proximal development (zpd)." To be effective, he argued, this guidance – or "instruction" as he called it – must always be in advance of development. But not arbitrarily so. For a learner in any situation, there is a zone of proximal development – a window of potential learning that lies between what he or she can manage to do unaided and what he or she can achieve with help. It is when appropriately pitched in this zone that instruction can optimally benefit the learner; for, under these conditions, "learning awakens a variety of developmental processes that are able to operate only when the child is interacting with people in his environment and in cooperation with his peers" (Vygotsky, 1978, p. 90).

Thinking together about the grade two science program with which we were concerned, we had little doubt that the framework we have just outlined would help us to make sense of the issues of learning and teaching that we wished to investigate. And, with its recognition of the active roles of both learners and teachers and its emphasis on collaborative activity, the notion of working in the zpd seemed likely to provide a fruitful starting point for an examination of the particular classroom events that had occurred and been recorded. However, as we thought about it more deeply, we soon came to realize that, although illuminating as a general orientation, Vygotsky's account of the zpd offers little specific guidance for particular classroom situations. We decided to start our investigation, therefore, by reviewing the data we had recently collected in order to see when, and to what extent, participants' behaviour seemed to meet the criteria he provided. In this way, we hoped to develop a clearer understanding of the different modes of working in the zpd that might help us to conceptualize and plan our future activities.

The Power of an Elastic Band

The theme for the unit we are about to describe was "energy," approached through a practical investigation of the energy that is stored in a stretched or twisted elastic band. We thought that designing and testing vehicles powered by an elastic band would provide an opportunity for "hands-on" experimentation that was within the capabilities of seven-year-olds, while, from a theoretical point of view, children's attempts to explain and predict the results of possible modifications in design seemed likely to generate "minds-on" activity that would provide a very tangible introduction to the broad theme of energy in some of its various manifestations.

We started by brainstorming what the children already knew about energy, its uses and sources, and on this basis constructed the first of many weblike representations of their understanding. Then, rather than asking what specific questions they might like to explore, we moved immediately into the construction of elastic-powered rollers, in the belief that this would stimulate the children's curiosity and also provide a focus for their inquiries. Drawing on a suggestion found in *An Early Start to Technology* (Richards, 1990), we invited the children to bring from home plastic containers of a cylindrical shape, such as empty bottles that had contained fizzy drinks or hand lotion, and then we helped them to construct their rollers. This involved drilling small holes in the the cap and the base of the container, through which an elastic band was threaded; one protruding end of the elastic band was then secured at the base and the other twisted round one end of a pencil or length of dowel, with a button to act as a washer between container cap and dowel. By winding the dowel, the elastic inside the container became progressively more twisted, thus storing energy, which, when the roller was placed on the floor, caused it to roll for some distance as the elastic unwound.

The preceding description is somewhat idealized, however. Several children had difficulty in making a roller that would actually move and others were frustrated by elastic bands that broke through overwinding, thus requiring them to go through the most difficult parts of the construction process for a second or third time. Nevertheless, these mishaps gave rise to some quite animated discussion in the review sessions with which each lesson ended, and several important conclusions were drawn from these experiences which were duly recorded on the charts that were compiled during each session.

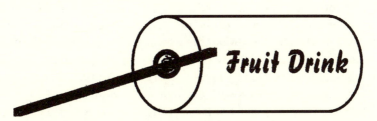

Figure 9.1 Example of an elastic-powered roller made from a fizzy drink can. From Richards, 1990.

One question in which everyone was interested was how far a roller would travel for a given number of turns of the dowel. In fact, some of the children approached this issue quite competitively. Unfortunately, the question proved impossible to answer in any systematic manner, due to the less than perfect functioning of many of the rollers and to the difficulty of defining a "baseline" for counting the number of turns.

However, probably the most significant of the unanticipated discoveries was that, while some rollers travelled in a straight line, others circled to right or left. Naturally, we were all interested in discovering why this happened and, as we addressed this problem together at the end of the session, several interesting explanations were suggested.

Originally, our plan was to conclude the unit after the experiments with the rollers. However, given the less than satisfactory results obtained and the obvious interest of the children and their desire to continue, we decided to attempt to apply what had already been discovered to the design, construction and testing of elastic-powered "cars." The design was simple. Using a cardboard box as the chassis, lengths of dowel were passed through the box at front and rear, and wheels were glued on to these axles. An elastic band was then secured round the middle of the rear axle and attached to the front of the car with a paper clip. Pushing the car backwards caused the elastic to wind round the axle, stretching the remainder of the elastic band in the process. This became the source of power which, when the car was released, caused it to run forward. However, once again, unforeseen problems arose. In some cases, the tension of the elastic band bent the axle and caused the wheels to rub against the chassis. And in almost all cases, when a well-wound car was released on the polished classroom floor, the driving wheels failed to grip and therefore spun without moving the car.

Although, from the point of view of moving ahead with the experiments we had planned, these problems were somewhat disconcerting, they proved, in the long run, to be the most valuable part of the whole experience. For, in order to overcome them, the children were forced to try to diagnose the cause of the problem and then to find workable solutions. In the end, however, either by fastening additional elastic bands round the wheels like snow chains or by sticking masking tape round the circumference of the wheels like tires, most of them succeeded and were able to proceed to work on what was considered to be the central question – that of discovering the relationship between the number of times the elastic band was wound round the axle and the distance that the car traveled when released. During the next two or three lessons, trials were conducted under varying conditions and with increasing accuracy, and the results were recorded in a tabular form that was designed for the purpose. Finally, there took place a lengthy whole-class discussion to consider what had been observed and to attempt to explain the results. This culminated in a conclusion that no one – neither teachers nor children – had known in advance: Distance traveled equals the number of times the elastic is wound round the axle multiplied by the circumference of the wheel.

Having thus briefly summarized the way in which the unit developed, we should now like to consider some of the events in more detail. Our purpose is to explore whether the notion of "working in the zone of proximal development" helps us to understand their significance and, at the same time, to evaluate the adequacy of that notion, as initially formulated.

Exploring the Zone of Proximal Development (zpd)

To aid us in this task, we have distinguished – as Vygotsky did – between two different modes of working in the zpd, namely adult–child and child–child. These modes are not mutually exclusive of one another but, rather, are interdependent. They do not necessarily occur on separate occasions within the classroom nor are there clearly established boundaries between them. However, in order to focus on attributes within each mode, we will start by discussing them separately. First, we will consider the adult–child relationship, focusing on how the adults helped the students in the zpd, both individually and as a community.

Adult Assistance in the zpd

On an individual level, we had many opportunities to assist students while they constructed their rollers and cars and then conducted tests. On the level of the classroom community, by contrast, the opportunity to help students consolidate and extend their learning occurred in the whole-class discussions that typically began and ended the weekly lessons. Essentially, then, there are two forms of the zpd relationship between adult and child to be considered: working in the individual child's zpd, and in the larger, communal zpd.

Some attributes of the adult's role were common to both situations. For example, because of the structure of the learning environment, which enabled the students to be engaged in authentic activity that was context dependent, we were able to observe the students' actions, both individually and as a group, and then intervene in ways that we hoped would facilitate their further understanding. In both situations, a key feature of the teacher role was that it was generally responsive rather than initiatory.

As an illustration of a group situation, let us consider the start of each lesson, when we would spend ten-to-fifteen minutes as a whole-class planning the task for the day. As teachers, we started each session with a specific direction in mind, but this was often altered as we reviewed the previous learnings with the students and listened to their immediate questions or problems. This opening discussion was vital because it provided an opportunity to consolidate knowledge and extend understanding, based on previous sessions' learnings and discoveries and, on that foundation, decide on the next step.

Because we were not committed to "covering" a predetermined lesson plan, we were able to be responsive to the students in the light of what we perceived to be the most appropriate direction. For example, in the instance below, we had thought we would move students into attempting to answer their own individual questions. They had already spent several weeks experimenting with their cars, and we had begun to build a base of community knowledge that was recorded on charts that were displayed for all to see. In planning the lesson, we had decided that we would invite the students to pose questions on the basis of their results to date and then form small groups to try to answer their questions. However, once the lesson started, we sensed that the students needed more experience in conducting tests and creating charts in which to record their results before they were ready to design and carry out their own investigations. In responding in this way, we were working in the communal zpd. And so we developed a chart together and the students set about exploring the same question, namely: "How far will the car travel with masking tape on the wheels, with no masking tape on the wheels, and with rubber bands on the wheels for different turns of the axle?"

Independent Group Activities

We then gave the students fifty-to-sixty minutes to work on their vehicles in independent groups. During this time, the adults circulated to offer assistance as needed, responding within an individual's zpd. Working in this way afforded us a window into an individual's thinking and ability level; it also helped us determine the direction in which to proceed as a community. Below is an example of an individual encounter; it occurred as Whitney and her friends were having some difficulty in conducting satisfactory trials to answer the above question. As Mary Ann (Teacher 2 in the following transcript) discovered, they had not been aligning the car with the end of the tape measure and so had not obtained accurate measurements of the distance that the car traveled with each additional turn of the elastic. After talking with all three girls for a moment, the teacher turns to Whitney and asks her to show how they had been carrying out their trials.

> *06 Teacher 2:* Show me how you do it
>
> *07 Carrie:* You have to – you know – use the mark on the wheel(pointing to the mark)
>
> *08 Teacher 2:* Have you been using the mark to count . how many times you're rolling it?. . Have you?
>
> *09 Whitney:* (nods somewhat uncertainly)
>
> *10 Teacher 2:* Yeah OK, show me then . how you do it for four (Whitney tentatively rolls her car back, making several fresh starts)
>
> *11 Whitney:* It won't – it's not going four, though
>
> *12 Teacher 2:* Ah-ha! Were you counting it when it went three? And two? (Whitney nods)
>
> *13 Teacher 2:* OK, let me try it

At this point, having watched Whitney's actions in order to establish what her group had been able to do on their own, the teacher takes the car and demonstrates how to use the mark on the wheel to count the turns of the wheel as the car is pushed backwards. She then instructs Whitney to place the tape measure so that the zero is lined up with the point where the back wheels touch the floor. When this has been done correctly, the teacher releases the car and it rolls forward, veering slightly to the right. Together, teacher and Whitney read off the distance traveled from the tape measure: seventy-eight centimeters. Before leaving, the teacher checks to make sure Whitney has understood the significance of what they have just done together and suggests that the group should carry out their trials again, paying attention to the accuracy of their procedures.

> *19 Teacher 2:* Hmm! Are you sure when you went– . . when you went three that you measured it that way? . . because do you think if you wound it three times it would go that far?
>
> *20 Carrie:* <u>I don't think so</u> (Whitney shakes her head in agreement)

21 Teacher 2: Now . . did <u>you</u> make sure that (= tape measure) was lined up at the starting?

23 Whitney: Um– (shakes her head)

24 Teacher 2: No, OK, why don't you start again then, cos that's what you need
to do . . so erase what you did before, now you know how to do it

This functional assistance leads Whitney to a better understanding of how to conduct a scientific test and of how to use the tape as a tool for measuring the distance traveled. In the follow-up discussion at the end of the lesson, the event also afforded the teachers an opportunity to discuss the concepts of a fair test and an accurate measurement. The episode can be seen, then, as an instance of the triple transformation referred to above. First, Whitney's and Carrie's capacity for participation in the activity was transformed through their interaction with their teacher. Second, they were able to continue after the teacher had left, effectively transforming the situation so that their subsequent trials were more accurate. Third, in taking over the use of these tools and practices, they transformed them into their own individual resources which they adapted to suit the needs of subsequent situations.

Finally, when we later reflected on this episode as we discussed the video recording, there was also a transformation in our own understanding of how teachers can most effectively help children to learn. Guidance and instruction are most helpful, we realized, when they are given in the context of a particular activity in which teacher and student are engaged together. For it is by observing how the student is attempting to carry out the activity that the teacher can judge what form of assistance is most useful; and it is when that assistance enables the student to achieve success in what she is already trying to do that she most readily understands the significance of the new action and is able to appropriate it and so to transform her repertoire of actions for use in similar situations.

Whole-Class Review

After this independent worktime, we usually gather the class together to review the day's activities. This ten-to-fifteen minutes period gives the students a chance to share the learnings and discoveries from what they have been doing in their separate groups. Often, the students share the problems they have encountered and, as a group, we have the opportunity to learn from the individual situations. During this time, the adults serve as facilitators, responding to the students' observations and comments. These sessions give us the chance to help them extend their knowledge and apply their learnings further. Because part of our goal is to build a community of scientific inquirers, we consider this coming together at the end of each session to be essential. The enthusiasm and curiosity generated by the "hands-on" activities are utilized in helping them to develop the "minds-on" knowledge and skills of scientists.

We also use this time to discuss issues and problems that we have noticed to be common to several groups during the independent work-time. For example, the difficulty experienced by Carrie and Whitney in conducting an accurate test was shared with the entire group, and we discussed the need for precision when measuring, so that the test would yield accurate results. At the beginning of the next week's session they were reminded of what had been discussed so that, as they continued their investigations, they needed less assistance with regard to the accuracy of measuring. As a result, they began to take over responsibility for the task themselves and, because the discussion of accuracy grew out of their needs and purposes, it had more meaning for them.

In the review that occurred at the end of the whole unit, the need for accuracy in testing surfaced again when several of the students talked about what they would do in the next unit. The evidence of the progress they had made in this respect can be seen from the following excerpt, as together we consider how they might find out about air.

> *252 Matthew:* We could make a paper airplane, and we could use a fan and see if it could push it?
>
> *253 Teacher 2:* OK
>
> *254 Teacher 1:* So you'd take an object that uses air and see HOW it uses air?
>
> *255 Teacher 2:* Do you think you could try to do a TEST?
>
> *256 Julia:* Yeah, you could try to see how far and like see how strong the wind is and then how far it would go **** and then turn on the fan and see how far it would go ***

At this point there is an interruption. A little later, Julia repeats her suggestion in slightly different terms:

> *264 Julia:* You would have to, like, put the measuring tape from where it started and then the plane, and then you'd see how far it would go,

and then where it fell, if it was too short then you'd have to add another one (i.e. another tape measure)

265 Teacher 2: And you also know something about recording, how to record the information from a test... What did we do with the cars?

266 Lindsay: What we would do was, we would wind it back a certain number (of turns) with the mark and it would stop . then we knew – we would put the measuring tape down exactly at it and would let it go, and then measure where it's at by the back wheel

267 Sara: Yeah, because it wouldn't be accurate if you just- because some people put (adhesive) tape on their measuring tape, but they couldn't move it . but they couldn't put it exact, or they HAD to pick it up and move it to the wheels, and it wasn't accurate

268 Teacher 1: And so that's another thing you learned about needing to make your measurements accurate

For us, as teachers, the above transcript provided evidence of our growing ability to be responsive to the students' current goals and stage of development. At the same time, we were providing the context and the support needed, within their zpd, for them to increase their potential for future participation. As our investigation proceeded, we made the important discovery that this responsive approach in our interactions with students was an essential part of successfully providing assistance in the zpd.

Peer Assistance in the zpd

Sociocultural theory suggests that the principal goal of education is to provide an environment in which students, however diverse their background, can engage in productive, purposeful activities and, in the process, learn to use the cultural tools and practices that have been developed to mediate the achievement of the goals of these activities (Lave and Wenger, 1991). In the previous section, we have illustrated some of the ways in which teachers can facilitate this learning through their responsive interventions. However, as Vygotsky made clear, this learning can also be assisted by other students, through the help they give each other as they work together collaboratively on jointly undertaken tasks.

The importance of peer assistance became very apparent to us as we reviewed the recordings we had made, both of the small-group practical work and of the whole-class discussions. Observing their interactions, we noticed several ways in which children provided assistance in each other's zones of proximal development.

One important form that this took arose from their personal and collaborative involvement in actually making the tools for their investigations, in particular their own cars. There was a strong element of ownership here, as they were the "authors" of their own experiments. For this reason, they were very willing to both give and receive help in order to make sure their cars "worked" and that they followed correct procedures.

In the following episode, children are working with partners to test how far their cars will go with increasing numbers of turns of the elastic round the axle. They are also investigating three conditions: bare wheels, elastic round wheels, and masking tape round wheels, in order to test the hypothesis that increasing the wheels' grip will increase the distance travelled. Julia and Simon are working together. In her science log, Julia is preparing her table of results, following the format previously agreed and shown on the board. She is writing, in advance, the number of turns to be tested on each trial. Simon looks over to see how Julia is constructing her table. Noticing this, Julia takes Simon's book and turns to the next blank page.

> *04 Julia:* There . . just . . . do that . . (demonstrating to Simon how to prepare his table) and then turn it like that, draw a line and then **
>
> *05 Simon:* <u>No</u>, I'm doing it this way (turning back to the previous page in his book, which is two-thirds written on)
>
> *06 Julia:* But you're going to have to write that stuff and that's not going to be enough room (pointing to Simon's page)
> You have to write "rubber band," "no rubber band," "masking tape" (Simon follows Julia's suggestion and starts on a fresh page)

A few minutes later, they have finished their tables and are ready to start their trials. Julia suggests that Simon have the first turn. When she sees that he is having difficulties, she instructs him in how to do it. Simon starts to push his car backwards to wind it up, while Julia monitors his actions.

> *12 Julia:* Did you put a mark – how many times–?

When Simon seems uncertain, Julia takes over and pushes the car back, counting the turns, while Simon watches. Together, they count three turns. Then Julia places the car with its front wheels approximately lined up with the end of a tape measure stretched out on the floor and releases it. When it stops, she marks the point the front of the car has reached along the tape measure and they both read off the distance.

16 Julia: Oh . . thirty-two- you- OK

17 Simon: Thirty-three

18 Julia: Thirty-three. . . put "thirty-three" on your chart

19 Simon: "No rubber bands" (writing in his science log)

20 Julia: Thirty-three . put . put "cm" (leaning over to supervise)

21 Simon: "Cm" (adding this to his entry)

As Julia and Simon worked together, Julia was obviously directing Simon: showing him how to make a chart and how to mark his wheel to make an accurate test. Simon was in no way resentful of this; he simply accepted and used the advice. On a videotape, we later observed Simon working with Alex and directing him in a similar way. In other words, Simon had not only appropriated the specific experimental procedures from working with Julia; he had also appropriated the practice of assisting others and was able to join in building and extending opportunities for inquiry in our classroom.

In the large group discussions, students frequently compared their cars and this led to problem solving and an increase in effective participation that helped them to extend their understanding. Even those children who were not verbalizing their ideas were totally focused, as we observed in the course of watching many video recordings and noting the attentive watching and listening. Those children who had not made connections while doing their tests were given new insights from the connections and understandings expressed by their peers. They were then able to take the ideas gleaned from the whole-class discussion and apply them in further tests on their own cars.

Similar comparisons took place in the small groups while they were working together. For example, here is how Julia described what she had learned while working with Gaelan.

> *78 Julia:* Gaelan – when we put our um– seeing how far our cars were going, he did the thing with the paper and we did it marked on the wheel and he had a good idea . After eighteen – like I think it was around eighteen or something, I'm not sure – after we did that . um . I would have a guess how far it would go if I gave it two turns, and it went two turns around
>
> *79 Teacher 1:* So you were predicting

During the course of a discussion, children would often turn to each other when a problem arose and ask questions of each other, request a clarification, or offer an alternative suggestion. In this way, the group as a whole was able to transform the knowledge they had each constructed from their own experiences into "common knowledge" (Edwards and Mercer, 1987), building a deeper level of understanding in their *social* talk from which each appropriated *individually* what made sense in terms of the understanding with which he or she started. This is clearly apparent in the following excerpts from a whole-class discussion that occurred toward the end of the unit.

Many of the children had discovered that, when the elastic had been wound a considerable number of turns, the driving wheels of their cars spun without gripping, and several design modifications had been attempted to overcome this problem. Annalise and Carrie had both tried 'adding weight', Annalise by pressing down on her car as she released it and Carrie by actually putting a 50 g weight on top. However, while Carrie's strategy had been successful, Annalise's had resulted in her car slowing down. As they discussed these differing results in an attempt to resolve the apparent discrepancy, Lindsay – who had also used the strategy of applying pressure, and who had been listening carefully to Annalise's account – suggested that, for this strategy to be successful, "you would just have to have the right pressure."

But it was also important to understand why applying appropriate weight or pressure would have this effect. Without it, as Lindsay observed, the wheels would just spin – an observation that several other children corroborated. At this point, Julia refers to her experience with a different attempted solution:

> *Julia:* That's exactly what happened to my car when I put it on the floor without rubberbands on . . it skidded on the ground. You need something to push the wheels down so they can-

and this prompts Annalise to break in with a new idea:

> *Annalise:* And more friction . . to grip the way on the ground

and this, in turn, leads another child to introduce the term "traction."

Summing up the discussion at this point, Barbara restates their collaboratively produced explanation as follows:

> *Teacher 1:* So MAYBE what was happening with Carrie's car is that just putting that LITTLE BIT of extra weight meant that the wheels were touching the ground more – or MORE of the wheel was touching the ground, so it was able to get better traction

What was remarkable about this discussion, and others like it, was the extent to which the helpful contributions came from the children. Perhaps because they had shared similar experiences, it was they who seemed best able to understand each other's difficulties and so to provide the most appropriate assistance. In the above example, as we have seen, it was Lindsay and Julia who made the contributions that enabled Annalise to move from her initial very specific observation to a much more general understanding – a personal transformation that was, to a considerable extent, shared by the other members of the class, as the subsequent discussion made clear.

Of course, this does not mean that teachers have no role to play. The success of the whole-class discussion just referred to was critically dependent on our structuring moves – reformulations, requests for elaboration and occasional summaries of what had been established. Indeed, it is by contributing to the discussion in these ways that we believe we can best assist the children's current participation in the *inter-mental* genres of problem-solving discourse and thus provide a model from which they can, over time, appropriate the resources for *intra-mental* problem solving in the discourse of "inner speech." But, in restricting our contributions – for the most part – to structuring moves, we created a "forum," as Bruner (1990) characterizes this form of classroom discussion, in which the children were able to offer their own ideas and have them evaluated and extended by their peers as well as by their teachers.

For us, as teachers, this was an important discovery. Learning, we realized, does not depend on a one-way flow of knowledge from teacher to students. When all are interested in solving a problem, any member of the group may make a contribution that helps toward a solution. Put differently, providing assistance in the zpd is a function, not of role or status, but of the collaboration itself: Each participant can potentially act in ways that assist the others, and all can learn from the others' contributions.

The Key Role of Language

As several of the preceding examples have shown, an important part of the collaboration that took place around the building and testing of the cars and in the follow-up discussions involved the development of an appropriate scientific and technical language to enable the children to communicate their ideas and discoveries. They not only talked about and labeled diagrams of their cars, using words like "axle," "hub," and "wheel circumference," but also used and explained terms like "friction," "traction," and "pressure." This language came, not from the adults presenting and defining these terms in formal lessons, but from the practical experiences and experimenting that the children themselves were engaged in. In this way, they were recapitulating the manner in which the formal registers of scientific description and explanation were developed, over many centuries, by practicing scientists as tools to assist them in the activity of doing science (Halliday and Martin, 1993).

Recording ideas in writing played a particularly significant role in this burgeoning of scientific language. For example, following one of the practical sessions, Alexandra wrote in her science journal: "Today our group made sure we got acurat answers on how far our cars move. First we looked at Jansens car. After 2 minutes me and katie realizised that Jansons cars wheels were rubbing against the box thats called friction. Then the car wouldent go very far because there was to much friction."

We also made a practice of recording ideas that emerged in whole-class discussion on large sheets of chart paper, the exact formulation being negotiated by the teacher in collaboration with the children. This practice helped the children to focus on what was happening, and why. It also provided a collective record of our emerging understanding, to which individual children could refer as they made their own entries in their science journals.

Engaging in writing as well as in talking certainly helped the children to extend and consolidate their understanding of the concepts involved in this investigation of energy. They themselves were aware of its importance as an integral part of "doing science" and approached it enthusiastically. This was apparent from their comments in the interviews that were conducted at the end of the unit, which included a question asking if writing in science had helped their learning. Alexandra replied: "When you write stuff . . You can always remember it and then, when you share in groups you can write more stuff so . so whatever you share you learn more."

In her own way, Alexandra was restating a key precept of sociocultural theory: Artifacts, such as written texts, can also function as tools when they are used for problem solving on subsequent occasions. So, both the act of writing and the texts that are produced can assist learners in their zones of proximal development, as they use them as means for formulating and extending their understanding of the activity in which they are engaged.

Teachers Learning in the zpd

In the writing of this chapter and in the work that it reports, our focus has been on exploring how teachers can best provide for the learning and development of others. And we have certainly found that the concept of the zone of proximal development has helped us in our task. However, in concluding, we feel it is essential to emphasize that this concept applies equally to our own learning. Like the students we teach, we too need to extend our understanding and improve or change our practice and, as we have discovered, we too can be assisted in doing so through the use of tools such as video and audio recordings, through reading the work of other educators and, most particularly, through exploratory and constructive discussion with colleagues who share our commitment to learning.

To begin with, as we reflected together on the way the unit on elastic-powered vehicles had developed, we were most aware of *what* we had learned. And there was certainly a lot to be said about that. Perhaps it can best be summed up in the recognition, expressed by Barbara and Mary Ann, that authentically to assist others in their zone of proximal development necessitates a shift in one's understanding of one's role as teacher. What is involved is not just a rethinking of one's goals, considered in terms of desired learning outcomes, but also a recognition that the nature of the journey that teachers and learners make toward those outcomes is equally important.

As classroom teachers, we felt a large responsibility for "covering the curriculum." However, what we came to recognize was that we had neglected the fact that we were not alone: that covering the curriculum also required students' active collaboration. The question we then began to ask ourselves was whether we trusted the students enough to guide us in fulfilling this responsibility. Over the preceding two years, we had observed many exciting and authentic learning situations develop when students had an active role in the direction and course of study, but we had been reluctant to trust the implications of these observations. As a result of the present investigation, however, we recognized that a major shift had occurred in our understanding of our curricular responsibilities. As Mary Ann wrote:

We have come to identify that the most important thing we do in our science class is listen. We listen in order to ask questions. Because our focus has shifted to assisting students in their zpds, we are able to listen to the students and to each other. We did not know this was the shift we needed to make, nor did we anticipate it at the outset, but it was the most significant learning for us.

In coming to understand more fully what it means to teach and learn in the zone of proximal development, we have identified the act of being responsive and the shift in perception of our role as being necessary to authentically help anyone in their zpd. These two elements have been the most significant contributing factors to our feelings of success in science instruction this year. And, as with all learning, they have carried over into all other areas of our teaching.

The change in us, as teachers, was reflected in our interactions with the children and in the changed climate of the classroom. Students' questions and knowledge were as valued in the learning process as those of the teachers. Consequently, the students were supported in their efforts to make sense of their world and were motivated to take risks to further their own understandings. Because of this act of being responsive, both to the students and to each other, the knowledge constructed over the course of the unit was much deeper and more meaningful than we had anticipated.

Thinking about the changes that had taken place as most obviously manifested in the quality of classroom interaction led us back to thinking about the *how* of our own learning, and we all quickly realized that interaction with each other had played a critical part. Of particular importance was the discussion of particular events that had struck one or other of us as significant.

As already mentioned, Barbara and Mary Ann met regularly after school to review each week's lesson and to prepare for the next, and Gordon joined them on several occasions. And it was in these meetings that some of the most important insights were developed. Because of our complete involvement in the ongoing activity, it was difficult for us, as classroom teachers, to take an objective view of what was happening in our classroom; the perspective of a participant–observer thus helped us to reflect on the processes that were taking place and on the reasons for our decisions and actions in particular situations. In addition, the ability for all three of us to review the events we were interested in by replaying the videotapes we had made added significantly to the richness of our discussions.

For instance, in one session when we were reflecting on a whole-class discussion about the rollers the children had made, Mary Ann recalled a question she had put to the class, asking them to compare two rollers: "Can you see a similarity between the two rollers that would make them go in a straight line?" Gordon's question was, "Where did that question come from? What led to the asking of that question?" This encouraged Mary Ann and Barbara to reflect on how, while acknowledging and valuing the students' ways of thinking about an issue or problem, a teacher's questions can direct the discussion to another level of understanding. It also prompted them to recognize that the questions themselves were an indication of their own increasing ability to "let go" and to listen to the children for direction.

This, in turn, led us once more to the important recognition that as
ing in the zpd is not unidirectional. As teachers, we can help learner
the questions we ask and the guidance we give. But we can ourselves
receive help and guidance from the questions and suggestions of lear
– if only we are ready to accept them. When we allow this to happen, l
ever, we set in motion a radical transformation. Instead of being a
where inert and impersonal knowledge is transmitted to passive receivers,
the classroom becomes a *community of inquiry*, in which knowledge is collaboratively constructed, as all participants engage together in activities to
which all are committed and to which each contributes as he or she best
can, according to the demands of the specific situation (Rogoff, 1994).
In such a community, as we have discovered, jointly undertaken activity
creates a context in which *all* participants – teachers and teacher educators, as well as students – can assist each other in their zones of proximal
development, as each teaches and learns from the others.

10   The Zone of Proximal Development and Its Implications for Learning and Teaching

There can be little doubt that, in the English-speaking world at least, it is the "zone of proximal development" that has been Vygotsky's most important legacy to education.[1] Indeed, it is the only aspect of Vygotsky's genetic theory of human development that most teachers have ever heard of and, as a result, it is not infrequently cited to justify forms of teaching that seem quite incompatible with the theory as a whole. This centenary conference therefore seems an appropriate occasion to review Vygotsky's exposition of the zpd and to consider the ways in which this seminal concept has been modified and extended in subsequent work.

Although the zpd is often said to be a central concept within his theory, its explicit formulation appeared quite late in Vygotsky's writings and then in two rather different contexts. One version, translated into English as "Interaction between Learning and Development" (chapter 6 of *Mind in Society*, 1978), occurred in a posthumously published collection of essays entitled *Mental Development of Children and the Processes of Learning* (Vygotsky, 1935). Here, the immediate context in which the concept of the zpd is presented is that of the assessment of children's intellectual abilities and, more specifically, as a more dynamic conception of intellectual potential than that represented by an IQ score. Vygotsky defines the zone of proximal development as "the distance between the actual developmental level as determined by independent problem solving and the level of potential development as determined through problem solving under adult guidance or in collaboration with more capable peers" (1978, p. 86). In other words, operationally, it is the zone defined by the difference between a child's test performances under two conditions: with or without assistance.

The second version occurs in Vygotsky's last major work, *Thinking and Speech* (1934/1987), and is embedded in Chapter 6, in which he discusses

"The Development of Scientific Concepts in Childhood." Here, the emphasis falls more heavily on instruction and, in particular, on its role in relation to the development of those higher mental functions that are characterized by conscious awareness and volition. In this context, the significance of the zpd is that it determines the lower and upper bounds of the zone within which instruction should be pitched. "Instruction is only useful when it moves ahead of development" (p. 212), "leading the child to carry out activities that force him to rise above himself" (p. 213). How instruction is conceived to operate in practice is briefly sketched in a description of the hypothesized processes leading to the child's solving of a test problem involving a causal relationship in the social sciences. Vygotsky writes: "The teacher, working with the school child on a given question, explains, informs, inquires, corrects, and forces the child himself to explain. All this work on concepts, the entire process of their formation, is worked out by the child in collaboration with the adult in instruction. Now [i.e. in the test situation], when the child solves a problem ... [he] must make independent use of the results of that earlier collaboration" (pp. 215–16).

Written at about the same time, these two expositions have several common features, including the emphasis on learning leading development, and on the role of adult assistance and guidance in enabling the child to do in collaboration with more expert others what he or she is not yet able to do alone. These are memorably summed up in the contrast Vygotsky makes between development in animals and humans: "animals are incapable of learning in the human sense of the term; human learning presupposes a specific social nature and a process by which children grow into the intellectual life of those around them" (1978, p. 88). In this sentence, one can see how the zpd was probably destined to play a pivotal role in the larger theory that Vygotsky was constructing. Unfortunately, however, he did not live to work out the implications of what is here only sketched. Instead, what we have in the work that was completed is, on the one hand, some provocative and generative metaphors and, on the other, two rather specific applications of the concept of the zpd that may appear to be rather out of keeping with contemporary Vygotskian-inspired educational practice.

On the basis of these two texts alone, therefore, there remain a number of questions about how the concept should be understood. For example, did Vygotsky consider that, at any particular point in a child's development, the zpd was a fixed and quantifiable attribute of that particular child? And did it apply only to intellectual development? Was the assistance that could be given by others restricted to deliberate instruction of the kind described above? And did it necessarily have to be given in face-to-face verbal interaction? And, perhaps most important, should the account he offered of learning-and-teaching in the zpd be taken as universal and normative or as merely descriptive of the practices of a particular stratum of the society in which he lived?

It is a central tenet of cultural historical theory, however, that tools – including cognitive artifacts – are created at a particular moment in the historical trajectory of a culture, in response to the demands of the activity in which they are used, and that they continue to be modified, in use, by those who continue the activity. The concept of the zone of proximal development is just such a cognitive artifact/tool. As Wertsch (1985) suggests, it was formulated by Vygotsky to tackle two specific problems, as these were construed at a particular moment in his ongoing construction of a more general theory of development; moreover, as well as being incomplete, his exposition of the concept bears the stamp of the more general intellectual and practical concerns of his generation in postrevolutionary Russia. However, since its first formulation, the zpd has continued to serve a valuable role as a tool for thinking about human development by theorists and researchers in other cultural and historical contexts. Not surprisingly, therefore, it has itself undergone considerable modification in the process. In the remainder of this chapter, I shall offer a brief overview of what I see to be the main trends in this development.

Assessment

Some of the earliest attempts to apply Vygotsky's concept occurred in the context of testing. Picking up his concern with appropriate assessment, attempts were made to use the concept of the zpd in the administration of tests under two conditions: without and with assistance. Typically, the aim of such assessment was, and continues to be, the categorization of individual students with a view to their appropriate placement in educational programs, often of a remedial kind (Campione and Brown, 1987; Feuerstein, 1979). In these applications, the tests used have typically been "standardized" in form and administered on a single occasion in a setting removed from ongoing classroom or home activities. However, it could be argued that, although compatible with Vygotsky's (1978) discussion of the value of the concept of the zpd for diagnostic assessment, the practice of administering such decontextualized tests is at variance with the requirement that assessment be related to the cultural activities in which the tested subject habitually engages. Certainly, this seems to be the implication of Cole's (1985) criticism of cross-cultural research that fails to embed testing in activity contexts familiar to those who are tested.

Since the purpose of assessment of the zpd is to enable the provision of appropriate instruction, such assessment, it might be argued, is more appropriately carried out in the context of particular students' engagement in an educational activity (Allal and Ducrey, 1996). Here, the aim is the diagnosis of the student's ability to cope with the specific task and of the nature of the difficulties that he or she is experiencing so that, when the teacher intervenes, the intervention is tailored to the student's actual needs rather than to the assumed needs of students in general at that age or grade level. This mode of diagnostic assessment has been employed at two levels, corresponding to the distinction that is frequently made between summative and formative assessment. At the summary level, a student's performance on an end-of-unit test or assignment can be made the basis on which the teacher then works with the student individually or in a small, relatively homogeneous group. The practices of "reciprocal teaching," developed by Palincsar and Brown (1984), would seem to fit into this category. The assistance given under these conditions can be seen as "remedial," designed to enable the student to master some specific skill or those parts of the unit with which he or she had not been successful under normal instruction. While such practices are certainly compatible with Vygotsky's theory, they might in many cases equally be characterized as a regular feature of good traditional pedagogy.

A more dynamic conception of diagnostic assessment can be found in a number of pedagogical approaches that explicitly make appeal to the concept of the zpd. Here, the assessment is both formative and informal, and occurs as the teacher, either as a coparticipant or as a bystander, observes how students are tackling particular tasks and, on this basis, attempts to intervene in a manner that is both responsive to the students' needs and intended to assist them to achieve mastery of the task (Schneuwly and Bain, 1993). Although geared to the responses of a group, rather than of an individual student, this dynamic use of assessment to guide teaching is also the basis of what Tharp and Gallimore (1988) refer to as "instructional conversation." It is this latter, situated use of assessment that Allal and Ducrey (1996) consider best fulfills Vygotsky's concern to use assessment to guide instruction.

Instruction

All the above assessment practices are undertaken with a view to providing appropriate instruction. However, the judgments that they lead to are of quite different orders of specificity with respect to the nature of the instruction that is deemed appropriate. In introducing the notion of the zpd in relation to the assessment of children with "delayed development," Vygotsky (1978) was essentially arguing for appropriate placement based on the child's learning potential. His chief concern was that the placement should ensure that the child had the opportunity for "good learning," i.e. learning that is in advance of his or her development. What form of instruction might best provide such opportunities was not addressed on that occasion.

In the chapter in *Thinking and Speech* in which Vygotsky focuses more directly on instruction, the emphasis is on enabling the mastery of scientific concepts, which are seen as psychological tools that mediate higher mental functioning. The zpd is used in this context to identify the window for instruction: "instruction is maximally productive when it occurs at a certain point in the zone of proximal development" (1987, p. 212). However, although he emphasizes the "decisive influence" that instruction has on the course of development (p. 213), Vygotsky does not treat the nature of instruction itself as problematic, seemingly accepting the current practices with which he was familiar as adequate, provided they were appropriately in advance of development.

The one place in which Vygotsky gives a clearer indication of the form that "good instruction" might take is in his discussion of the Montessori approach to the early stages of literacy learning. The passage is worth quoting at some length.

Teaching should be organized in such a way that reading and writing are necessary for something. If they are used only to write official greetings to the staff or whatever the teacher thinks up (and clearly suggests to them), then the exercise will be purely mechanical and may soon bore the child; his activity will not be manifest in his writing and his budding personality will not grow. Reading and writing must be something the child needs ... writing must be "relevant to life" – in the same way that we require a "relevant" arithmetic. A second conclusion, then, is that writing should be meaningful for children, that an intrinsic need should be aroused in them, and that writing should be incorporated into a task that is necessary and relevant for life. (1978, pp. 117–18)

Vygotsky is here writing about children of preschool age and, as he says elsewhere, "instruction takes on forms that are specific to each age level"

(1987, p. 213). We cannot be certain, therefore, whether he considered that the meaningfulness of educational activities to the learner and their relevance to life were essential characteristics of instruction at *all* ages and stages of development. However, recent commentators have for the most part assumed that this is what is implied by his theory as a whole.

As a result of Vygotsky's lack of specificity about the nature of instruction - at least in the context of his discussion of the zpd – there is considerable diversity in the instructional approaches that have been developed on the basis of his ideas. One crucial difference is in the role that students are given in shaping the goals of learning activities. On the one hand, there are approaches in which the zpd is appealed to only in determining the level at which instruction is pitched. Here, it is assumed that it is possible to establish the zpd of the class as a whole and to modify instructional input and task demands accordingly (Hedegaard, 1990). A further refinement might involve the formation of groups within the class, with tasks of different levels of difficulty being assigned according to the group's zpd. In neither case, however, would the students' interests and goals typically play a significant role in determining the teacher's preestablished instructional plans.

An alternative view places much greater emphasis on the importance of educational activities being meaningful and relevant to students *at the time that they engage in them* (Wells, 1995). Adopting this approach involves the teacher in negotiating the curriculum and in accepting that the most valuable learning opportunities are often those that emerge when students are encouraged to share the initiative in deciding which aspects of a class topic they wish to focus on and how they intend to do so. In such a context, the concept of the zpd is interpreted very differently. Not only is it assumed that the zpd applies to individuals rather than to collectives, such as a group or class, but, more importantly, it is treated as an attribute, not of the student alone, but of the student in relation to the specifics of a particular activity setting. In other words, the zone of proximal development is *created in the interaction* between the student and the coparticipants in an activity, including the available tools and the selected practices, and depends on the nature and quality of that interaction as much as on the upper limit of the learner's capability. A corollary of this view is that, while it may be possible to determine, in general terms, what activity settings and modes of interaction are likely to be conducive to effective learning and, on that basis, to propose the goals for class or group activities, the teacher always has to be responsive to the students' goals, as these emerge in the course of activity, and by collaborating with them in the achievement of their individual goals, to enable them to extend their mastery and at the same time their potential for further development. From a teacher's perspective, therefore, one is always aiming at a moving target.[2]

Semiotic Mediation

Learning and teaching in the zpd is clearly dependent on social interaction and, in educational settings, this most typically involves face-to-face interaction mediated by speech. The development of the higher mental functions, as envisaged by Vygotsky, is largely achieved through the construction on the intra-mental plane of the discourse practices that are first encountered on the inter-mental plane of activity-related social interaction. As Leont'ev puts it, summarizing Vygotsky's fundamental insight: "Higher psychological processes unique to humans can be acquired only through interaction with others, that is, through *interpsychological* processes that only later will begin to be carried out independently by the individual. When this happens, some of these processes lose their initial, external form and are converted into intrapsychological processes" (1981, p. 56).

Indeed, the final chapter of *Thinking and Speech* is essentially an expansion of this last sentence as, tracing the differentiation of the child's initial "social speech" into speech for others and "egocentric" speech for self which, in turn, becomes converted into the intrapsychological activity of "inner speech," Vygotsky charts the development of the medium in which individual thinking is realized. As he puts it, "thought is born through words" (1987, p. 282).

There is no doubt that, in Vygotsky's view, speech played a critical role in the child's learning in the zpd and, hence, in the associated processes of instruction and collaborative assistance. However, as is increasingly being recognized, to focus exclusively on face-to-face interaction mediated by speech is seriously to limit our understanding of the range of modes of semiotic mediation that play a role in both interpersonal and intrapersonal thinking and problem solving; it also limits our understanding of the variety of ways in which learning in the zpd is facilitated (Smagorinsky, 1995).

In his exposition of the concept of psychological tools, Vygotsky himself made clear that the means of semiotic mediation are not limited to speech. He also included: "various systems for counting; mnemonic techniques; algebraic symbol systems; works of art; writing; schemes, diagrams, maps, and mechanical drawings; all sorts of conventional signs; and so on" (1981, p. 137). To these, we might also wish to add the various modes of artistic expression, such as dance, drama, and musical performance. All these modes of representation are simultaneously means of communication and tools for thinking with, both when with others and when alone (John-Steiner, 1987). To recognize this is to enlarge considerably the range of applicability of the concept of learning and teaching in the zpd.

Broadening the range of modes of semiotic mediation considered also leads to the recognition that there are other sources from which learners can receive assistance in the zpd, in addition to deliberate instruction or the assistance of others who are physically present in the situation. As has been pointed out, all artifacts – both material and symbolic – are embodiments of the knowing that was involved in their production (Wartofsky, 1979) and can thus, in appropriate circumstances, make that knowing available to others, provided that the learning that is required is within the potential user's zpd. While this is certainly the case with material artifacts, as when a new and more efficient tool becomes available for carrying out a familiar task, it is even more true of symbolic artifacts, such as written texts, charts and mathematical formulae. For those who are able to read them, such texts can provide a powerful means of self-instruction, as the reader appropriates the thoughts of others and makes them his or her own. However, as Lotman (1988) makes clear, texts are not only valuable when read "univocally," in an attempt to reconstruct the author's intended meaning; treating the text "dialogically" can be even more productive, as the reader uses it as "a thinking device" to develop meanings that are new not only for the reader but perhaps also for the culture as a whole (Wertsch, 1998). By the same token, it is probably through the dialoguing with real or imagined others that is an essential part of the process of textual composition that even the most knowledgeable others are able to continue to learn in the zpd.

Internalization: From Inter-mental to Intra-mental

The concept of "internalization" played a central role in Vygotsky's theory of learning and development; in fact, it might be said to be the end for which interaction in the zpd was conceived as the means. As he put it: "all higher mental functions are internalized social relationships" (1981, p. 164). Yet, central though the concept is, it is probably the aspect of his theory that has been the most hotly contested. For some, the concept simply lacks explanatory power; for others, it is the implied mind–body dualism that is unacceptable. But whatever the specific objection, the general thrust of this line of argument has been to question, and even to reject, the sharp distinction that Vygotsky seems to draw between internal and external, and between social (inter-mental) and individual (intra-mental) functioning.

It is not that individuals do not develop more complex (higher) modes of functioning with respect to the activities in which they engage, as they increasingly bring their actions under semioticized self-control, but that these modes of functioning are not independent of the social practices in and for which they develop. Neither in learning nor in use after mastery does it therefore seem appropriate to talk of a movement between inner and outer, such as is implied by the terms "internalization" and "externalization." This position is forcibly stated by Lave and Wenger in setting out their alternative theory of "legitimate peripheral participation":

In a theory of practice, cognition and communication in, and with, the social world are situated in the historical development of ongoing activity.... First, the historicizing of the processes of learning gives the lie to ahistorical views of "internalization" as a universal process. Further, given a relational understanding of person, world, and activity, participation, at the core of our theory of learning, can be neither fully internalized as knowledge structures nor fully externalized as instrumental artifacts or overarching activity structures. Participation is always based on situated negotiation and renegotiation of meaning in the world. (1991, p. 51)

More will be said below about Vygotsky's ahistorical universalizing tendencies but, in the present context, the issue that most needs to be addressed is the sharp distinction that he appears to draw between social and individual and, perhaps even more important, the temporal sequence in which functions are said to appear on the two planes.

From a strictly ontogenetic perspective, it is not inappropriate to argue, as Vygotsky does, that higher mental functions are first social and external, in the sense that they are already implicated in ongoing social activity before any particular individual enters into the activity and gradually becomes able to organize his or her participation in terms of an individual construction of the relevant cultural practices. It is also true that, from the same perspective, an individual's participation changes, over time, from a stage in which assistance and guidance are needed to a stage in which the same individual is generally able to function 'autonomously' and even to provide assistance and guidance to others. However, in using the term "internalization" to describe this transformation in and of participation, Vygotsky also appears to be proposing a temporal sequence on the microgenetic plane, such that, in learning, there is a stage at which the higher mental functions are external to the learner and a subsequent stage at which they are internal. The problem with this latter proposition is that it also implies a spatial movement in which what is learned passes from outside to inside the skin of the learner. And it is this that many commentators find objectionable.

The root of the problem seems to lie in Vygotsky's tendency to focus on the process of learning solely from the perspective of the inner transformation that takes place as a result of the learner's participation. And this leads him to set up an opposition between individual and social that seems to lose sight of the fact that, at every stage, the learner is necessarily a participant in, and therefore a part of, the community whose practices he or she is learning (Rogoff, 1990). The distinction between individual and social is thus not to be understood as a spatial separation between two distinct entities, such that functions can pass between them, but rather as the adoption of one or other of two different analytic perspectives on an individual's participation in activity, where the activity is inherently social and cultural, although carried out at any time by particular individual participants. In other words, the ongoing activity can be seen either from the perspective of the individual participants acting with mediational means, or from that of the social practices in which they and the mediational means are involved (Wertsch et al., 1995). And this remains the case whether the component actions are undertaken solo or in collaboration with others. Both perspectives are equally valid, although which perspective is foregrounded will vary with the purposes of the analysis.

The value of the concept of the zpd is that it enables us to adopt both of these perspectives simultaneously. For what it highlights for us is, on the one hand, the reciprocity with which the participants adjust their manner of participation to take account of each other's current levels of knowledge and skill in carrying out the activity and, on the other, the transformation that takes place, in the process, in their individual potential for participation. It is also important to add that, as a result of the ways in which new participants take part, both the purposes and the means of joint action are themselves constantly undergoing transformation.

Elsewhere (Wells, 1993a), I have proposed that learning to dance is a particular case that can serve as an analogy for what is involved, more generally, in learning and teaching in the zpd. Dancing is a cultural activity that is far older than any individual participant and, although new forms emerge and are, in turn, replaced by still newer, the basic patterns tend to persist from one generation to the next. In learning to dance, therefore, the newcomer is joining an ongoing community of practice. To begin with, as the novice takes the first faltering steps, he or she is carried along by the rhythm of the music and guided by the movements of the other dancers (and even, in some, characteristically Western, genres, quite forcibly "led" by his or her partner). Before long, however, the novice begins to get a feel for the dance and is soon able to participate on equal terms, both creating new variations that are taken up by others and adapting easily to those that they introduce.

In explaining this learning process, talk of internalization seems unnecessary; no knowledge passes explicitly to the novice from the more expert participants, as they move together with increasing synchrony. Rather, within the framework provided by the structure of the activity as a whole, of which the entraining movements of the other participants are just one part, the novice gradually constructs the organizing cognitive structures for him or herself and brings his or her actions into conformity with the culture-given pattern. In the words with which W. B. Yeats concludes his poem, *Among School Children*: "How can we know the dancer from the dance?"

The Significant Other

Much of the discussion of the zpd has assumed that, in order to learn, the young novice needs the assistance of a more expert person who participates with him or her in the activity. Certainly, parents and teachers are the most important providers of guidance and assistance in relation to the child's learning, in early childhood and even beyond. But they are not the only significant others in this respect. Vygotsky made this clear when he wrote: "learning awakens a variety of internal developmental processes that are able to operate only when the child is interacting with people in his environment and in cooperation with his peers" (1978, p. 90). Indeed, the current emphasis on "cooperative learning" in North America can be attributed, in part, to the significant role that Vygotsky, as well as Piaget, attributed to peer group activities in fostering learning.

On page eighty-six of the same text, Vygotsky actually specifies "more capable peers" but, as has become apparent from a range of studies of group work (Forman and McPhail, 1993; Tudge, 1990), it is not necessary for there to be a group member who is in all respects more capable than the others. This is partly because most activities involve a variety of component tasks such that students who are expert in one task, and therefore able to offer assistance to their peers, may themselves need assistance on another task. But it can also happen that in tackling a difficult task as a group, although no member has expertise beyond his or her peers, the group as a whole, by working at the problem together, is able to construct a solution that none could have achieved alone. In other words, each is "forced to rise above himself" and, by building on the contributions of its individual members, the group collectively constructs an outcome that no single member envisaged at the outset of the collaboration.

Educators have typically had little faith in the potential for learning inherent in tackling problems to which no one knows the answer. However, it must have been through the "pooling of ignorance" in the face of new ecological challenges that our ancestors gradually developed the cultural resources of tools and practices that provided the basis for subsequent generations' common knowledge. And still today, outside the classroom, it is often in conditions where no one member of the group has a clear idea of how to proceed that many of the most significant advances in understanding are made. It seems, therefore, for learning to occur in the zpd, it is not so much a more capable other that is required as a willingness on the part of all participants to learn with and from each other.

Telos: The End-Point of Development

Implicit in Vygotsky's discussion of the "awakening" role of instruction in relation to development there seems to be an assumption that the development that results from learning can be treated unequivocally as progress. This is most apparent in the chapter on spontaneous and scientific concepts (Vygotsky, 1987, chap. 6), where the mastery of scientific concepts is clearly presented as making possible a higher mode of mental functioning than is possible with spontaneous concepts alone. Here, "higher" appears not simply to denote later in the sequence of ontogenetic development, but evaluatively to connote a superior mode of functioning. The same assumption, transferred to the plane of cultural history, can also be seen to underlie the studies conducted by Luria in Central Asia in the 1930s in collaboration with Vygotsky. The presupposition on which these studies were apparently based was that mastery of the abstract and decontextualized modes of thinking made possible by the use of scientific concepts would provide a criterion for distinguishing between "primitive" and "advanced" societies (Luria, 1976) and, hence, for the planning of educational interventions designed to bring all societies to the advanced level of intellectual functioning of which they were potentially capable.

As Bruner (1996) and Wertsch and Tulviste (1991), among others, have argued, such a view can be seen as consistent with Vygotsky's evolutionary approach to culture, and also with the revolutionary ideological spirit in which he conceived his task of reconstructing psychology as a basis for emancipatory action and as a more adequate foundation for the study of human behavior. In the decades since his death, however, there have arisen a number of grounds for challenging what many now consider to be an overly optimistic belief in the universal superiority of scientific rationalism and an unquestioning acceptance of the progressive and benign consequences of schooled instruction. Here I shall consider three that have, in recent years, increasingly been voiced.

The first problem concerns the assumption of the superiority in all situations of thinking based on scientific as opposed to everyday concepts. Habermas (1971), for example, writing from the perspective of social theory, criticizes the increasing hegemony of technical rationality in Western societies, arguing that, although it has a crucial role to play in contemporary life, it must be complemented by both practical and critical-emancipatory modes of knowing. A somewhat similar challenge has come from cultural anthropologists, whose studies of non-Western cultures have led them to reject the view that treats the trajectory of European cultural history as the point of reference for evaluating other cultures. Within Western societies, too, the influx of immigrants from a wide range of different cultures has led to a de facto multiculturalism that is demanding a reevaluation of the assumed superiority of white, male, middle-class values and, hence, also of the technical rationality on which it is based.

Nevertheless, it is not clear that the ways in which Vygotsky used the terms "primitive" and "advanced" when explaining and comparing the development of mental functions in the three different contexts of general human history, contemporary preliterate cultures, and children in contemporary Western societies, really do lay him open to the charge of "Eurocentrism," as Wertsch and Tulviste (1992) have suggested. As Minick (1987) points out, Vygotsky's theory was itself constantly evolving, as he read and critiqued the work of others and carried out his own research, with the result that his written oeuvre is not internally consistent in this respect; furthermore, as Scribner (1985) shows, Vygotsky was emphatic in rejecting a recapitulationist position. The intellectual development of a child in any contemporary culture through the appropriation of resources already in use in his or her social environment, he insisted, constitutes a very different kind of development from that which was involved in the gradual creation of these resources over many generations in the phylogenetic development of the species. In fact, Scribner argues, Vygotsky's habit of using the term "primitive" when comparing these different situations can best be understood, not as substantively equating them, but as a methodological heuristic that he used at various points in his theory-building procedure.

A second criticism is based on the primacy given to cognition in much of the Vygotskyan-inspired study of human development, and the consequent neglect of the social, affective and motivational dimensions. However, the responsibility for this imbalance should not be laid at Vygotsky's door; it is due much more to the "cognitive revolution" of the 1960s and the central role that the metaphor of the mind as computer has played in recent work in cognitive science. That Vygotsky had a much more comprehensive and balanced conception of development is apparent from the final section of *Thinking and Speech*. "Thought has its origins in the motivating sphere of consciousness," he wrote, "a sphere that includes our inclinations and needs, our interests and impulses, and our affect and emotion. . . . A true and complex understanding of another's thought becomes possible only when we discover its real, affective–volitional basis" (1987, p. 282). To which he might have added the converse, namely that "feeling is forever given shape through thought," which is structured by our cultural forms of understanding (Rosaldo, 1984, p. 143). A further indication of the holistic nature of Vygotsky's mature understanding of development is to be found in the extension of his ideas in the work of his colleague, Leont'ev (1978), on motivation, emotion, and personality.

The third, and most recent, reevaluation of Vygotsky's account of the zpd questions the assumption of inevitable progress at the level of ontogenetic development. Since the development of the individual is dependent on the tools and practices that are made available for appropriation in the activities in which he or she participates, it is just as possible for the learner's interpersonal experiences to constrain or even distort his or her development as to enable the development of a socially and emotionally balanced personality (Engeström, 1996). Clearly, many children do experience appalling deprivation and cruelty at the hands of others and the learned coping strategies and conflicted self-image that result have long-term harmful consequences for themselves and for society at large. Some have argued, too, that the coercion that is a pervasive characteristic of formal schooling in almost every culture constitutes an unrecognized but systematic limitation of the creativity and originality of which all human beings are capable.

In the light of these important reservations, it is now no longer possible to accept a conception of learning in the zpd that assumes either a single end in view or a developmental trajectory that is free of contradiction and conflict. Decontextualized rational thinking is not the inevitable apogee of intellectual development, nor is it necessarily optimal in all situations. Here, Tulviste's (1991) emphasis on the heterogeneity of semiotic mediational means is important, as is Wertsch's (1991) metaphor of the tool-kit, from which a selection is made according to the culturally construed demands of different activity settings. Gardner's (1983) theory of "multiple intelligences" represents yet another attempt to escape from too narrow a view of intellectual development. But the development that is fostered by learning and teaching in the zpd is, in any case, not unidimensionally cognitive. Because the whole person is involved in activity undertaken with others, interaction in the zpd necessarily involves all facets of the personality. This is the force of the current emphasis on the zpd as a site of identity formation, which, in turn, has led to the recognition that an individual's developmental trajectory is rarely, if ever, free of social encounters that may engender inner as well as outer conflict and contradiction (Litowitz, 1993). Finally, it is now increasingly recognized that what is taken to constitute the ideal end point of development is itself a cultural construct; it varies from one culture to another and, in each culture, is implicated in the continuous processes of change that characterize cultural history everywhere.

Instead of viewing development as progress towards some ideal, therefore, there is an increasing tendency to focus on the transformative nature of learning in the zpd, with an emphasis on diversity rather than on improvement. This conceptualization of learning as transformation is already to be seen, at least embryonically, in Vygotsky's formulation of the general genetic law of cultural development. Having stated the major proposition that, in development, any function first appears between people and only subsequently within the child, he goes on to add: "It goes without saying that internalization transforms the process itself and changes its structure and functions" (1981, p. 163). However, it could be argued that more is involved than a transformation of the process alone. Whenever an individual engages, with the assistance of one or more others, in tackling and solving a problem that arises in the course of action, there are, potentially, multiple transformations. First, there is a transformation in the individual in terms of his or her capacity to participate more effectively in future actions of a related kind and, hence, a transformation of his or her identity; second, where the problem demands a novel solution, the invention of new tools and practices or the modification of existing ones transforms the culture's tool-kit and its repertoire for problem solving; and third, there is the transformation in the activity setting brought about by the problem-solving action which, in turn, opens up further possibilities for action. Finally, to the extent that one or more members of the group has changed the nature of his or her participation, there is also transformation in the social organization of the group and in the ways in which the members relate to each other. These transformations may usually be quite small, and they may not always be positively evaluated by all the participants involved. Nevertheless, it is such small transformations that, successively and cumulatively, lead to the actual outcomes of the activities in which they occur and, in the process, contribute to the construction of the developmental trajectories of individual participants, of collaborating groups and, thus, of whole cultures.

Vygotsky tended to emphasize the revolutionary nature of the transformations that take place periodically in the developmental trajectories of both individuals and whole cultures. Today, we are probably more aware of the constantly emerging nature of the activities in which we engage and of the extent to which they overlap and impinge on each other. This has certainly led to a more complex conception of development, but it has perhaps also led to a recognition of the developmental significance of each and every activity and, thus, of the transformative potential of the manner in which we participate, of the tools we select from the available tool-kit, and of the way in which we use and reshape them in action.

The Role of the Teacher

Although Vygotsky emphasized the critical role of instruction in the zpd, he had relatively little to say about teachers and teaching. However, as we consider the way in which his ideas are interpreted today, it is perhaps here that there has been the greatest change, as is evidenced by the attention that is now given to teacher development.

The reasons for this are not hard to find. One of the most hopeful – due in no small part to the influence of Vygotsky's concept of the zpd – is the increased understanding among educators that teaching involves much more than appropriately selecting and delivering a standardized curriculum and assessing the extent to which it has been correctly received. Teaching certainly involves preparation, instruction and assessment; but to be truly effective it also involves the ongoing co-construction of each student's zpd and on-the-spot judgments about how best to facilitate his or her learning in the specific activity setting in which he or she is engaged. Of equal importance is the growing recognition of the multifaceted nature of development, and of the need to respond to the diversity among the student population with more open-ended envisionments of their possible futures. To these must be added the increasing rate of cultural change, particularly in the technologies that amplify the traditional modes of semiotic mediation. Taken together, these changes in what is expected of teachers have finally led those who administer public education to recognize the complexity of the responsibility that is placed on those who guide young people's development and, therefore, on the need for adequate teacher development.

For the most part, however, 'teacher development' has meant teacher training, that is to say, something that is *done to* teachers. Only recently has this begun to give way to a more agentive view of development: teachers learning in their zones of proximal development, constructing their understanding of the art of teaching through reflective practice, and drawing for guidance and assistance upon the same range of sources that is available to other learners (Tharp and Gallimore, 1988).

In this context, it is worth mentioning the growing number of teachers who are undertaking classroom-based action research as a means of simultaneously improving the learning opportunities they provide for the particular students in their care, and of increasing their own understanding of the principles that underpin these improvements. As might be expected, linguistic mediation has frequently been the object of their inquiries, particularly the quality of whole-class and small-group interaction (Mercer, 1995); however, some teachers are also beginning to investigate the potential of other, nonlinguistic, semiotic modes for mediating learning in the zpd (Gallas, 1994), while others are challenging the ideological underpinnings of the discourses of power that regulate what will count as learning (Gee, 1992; Lemke, 1988).

A further significant feature of the growing practice of teacher research is the emphasis on community and collaboration with other teachers. As with peer groups solving problems in the classroom, teachers providing "horizontal" support for each other often construct novel solutions to the problems they face that are more appropriate to their particular circumstances than the standard practices recommended by experts outside the classroom; in this way, they both challenge the traditional, "vertical," model of teacher development, and enlarge and diversify the repertoire of strategies available for supporting learning. Equally important, they transform their own identities as teachers, as they take greater responsibility for their own learning and for the learning opportunities they provide for their students (Chang-Wells and Wells, 1997). And when, as is quite frequently the case, they also include their students as well as their colleagues as collaborators in their inquiries, a new, more equal and reciprocal interpretation of the concept of learning and teaching in the zpd is born (Hume, 1998) – one that Vygotsky would recognize, I believe, as a very worthwhile transformation of his initial formulation.

Conclusion: Toward a New Conception of Education

Since Vygotsky first coined the phrase "zone of proximal development," the concept that it names has itself undergone very considerable development. Starting as an insight about the need for psychological assessment to be dynamic and forward looking so that it might maximize the effectiveness of instruction, the concept of the zpd has been expanded in scope and become more fully integrated into the theory as a whole.

As was suggested above, Vygotsky tended to characterize the zpd in terms of individual assessment and instruction, concerned chiefly with generalized intellectual development, and dependent upon face-to-face interaction. However, subsequent discussion and use of the concept in the exploration of its applicability in a variety of settings has considerably extended this characterization by emphasizing the holistic nature of the learning that takes place in the zpd and by making clear that it involves not simply speech but a wide range of mediational means, and not simply dyads in face-to-face interaction but all participants in collaborative communities of practice.

Viewed from the perspective of education, the most salient features of this expanded interpretation of the zpd are, in my view, the following. First, rather than being a "fixed" attribute of the learner, the zpd constitutes a potential for learning that is created in the interaction between participants as they engage in a particular activity together; furthermore, although there is, in principle, an upper bound with respect to what participants are able to take from their task-related interaction at any moment, this upper bound is, in practice, unknown and indeterminate; it depends as much on the manner in which the interaction unfolds as on any independent estimate of the participants' current potential. In this sense, the zpd emerges in the activity and, as participants jointly resolve problems and construct solutions, the potential for further learning is expanded as new possibilities open up that were initially unforeseen. Second, as an opportunity for learning with and from others, the zpd applies potentially to all participants, and not simply to the less skillful or knowledgeable. From this it follows that it is not only children who can learn in the zpd; learning continues over the life-span, and can at all ages and stages be assisted by others, including those who are younger and less mature. Third, the sources of guidance and assistance for learning are not limited to human participants who are physically present in the situation; absent participants, whose contributions are recalled from memory or encountered in semiotic artifacts, such as books, maps, diagrams, and works of art, can also function as significant others in the zpd. Finally, more is involved than cognition alone. Learning in the zpd involves all aspects of the learner – acting, thinking, and feeling; it not only changes the possibilities for participation but also transforms the learner's identity. And, because individuals and the social world are mutually constitutive of each other, transformation of the learner also involves transformation of the communities of which he or she is a member and of the joint activities in which they engage.

This enlarged conception of the zpd has contributed significantly to changing views of the role of joint activity and interaction in the classroom, as is to be seen in reform efforts in curricular areas as different as mathematics (Cobb et al., 1990), history (Pontecorvo and Girardet, 1993), literacy (Brossard and Magendie, 1993; McMahon and Raphael, 1997), and second and foreign language teaching (Lantolf and Appel, 1994), and in the efforts made to integrate exceptional students into mainstream classrooms (Englert, 1992). It has also been influential in the increased value that is attributed to collaboration in classroom activities (Sharan and Sharan, 1992), as students are encouraged to work on group projects, sharing their ideas with peers – their problems, questions, and wonderings, as well as their tentative solutions – rather than treating the classroom as a site of individualistic competition (Scardamalia et al., 1994; Brown and Campione, 1994). This has led, in turn, to a different conception of the role of the teacher; rather than being primarily a dispenser of knowledge and assigner of grades, the teacher sees him or herself as a fellow learner whose prime responsibility is to act as leader of a community committed to the co-construction of knowledge (Rogoff, 1994; Wells and Chang-Wells, 1992).

The second major effect of continued exploration of the zpd has been to highlight its interdependence with all the main threads in Vygotsky's theory: the dialectical relationship between individual and society, each creating, and being created by, the other; the mediation of action by material and semiotic tools and practices; the multiple levels on which previous development both enables and constrains current action and interaction; and activity as the site in which these threads are woven together as the resources of the past are deployed in the present to construct an envisaged future. All activity involves change, and learning is that aspect of change that is brought into focus when activity is considered from the perspective of the human participants who are involved. In this pattern, learning and teaching in the zpd provide both the assurance of a degree of cultural continuity and the opportunity for creative transformation and further development.

At the same time, the concept of development has itself been undergoing change. Vygotsky's revolutionary vision of development as progress to the ideal society is now seen to be untenable. On the phylogenetic level, there is no biologically given end point for development, although the continued existence of a species over successive transformations is evidence that the trajectory it has followed is still ecologically viable. On the cultural historical level, too, there is no universal goal to which all cultures aspire; as was argued above, development is always construed in relation to the values obtaining in particular times and places and, even within a particular culture, these values may be contested. When we describe or evaluate development on the ontogenetic plane, therefore, we should be clear that, in so doing, we are privileging one particular set of values and, by implication, rejecting or according less value to other possibilities that might prove to be just as – or even more – viable for the individuals concerned and for society as a whole (Lemke, 1995).

However, this new understanding of development in no way reduces the educational significance of Vygotsky's concept of working in the zpd; on the contrary, it serves to bring into focus the critical nature of the decisions that teachers have always had to make concerning the kinds of activities in which they engage with students and the manner in which they do so. When it was assumed that there was an ideal, predetermined end in view for development, it was possible for the teacher simply to rely on tradition or authority in making curricular decisions. However, that is no longer the case. As well as with the means to be used in awakening the potential for development, the teacher must also be concerned with the diverse directions that development may take; as well as making available to students the legacy of the past, the teacher must also support and guide them as they create their own alternative versions of the future.

Teaching thus becomes more than ever a matter of making choices, and ones that are not simply practical in their implications but also moral, in that they concern ethics and values (Cole, 1996b).

The list below summarizes the characteristics of this expanded conception of the zone of proximal development.

1. The zpd may apply in any situation in which, while participating in an activity, individuals are in the process of developing mastery of a practice or understanding of a topic.

2. The zpd is not a context-independent attribute of an individual; rather it is constructed in the interaction between participants in the course of their joint engagement in a particular activity.

3. To teach in the zpd is to be responsive to the learner's current goals and stage of development and to provide guidance and assistance that enables him/her to achieve those goals and, at the same time, to increase his/her potential for future participation.

4. To learn in the zpd does not require that there be a designated teacher; whenever people collaborate in an activity, each can assist the others, and each can learn from the contributions of the others.

5. Some activities have as one of their outcomes the production of an artifact, which may be used as a tool in a subsequent activity. Representations – in e.g. art, drama, spoken, or written text – of what has been done or understood are artifacts of this kind; engaging with them can provide an occasion for learning in the zpd.

6. Learning in the zpd involves all aspects of the learner and leads to the development of identity as well as of skills and knowledge. For this reason, the affective quality of the interaction between the participants is critical. Learning will be most successful when it is mediated by interaction that expresses mutual respect, trust and concern.

7. Learning in the zpd involves multiple transformations: of the participants' potential for future action and of the cognitive structures in terms of which it is organized; of the tools and practices that mediate the activity; and of the social world in which that activity takes place.

8. Development does not have any predetermined end, or telos; although it is characterized by increasing complexity of organization, this does not, in itself, constitute progress. What is considered to be progress depends on the dominant values in particular times and places, which are both contested and constantly changing. The zpd is thus a site of conflict and contradiction as well as of unanimity; the transformations it engenders lead to diversity of outcome which may radically change as well as reproduce existing practices and values.

At this time when confidence in public schooling is at a low ebb, there is both a need and an opportunity to make radical changes in the way in which it is organized. In this context, as increasing numbers of educators are recognizing, Vygotsky's genetic theory of learning and development can provide a starting point for rethinking the principles on which education should be based. And in that rethinking, the concept of the zone of proximal development has a central role to play. For, far from being simply a new and better pedagogical method, the zpd offers an insightful and theoretically coherent way of thinking about the complex nature of the transformations that are involved in learning and of the multiple ways in which learning can be assisted. However, as was pointed out at the outset, it is a central tenet of Vygotsky's theory that theories, like all other artifacts, are the products of the particular conditions in which they are created; if they are to be useful in other times and places, therefore, they must be treated, not as repositories of truth that are fixed and immutable but as helpful tools for thinking with, which can themselves be improved in the process. It thus follows that, if Vygotsky's theory is to provide the guidance that many believe it should, we should treat his ideas as a source of assistance in *our* zones of proximal development. We should certainly read his texts and try to understand what he had to say; but, in appropriating his ideas and putting them to use, we should also be willing to transform those ideas so that they can be of greatest use to us in meeting the demands of our own situations.

Notes

1. This chapter is based on my comments, as discussant, in the Symposium, "The ZPD: relationships between education and development," at the IInd Conference for Sociocultural Research, Geneva, 11–15 September 1996.

    I should like to acknowledge the initiating role played by the other members of the symposium in prompting me to write this paper: P. Adey, L. Allal and G. Pelgrims Ducrey; J. Lompscher; T. Murphey; T. Schack, H.-J. Lander; and O. Stoll. I should also like to thank the many contributors to XLCHC (now XMCA) for the stimulating discussions of the issues that are presented here. This paper should be read as part of that ongoing dialogue.

2. This metaphor was suggested by Merrill Swain (personal communication).

Appendix I

A Social Constructivist Model of Learning and Teaching

Vygotskian theory suggests that the principal goal of education is to provide an environment in which students, however diverse their background, engage collaboratively in productive, purposeful activities which enable them to:

- take over the culture's tool-kit of skills, knowledge and values so that they are able to participate effectively in the practices of the larger society
- develop the disposition to act creatively, responsibly and reflectively in achieving their own potential and constructing a personal identity

These aims seem most likely to be achieved by:

1. Creating a classroom community which shares a commitment to caring, collaboration, and a dialogic mode of making meaning
2. Organizing the curriculum in terms of broad themes for inquiry that encourage a willingness to wonder, to ask questions, and to collaborate with others in building knowledge, both practical and theoretical, to answer them
3. Negotiating goals that:
   - challenge students to develop their interests and abilities
   - are sufficiently open-ended to elicit alternative possibilities for consideration
   - involve the whole person – feelings, interests, personal and cultural values, as well as cognition
   - provide multiple opportunities to master the culture's tools and technologies through purposeful use

- encourage both collaborative group work and individual effort;
- give equal value to thoughtful processes and excellent products.

4. Ensuring that there are occasions for students to:

- use a variety of modes of representation as tools for achieving joint and individual understanding
- present their work to others and receive critical, constructive feedback
- reflect on what they have learned, both individually and as a community
- receive guidance and assistance in their zones of proximal development.

Appendix II

Categories for the Analysis of Discourse

The analysis of the two episodes in Chapter 7 is carried out at three levels. At the first level, each *episode* is segmented into *sequences*, which are numbered consecutively. At the second level, each *sequence* is segmented into *exchanges*; and at the third, each *exchange* is segmented into *moves*, either *initiate*, *respond* or *follow-up*. Each move is further categorized according to its Prospectiveness and its topic-oriented function.

At the levels of *exchange* and *move*, codings of categories are entered in four columns.

Column 1: Exchange Type
Nuc.   Nuclear exchange
Dep.   Dependent exchange
Emb.   Embedded exchange

Column 2: Move Type
I   Initiating move
R   Responding move
F   Follow-up move

Column 3: Prospectiveness
D   Demand
G   Give
A   Acknowledge

Column 4: Function
Req. inform   Request information
Req. suggest   Request suggestion
Req. opinion   Request opinion

Req. justif.	Request justification/explanation
Req. pos/neg	Request 'Yes'/'No' answer
Req. confirm	Request confirmation
Req. repeat	Request repetition
Check	Check for understanding
Bid	Request to speak
Inform	Give information
Suggest	Give suggestion
Opinion	Give opinion
Justif.	Give justification/explanation
Confirm	Give confirmation
Qualify	Qualify previous contribution
Clarify	Clarify own previous contribution
Extend	Extend previous contribution
Exemplify	Give relevant example
Pos/neg	Give 'Yes' or 'No' answer
Repetition	Repeat own previous contribution
Nominate	Nominate next speaker
Acknowledge	Acknowledge
Accept	Accept previous contribution
Reject	Reject previous contribution
Evaluate	Evaluate previous contribution
Reformulate	Reformulate previous contribution

Note: The complete coding scheme contains other *function* categories, notably those concerned with *action* and with *attitude*. It also distinguishes between *information* that is known only to the speaker and *information* that all participants are expected to know. The complete scheme is available from the author on request.

References

Alexander, P. A., Schallert, D. L., & Hare, V. C. 1991. Coming to terms: How researchers in learning and literacy talk about knowledge. *Review of Educational Research, 61*, 315–343.

Allal, L., & Ducrey, G. P. 1996. Assessment of or in the zone of proximal development., *II International Conference for Sociocultural Research*. Geneva, September 1996.

Allen, P. W. B. 1993. *The integration of ESL students into mainstream science classrooms: A Canadian case-study*. Toronto: Ontario Institute for Studies in Education/University of Toronto: Unpublished paper.

Applebee, A. N. 1996. *Curriculum as conversation: Transforming traditions of teaching and learning*. Chicago: University of Chicago Press.

Atwell, N. 1991. *Side by side: Essays on teaching to learn*. Portsmouth, NH: Heinemann.

Bakhtin, M. N. 1981. *The dialogic imagination*. Austin: University of Texas Press.

Bakhtin, M. M. 1986. *Speech genres and other late essays*. (Y. McGee, Trans.). Austin: University of Texas Press.

Barnes, D. 1976/1992. *From communication to curriculum*. Harmondsworth, UK: Penguin.

Barnes, D., Britton, J., & Rosen, H. 1969. *Language, the learner and the school*. Harmondsworth, UK: Penguin.

Barnes, D., & Todd, F. 1977. *Communicating and learning in small groups*. London: Routledge & Kegan Paul.

Barlett, F. C. 1932. *Remembering: A study in experimental and social psychology*. Cambridge: Cambridge University Press.

Bates, E. 1976. *Language and cognition: The acquisition of pragmatics*. New York: Academic Press.

Bateson, G. 1972. *Steps to an ecology of mind*. New York: Ballantine.

Bazerman, C. 1994. Systems of genres and the enactment of social intentions. In A. Freedman & P. Medway (Eds.), *Genre and the new rhetoric*. London: Taylor and Francis.

Bereiter, C. 1994a. Implications of postmodernism for science, or, science as progressive discourse. *Educational Psychologist, 29* (1), 3–12.

1994b. Constructivism, socioculturalism, and Popper's World 3. *Educational Researcher 23* (7): 21–23.

Bereiter, C., & Scardamalia, M. 1987. *The psychology of written composition*. Hillsdale, NJ: Erlbaum.

    1996. Rethinking learning. In D. R. Olson and N. Torrance (Eds.), *The handbook of education and human development* (pp. 485–513). Cambridge, MA: Blackwell.

Berkenkotter, C. 1994. Scientific writing and scientific thinking: Writing the scientific habit of mind. *"Lev Vygotsky and the Human Sciences" Conference*. Moscow.

Bernstein, B. 1971. *Class, codes and control Vol. I: Theoretical studies towards a sociology of language*. London: Routledge & Kegan Paul.

    1975. *Class, codes and control, Vol. 3: Towards a theory of educational transmissions*. London: Routledge & Kegan Paul.

Berry, M. 1981. Systemic linguistics and discourse analysis: a multi-layered approach to exchange structure. In M. C. Coulthard & M. Montgomery (Eds.), *Studies in discourse analysis* (pp. 120–45). London: Routledge and Kegan Paul.

Brazil, D. 1981. The place of intonation in a discourse model. In M. C. Coulthard & M. Montgomery (Eds.), *Studies in discourse analysis* (pp. 12–145). London: Routledge and Kegan Paul.

Britton, J. 1970. *Language and learning*. London: Allen Lane.

    1982. *Prospect and retrospect: Selected essays of James Britton*. (G. Pradl ed.). London: Heinemann.

Brossard, M., & Magendie, A. 1993. Situations scolaires et apprentissage de l'écrit. In G. Chauveau, E. Rogovas-Chauveau, & M. Remond (Eds.), *L'enfant apprenti lecteur* (pp. 151–9). Paris: L'Harmattan Gresos.

Brown, A. L. 1975. The development of memory: Knowing, knowing about knowing, and knowing how to know. In H. W. Reese (Ed.), *Advances in child development and behavior* (Vol. 10, pp. 103–52). New York: Academic Press.

Brown, A. L., Ash, D., Rutherford, M., Kakagawa, et al. 1993. Distributed expertise in the classroom. In G. Salomon (Ed.), *Distributed cognitions: Psychological and educational considerations* (pp. 188–228). Cambridge: Cambridge University Press.

Brown, A. L., & Campione, J. C. 1994. Guided discovery in a community of learners. In K. McGilly (Ed.), *Integrating cognitive theory and classroom practice: Classroom lessons* (pp. 229–72). Cambridge, MA: MIT Press/Bradford Books.

Brown, A. L., & Palincsar, A. S. 1989. Guided, cooperative learning and individual knowledge acquisition. In L. B. Resnick (Ed.), *Knowing, learning and instruction: Essays in honor of Robert Glaser* (pp. 393–452). Hillsdale, NJ: Erlbaum.

Bruner, J. S. 1962. *On knowing: Essays for the left hand*. Cambridge, MA: Harvard University Press.

    1983. *Child's Talk*. New York: Norton.

    1986. *Actual minds, possible worlds*. Cambridge, MA: Harvard University Press.

    1987. Prologue. In R. W. Rieber & A. S. Carton (Eds.), *The collected works of L. S. Vygotsky. Vol. 1 Problems of general psychology*. New York: Plenum.

    1990. *Acts of meaning*. Cambridge, MA: Harvard University Press.

    1996a. *The culture of education*. Cambridge, MA: Harvard University Press.

    1996b. Celebrating divergence: Piaget and Vygotsky. *IInd International Conference for Sociocultural Research and 'The Growing Mind'*, Geneva, 15 September 1996.

    1997. Conference on *Theory of Mind*. Toronto, April 1997.

Bruner, J. S., & Greenfield, P. M. 1972. Culture and cognitive growth. In J. S. Bruner (Ed.), *The relevance of education*. London: Allen and Unwin.

Budilova. 1972. *Filosofskie probremy v sovetckoi psikxologii*. Moscow: Izdatel'stva (Nayka). [Philosophical problems of Soviet psychology.].

Campione, J. C., & Brown, A. L. 1987. Linking dynamic assessment with school achievement. In C. S. Lidz (Ed.), *Dynamic assessment: An interactional approach to evaluating learning potential* (pp. 82–115). New York: Guilford Press.

Cazden, C. B. 1988. *Classroom discourse: The language of teaching and learning*. Portsmouth, NH: Heinemann.

Chambers, A. 1993. *Tell me: Children, reading and talk*. Stroud, UK: Thimble Press.

Chang-Wells, G. L., & Wells, G. 1993. The dynamics of discourse: Literacy and the construction of knowledge. In E. A. Forman, N. Minick, & C. A. Stone (Eds.), *Contexts for learning: Sociocultural dynamics in children's development* (pp. 58–90). New York: Oxford University Press.

Chang-Wells, G. L., & Wells, G. 1997. Modes of discourse for living, learning and teaching. In S. Hollingsworth (Ed.), *International action research and educational reform* (pp. 147–56). London and Philadelphia: Falmer Press.

Christie, F. 1989. Language development in education. In R. Hasan & J. R. Martin (Eds.), *Language development: Learning language, learning culture. Meaning and choice in language: Studies for Michael Halliday* (pp. 152–98). Norwood, NJ: Ablex.

Christie, F. 1991. Pedagogical and content registers in a writing lesson. *Linguistics and Education*, *3*, 203–224.

Christie, F. 1993. Curriculum genres: Planning for effective teaching. In B. Cope & M. Kalantzis (Eds.), *The powers of literacy: A genre approach to teaching writing* (pp. 154–78). Pittsburgh: University of Pittsburgh Press.

Christie, F., Gray, B., Gray, P., Macken, et al. 1990. *Language: A resource for meaning, Levels 1–4*. Sydney: Harcourt Brace Jovanovich.

Clay, M. M., & Cazden, C. B. 1990. A Vygotskian interpretation of Reading Recovery. In L. C. Moll (Ed.), *Vygotsky and education: Implications and applications of socio-historical psychology* (pp. 206–20). New York: Cambridge University Press.

Cobb, P., Wood, T., & Yackel, E. 1990. Classrooms as learning environments for teachers and researchers. In R. B. Davis, C. A. Maher, & N. Noddings (Eds.), *Constructivist views on the teaching and learning of mathematics. Journal for Research in Mathematics Education Monograph No. 4* (pp. 125–146). Reston, VA: National Council of Teachers of Mathematics.

Cobb, P., Wood, T., Yackel, E., & McNeal, B. 1992. Characteristics of classroom mathematics traditions: An interactional analysis. *American Educational Research Journal*, *29* (3), 573–604.

Cole, M. 1985. The zone of proximal development: Where culture and cognition create each other. In J. V. Wertsch (Ed.), *Culture, communication and cognition: Vygotskian perspectives* (pp. 146–61). New York: Cambridge University Press.

Cole, M. 1993. Remembering the future. In G. Harman (Ed.), *Conceptions of the human mind. Essays in honor of George A. Miller* (pp. 247–65). Hillsdale, NJ: Erlbaum.

Cole, M. 1994. A conception of culture for a communication theory of mind. In D. R. Vocate (Ed.), *Intrapersonal communication: Different voices, different minds* (pp. 77–98). Hillsdale, NJ: Erlbaum.

1996a. *Cultural psychology: A once and future discipline*. Cambridge, MA: The Bellknap Press of Harvard University Press.

1996b. A cultural–historical approach to the sciences of the artificial., IInd International Conference for Sociocultural Research, Geneva, September 1996.

Cole, M., & Engeström, Y. 1993. A cultural-historical approach to distributed cognition. In G. Salomon (Ed.), *Distributed cognitions: Psychological and educational considerations* (pp. 1–46). Cambridge: Cambridge University Press.

Collins, A., Brown, J. S., & Newman, S. E. 1989. Cognitive apprenticeship: Teaching the crafts of reading, writing, and mathematics. In L. B. Resnick (Ed.), *Knowing, learning, and instruction: Essays in honor of Robert Glaser* (pp. 453–94). Hillsdale, NJ: Erlbaum.

Collins, J. 1982. Discourse style, classroom interaction and differential treatment. *Journal of Reading Behavior, 14*, 429–37.

Coulthard, M. C. 1977. *An introduction to discourse analysis*. London: Longman.

Countryman, J. 1992. *Writing to learn mathematics: Strategies that work, K–12*. Portsmouth, NH: Heinemann.

Crain-Thoreson, C. 1993. The subtext of parent/child story reading. Western Washington University, Department of Psychology, unpublished paper.

Crowder, E. M. 1996. Gestures at work in sense-making science talk. *Journal of the Learning Sciences, 5*(3), 173–208.

D'Arcy, P. 1989. *Making sense, shaping meaning*. Portsmouth, NH: Boynton/Cook and Heinemann Educational Books.

Dascal, M. 1995. The dispute over the primacy of thinking or speaking. In M. Dascal, D. Gerhardus, K. Lorenz, & G. Meggle (Eds.), *Philosophy of language: A handbook of contemporary research* (Vol. 2, pp. 1024–41). Berlin: Walter de Gruyter.

Deacon, T. W. 1997. *The symbolic species: The co-evolution of language and the brain*. New York: Norton.

de Jong, T., & Ferguson-Hessler, M. G. M. 1996. Types and qualities of knowledge. *Educational Psychologist, 31*(2), 105–14.

Derewianka, B. 1991. *Exploring how texts work*. Rozelle, NSW: Primary English Teaching Association (Australia).

Dewey, J. 1938. *Education and experience*. New York: Collier Macmillan.

1956. *The school and society & The child and the curriculum*. Chicago: University of Chicago Press.

Dias, P. X., & Hayhoe, M. 1988. *Developing response to poetry*. Milton Keynes, UK: Open University Press.

Dixon, J. 1987. The question of genres. In I. Reid (Ed.), *The place of genre in learning: Current debates*. Geelong Vic.: Deakin University, Centre for Studies in Literary Education.

Donald, M. 1991. *Origins of the modern mind: Three stages in the evolution of culture and cognition*. Cambridge, MA: Harvard University Press.

Donoahue, Z., Van Tassell, M. A., & Patterson, L. (Eds.). 1996. *Research in the classroom: Talk, text and inquiry*. Newark, DE: International Reading Association.

Driver, R. 1983. *The pupil as scientist?* Milton Keynes, UK: Open University Press.

Dyson, A. H. 1989. *Multiple worlds of child writers: Friends learning to write*. New York: Teachers College Press.

1993. *Social worlds of children learning to write in an urban school.* New York: Teachers College Press.

Edelman, G. 1992. *Bright air, brilliant fire.* New York: Basic Books.

Edwards, A. D., & Westgate, D. 1994. *Investigating classroom talk.* London: Falmer Press.

Edwards, D. 1993. But what do children really think? Discourse analysis and conceptual content in children's talk. *Cognition and Instruction, 11*(3–4), 207–25.

1997. *Discourse and cognition.* London: Sage.

Edwards, D., & Mercer, N. 1987. *Common knowledge.* London: Methuen/Routledge.

Edwards, D., & Potter, J. 1992. *Discursive psychology.* London: Sage.

Egan, K. 1997. *The educated mind.* Chicago: University of Chicago Press.

Eggins, S., & Slade, D. 1997. *Analysing casual conversation.* London: Cassell.

Engeström, Y. 1987. *Learning by expanding: An activity-theoretical approach to developmental research.* Helsinki: Orienta-Konsultit.

1990. *Learning, working and imagining: Twelve studies in activity theory.* Helsinki: Orienta-Konsultit.

1991a. Activity theory and individual and social transformation. *Activity Theory, 7/8,* 6–17.

1991b. Non scolae sed vitae discimus: Toward overcoming the encapsulation of school learning. *Learning and Instruction, 1,* 243–59.

1996. Development as breaking away and opening up: A challenge to Vygotsky and Piaget. IInd International Conference for Sociocultural Research and "The Growing Mind," Geneva, 15 September 1996.

Englert, C. S. 1992. Writing instruction from a sociocultural perspective: The holistic, dialogic, and social enterprise of writing. *Journal of Learning Disabilities, 25*(3), 153–172.

Fédération étudiante universitaire du Québec. 1995. Mémoire à la Commission des États généraux sur l'éducation. Québec: FEUQ.

Feldman, C. F., & Kalmar, D. A. 1996. Autobigraphy and fiction as modes of thought. In D. R. Olson & N. Torrance (Eds.), *Modes of thought: Explorations in culture and cognition* (pp. 106–22). New York: Cambridge University Press.

Feuerstein, R. 1979. *The dynamic assessment of retarded performers: The Learning Potential Assessment Device, theory, instruments, and techniques.* Baltimore: University Park Press.

Flower, L. S., & Hayes, J. R. 1980. The dynamics of composing: Making plans and juggling constraints. In L. W. Gregg & E. R. Steinberg (Eds.), *Cognitive processes in writing.* Hillsdale, NJ: Erlbaum.

Forman, E. A. 1996. Learning mathematics on participation in classroom practice: Implications of sociocultural theory for educational reform. In L. P. Steffe, P. Nesher, P. Cobb, G. A. Goldin, and B. Green, *Theories of mathematical learning.* Hillsdale, NJ: Erlbaum.

Forman, E. A., & McPhail, J. 1993. Vygotskian perspectives on children's collaborative problem-solving activities. In E. A. Forman, N. Minick, & C. A. Stone (Eds.), *Contexts for learning: Sociocultural dynamics in children's development* (pp. 213–29). New York: Oxford University Press.

Forman, E. A., Minick, N., & Stone, A. (Eds.). 1993. *Contexts for learning: Sociocultural dynamics in children's development.* New York: Oxford University Press.

Franklin, U. 1996. Introduction, Conference on *Towards an Ecology of Knowledge*. University of Toronto, May 1996.

Gal'perin, P. Y. 1969. Stages in the development of mental acts. In M. Cole & I. Maltzman (Eds.), *A handbook of contemporary Soviet psychology*. (pp. 249–73). New York: Basic Books.

Gallas, K. 1994. *The languages of learning: How children talk, write, dance, draw, and sing their understanding of the world*. New York: Teachers College Press.

1995. *Talking their way into science: hearing children's questions and theories, responding with curricula*. New York: Teachers College Press.

Gamberg, R., Kwak, W., Hutchings, M., Altheim, J., et al. 1988. *Learning and loving it: Theme studies in the classroom*. Toronto: OISE Press; Portsmouth, NH: Heinemann.

Gardner, H. 1983. *Multiple intelligences: the theory in practice*. New York: Basic Books.

1989. *Art, mind, and education: Research from Project Zero*. Urbana, IL: University of Illinois Press.

Gee, J. P. 1992. *The social mind: Language, ideology and social practice*. New York: Bergin and Garvey.

Gianotti, M. A. 1994. Moving between worlds: Talk during writing workshop. In G. Wells et al., *Changing schools from within: Creating communities of inquiry*. (pp. 37–59). Toronto: OISE Press; Portsmouth, NH: Heinemann.

Golding, W. 1955. *The inheritors*. London: Faber and Faber.

Goodwin, C., & Heritage, J. C. 1990. Conversation analysis. *Annual Review of Anthropology*, *19*, 283–307.

Goody, J. 1987. *The interface between the oral and the written*. Cambridge: Cambridge University Press.

Green, J. L., & Dixon, C. N. 1993. Talking knowledge into being: Discursive and social practices in classrooms. *Linguistics and Education*, 5(3–4), 231–39.

Green, J. L., Kantor, R., & Rogers, T. 1990. Exploring the complexity of language and learning in the classroom.. In B. Jones & L. Idol (Eds.), *Educational values and cognitive instruction: Implications for reform* (Vol. II,). Hillsdale, NJ: Erlbaum.

Grice, H. P. 1975. Logic and conversation. In P. Cole & J. L. Morgan (Eds.), *Syntax and semantics III: Speech acts*. (pp. 41–58). New York: Academic Press.

Griffin, P., & Mehan, H. 1981. Sense and ritual in classroom discourse. In F. Coulmas (Ed.), *Explorations in standardized communication situations and prepatterned speech*. The Hague: Mouton.

Habermas, J. 1971. *Knowledge and human interests*. Boston: Beacon.

1983. *The theory of communicative action*. Boston, MA: Beacon Press.

Hacking, I. 1990. *The taming of chance*. Cambridge: Cambridge University Press.

Hall, R. 1990. *Making mathematics on paper: Constructing representations of stories about related linear functions*. (Technical Report (Doctoral Dissertation) 90–17). Irvine, CA: University of California, Department of Information and Computer Science.

Halliday, M. A. K. 1970. Language structure and language function. In J. Lyons (Ed.), *New horizons in linguistics*. Harmondsworth, UK: Penguin.

1973a. *Explorations in the functions of language*. London: Arnold.

1973b. Foreword. In D. Mackay, B. Thompson, & P. Schaub (Eds.), *Breakthrough to literacy (American edition)*. Glendale, CA: Bowmar.

1975. *Learning how to mean*. London: Arnold.

1978. *Language as social semiotic: The social interpretation of language and meaning.* London: Arnold.

1984. Language as code and language as behaviour: A systemic functional interpretation of the nature and ontogenesis of language. In R. Fawcett, M. A. K. Halliday, S. M. Lamb, & A. Makkai (Eds.), *The semiotics of culture and language, Vol. 1* (pp. 3–35). London: Frances Pinter.

1985. *Spoken and written language.* Geelong, Vic.: Deakin University (Republished by Oxford University Press, 1989).

1988. On the language of physical science. In M. Ghadessy (Ed.), *Registers of written English: Situational factors and linguistic features* (pp. 162–78). London: Frances Pinter.

1990. Some grammatical problems in scientific English. *Australian Review of Applied Linguistics, Series S, 6,* 13–37.

1993a. Towards a language-based theory of learning. *Linguistics and Education, 5,* 93–116.

1993b. *Language in a changing world.* Sydney: Applied Linguistics Association of Australia, Occasional Paper 13.

1994. *An introduction to functional grammar (second edition).* London: Arnold.

Halliday, M. A. K., & Hasan, R. 1976. *Cohesion in English.* London: Longman.

1985. *Language, context and text: Aspects of language in a social-semiotic perspective.* Geelong, Vic.: Deakin University (Republished by Oxford University Press, 1989).

Halliday, M. A. K., & Martin, J. R. 1993. *Writing science: Literacy and discursive power.* London: Falmer Press.

Harste, J. 1993. Literacy as curricular conversations about knowledge, inquiry and morality. In M. R. Ruddell & R. B. Ruddell (Eds.), *Theoretical models and processes of reading* (4th ed.).

Hasan, R. 1985. The structure of a text. In M. A. K. Halliday & R. Hasan, *Language, context and text: Aspects of language in a social-semiotic perspective.* Geelong, Vic.: Deakin University.

1986. The ontogenesis of ideology: An interpretation of mother-child talk. In T. Threadgold, E. A. Gros, G. Kress, & M. A. K. Halliday (Eds.), *Language, semiotics and ideology* (pp. 125–46). Sydney: Sydney Association for Studies in Society and Culture.

1989. Semantic variation and sociolinguistics. *Australian Journal of Linguistics, 9,* 221–76.

1992. Meaning in sociolinguistic theory. In K. Bolton & H. Kwok (Eds.), *Sociolinguistics today: International perspectives.* London: Routledge.

Hasan, R., & Cloran, C. 1990. A sociolinguistic interpretation of everyday talk between mothers and children. In M. A. K. Halliday, J. Gibbons, & H. Nicholas (Eds.), *Learning, keeping and using language.* Amsterdam: John Benjamins.

Hasan, R., & Martin, J. R. (Eds.). 1989. *Language development: Learning language, learning culture. Meaning and choice in language: Studies for Michael Halliday.* Norwood, NJ: Ablex.

Hatano, G. 1993. Time to merge Vygotskian and constructivist conceptions of knowledge acquisition. In E. A. Forman, N. Minick, & C. A. Stone (Eds.), *Contexts for learning: Sociocultural dynamics in children's development* (pp. 153–66). New York: Oxford University Press.

Hatano, G., & Inagaki, K. 1991. Sharing cognition through collective comprehension activity. In L. B. Resnick, J. M. Levine, & S. D. Teasley (Eds.), *Perspectives on socially shared cognition* (pp. 331–48). Washington, DC: American Psychological Association.

Hatch, T., & Gardner, H. 1993. Finding cognition in the classroom: an expanded view of human intelligence. In G. Salomon (Ed.), *Distributed cognitions: Psychological and educational considerations* (pp. 164–87). Cambridge: Cambridge University Press.

Heap, J. 1989. Language as social action. *Theory into Practice*, *28*(2), 148–53.

    1985. Discourse in the production of classroom knowledge: Reading lessons. *Curriculum Inquiry*, *15*(3), 247–79.

Heath, S. B. 1983. *Ways with words*. Cambridge: Cambridge University Press.

Hedegaard, M. 1990. How instruction influences children's concepts of evolution. *Mind, Culture, and Activity*, *3*, 11–24.

Hicks, D. 1995. Discourse, learning, and teaching. *Review of Research in Education*, *21*, 49–95.

Holzman, L. 1995. Creating developmental learning environments. *School Psychology International*, *16*, 199–212.

Hume, K. 1998. Co-researching with students: An activity for a knowledge building community. *Networks*, http://www.oise.utoronto.ca/~ctd/networks/.

Hutchins, E. 1995. *Cognition in the wild*. Cambridge, MA: MIT Press.

Ilyenkov, E. V. 1977. The concept of the ideal. In P. N. Fedoseyev (Ed.), *Philosophy in the USSR: Problems of dialectical materialism* (pp. 71–99). Moscow: Progress.

Itakura, K. 1967. Instruction and learning of concept "force" in static based on Kasetsu Jikken-Jigyo (Hypothesis–Experiment–Instruction): A new method of science teaching (in Japanese). *Bulletin of National Institute for Educational Research*, *52*, 1–121.

Jefferson, G. 1972. Side sequences. In D. Sudnow (Ed.), *Studies in social interaction*. New York: The Free Press.

John-Steiner, V. 1987. *Notebooks of the mind*. New York: Harper and Row.

Kamberelis, G. 1995. Genre as institutionally-informed social practice. *Journal of Contemporary Legal Issues*, *6*, 115–171.

Kierstead, J. 1985. Direct instruction and experiential approaches: Are they really mutually exclusive? *Educational Leadership* (May 1985), 25–30.

Kinkead-Weekes, M., & Gregor, I. 1967. *William Golding: A critical study*. London: Faber and Faber.

Kress, G. 1997. *Before writing: Rethinking the paths to literacy*. London: Routledge.

Kuutti, K. 1996. Activity theory as a potential theory for human-computer interaction research. In B. Nardi (Ed.), *Context and consciousness: Activity theory and human computer interaction* (pp. 17–44). Cambridge, MA: MIT Press.

Labov, W., & Fanshel, D. 1977. *Therapeutic discourse: Psychotherapy as conversation*. New York: Academic Press.

Lampert, M. 1990. When the problem is not the question and the solution is not the answer: Mathematical knowing and teaching. *American Educational Research Journal*, *27*, 29–63.

    1992. Practices and problems in teaching authentic mathematics. In F. K. Oser, A. Dick, & J.-L. Patry (Eds.), *Effective and responsible teaching* (pp. 295–314). San Francisco: Jossey-Bass.

Lampert, M., Rittenhouse, P., & Crumbaugh, C. 1996. Agreeing to disagree: Developing sociable mathematical discourse. In D. R. Olson & N. Torrance (Eds.), *The handbook of education and human development* (pp.731–64). Cambridge, MA: Blackwell.

Langer, J. A., & Applebee, A. N. 1987. *How writing shapes thinking: A study of teaching and learning.* (Research Monograph Series 22). Urbana, IL: National Council of Teachers of English.

Langer, S. 1953. *Feeling and form; a theory of art.* New York: Scribner.

Lantolf, J. P., & Appel, G. 1994. Theoretical framework: An introduction to Vygotskian approaches to second language research. In J. P. Lantolf & G. Appel (Eds.), *Vygotskian approaches to second language research.* (pp. 1–31.). Norwood, NJ: Ablex.

Latour, B. 1987. *Science in action.* Cambridge, MA: Harvard University Press.

Latour, B., & Woolgar, S. 1986. *Laboratory life: The construction of scientific facts.* (2nd ed.). Princeton, NJ: Princeton University Press.

Lave, J. 1977. Tailor-made experiments and evaluating the intellectual consequences of apprenticeship training. *Quarterly Newsletter of the Laboratory of Comparative Human Cognition, 1,* 1–3.

Lave, J., & Wenger, E. 1991. *Situated learning: Legitimate peripheral participation.* New York: Cambridge University Press.

Lemke, J. L. 1985. *Using language in the classroom.* Geelong, Vic.: Deakin University Press. (Republished by Oxford University Press, 1989).

1988. Genres, semantics and classroom education. *Linguistics and Education, 1,* 81–99.

1990. *Talking science: Language, learning, and values.* Norwood, NJ: Ablex.

1993a. Intertextuality and educational research. *Linguistics and Education, 4*(3–4), 257–268.

1993b. When is a strategy? : E-mail message, XLCHC, 29 October 1993.

1995. *Textual politics: Discourse and social dynamics.* Bristol, PA: Taylor & Francis.

Leont'ev, A. N. 1978. *Activity, consciousness, and personality.* Englewood Cliffs, NJ: Prentice Hall.

1981. The problem of activity in psychology. In J. V. Wertsch (Ed.), *The concept of activity in Soviet psychology* (pp. 37–71). Armonk, NY: Sharpe.

Litowitz, B. 1993. Deconstruction in the zone of proximal development. In E. A. Forman, N. Minick, & C. A. Stone (Eds.), *Contexts for learning: Sociocultural dynamics in children's development* (pp. 184–96). New York: Oxford University Press.

Lotman, Y. M. 1988. Text within a text. *Soviet Psychology, 26*(3), 32–51.

1990. *Universe of the mind: A semiotic theory of culture.* London: I.B. Tauris.

Luke, A. 1995. Text and discourse in education: An introduction to critical discourse analysis. *Review of Research in Education, 21,* 3–48.

Luria, A. R. 1976. *Cognitive development: Its cultural and social foundations.* Cambridge, MA: Harvard University Press.

1978. *The making of mind: A personal account of Soviet psychology.* (M. Cole and S. Cole, eds.). Cambridge, MA: Harvard University Press.

MacLure, M., Phillips, T., & Wilkinson, A. (Eds.). 1988. *Oracy matters.* Milton Keynes, UK: Open University Press.

Martin, J. R. 1985. Process and text: Two aspects of human semiosis. In J. D. Benson & W. S. Greaves (Eds.), *Advances in discourse processes: Systemic perspectives on discourse* (Vol. 15, pp. 248–274). Norwood, NJ: Ablex.

Martin, J. R. 1989. *Factual writing: Exploring and challenging social reality*. London: Oxford University Press.

Martin, J. R. 1992. *English texts*. Amsterdam: John Benjamins.

Martin, J. R. 1993. A contextual theory of language. In B. Cope & M. Kalantzis (Eds.), *The powers of literacy: A genre approach to teaching writing* (pp. 116–36). Pittsburgh: University of Pittsburgh Press.

Martin, J. R., Christie, F., & Rothery, J. 1987. Social processes in education: A reply to Sawyer and Watson. In I. Reid (Ed.), *The place of genre in learning: Current debates*. Geelong, Vic.: Deakin University, Centre for Studies in Literary Education.

Matusov, E. 1996. Intersubjectivity without agreement. *Mind, Culture, and Activity*, *3*, 25–45.

Maybin, J., Mercer, N., & Stierer, B. 1992. "Scaffolding" learning in the classroom. In K. Norman (Ed.), *Thinking voices: The work of the National Oracy Project*. (pp. 186–95). London: Hodder & Stoughton.

McMahon, S. I., Raphael, T. E., with Goatley, V. J., & Pardo, L. S. (Eds.). 1997. *The Book Club connection*. New York: Teachers College Press.

McNeill, D. 1992. *Hand and mind: What gestures reveal about thought*. Chicago: University of Chicago Press.

Mehan, H. 1979. *Learning lessons: Social organization in the classroom*. Cambridge, MA: Harvard University Press.

Mercer, N. 1992. Talk for teaching and learning. In K. Norman (Ed.), *Thinking voices: The work of the National Oracy Project*. (pp. 215–223). London: Hodder and Stoughton for the National Curriculum Council.

Mercer, N. 1995. *The guided construction of knowledge*. Clevedon UK: Multilingual Matters.

Mercer, N., & Fisher, E. 1993. How do teachers help children to learn? An analysis of teachers' interventions in computer-based activities. *Learning and Instruction*, *2*, 339–355.

Michaels, S. 1981. "Sharing time": Children's narrative styles and differential access to literacy. *Language in Society*, *10*, 423–42.

Miller, C. R. 1984. Genre as social action. *Quarterly Journal of Speech*, *70*, 151–167.

Minick, N. 1987. The development of Vygotsky's thought: An introduction. In R. W. Rieber & A. S. Carton (Eds.), *The collected works of L. S. Vygotsky. Vol.1 Problems of general psychology*. New York: Plenum.

1989. Mind and activity in Vygotsky's work: An expanded frame of reference. *Cultural Dynamics*, *2*(2), 162–87.

Moll, L. C. (Ed.). 1990. *Vygotsky and education: Instructional implications and applications of sociohistorical psychology*. New York: Cambridge University Press.

Moll, L. C., & Greenberg, J. B. 1990. Creating zones of possibilities: Combining social contexts for instruction. In L. C. Moll (Ed.), *Vygotsky and education: Instructional implications and applications of sociohistorical psychology*. (pp. 319–48). Cambridge: Cambridge University Press.

Murray, D. 1978. Internal revision: A process of discovery. In C. R. Cooper & L. Odell (Eds.), *Research on composing*. (pp. 85–103). Urbana, IL: National Council of Teachers of English.

Nelson, K. 1996. *Language in cognitive development: The emergence of the mediated mind*. New York: Cambridge University Press.

Newman, D., Griffin, P., & Cole, M. 1989. *The construction zone: Working for cognitive change in school.* Cambridge: Cambridge University Press.

Newman, J. (Ed.). 1989. *Finding our own way.* Portsmouth, NH: Heinemann Educational Books.

Nickerson, R. S. 1993. On the distribution of cognition: Some reflections. In G. Salomon (Ed.), *Distributed cognitions: Psychological and educational considerations* (pp. 229–61). New York: Cambridge University Press.

Nicolopoulou, A. 1989. The invention of writing and the development of numerical concepts in Sumeria: Some implications for developmental psychology. *The Quarterly Newsletter of the Laboratory of Comparative Human Cognition, 11*(4), 114–24.

1991. E-mail message : xlchc, 1 January 1991.

Norman, K. (Ed.). 1992. *Thinking voices: The work of the National Oracy Project.* London: Hodder & Stoughton.

Nuthall, G. A. (in press). Students' memory for classroom experience and learning activities in science and social studies units. *Cognition and Instruction.*

Nuthall, G. A., & Alton-Lee, A. G. 1995. Assessing classroom learning: How students use their knowledge and experience to answer achievement test questions in science and social studies. *American Educational Research Journal, 32,* 185–223.

Nystrand, M. 1997. *Opening dialogue: Understanding the dynamics of language and learning in the English classroom.* New York: Teachers College Press.

Nystrand, M., & Gamoran, A. 1991. Student engagement: When recitation becomes conversation. In H. C. Waxman & H. J. Walberg (Eds.), *Effective teaching: Current research.* (pp. 257–76). Berkeley, CA: McCutchan Publishing Corp.

Oatley, K. 1996. Inference in narrative and science. In D. R. Olson & N. Torrance (Eds.), *Modes of thought: Explorations in culture and cognition* (pp. 123–40). New York: Cambridge University Press.

O'Connor, M. C. & Michaels, S. 1996. Shifting participant frameworks: orchestrating thinking practices in group discussions. In D. Hicks (Ed), *Discourse, learning, and schooling* (pp. 63–103). New York: Cambridge University Press.

Olson, D., R. 1977. From utterance to text: The bias of language in speech and writing. *Harvard Educational Review, 47*(3), 257–281.

1994a. Aboriginal literacy. *Interchange, 25*(4), 389–394.

1994b. *The world on paper.* Cambridge: Cambridge University Press.

Olson, D. R., and Astington, J. W. 1993. Thinking about thinking. *Educational Psychologist, 28*(1), 7–23.

Olson, D. R., & Bruner, J. S. 1996. Folk psychology and folk pedagogy. In D. R. Olson & N. Torrance (Eds.), *The handbook of education and human development* (pp. 9–27). Cambridge, MA: Blackwell.

Ong, W. 1982. *Orality and literacy.* New York: Methuen.

Painter, C. 1989. Learning language: A functional view of language development. In R. Hasan & J. R. Martin (Eds.), *Language development: Learning language, learning culture. Meaning and choice in language: Studies for Michael Halliday.* (pp. 18–65). Norwood, NJ: Ablex.

Palincsar, A. S., & Brown, A. L. 1984. Reciprocal teaching of comprehension-fostering and monitoring activities. *Cognition and Instruction, 1,* 117–175.

Parker, R. P., & Goodkin, V. 1986. *Consequences of writing: Enhancing learning in the disciplines.* Upper Montclair, NJ: Boynton/Cook.

Parret, H. 1974. *Discussing language*. The Hague: Mouton.

Paulauskas, S. 1994. *The effects of strategy training on the aural comprehension of L2 adult learners at the high beginning/low intermediate proficiency level*. Unpublished Ph.D., University of Toronto, Toronto.

Pea, R. 1993. Practices of distributed intelligence and designs for education. In G. Salomon (Ed.), *Distributed cognitions: Psychological and educational considerations* (pp. 47–87). New York: Cambridge University Press.

Phillips, T. 1988. On a related matter: Why "successful" small-group talk depends upon not keeping to the point. In M. MacLure, T. Phillips, & A. Wilkinson (Eds.), *Oracy matters* (pp. 69–81). Milton Keynes, UK: Open University Press.

Piaget, J. 1932. *The language and thought of the child*. London: Routledge.

Pierce, K. M., & Gilles, C. J. (Eds.). 1993. *Cycles of meaning*. Portsmouth, NH: Heinemann.

Pontecorvo, C., & Girardet, H. 1993. Arguing and reasoning in understanding historical topics. *Cognition and Instruction*, *11*, 189–96.

Pontecorvo, C., Girardet, H., & Zucchermaglio, C. 1990. Reasoning together in understanding historical topics., *"Social Interaction and the Acquisition of Knowledge."* Universita di Roma, "La Sapienza."

Poole, D. 1990. Contextualizing IRE in an eighth grade quiz review. *Linguistics and Education*, *2*(3), 185–212.

Popper, K. R. 1972. *Objective knowledge: An evolutionary approach*. Oxford: Clarendon Press.

Popper, K. R., & Eccles, J. C. 1977. *The self and its brain*. Berlin: Springer–Verlag.

Premack, D. 1976. *Intelligence in ape and man*. Hillsdale, NJ: Erlbaum.

Reddy, M. 1979. The conduit metaphor – a case of frame conflict in our language about language. In A. Ortony (Ed.), *Metaphor and thought* (pp. 284–324). Cambridge: Cambridge University Press.

Resnick, L. 1987. Learning in school and out. *Educational Researcher*, *16*(9), 13–20.

Richards, R. 1990. *An early start to technology*. London: Simon & Schuster.

Rogoff, B. 1990. *Apprenticeship in thinking: Cognitive development in social context*. New York: Oxford University Press.

Rogoff, B. 1994. Developing understanding of the idea of Communities of Learners. *Mind, Culture, and Activity*, *1*(4), 209–29.

Rogoff, B., & Wertsch, J. V. (Eds.). 1984. *Children's learning in the "zone of proximal development."* San Francisco: Jossey-Bass.

Rosaldo, M. Z. 1984. Toward an anthropology of self and feeling. In R. A. Shweder & R. A. LeVine (Eds.), *Culture theory: Essays on mind, self, and emotion.* (pp. 137–57). Cambridge: Cambridge University Press.

Roseberry, A., Warren, B., & Conant, F. 1992. Appropriating scientific discourse: findings from language minority classrooms. *The Journal of the Learning Sciences*, *2*, 61–94.

Rosenblatt, L. 1978. *The reader, the text, the poem: The transactional theory of the literary work*. Carbondale, IL: Southern Illinois University Press.

Rothery, J. 1989. Learning about language. In R. Hasan & J. R. Martin (Eds.), *Language development: Learning language, learning culture. Meaning and choice in language: Studies for Michael Halliday.* (pp. 199–256). Norwood, NJ: Ablex.

Ryle, G. 1949. *The concept of mind*. London: Hutchinson.

Sacks, H., Schegloff, E. A., & Jefferson, G. 1994. A simplest systematics for the organizing of turn-taking for conversation. *Language, 50*(4), 696–735.

Salomon, G. 1993. No distribution without individuals' cognition: a dynamic interactional view. In G. Salomon (Ed.), *Distributed cognitions: Psychological and educational considerations* (pp. 111–38). New York: Cambridge University Press.

1993. (Ed.), *Distributed cognitions: Psychological and educational considerations*. New York: Cambridge University Press.

Sawyer, W. & Watson, K. 1987. Questions of genre. In I. Reid (Ed.), *The place of genre in learning: Current debates* (pp. 46–57). Geelong, Vic.: Deakin University, Centre for Studies in Literary Education.

Saxe, G. 1992. Studying children's learning in context: Problems and prospects. *Journal of the Learning Sciences, 2*(2), 215–234.

Scardamalia, M., & Bereiter, C. 1983. Child as co-investigator: Helping children gain insight into their own mental processes. In S. Paris, G. Olson, & H. Stevenson (Eds.), *Learning and motivation in the classroom*. Hillsdale, NJ: Erlbaum.

1992. Text-based and knowledge-based questioning by children. *Cognition and Instruction, 9*(3), 177–99.

Scardamalia, M., Bereiter, C., & Lamon, M. 1994. The CSILE project: Trying to bring the classroom into World 3. In K. McGilley (Ed.), *Classroom lessons: Integrating cognitive theory and classroom practice* (pp. 201–28). Cambridge, MA: MIT Press.

Schegloff, E. A. 1989. Reflections on language, development and the interactional character of talk-in-interaction. In M. Bornstein & J. S. Bruner (Eds.), *Interaction in human development*. Hillsdale, NJ: Erlbaum.

Schegloff, E. A., & Sacks, H. 1973. Opening up closings. *Semiotica, VIII* (289–327).

Schneuwly, B., & Bain, D. 1993. Mécanismes de régulation des activités textuelles: stratégies d'intervention dans les séquences didactiques. In L. Allal, D. Bain, & P. Perrenoud (Eds.), *Evaluation formative et didactique du français* (pp. 219–38). Neuchâtel: Delachaux et Niestlé.

Scribner, S. 1985. Vygotsky's uses of history. In J. V. Wertsch (Ed.), *Culture, communication and cognition: Vygotskian perspectives* (pp. 119–45). Cambridge: Cambridge University Press.

Scribner, S., & Cole, M. 1981. *The psychology of literacy*. Cambridge, MA: Harvard University Press.

Sharan, S., & Sharan, Y. 1992. *Expanding cooperative learning through group investigation*. New York: Teachers College Press.

Short, K. G., & Burke, C. L. 1991. *Creating curriculum: Teachers and students as a community of learners*. Portsmouth, NH: Heinemann.

Sinclair, J. McH., & Coulthard, M. C. 1975. *Towards an analysis of discourse: The English used by teachers and pupils*. London: Oxford University Press.

Smagorinsky, P. 1995. Constructing meaning in the disciplines: Reconceptualizing writing across the curriculum as composing across the curriculum. *American Journal of Education, 103*, 160–184.

Smolka, A. L. B., De Goes, M. C. R., & Pino, A. 1995. The construction of the subject: A persistent question. In J. V. Wertsch, P. d. Rio, & A. Alvarez (Eds.), *Sociocultural studies of mind* (pp. 165–84). Cambridge: Cambridge University Press.

Staton, J., Shuy, R. W., Peyton, J. K., & Reed, L. 1988. *Dialogue journal communication: Classroom, linguistic, social and cognitive views*. Norwood, NJ: Ablex.

Stock, P. L. 1995. *The dialogic curriculum: Teaching and learning in a multicultural society*. Portsmouth, NH: Heinemann.

Stubbs, M. 1983. *Discourse analysis: The sociolinguistic analysis of natural language*. London: Blackwell.

Swanson-Owens, D., & Newell, G. E. 1994. Using intervention protocols to study the effects of instructional scaffolding on writing and learning. In P. Smagorinsky (Ed.), *Speaking about writing: Reflections on research methodology*. (pp. 141–62). Thousand Oaks, CA: Sage.

Swartz, L. 1994. Reading response journals: One teacher's research. In G. Wells, et al., *Changing schools from within: Creating communities of inquiry* (pp. 99–128). Toronto: OISE Press; Portsmouth, NH: Heinemann.

Teale, W. H., & Sulzby, E. (Eds.). 1986. *Emergent literacy: Writing and reading*. Norwood, NJ: Ablex.

Tharp, R., & Gallimore, R. 1988. *Rousing minds to life*. New York: Cambridge University Press.

Tinker, R. F. 1993. Curriculum development and the scientific method. *Hands On, 16*(2), 2.

Tomasello, M. 1994. The question of chimpanzee culture. In R. Wrangham, W. McGrew, F. d. Waal, & P. Heltne (Eds.), *Chimpanzee cultures*. Cambridge, MA: Harvard University Press.

Tudge, J. 1993. Vygotsky, the zone of proximal development, and peer collaboration: Implications for classroom practice. In E. A. Forman, N. Minick, & C. A. Stone (Eds.), *Contexts for Learning: Sociocultural dynamics in children's development*. New York: Oxford University Press.

Tulviste, P. 1991. *Cultural–historical development of verbal thinking: A psychological study*. Commack, NY: Nova Science Publishers.

Turner, G. J. 1973. Social class and children's language of control at age five and age seven. In B. Bernstein (Ed.), *Class, codes and control 2: Applied studies towards a sociology of language* (pp. 135–201). London: Routledge & Kegan Paul.

Ueno, N. 1995. The reification of artifacts in ideological practice. *Mind, Culture, and Activity, 2*, 230–39.

Valsiner, J. 1994. Irreversibility of time and the construction of historical developmental psychology. *Mind, Culture, and Activity, 1*, 25–42.

Ventola, E. 1987. *The structure of social interaction: A systemic approach to the semiotics of service encounters*. London: Frances Pinter.

von Wright, G. H. 1971. *Explanation and understanding*. Ithaca, NY: Cornell University Press.

Vygotsky, L. S. 1925 (translated into English, 1971). *Psikhologiya iskussto [The psychology of art]*. (Scripta Technica, Inc., Trans.). Cambridge, MA: MIT Press.

  1934/1987. Thinking and speech. In R. W. Rieber & A. S. Carton (Eds.), *The collected works of L.S. Vygotsky, Volume 1: Problems of general psychology*. New York: Plenum.

  1935. *Mental development of children during education*. Moscow-Leningrad: Uchpedzig.

  1978. *Mind in society: The development of higher psychological processes*. Cambridge, MA: Harvard University Press.

1981. The genesis of higher mental functions. In J. V. Wertsch (Ed.), *The concept of activity in Soviet Psychology* (pp. 144–88). Armonk, NY: Sharpe.

Vygotsky, L. S., & Luria, A. R. 1930. *Etyudy po istorii povedeniya: Obez'yana, primitiv, rebenok. [Essays in the history of behavior: Ape, primitive, child.].* Moscow and Leningrad: Gosudarstvennoe Izdatel'stvo.

Walkerdine, V. 1988. *The mastery of reason: Cognitive development and the production of rationality.* London: Routledge.

Wartofsky, M. 1979. *Models, representation and scientific understanding.* Boston: Reidel.

Wegerif, R., & Mercer, N. 1997. A dialogical framework for researching peer talk. In R. Wegerif & P. Scrimshaw (Eds.), *Computers and talk in the primary classroom* (pp. 49–61). Clevedon, U.K.: Multilingual Matters.

Wegerif, R., & Scrimshaw, P. (Eds.). 1997. *Computers and talk in the primary classroom.* Clevedon, U.K.: Multilingual Matters.

Wells, G. 1981. *Learning through interaction: the study of language development.* Cambridge: Cambridge Uiversity Press.

1985. *Language development in the pre-school years.* Cambridge: Cambridge University Press.

1986. *The meaning makers: Children learning language and using language to learn.* Portsmouth, NH: Heinemann.

1990. Talk about text: Where literacy is learned and taught. *Curriculum Inquiry, 20*(4), 369–405.

1993a. Intersubjectivity and the construction of knowledge (in Italian). In C. Pontecorvo (Ed.), *La Condivisione della Conoscenza* (pp. 353–80). Rome: La Nuova Italia.

1993b. Working with a teacher in the zone of proximal development: Action research on the learning and teaching of science. *Journal of the Society for Accelerative Learning and Teaching, 18*, 127–222.

1994a. Doing, writing, and talking science: 'The development of scientific concepts' revisited., *"Lev Vygotsky and the Human Sciences."* Moscow.

1994b. Introduction: Teacher research and educational change. In G. Wells et al., *Changing schools from within: Creating communities of inquiry* (pp. 1–35). Toronto: OISE Press: Portsmouth, NH: Heinemann.

1994c. Watching ourselves grow. In G. Wells et al., *Changing schools from within: Creating communities of inquiry.* (pp. 237–75). Toronto: OISE Press: Portsmouth, NH: Heinemann.

1995. Language and the inquiry-oriented curriculum. *Curriculum Inquiry, 25*(3), 233–269.

Wells, G. (in press). Modes of meaning in a science activity. *Linguistics and Education.* (Ed.) (forthcoming). *Talk, text and inquiry.*

Wells, G., Bernard, L., Gianotti, M. A., Keating, et al. 1994. *Changing schools from within: Creating communities of inquiry.* Toronto: OISE Press: Portsmouth, NH: Heinemann.

Wells, G., & Chang-Wells, G. L. 1992. *Constructing knowledge together: Classrooms as centers of inquiry and literacy.* Portsmouth, NH: Heinemann.

1997. "What have you learned?": Co-constructing the meaning of time. In J. Flood, S. B. Heath, & D. Lapp (Eds.), *A Handbook for Literacy Educators: Research on Teaching the Communicative and Visual Arts.* (pp. 514–527) New York: Macmillan.

Wells, G., Chang, G. L., & Maher, A. 1990. Creating classroom communities of literate thinkers. In S. Sharan (Ed.), *Cooperative learning: Theory and research*. (pp 95–121). New York: Praeger.

Wertsch, J. V. (Ed.). 1981. *The concept of activity in Soviet psychology*. Armonk, NY: Sharpe.

1985. *Vygotsky and the social formation of mind*. Cambridge, MA: Harvard University Press.

1989. A sociocultural approach to mind: Some theoretical considerations. *Cultural Dynamics*, *2*, 140–61.

1991. *Voices of the mind: A sociocultural approach to mediated action*. Cambridge, MA: Harvard University Press.

Wertsch, J. V. 1998. *Mind as action*. Oxford: Oxford University Press.

Wertsch, J. V., del Rio, P., & Alvarez, A. (Eds.). 1995. *Sociocultural studies of mind*. Cambridge: Cambridge University Press.

Wertsch, J. V., Minick, N., & Arns, F. J. 1984. The creation of context in joint problem solving. In B. Rogoff & J. Lave (Eds.), *Everyday cognition: Its development in social context*. Cambridge: Cambridge University Press.

Wertsch, J. V., & Stone, C. A. 1985. The concept of internalization in Vygotsky's account of the genesis of higher mental functions. In J. V. Wertsch (Ed.), *Culture, communication and cognition: Vygotskian perspectives* (pp. 162–79). New York: Cambridge University Press.

Wertsch, J. V., & Tulviste, P. 1992. L. S. Vygotsky and contemporary developmental psychology. *Developmental Psychology*, *28*(4), 548–57.

White, L. 1942. On the use of tools by primates. *Journal of Comparative Psychology*, *34*, 369–374.

Whitehead, A. N. 1949. *The aims of education*. New York: New American Library Mentor Books.

Witte, S. P. 1992. Context, text, intertext: Toward a constructivist semiotic of writing. *Written Communication*, *9*(2), 237–8.

Wood, D. 1992. Teaching talk. In K. Norman (Ed.), *Thinking voices: The work of the National Oracy Project* (pp. 203–14). London: Hodder and Stoughton for the National Curriculum Council.

Wood, D., Bruner, J. S., & Ross, G. 1976. The role of tutoring in problem-solving. *Journal of Child Psychology and Child Psychiatry*, *17*, 89–100.

Yackel, E., Cobb, P., Wood, T., Wheatley, G., et al. 1990. The importance of social interaction in children's construction of mathematical knowledge. In T. J. Cooney (Ed.), *Teaching and learning mathematics in the 1990s* (pp. 12–21). Reston, VA: National Council of Teachers of Mathematics.

Zinchenko, V. P., & Gordon, V. M. 1981. Methodological problems in the psychological analysis of activity. In J. V. Wertsch (Ed.), *The concept of activity in Soviet psychology*. (pp. 72–133). Armonk, NY: Sharpe.

Index of Authors

Index of Subjects

360

Continued from the front of the book

The Learning in Doing series was founded in 1987 by Roy Pea and John Seely Brown